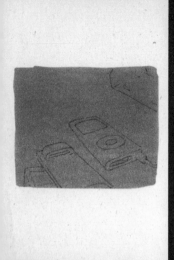

I bought an iPod the other day. I put off buying one just because they were so popular. What was I thinking?! Wow!! It's so useful! You can listen to hundreds of songs in a row! The machine itself is great, but the best part is the packaging. I couldn't bring myself to throw away the acrylic case my iPod came in even though I have no use for it. I hope someday I can design a book jacket so good that no one can throw it away.

-Tite Kubo

BLEACH is author Tite Kubo's second title. Kubo made his debut with *ZOMBIEPOWDER.*, a four-volume series for *WEEKLY SHONEN JUMP.* To date, *BLEACH* has been translated into numerous languages and has also inspired an animated TV series that began airing in the U.S. in 2006. Beginning its serialization in 2001, *BLEACH* is still a mainstay in the pages of *WEEKLY SHONEN JUMP.* In 2005, *BLEACH* was awarded the prestigious Shogakukan Manga Award in the *shonen* (boys) category.

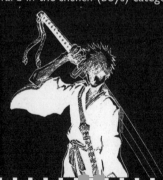

BLEACH
Vol. 27: goodbye, halcyon days.
The SHONEN JUMP Manga Edition
This volume contains material that was originally published in English in
SHONEN JUMP #69-71. Artwork in the magazine may have been altered
slightly from what is presented in this volume.

STORY AND ART BY
TITE KUBO

English Adaptation/Lance Caselman
Translation/Joe Yamazaki
Touch-Up Art & Lettering/Mark McMurray
Design/Sean Lee
Editor/Pancha Diaz

Editor in Chief, Books/Alvin Lu
Editor in Chief, Magazines/Marc Weidenbaum
VP, Publishing Licensing/Rika Inouye
VP, Sales & Product Marketing/Gonzalo Ferreyra
VP, Creative/Linda Espinosa
Publisher/Hyoe Narita

Printed in the U.S.A.

Published by VIZ Media, LLC
P.O. Box 77010
San Francisco, CA 94107

SHONEN JUMP Manga Edition
10 9 8 7 6 5 4 3 2 1
First printing, June 2009

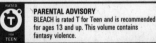

www.viz.com

www.shonenjump.com

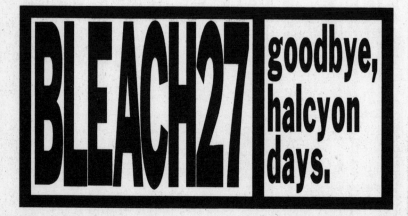

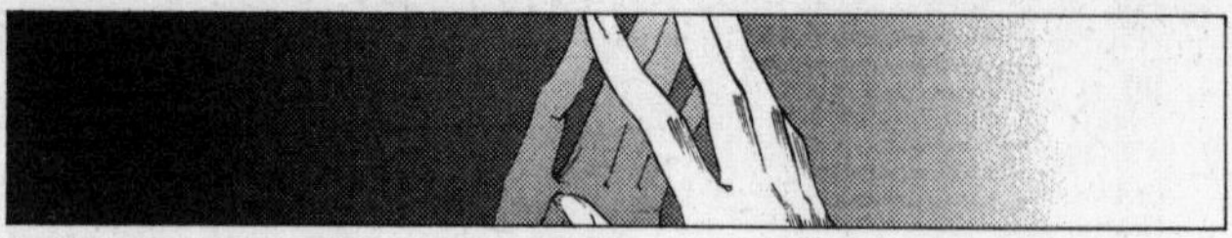

We have
Not one
In common
No two
Are shaped alike
The third
Because of that eye we lack
In the fourth
Direction there is no hope
The fifth
Is at the heart

BLEACH27 goodbye, halcyon days.

STARS AND

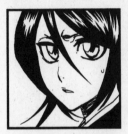

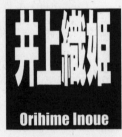

Orihime Inoue

Rukia Kuchiki

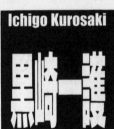

Ichigo Kurosaki

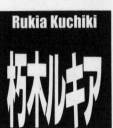

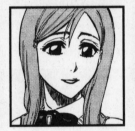

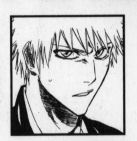

plot

When High School student Ichigo Kurosaki meets Soul Reaper Rukia Kuchiki his life is changed forever. Soon Ichigo is a soul-cleansing Soul Reaper too, and he finds himself having adventures--and problems--he never could have imagined. Now Ichigo and his friends face their greatest challenge yet in the form of the renegade Soul Reaper Aizen and his army of Arrancars, who are bent on killing the king of the Soul Society and wiping out Karakura in the process.

In the World of the Living, Ichigo and a small detachment of Soul Reapers prepare for war while Orihime, rejected for frontline service, goes to the Soul Society to improve her fighting skills. But when the Arrancars unexpectedly attack Karakura, Orihime heads for home, only to be confronted by the deadly Arrancar Ulquiorra!

BLEACH ALL

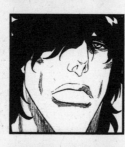

石田雨竜

Uryû Ishida

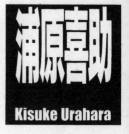

浦原喜助

Kisuke Urahara

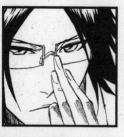

Chad Yasutora

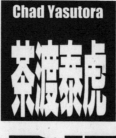

茶渡泰虎

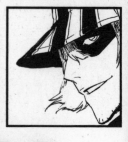

STORIES

BLEACH27

goodbye, halcyon days.

Contents

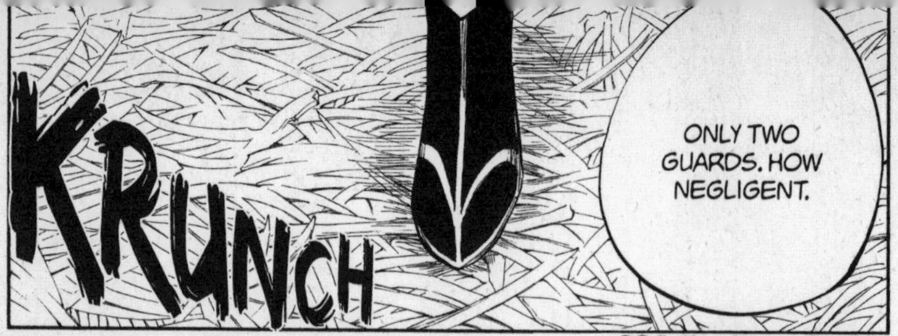
ONLY TWO GUARDS. HOW NEGLIGENT.
KRUNCH

234. Not Negotiation

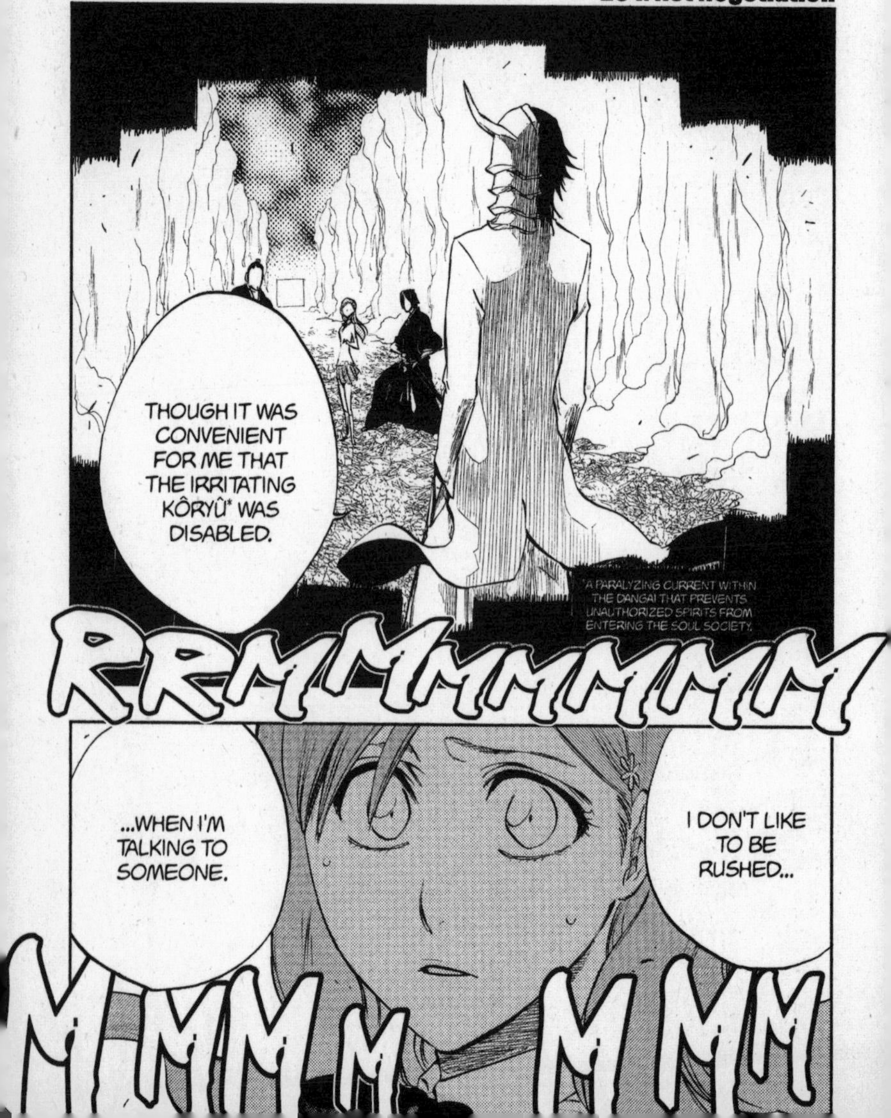
THOUGH IT WAS CONVENIENT FOR ME THAT THE IRRITATING KÔRYÛ* WAS DISABLED.
*A PARALYZING CURRENT WITHIN THE DANGAI THAT PREVENTS UNAUTHORIZED SPIRITS FROM ENTERING THE SOUL SOCIETY.
RRMMMMMMM
I DON'T LIKE TO BE RUSHED...
...WHEN I'M TALKING TO SOMEONE.
MMMM MMM

BLEACH -ブリーチ-

234. Not Negotiation

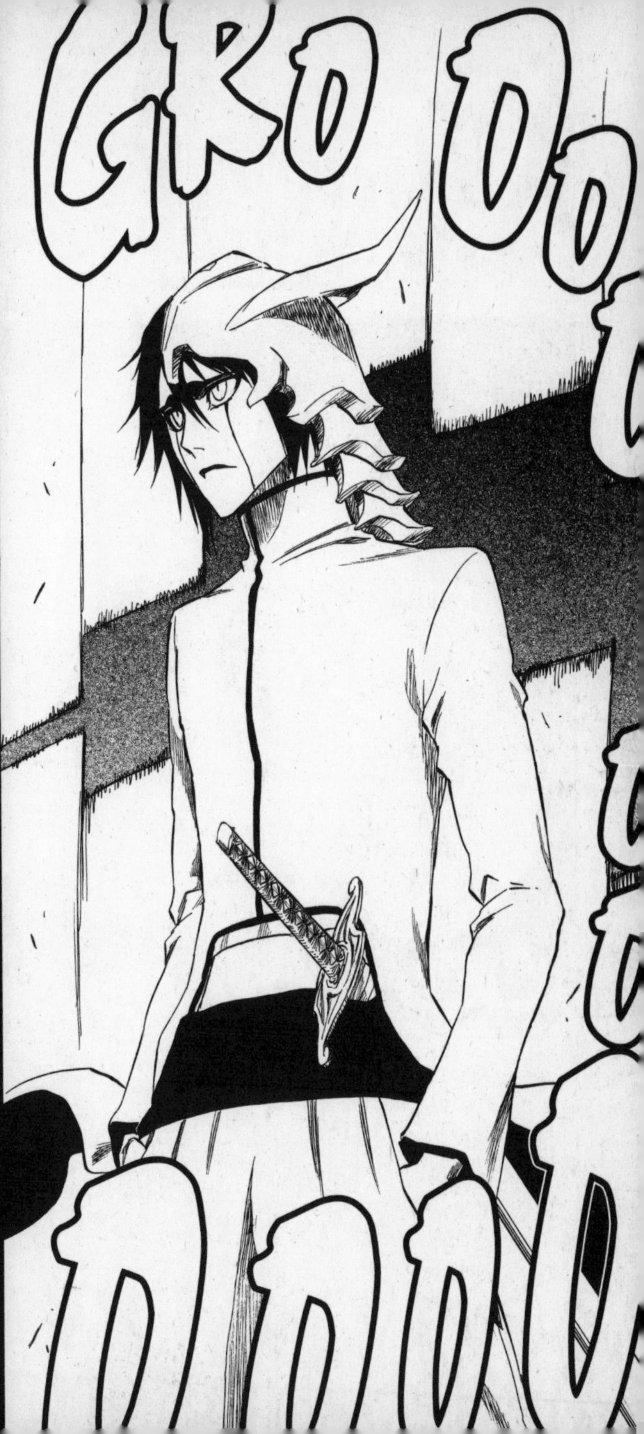
GROOO

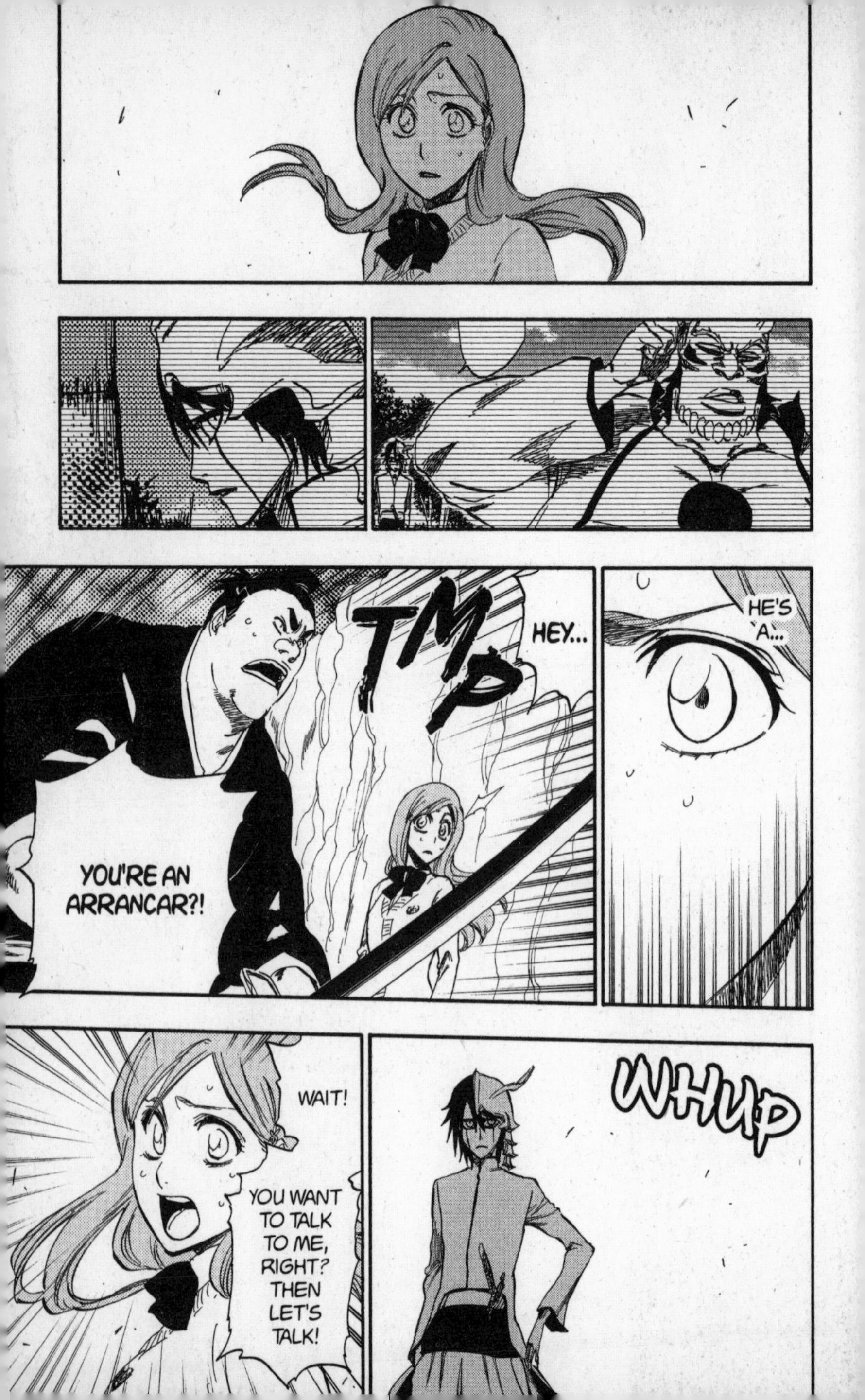
HE'S A...
HEY...
TMP
YOU'RE AN ARRANCAR?!
WHUP
WAIT!
YOU WANT TO TALK TO ME, RIGHT? THEN LET'S TALK!

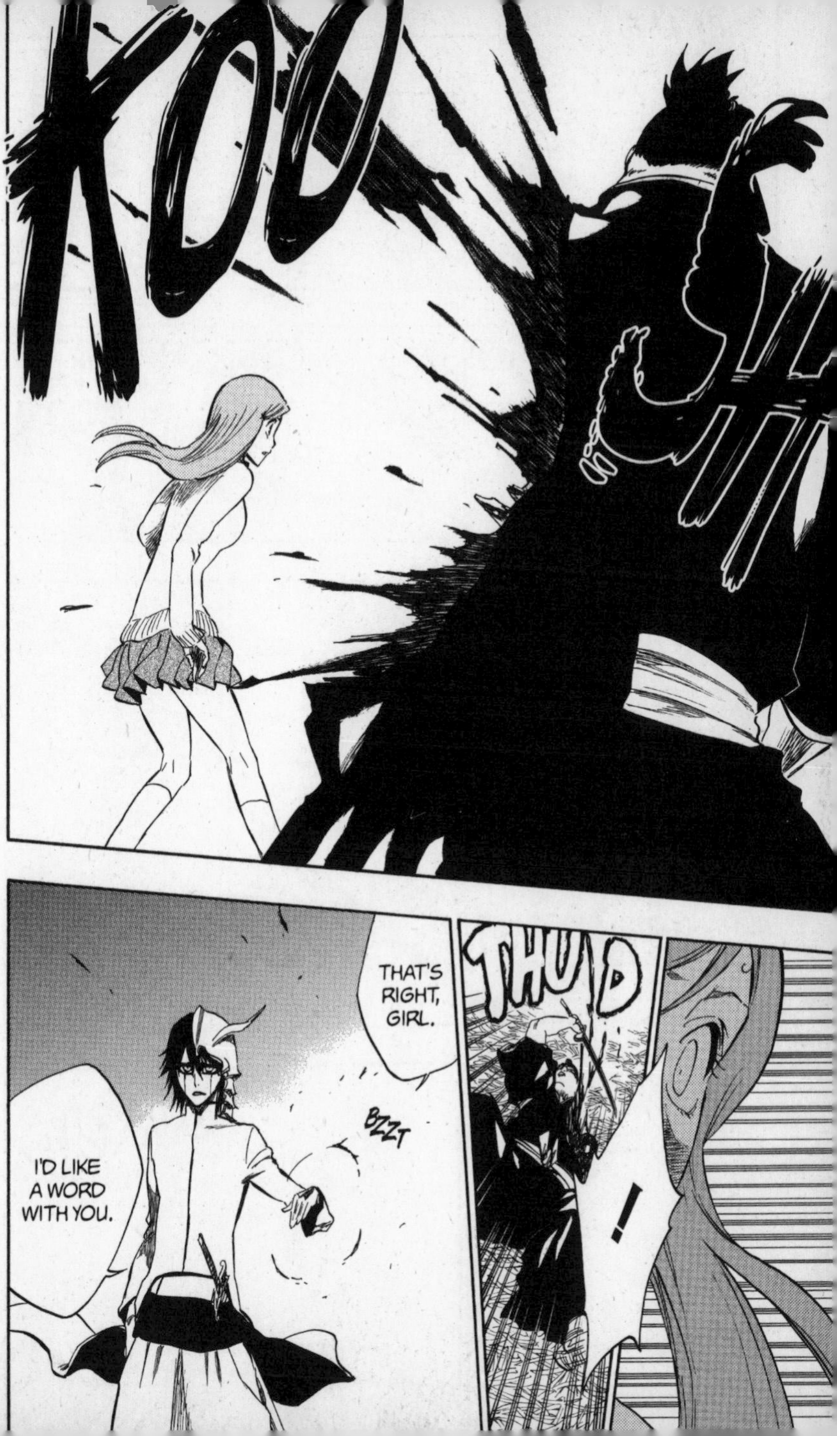
KOO
!
THUD
THAT'S RIGHT, GIRL.
BZZT
I'D LIKE A WORD WITH YOU.

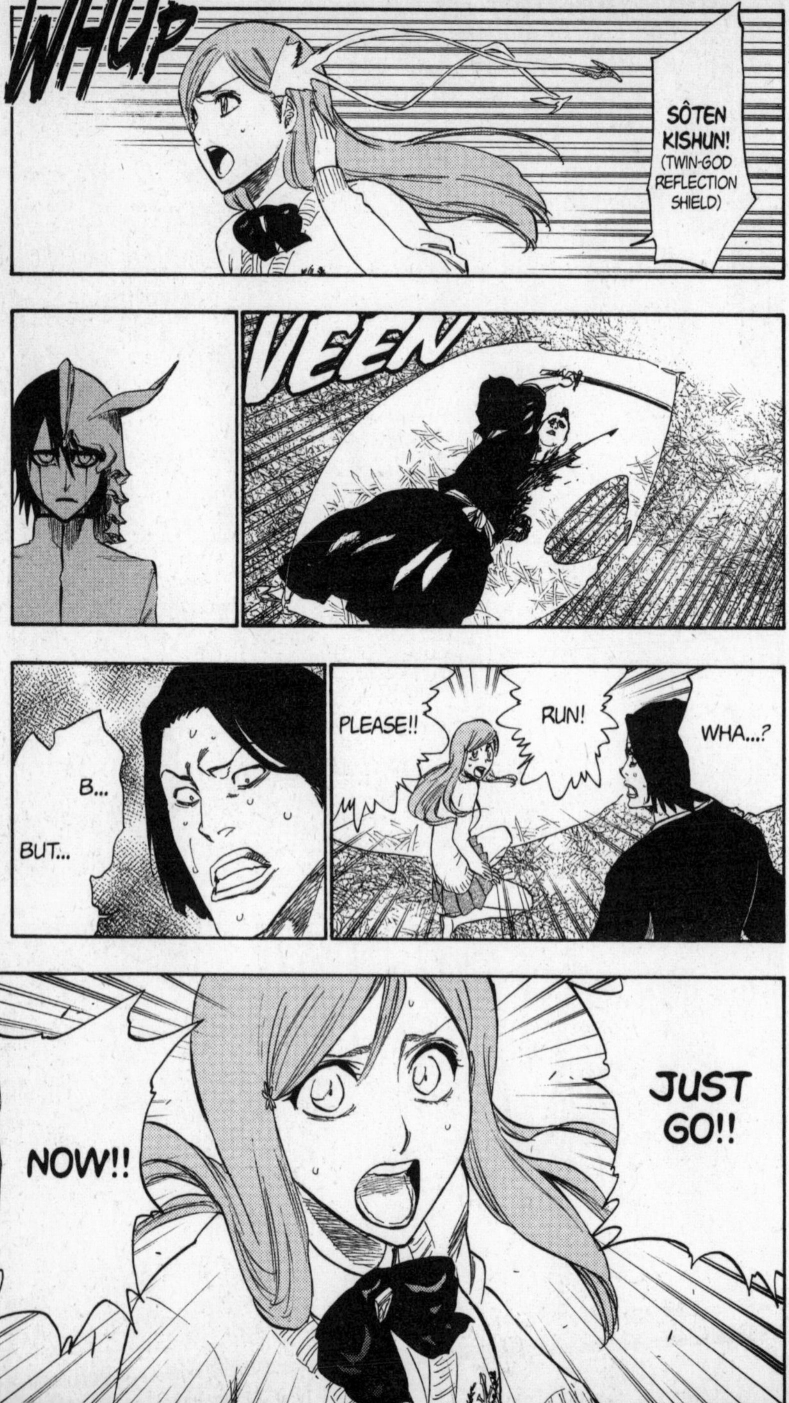
WHUP
SÔTEN KISHUN! (TWIN-GOD REFLECTION SHIELD)
VEEN
WHA...?
RUN!
PLEASE!!
B...
BUT...
JUST GO!!
NOW!!

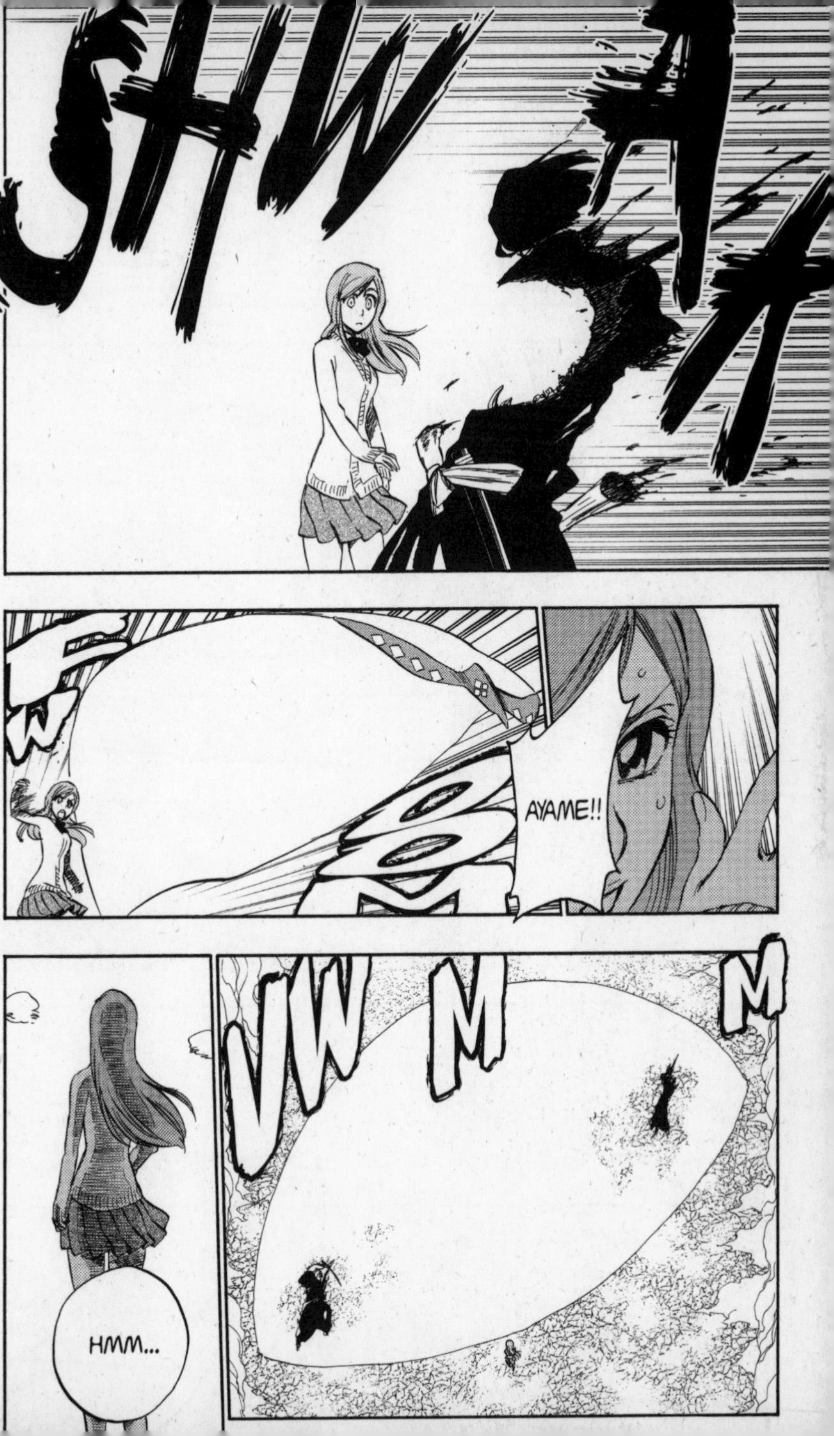
SHW
AYAME!!
VWMM
HMM...

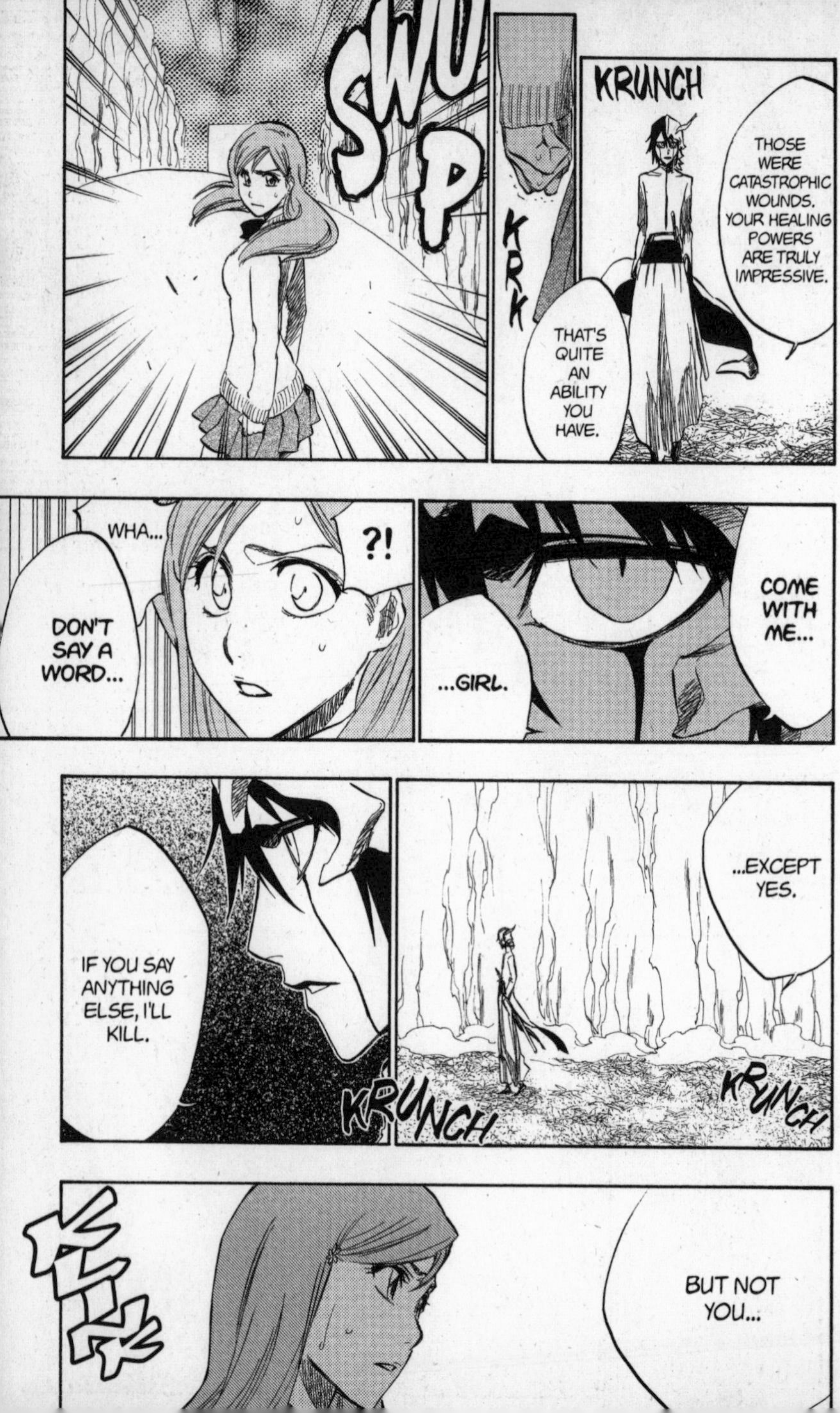
KRUNCH
THOSE WERE CATASTROPHIC WOUNDS. YOUR HEALING POWERS ARE TRULY IMPRESSIVE.
KRK
THAT'S QUITE AN ABILITY YOU HAVE.
SWUP
COME WITH ME...
...GIRL.
?!
WHA...
DON'T SAY A WORD...
...EXCEPT YES.
KRUNCH
IF YOU SAY ANYTHING ELSE, I'LL KILL.
KRUNCH
BUT NOT YOU...

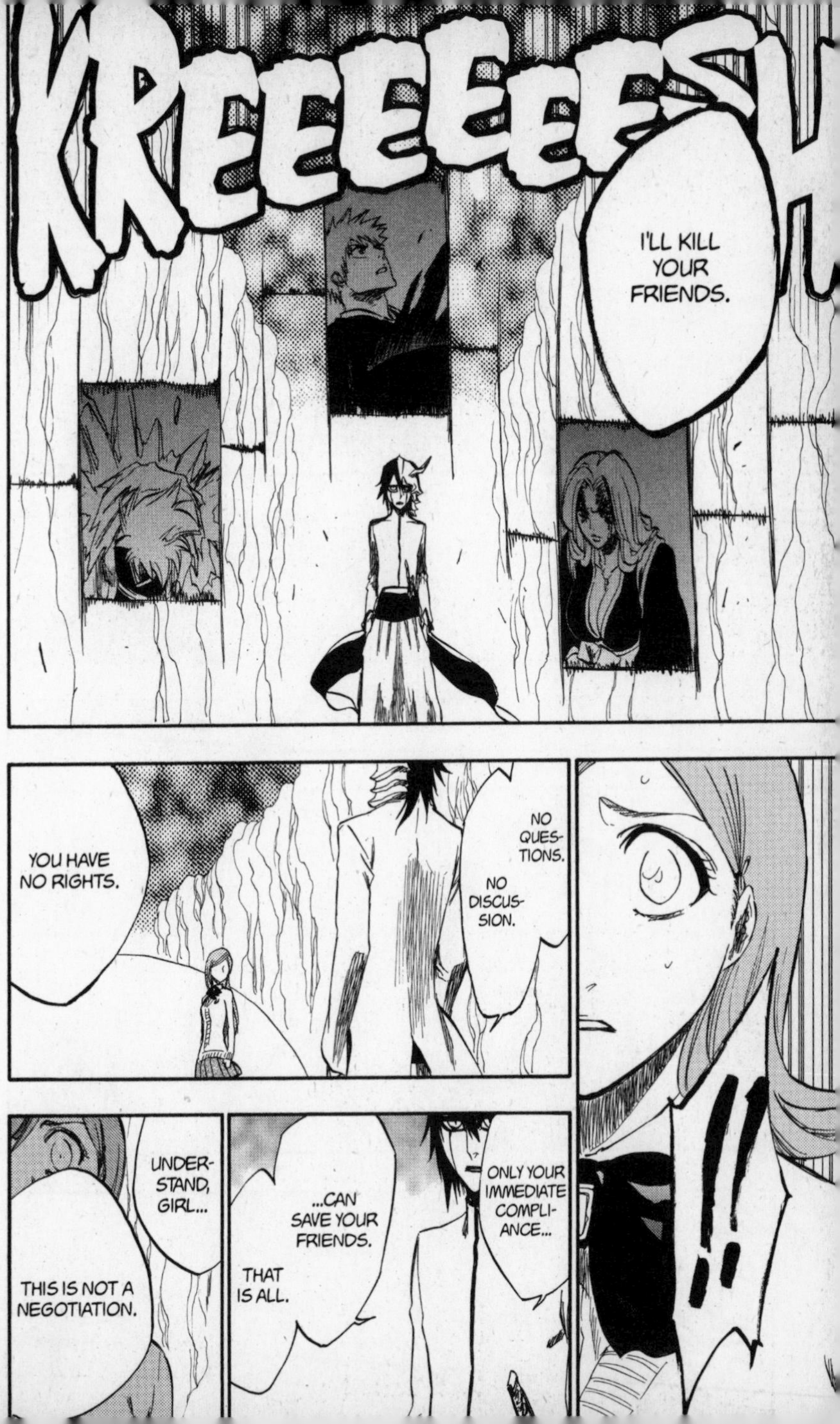
KREEEEEESH
I'LL KILL YOUR FRIENDS.
!!
NO QUESTIONS.
NO DISCUSSION.
YOU HAVE NO RIGHTS.
ONLY YOUR IMMEDIATE COMPLIANCE...
...CAN SAVE YOUR FRIENDS.
THAT IS ALL.
UNDERSTAND, GIRL...
THIS IS NOT A NEGOTIATION.

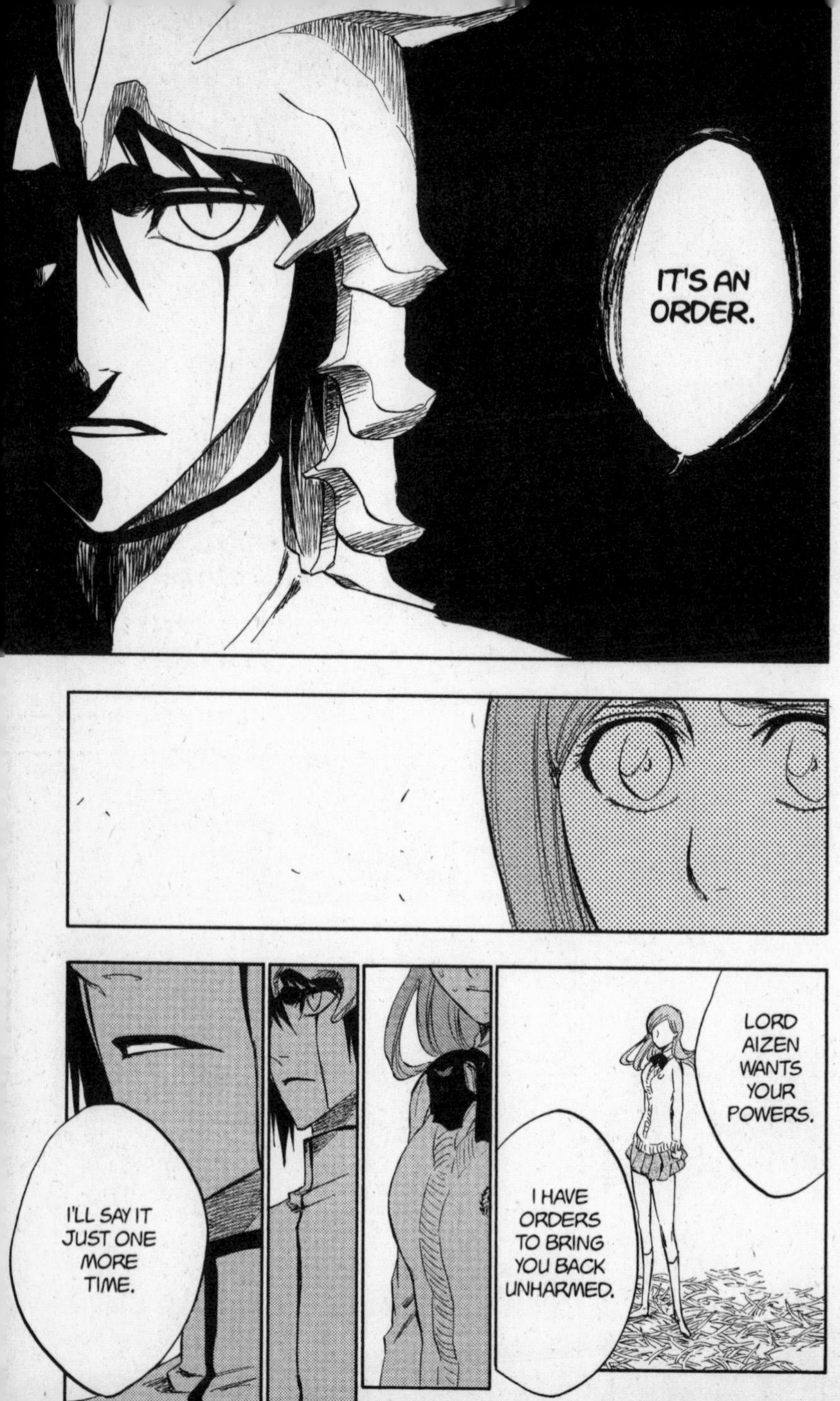
IT'S AN ORDER.
LORD AIZEN WANTS YOUR POWERS.
I HAVE ORDERS TO BRING YOU BACK UNHARMED.
I'LL SAY IT JUST ONE MORE TIME.

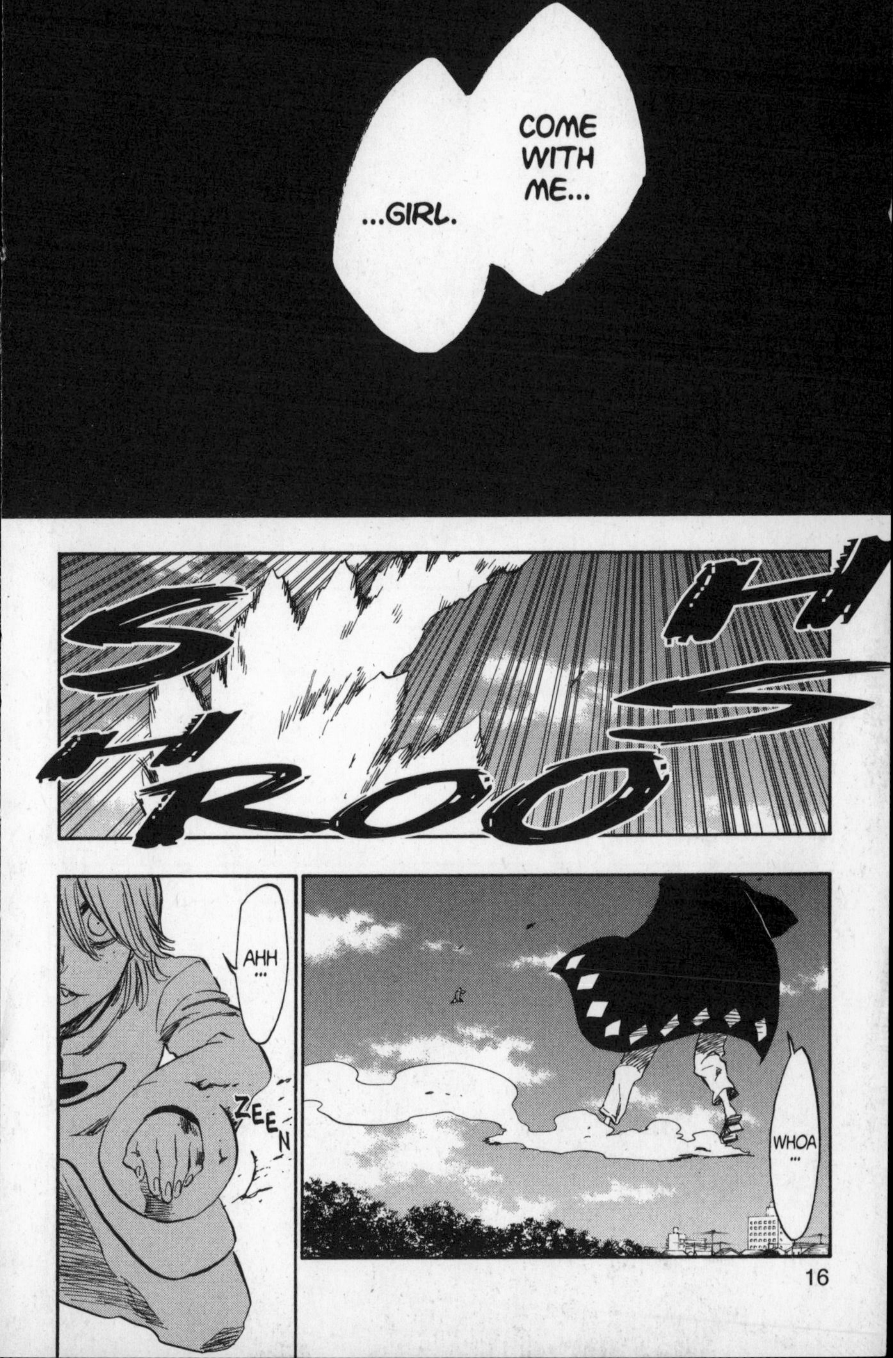
COME WITH ME...
...GIRL.
SHROOSH
WHOA...
AHH...
ZEEN

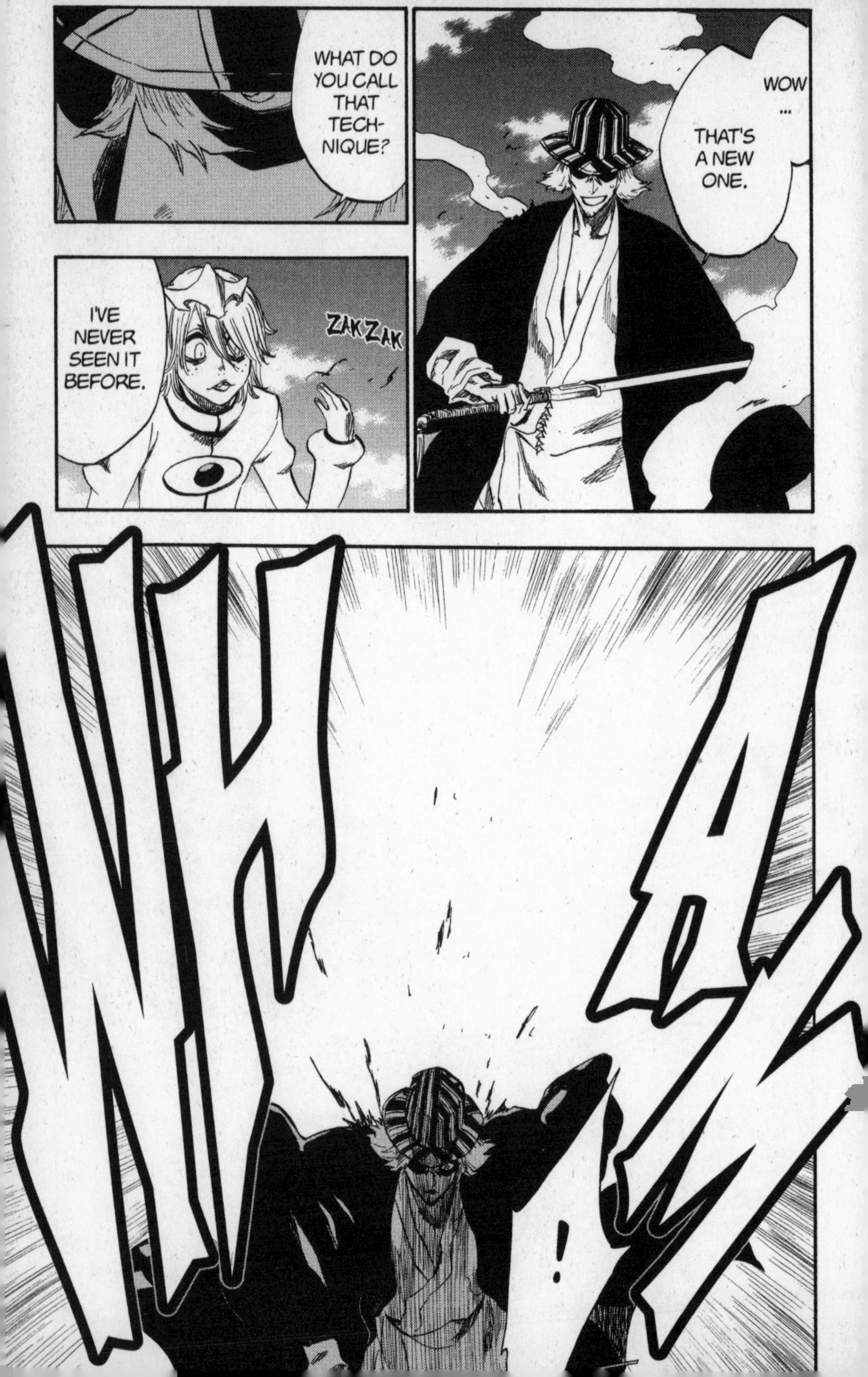
WOW ... THAT'S A NEW ONE.
WHAT DO YOU CALL THAT TECH-NIQUE?
I'VE NEVER SEEN IT BEFORE.
ZAK ZAK
WHAM
!

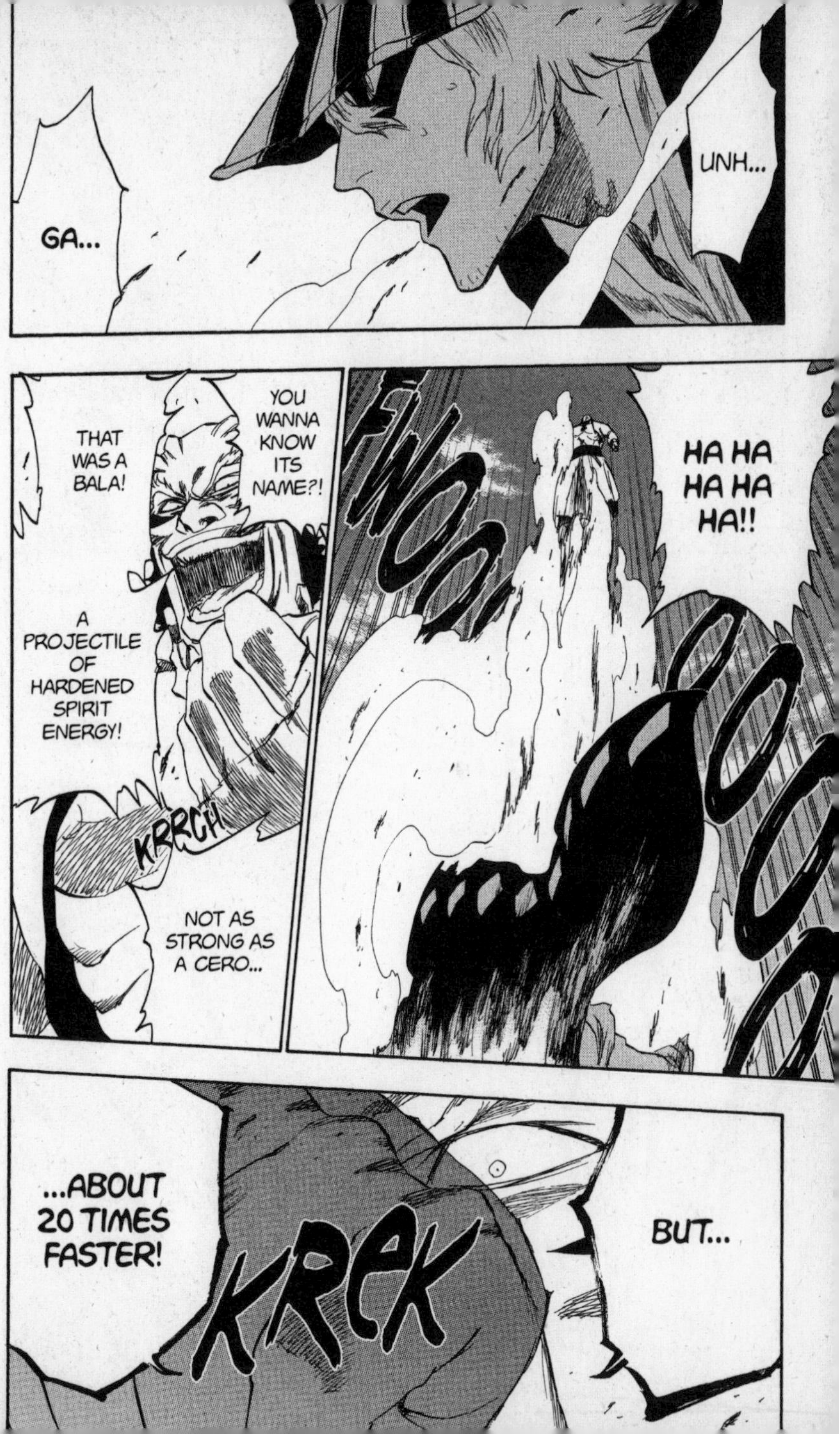
UNH...
GA...
HA HA HA HA HA!!
YOU WANNA KNOW ITS NAME?!
THAT WAS A BALA!
A PROJECTILE OF HARDENED SPIRIT ENERGY!
KRRCH
NOT AS STRONG AS A CERO...
BUT...
KREK
...ABOUT 20 TIMES FASTER!

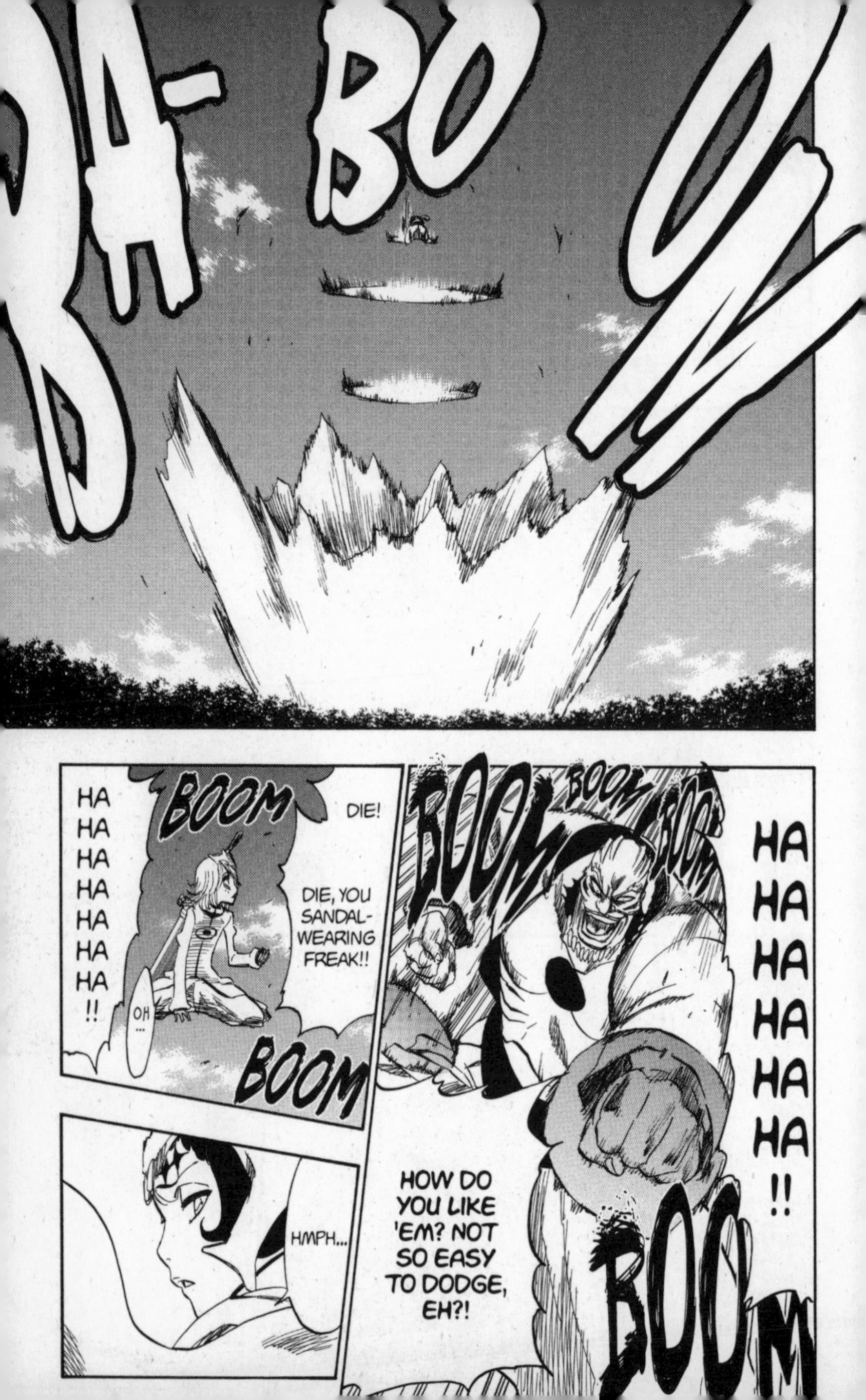
BA- BOOM
BOOM BOOM BOOM
HA HA HA HA HA HA HA HA!!
HOW DO YOU LIKE 'EM? NOT SO EASY TO DODGE, EH?!
BOOM
HA HA HA HA HA HA HA!!
BOOM
DIE!
DIE, YOU SANDAL-WEARING FREAK!!
OH...
BOOM
HMPH...

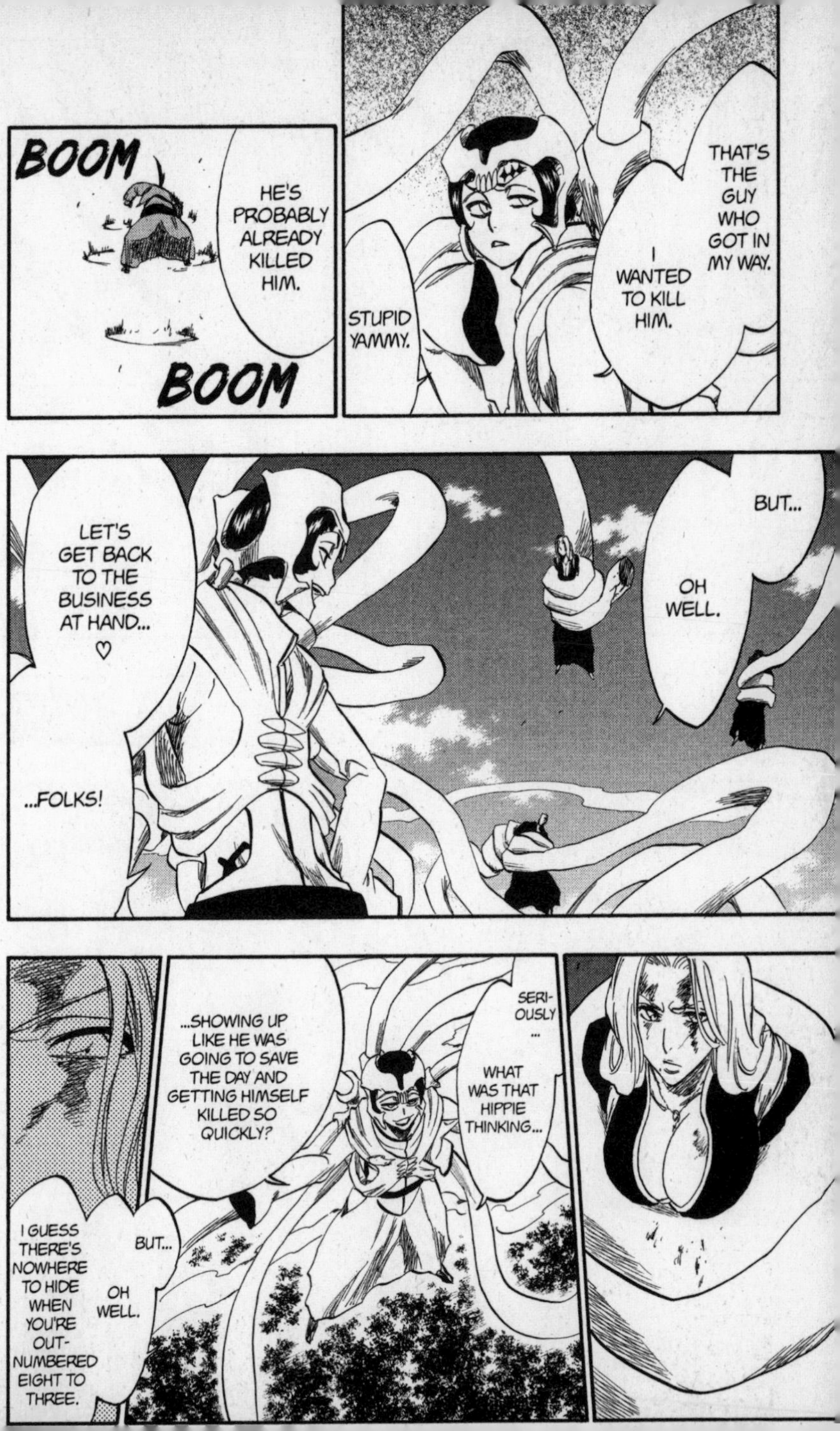
THAT'S THE GUY WHO GOT IN MY WAY.
I WANTED TO KILL HIM.
STUPID YAMMY.
BOOM
HE'S PROBABLY ALREADY KILLED HIM.
BOOM
BUT...
OH WELL.
LET'S GET BACK TO THE BUSINESS AT HAND... ♡
...FOLKS!
SERIOUSLY...
WHAT WAS THAT HIPPIE THINKING...
...SHOWING UP LIKE HE WAS GOING TO SAVE THE DAY AND GETTING HIMSELF KILLED SO QUICKLY?
BUT...
OH WELL.
I GUESS THERE'S NOWHERE TO HIDE WHEN YOU'RE OUT-NUMBERED EIGHT TO THREE.

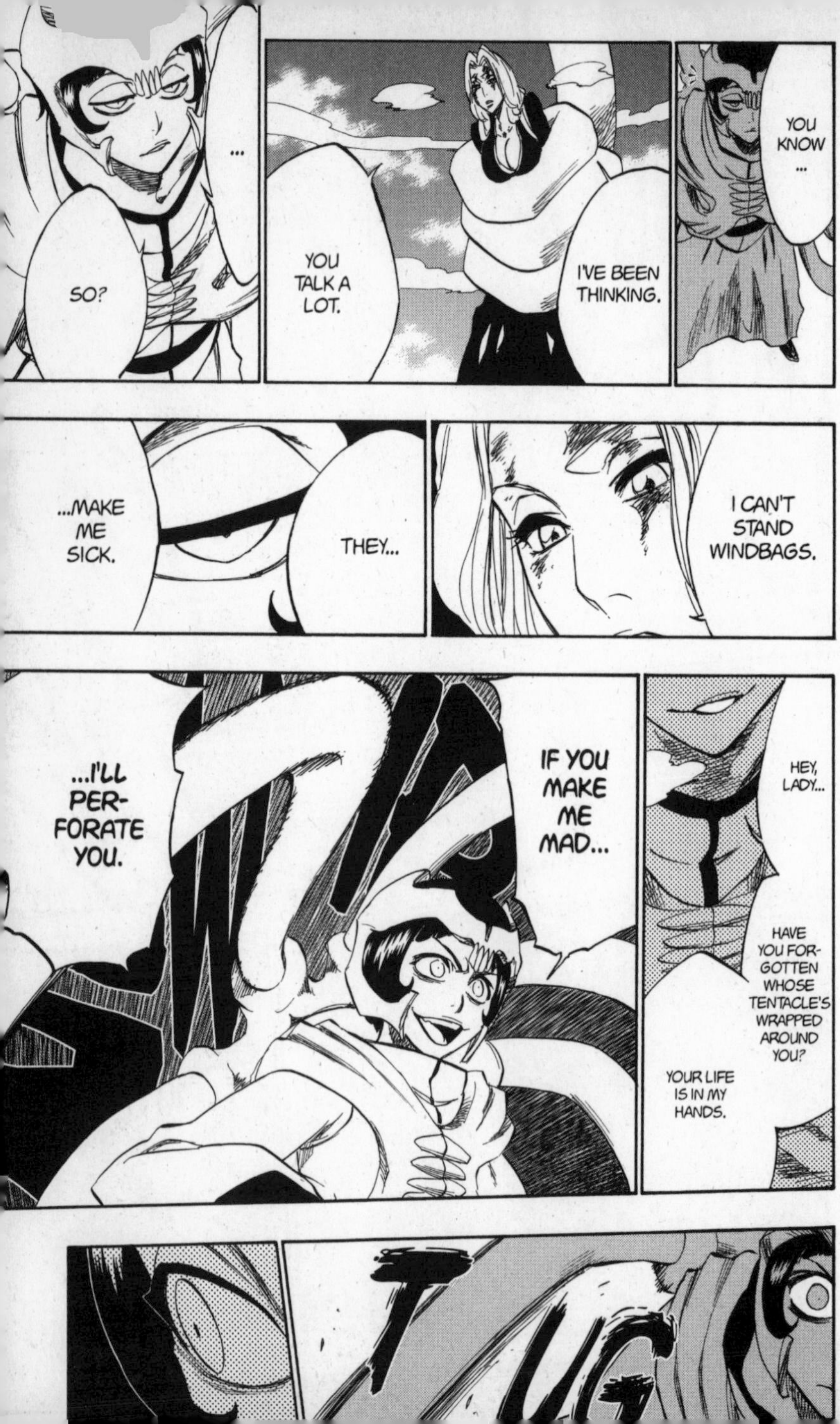
YOU KNOW ...
I'VE BEEN THINKING.
YOU TALK A LOT.
...
SO?
I CAN'T STAND WINDBAGS.
THEY...
...MAKE ME SICK.
HEY, LADY...
HAVE YOU FOR-GOTTEN WHOSE TENTACLE'S WRAPPED AROUND YOU?
YOUR LIFE IS IN MY HANDS.
IF YOU MAKE ME MAD...
...I'LL PER-FORATE YOU.

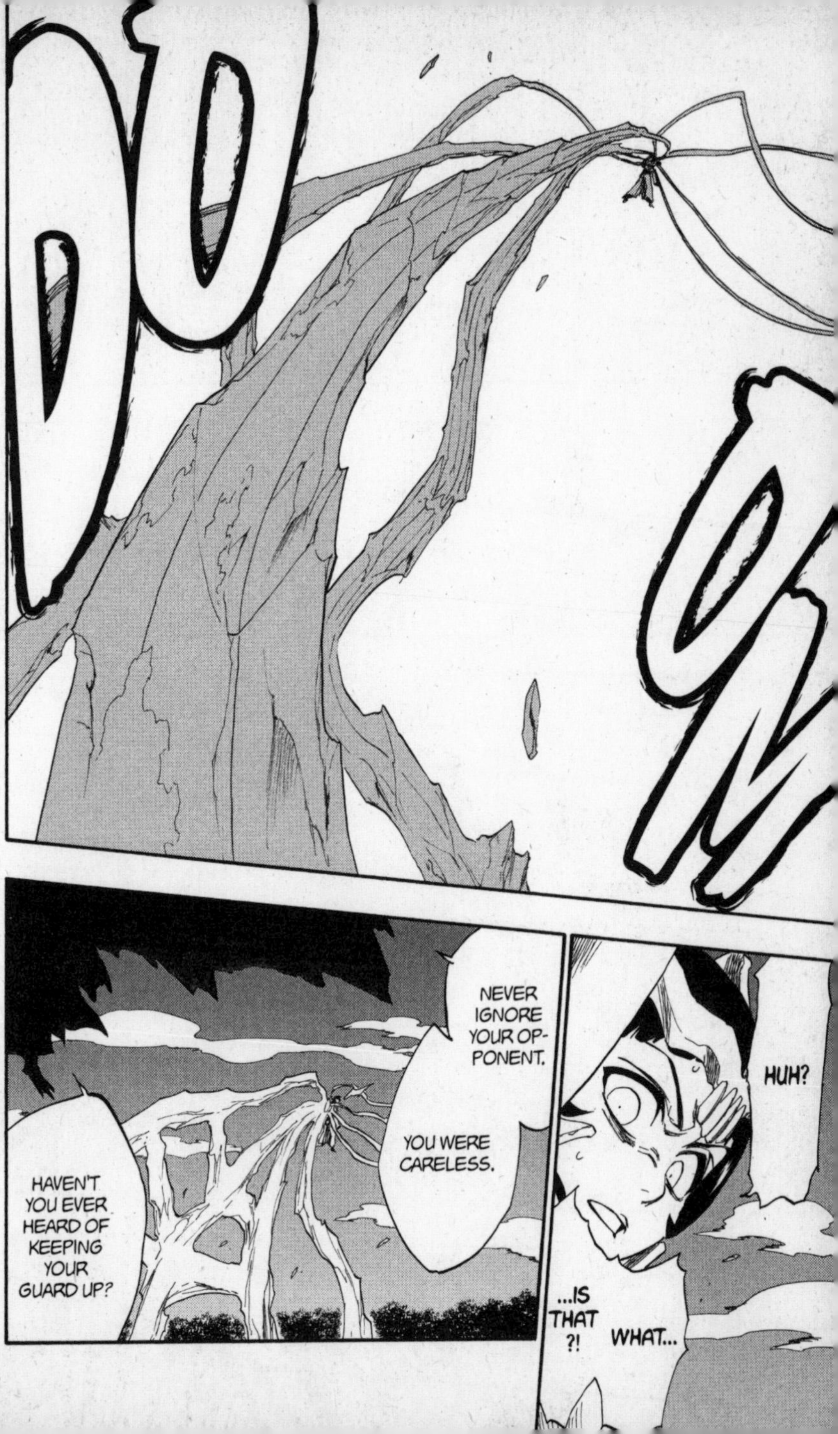
HUH?
WHAT...
...IS THAT?!
NEVER IGNORE YOUR OP-PONENT.
YOU WERE CARELESS.
HAVEN'T YOU EVER HEARD OF KEEPING YOUR GUARD UP?

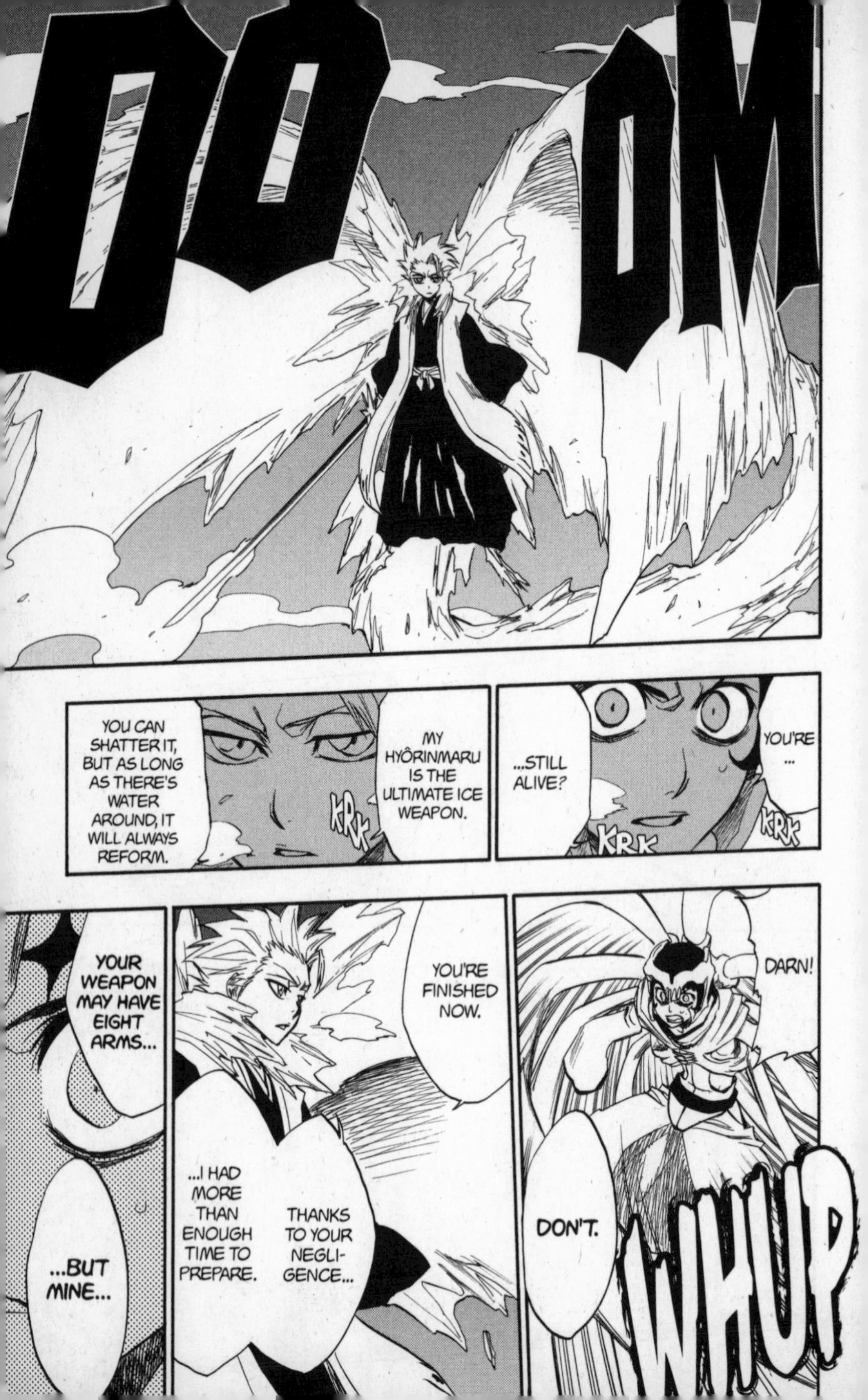
DOOM
YOU'RE ...
...STILL ALIVE?
KRK
KRK
MY HYÔRINMARU IS THE ULTIMATE ICE WEAPON.
YOU CAN SHATTER IT, BUT AS LONG AS THERE'S WATER AROUND, IT WILL ALWAYS REFORM.
KRK
DARN!
DON'T.
WHUP
YOU'RE FINISHED NOW.
THANKS TO YOUR NEGLI-GENCE...
...I HAD MORE THAN ENOUGH TIME TO PREPARE.
YOUR WEAPON MAY HAVE EIGHT ARMS...
...BUT MINE...

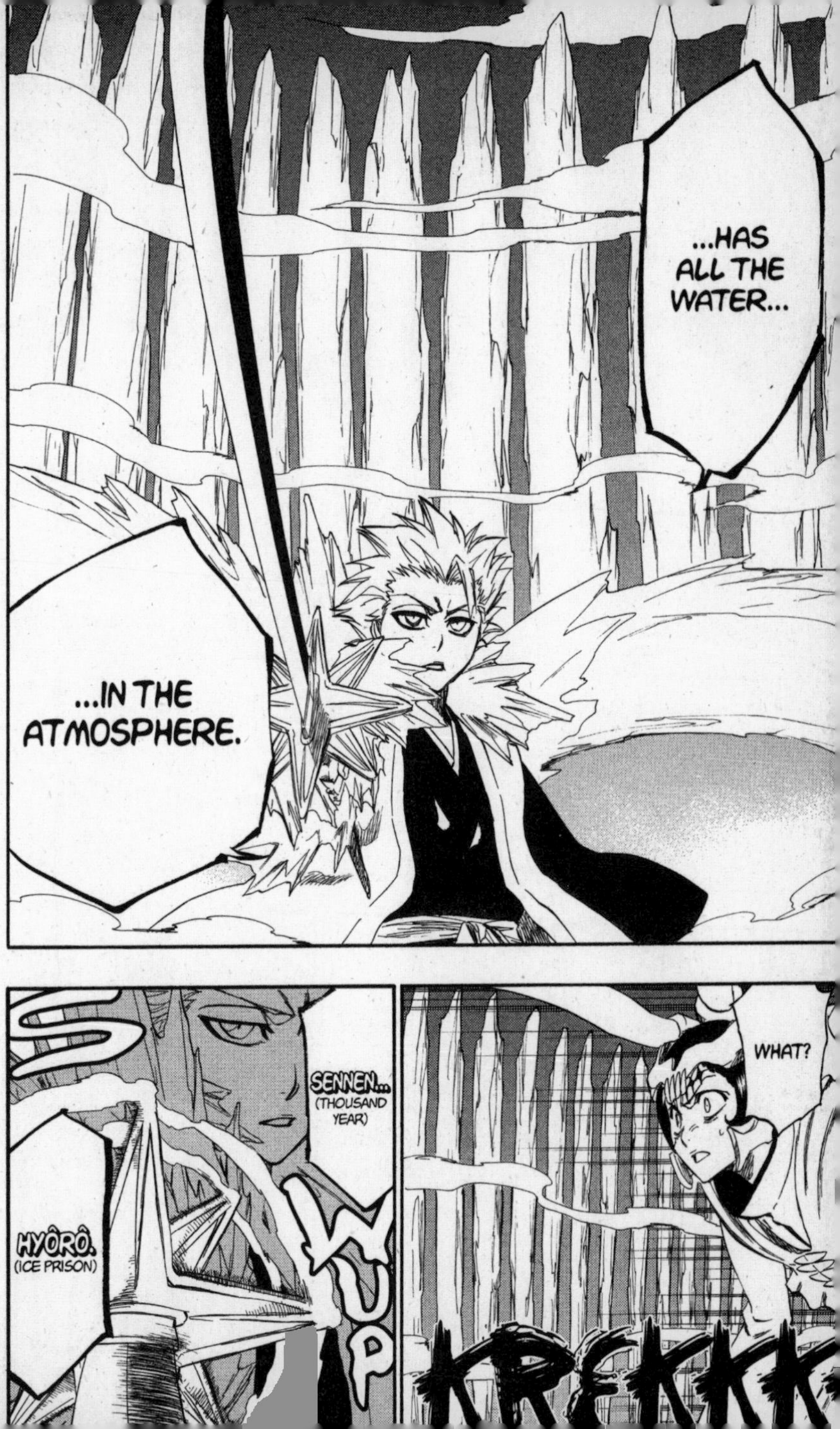
...HAS ALL THE WATER...
...IN THE ATMOSPHERE.
WHAT?
KRKKKK
SENNEN... (THOUSAND YEAR)
HYÔRÔ. (ICE PRISON)
WUP

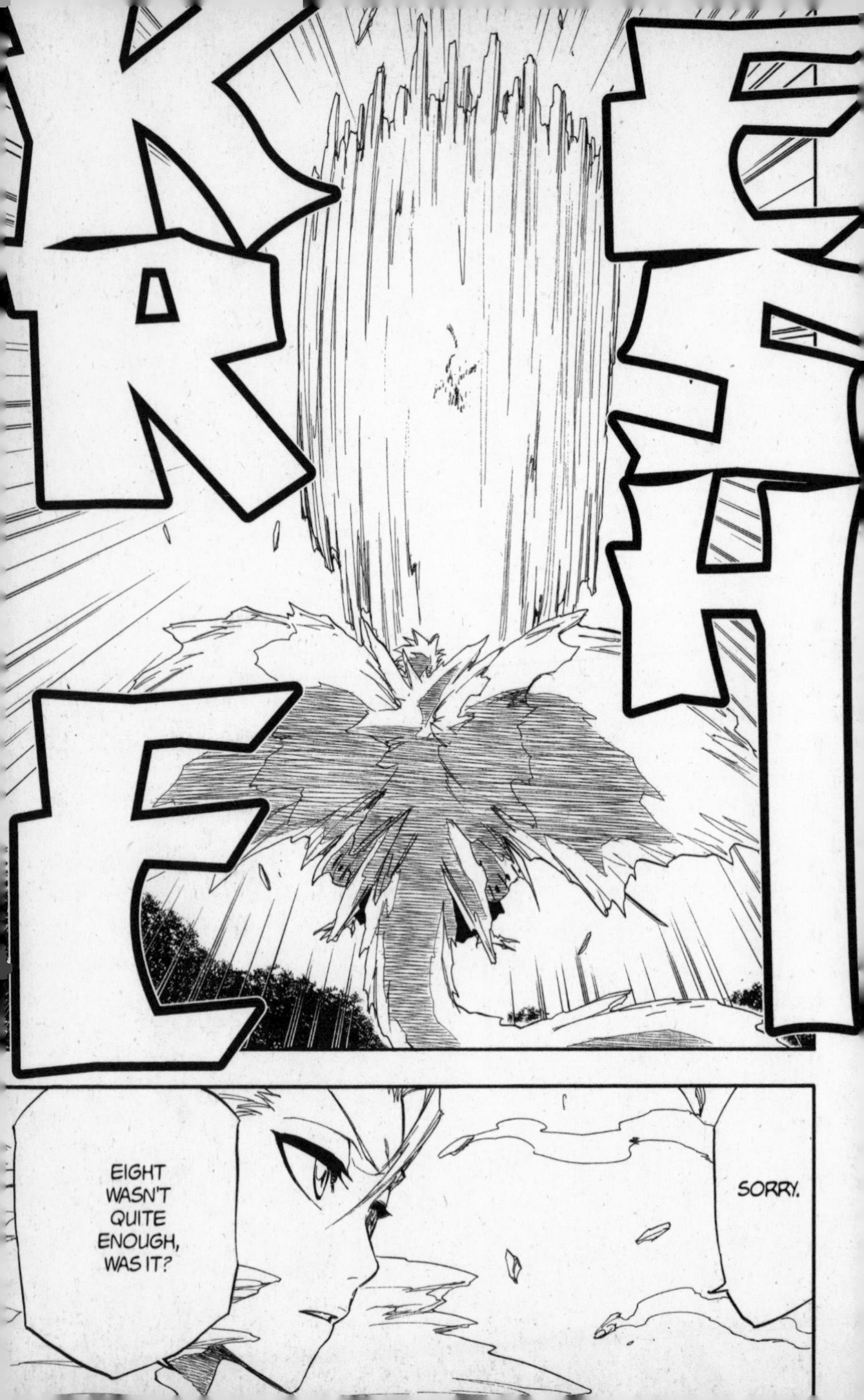
SORRY.
EIGHT WASN'T QUITE ENOUGH, WAS IT?

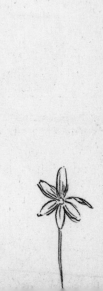

235. The Frozen Clutch

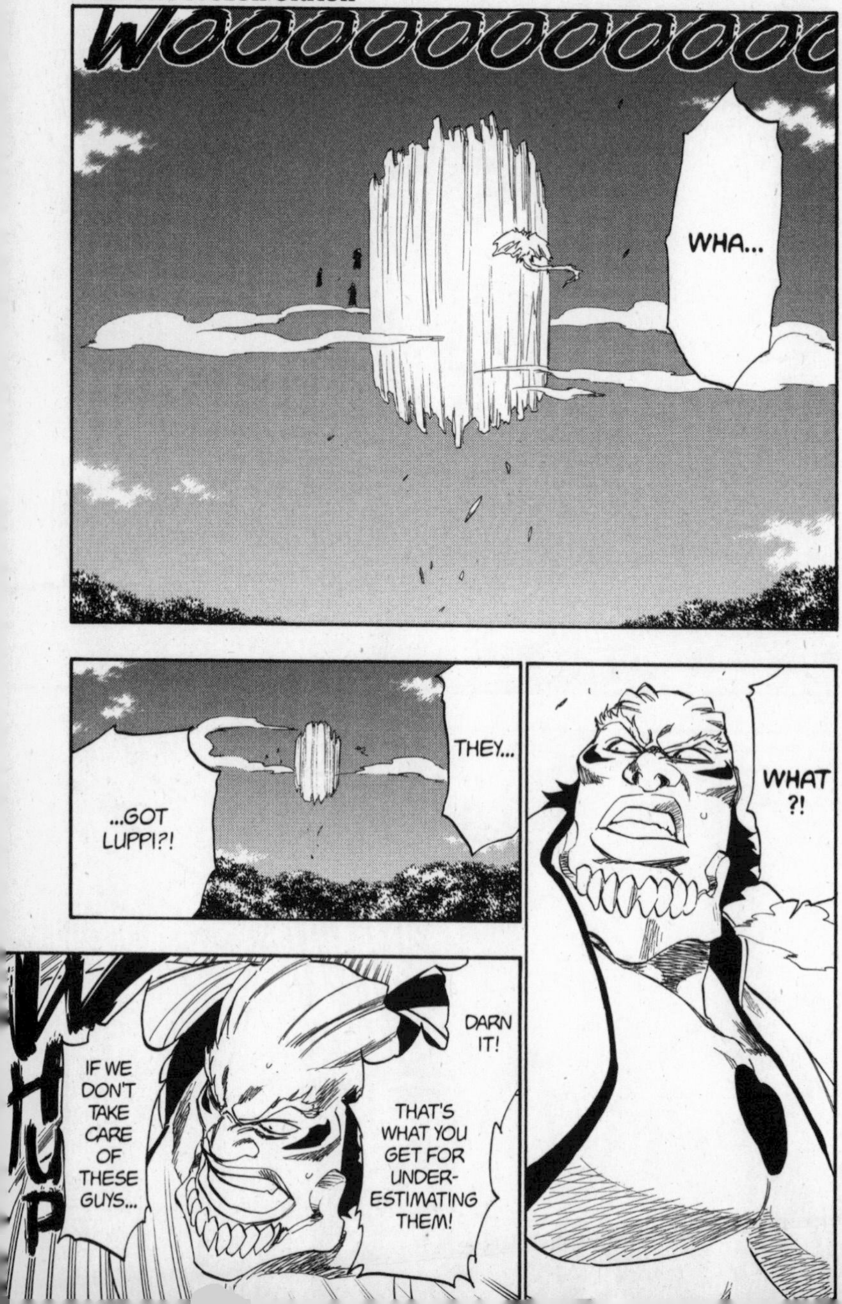
WOOOOOOOOOOO
WHA...
WHAT ?!
THEY...
...GOT LUPPI?!
DARN IT!
THAT'S WHAT YOU GET FOR UNDER-ESTIMATING THEM!
IF WE DON'T TAKE CARE OF THESE GUYS...
WHUP

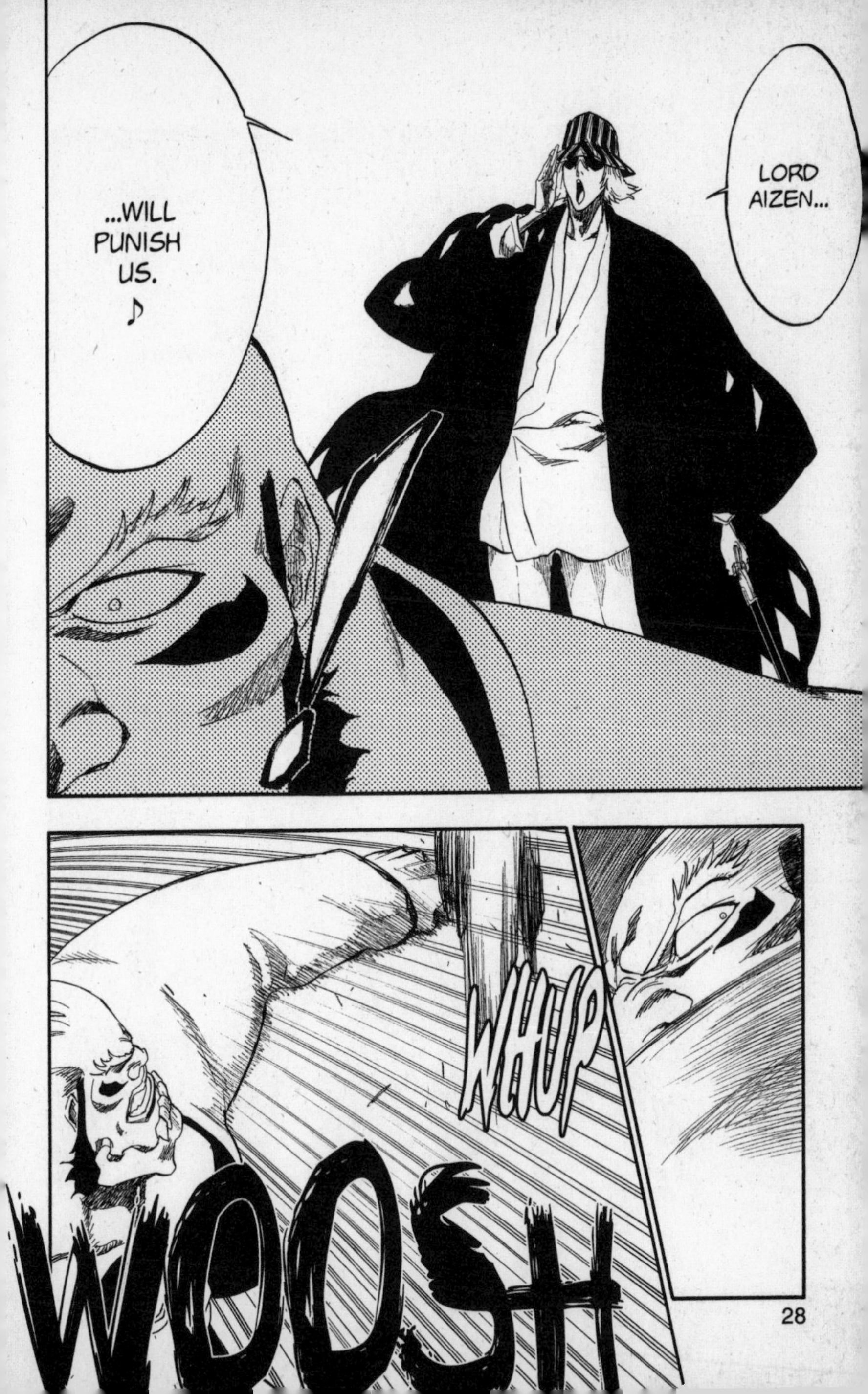
LORD AIZEN...
...WILL PUNISH US. ♪
WHUP
WOOSH

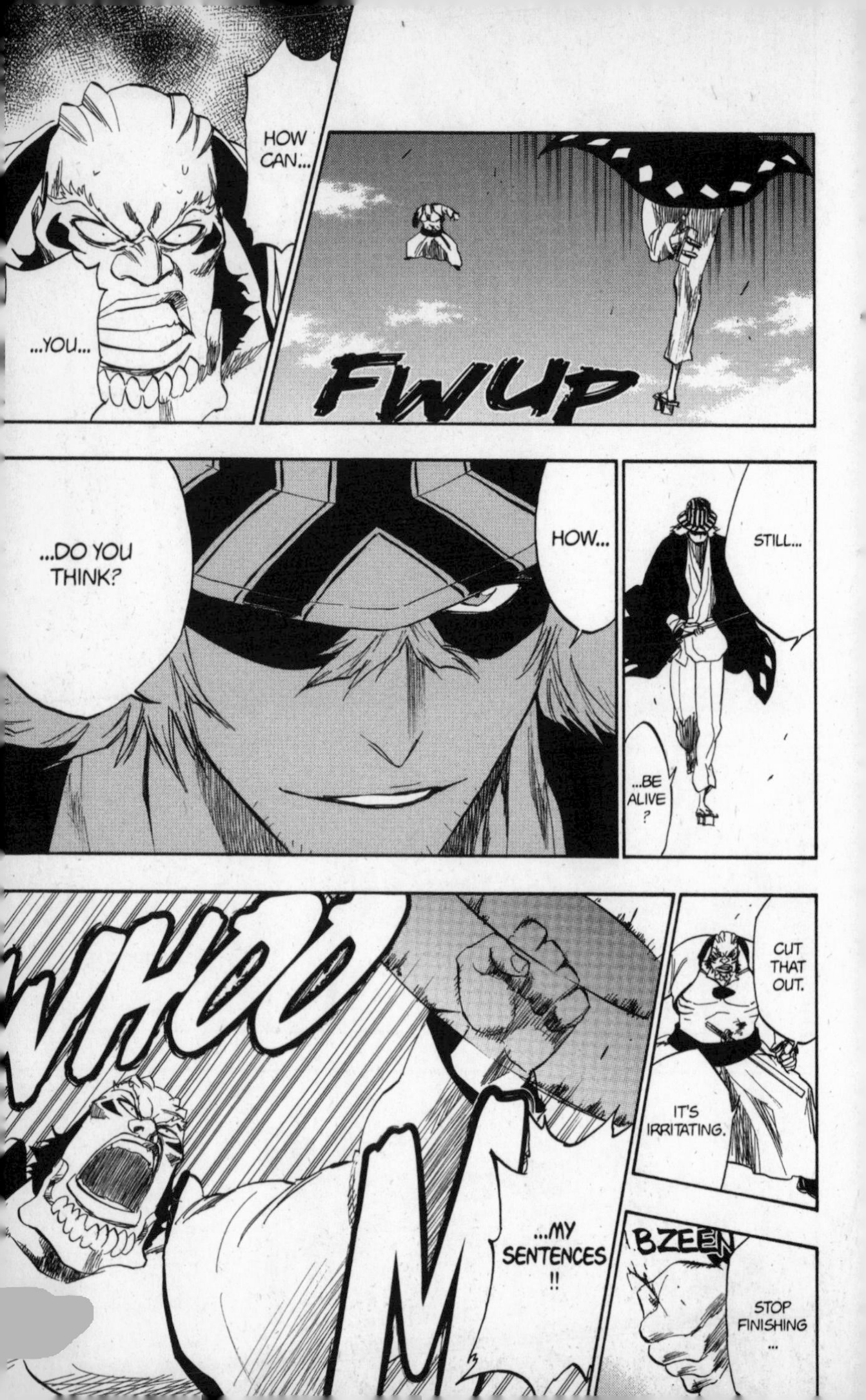
FWUP
HOW CAN...
...YOU...
STILL...
...BE ALIVE?
HOW...
...DO YOU THINK?
CUT THAT OUT.
IT'S IRRITATING.
BZEEN
STOP FINISHING...
...MY SENTENCES!!

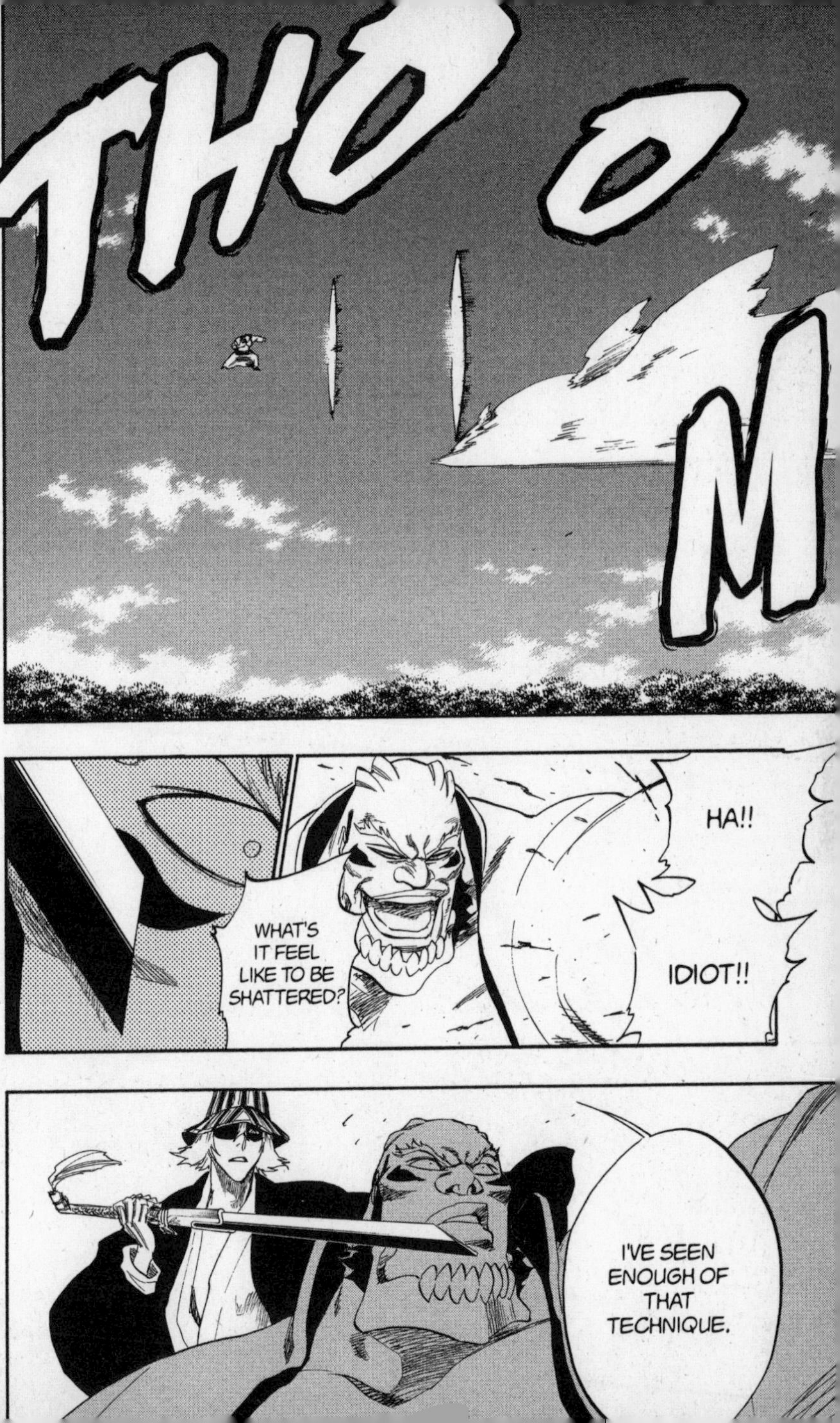
THOOOM
HA!!
WHAT'S IT FEEL LIKE TO BE SHATTERED?
IDIOT!!
I'VE SEEN ENOUGH OF THAT TECHNIQUE.

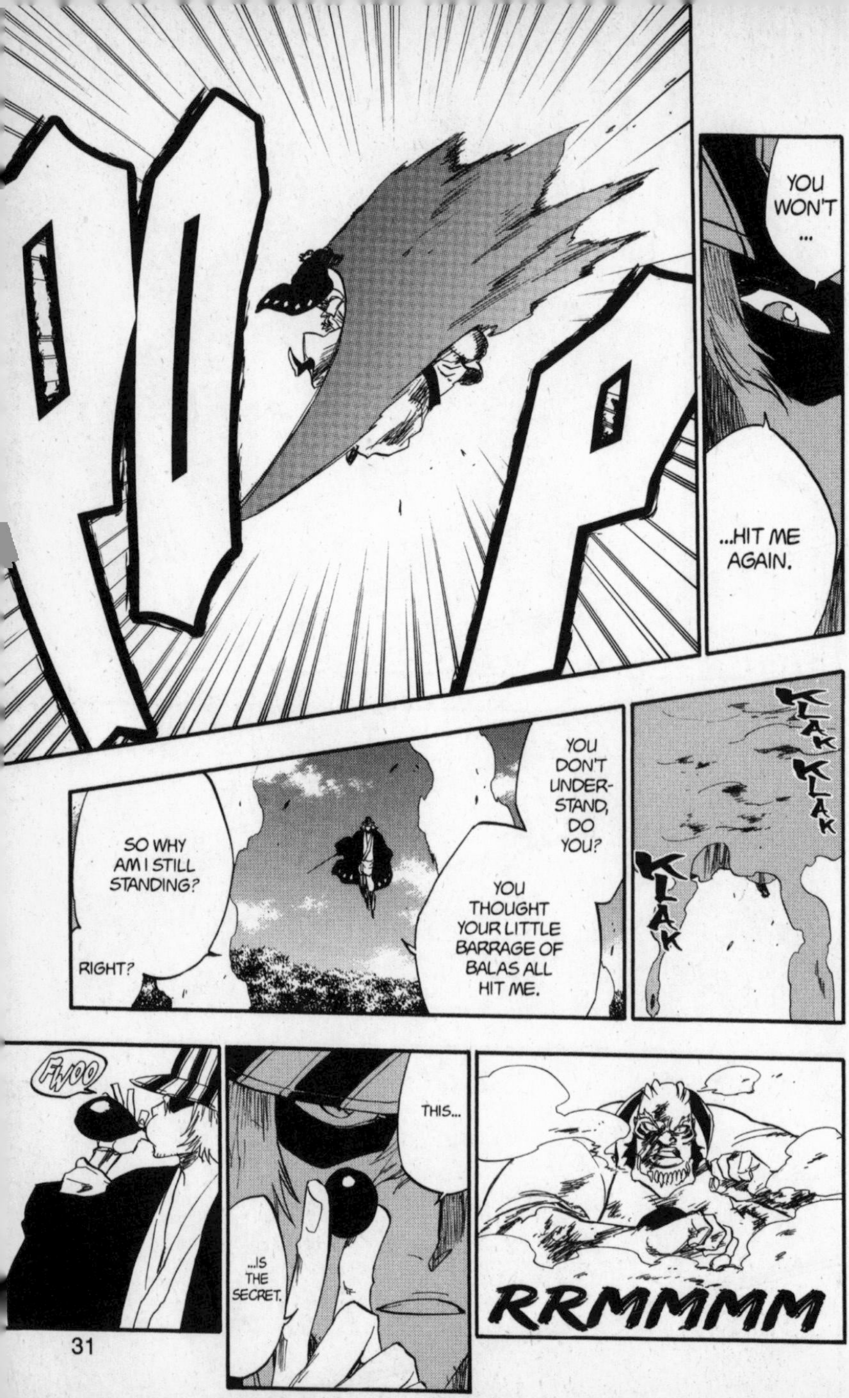
YOU WON'T ...
...HIT ME AGAIN.
KLAK KLAK
KLAK
YOU DON'T UNDER-STAND, DO YOU?
YOU THOUGHT YOUR LITTLE BARRAGE OF BALAS ALL HIT ME.
SO WHY AM I STILL STANDING?
RIGHT?
RRMMMMM
THIS...
...IS THE SECRET.
FWOO

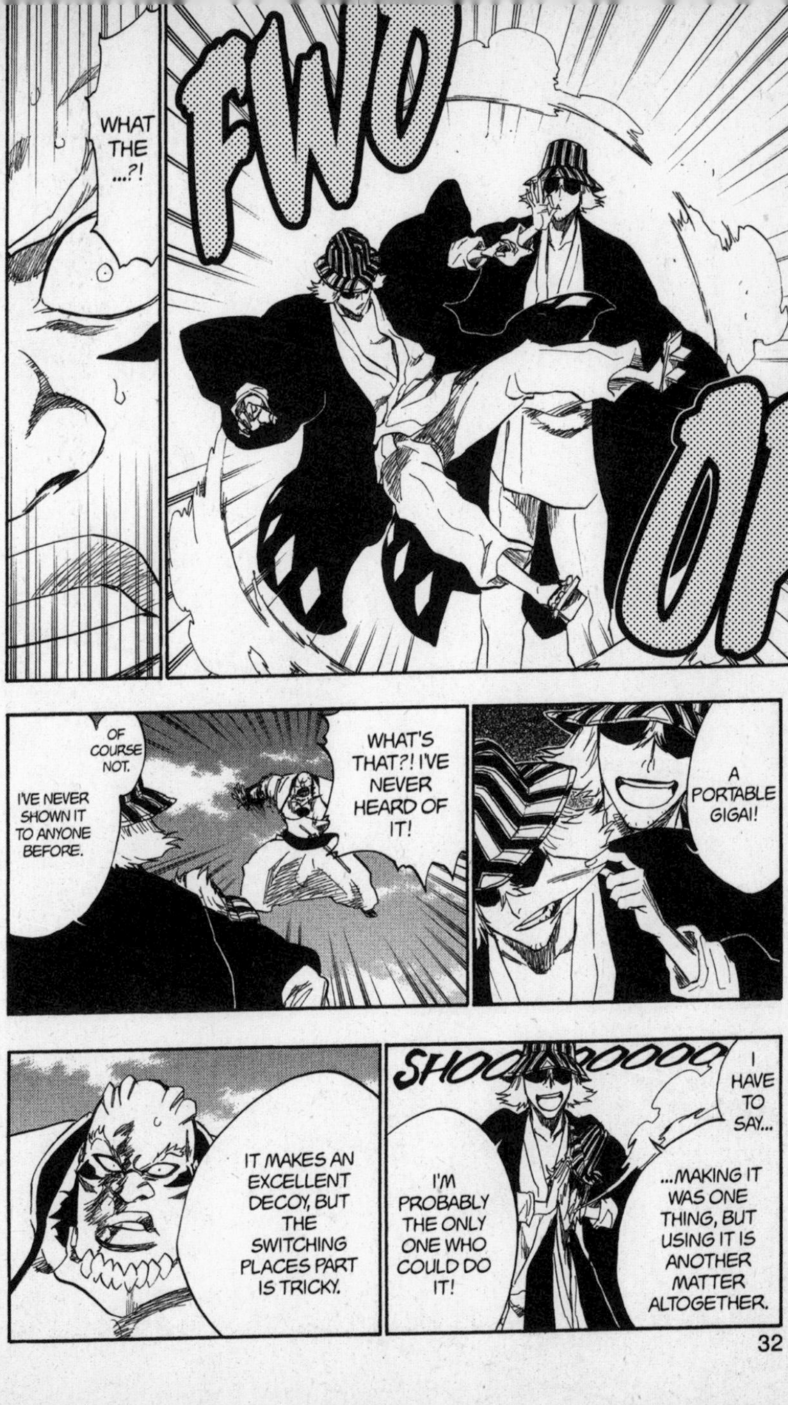
FWO
OF
WHAT THE ...?!
A PORTABLE GIGAI!
WHAT'S THAT?! I'VE NEVER HEARD OF IT!
OF COURSE NOT.
I'VE NEVER SHOWN IT TO ANYONE BEFORE.
SHOOOOOOOOO
I HAVE TO SAY...
...MAKING IT WAS ONE THING, BUT USING IT IS ANOTHER MATTER ALTOGETHER.
I'M PROBABLY THE ONLY ONE WHO COULD DO IT!
IT MAKES AN EXCELLENT DECOY, BUT THE SWITCHING PLACES PART IS TRICKY.

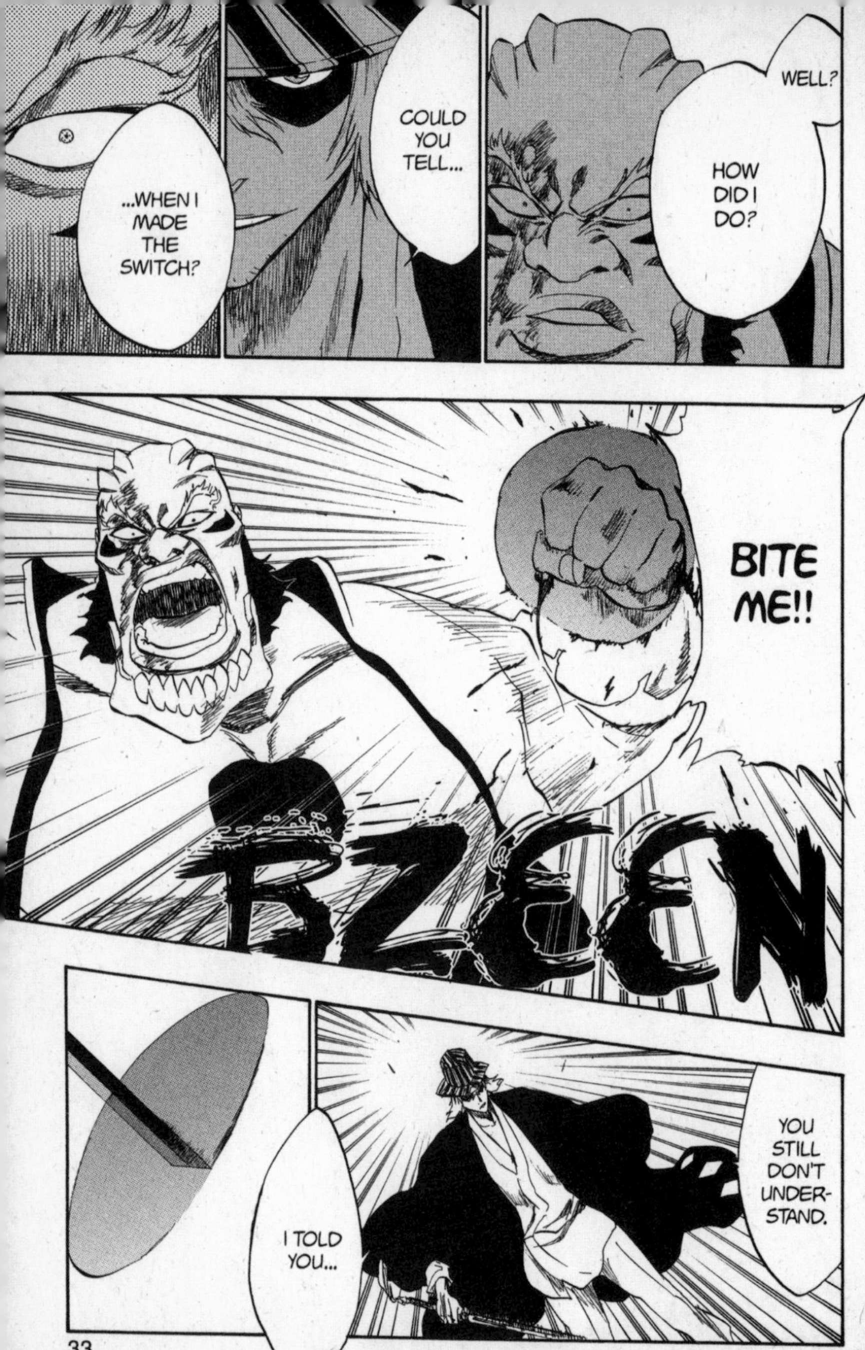
WELL?
HOW DID I DO?
COULD YOU TELL...
...WHEN I MADE THE SWITCH?
BITE ME!!
BZEEN
YOU STILL DON'T UNDER-STAND.
I TOLD YOU...

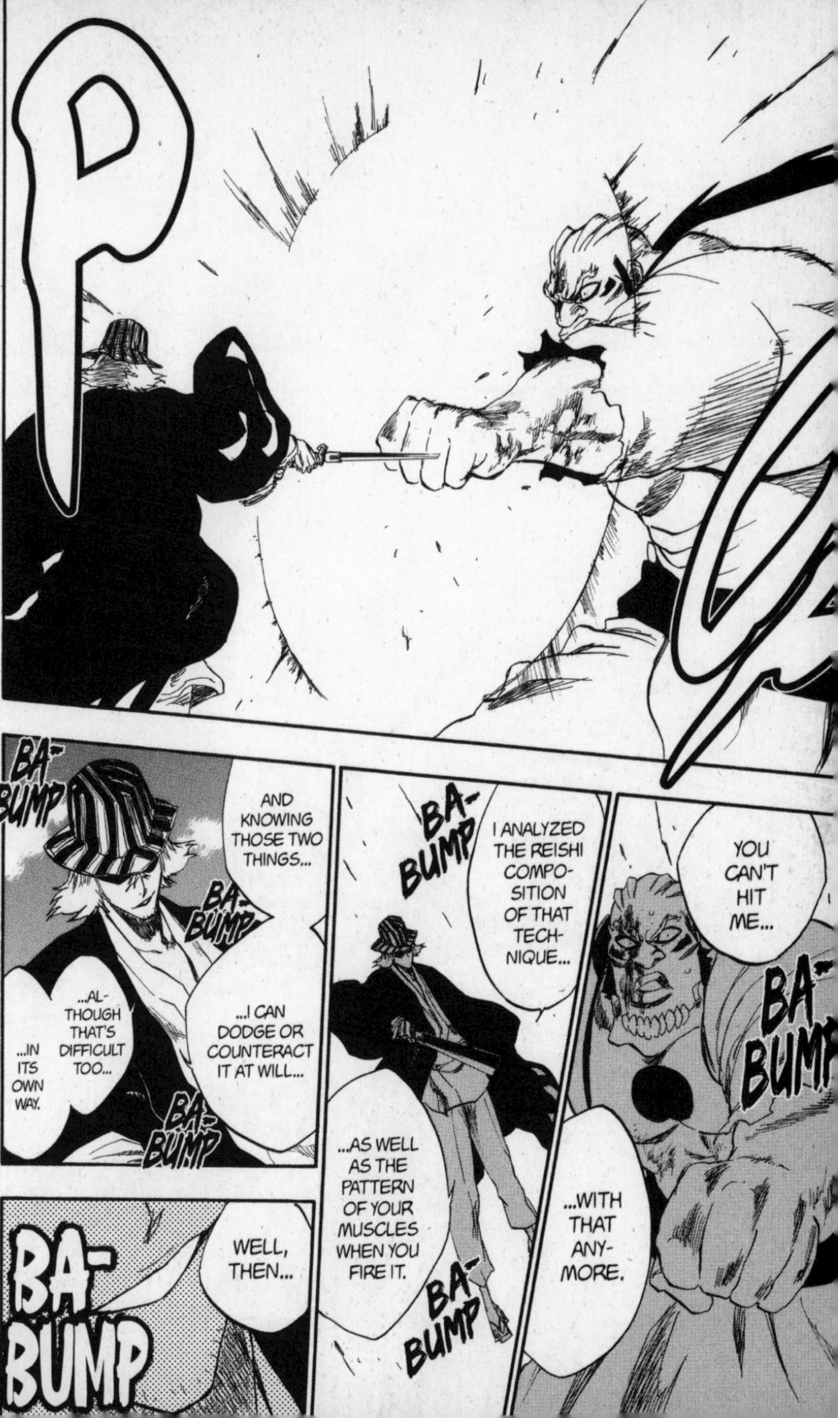
P
YOU CAN'T HIT ME...
BA-BUMP
...WITH THAT ANYMORE.
BA-BUMP
I ANALYZED THE REISHI COMPOSITION OF THAT TECHNIQUE...
...AS WELL AS THE PATTERN OF YOUR MUSCLES WHEN YOU FIRE IT.
BA-BUMP
BA-BUMP
AND KNOWING THOSE TWO THINGS...
BA-BUMP
...I CAN DODGE OR COUNTERACT IT AT WILL...
...ALTHOUGH THAT'S DIFFICULT TOO...
...IN ITS OWN WAY.
BA-BUMP
WELL, THEN...
BA-BUMP

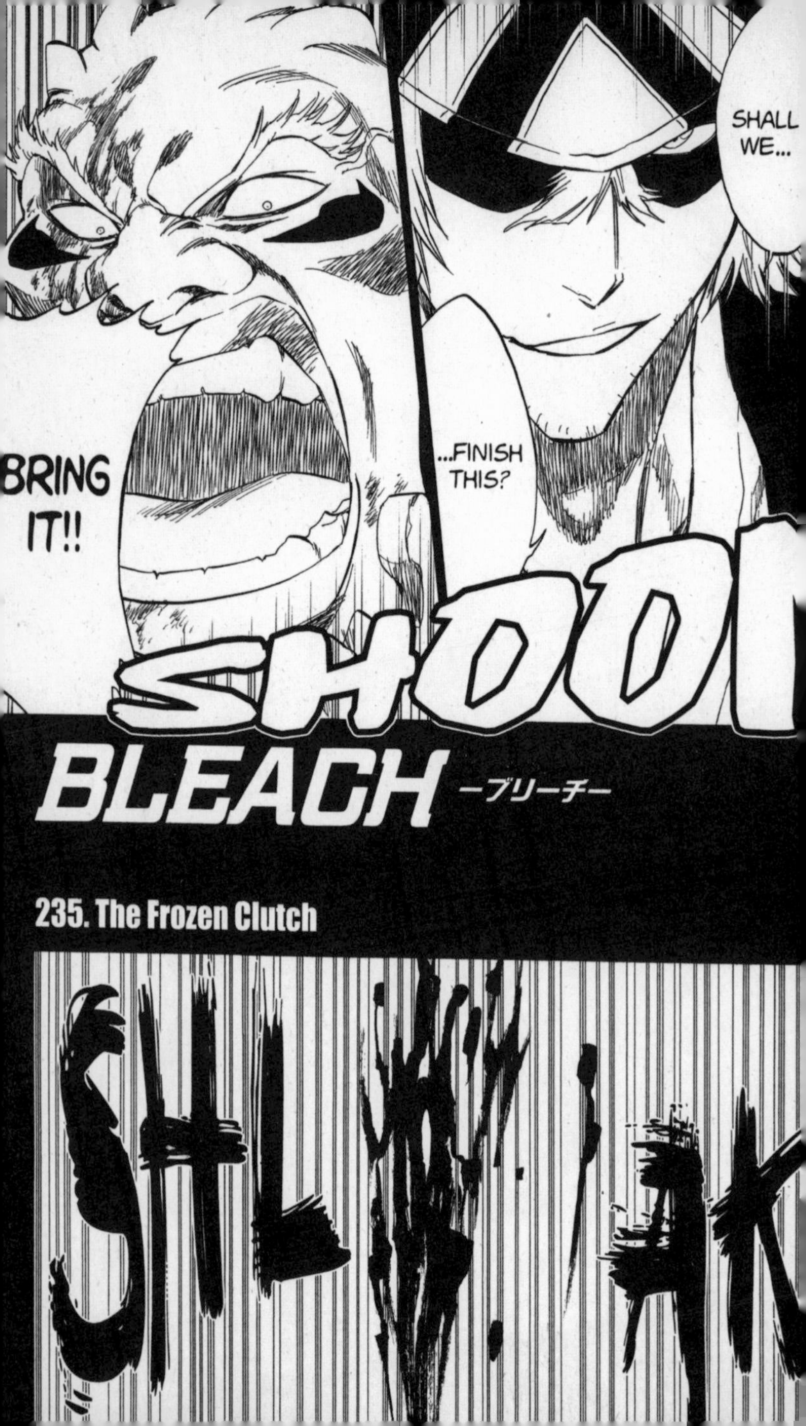
SHALL WE...
...FINISH THIS?
BRING IT!!
SHOO
BLEACH
ーブリーチー
235. The Frozen Clutch

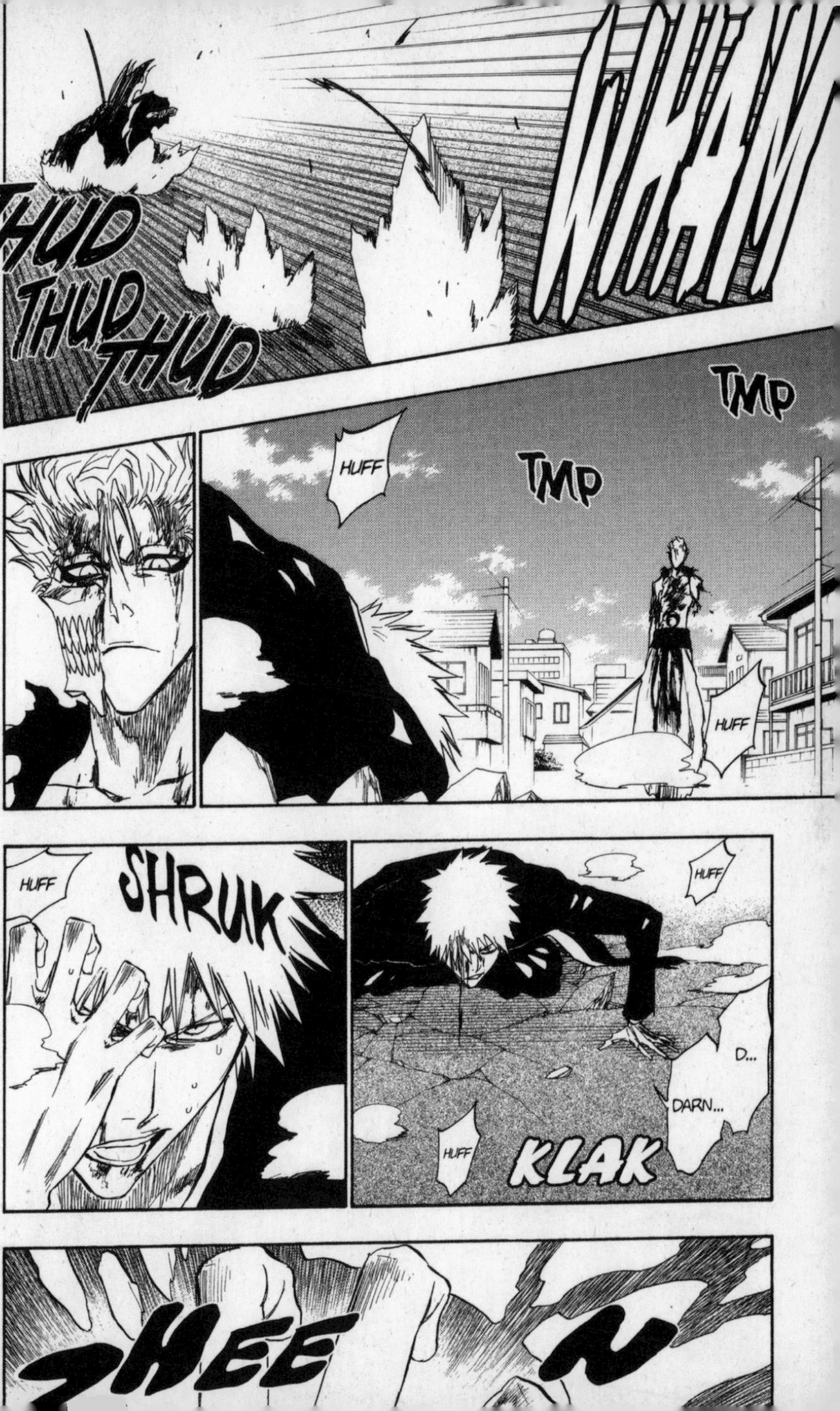
WHAM
THUD
THUD
THUD
TMP
TMP
HUFF
HUFF
HUFF
D...
DARN...
HUFF
KLAK
HUFF
SHRUK
SHEE N

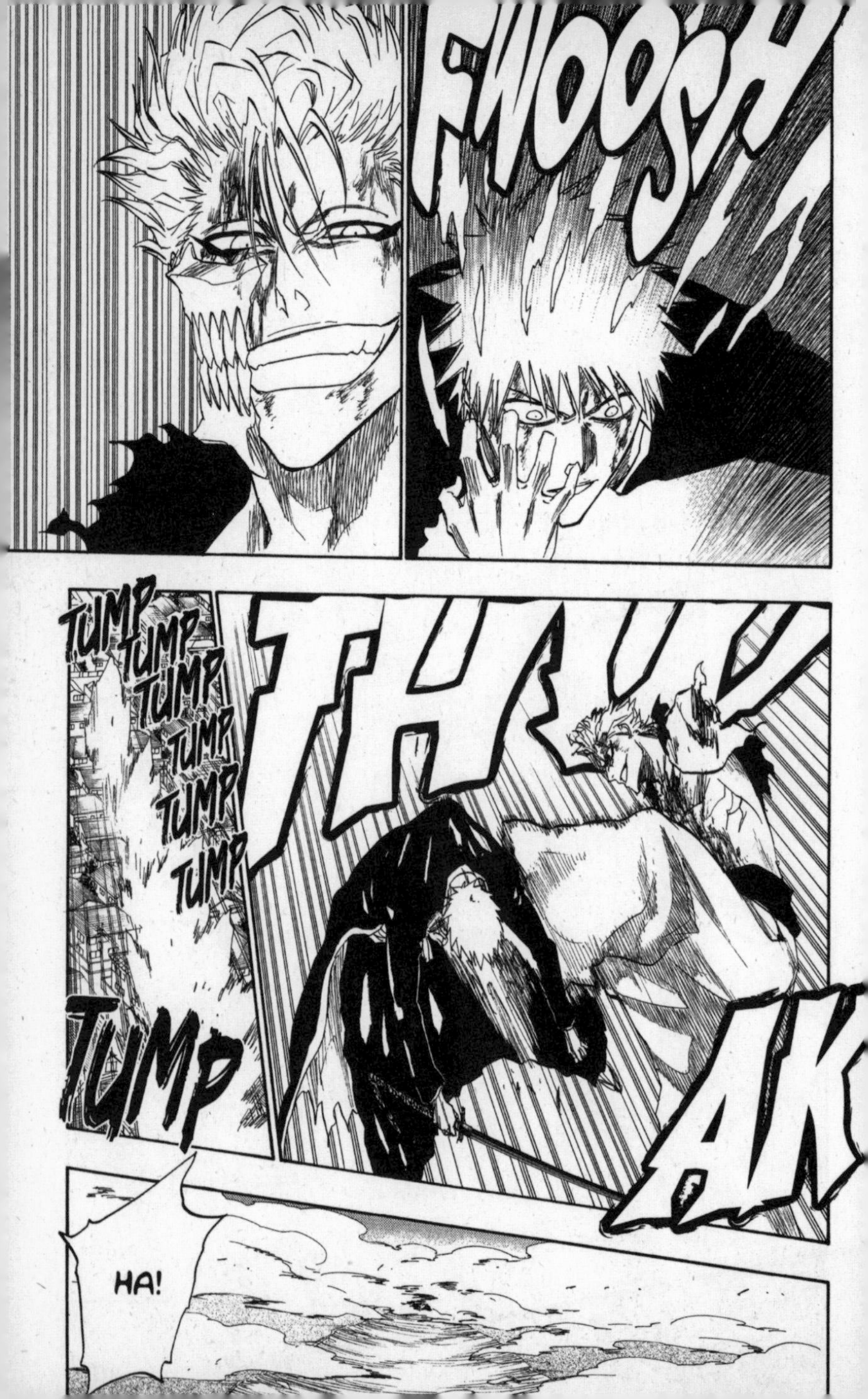
FWOOSH
THWAK
TUMP
TUMP
TUMP
TUMP
TUMP
TUMP
TUMP
TUMP
HA!

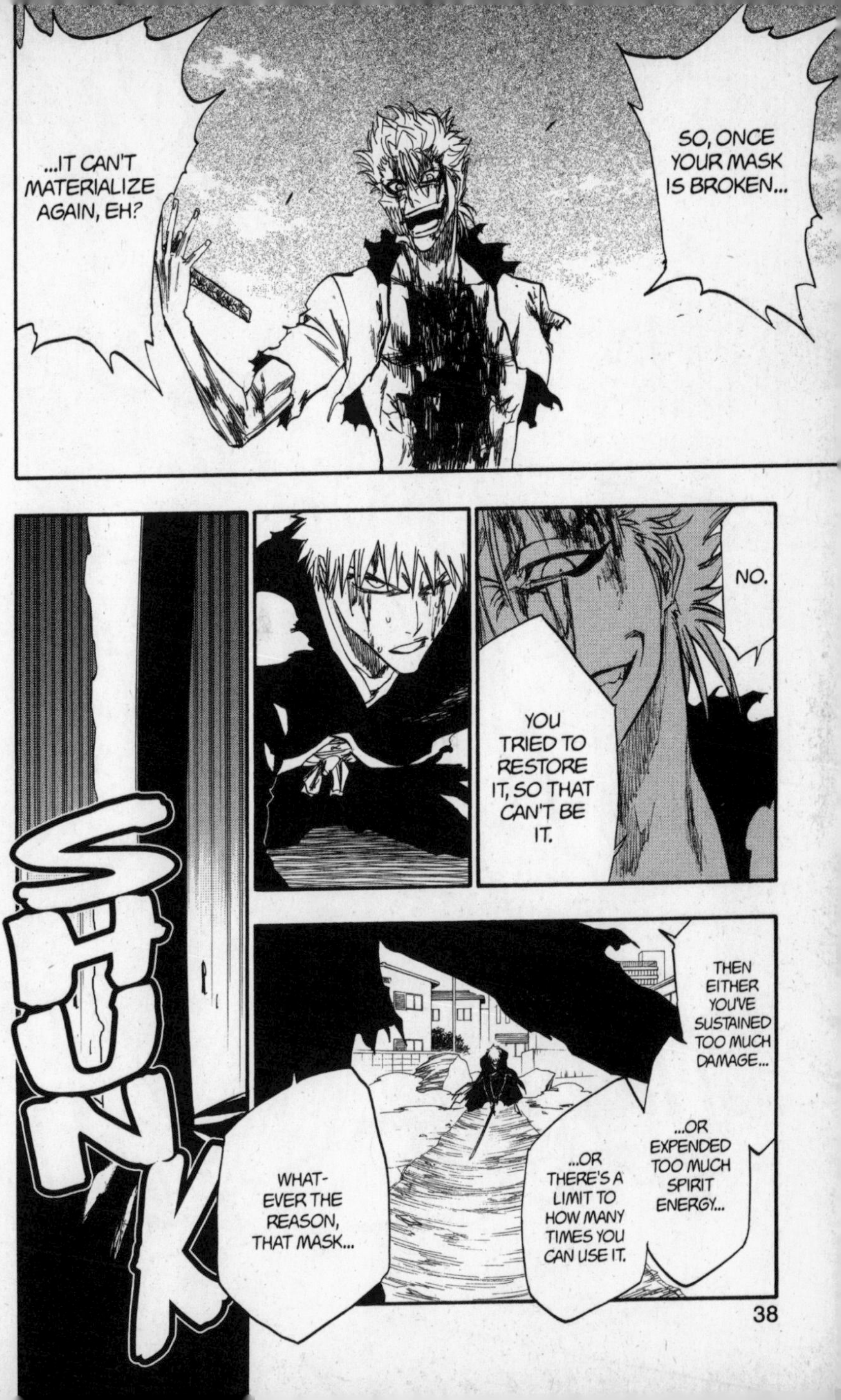
SO, ONCE YOUR MASK IS BROKEN...
...IT CAN'T MATERIALIZE AGAIN, EH?
NO.
YOU TRIED TO RESTORE IT, SO THAT CAN'T BE IT.
THEN EITHER YOU'VE SUSTAINED TOO MUCH DAMAGE...
...OR EXPENDED TOO MUCH SPIRIT ENERGY...
...OR THERE'S A LIMIT TO HOW MANY TIMES YOU CAN USE IT.
WHAT-EVER THE REASON, THAT MASK...
SHUNK

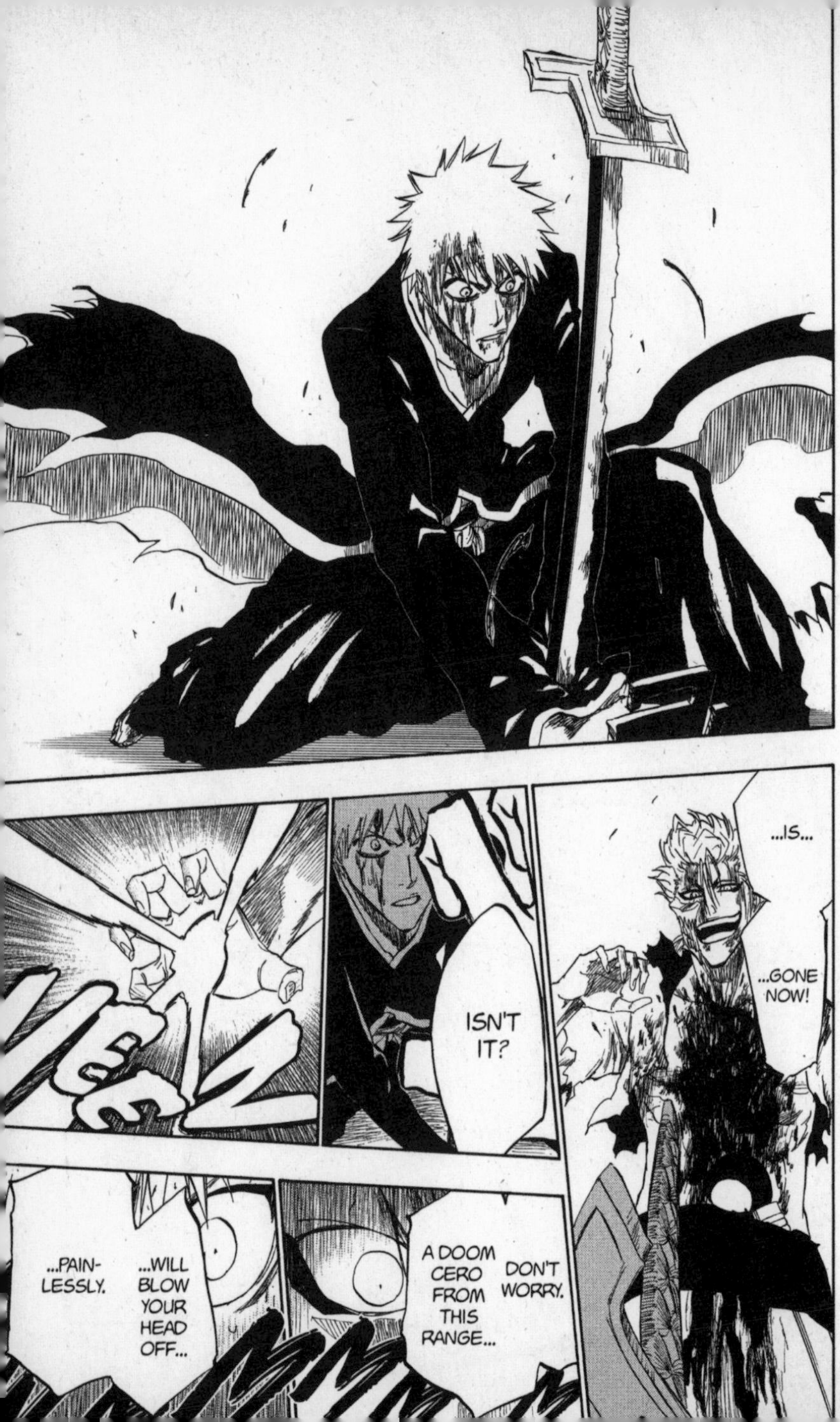
...IS...
...GONE NOW!
ISN'T IT?
DON'T WORRY.
A DOOM CERO FROM THIS RANGE...
...WILL BLOW YOUR HEAD OFF...
...PAIN-LESSLY.

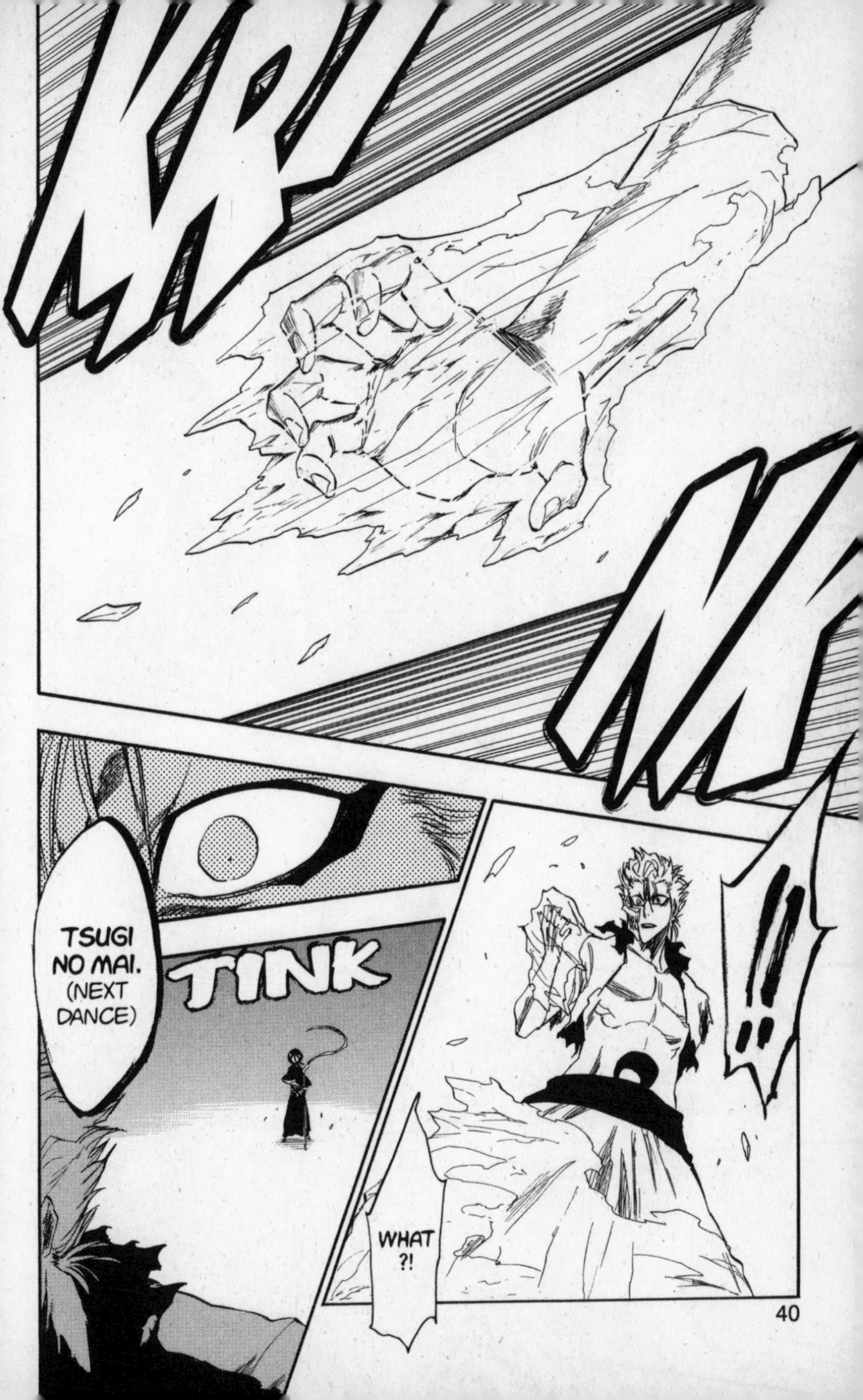
!!
WHAT ?!
TSUGI NO MAI. (NEXT DANCE)
TINK

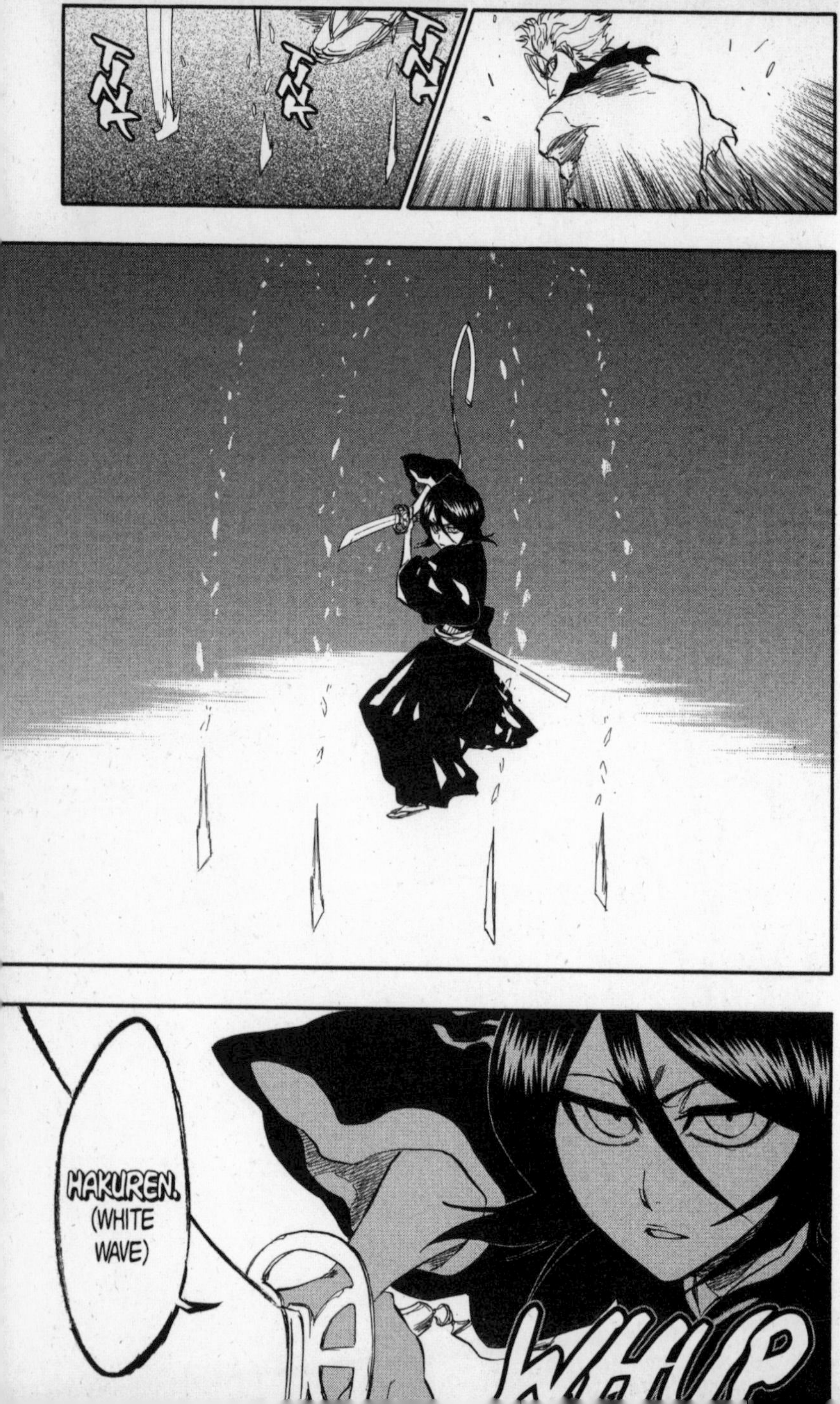
TINK
TINK
TINK
HAKUREN.
(WHITE
WAVE)
WHIP

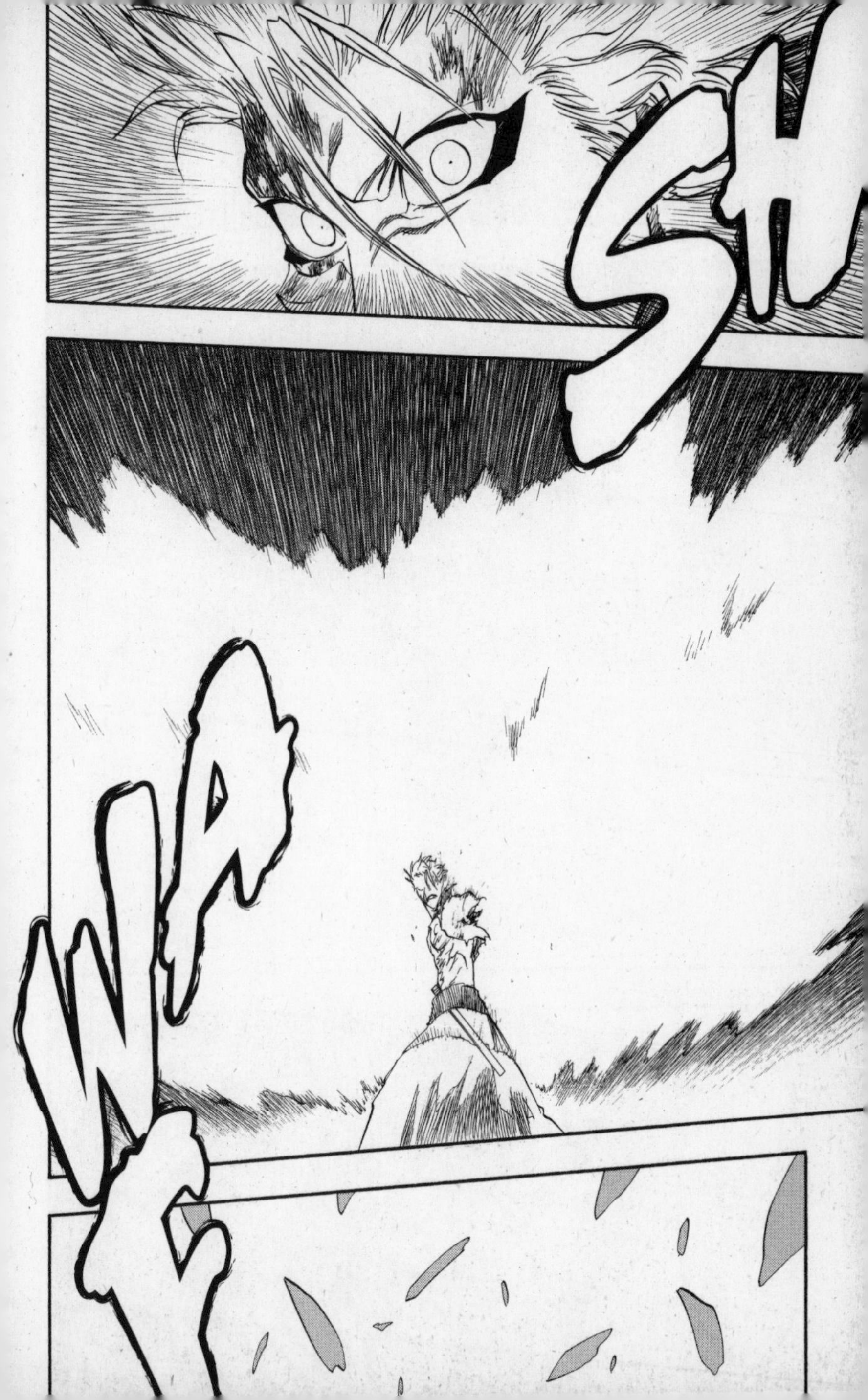
SH
WA

READ THIS WAY

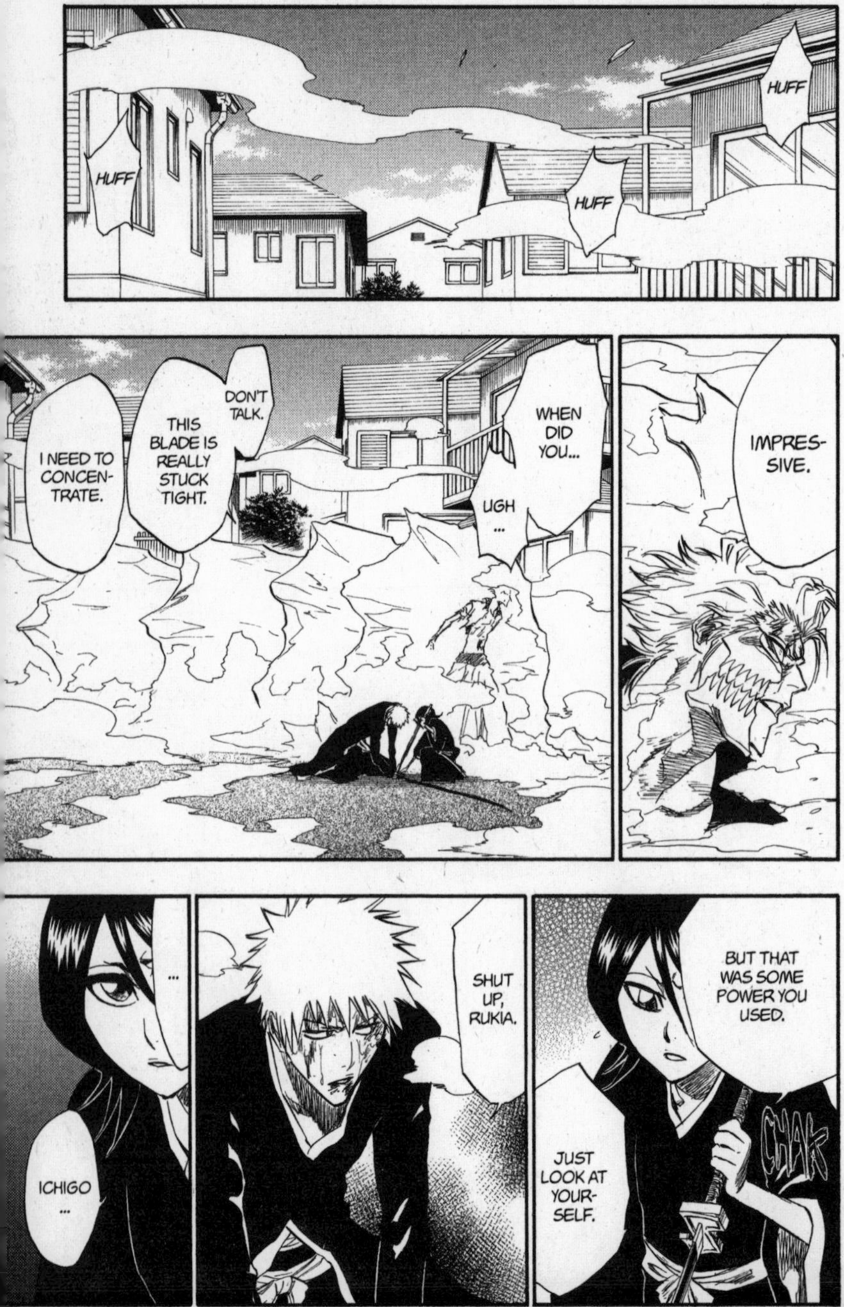
HUFF
HUFF
HUFF
IMPRES-SIVE.
WHEN DID YOU...
UGH ...
DON'T TALK.
THIS BLADE IS REALLY STUCK TIGHT.
I NEED TO CONCEN-TRATE.
BUT THAT WAS SOME POWER YOU USED.
JUST LOOK AT YOUR-SELF.
CHAK
SHUT UP, RUKIA.
...
ICHIGO ...

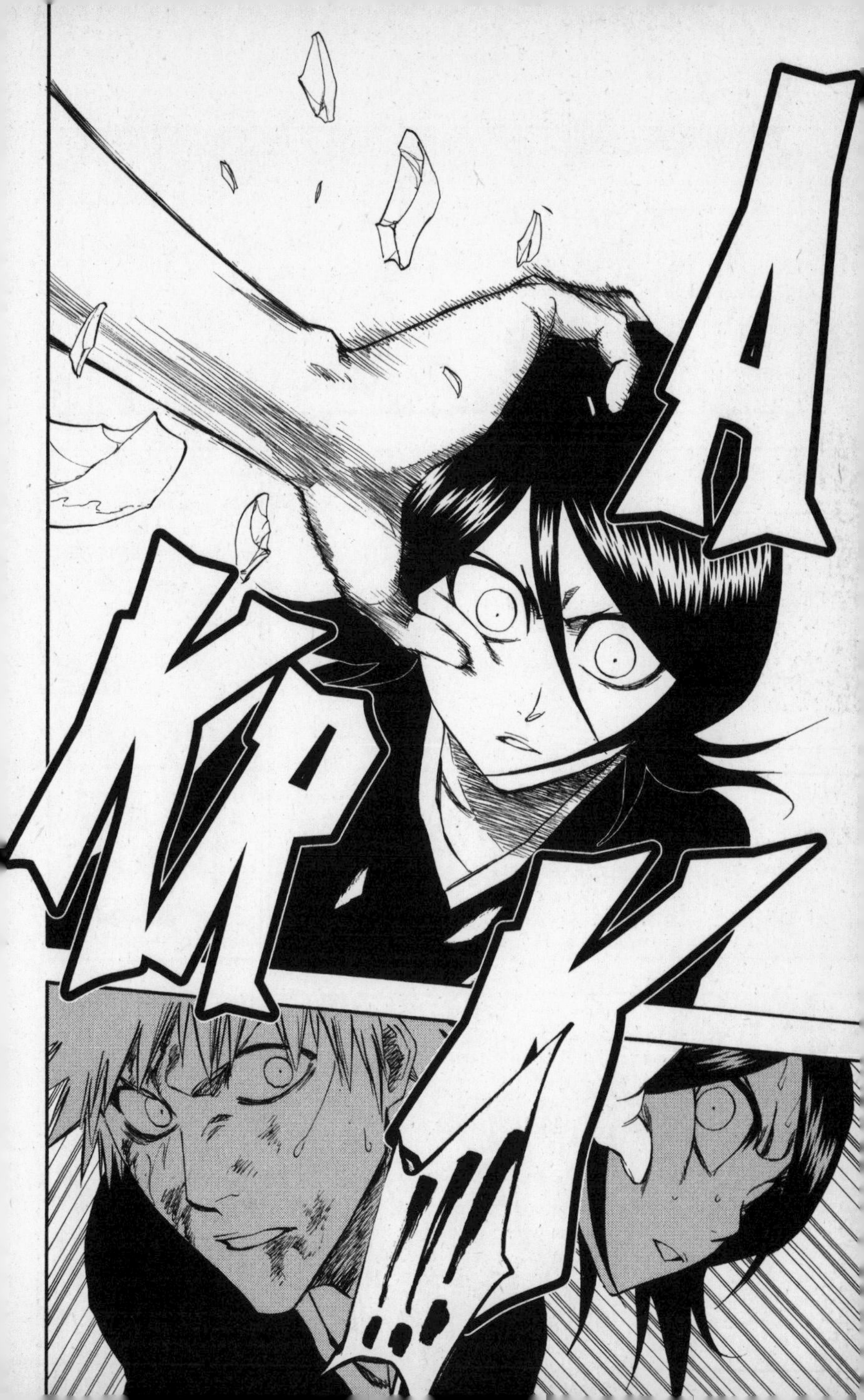

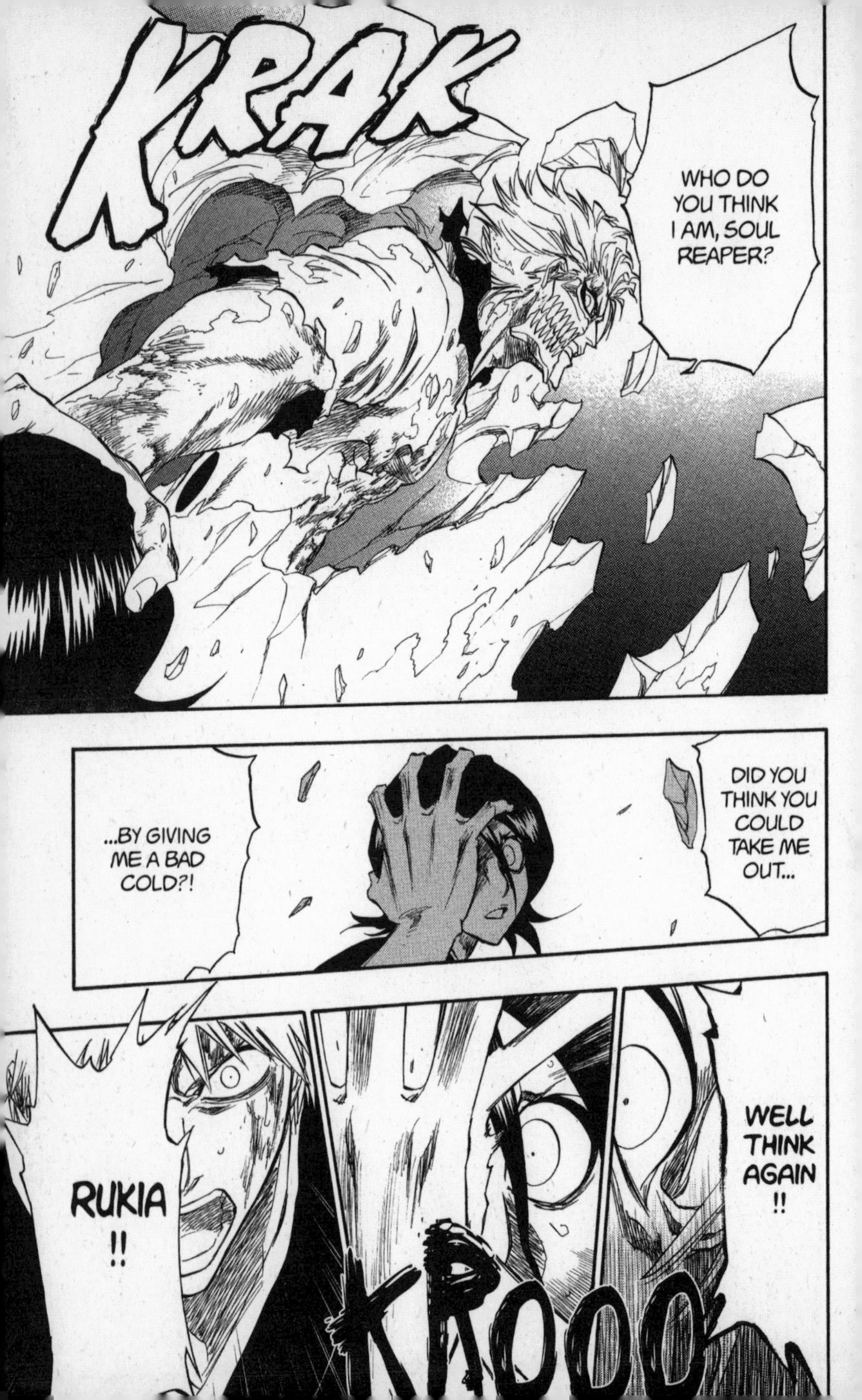
KRAK
WHO DO YOU THINK I AM, SOUL REAPER?
DID YOU THINK YOU COULD TAKE ME OUT...
...BY GIVING ME A BAD COLD?!
WELL THINK AGAIN !!
KROOOO
RUKIA !!

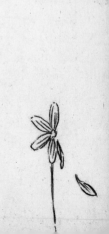

236. The Sun Already Gone Down

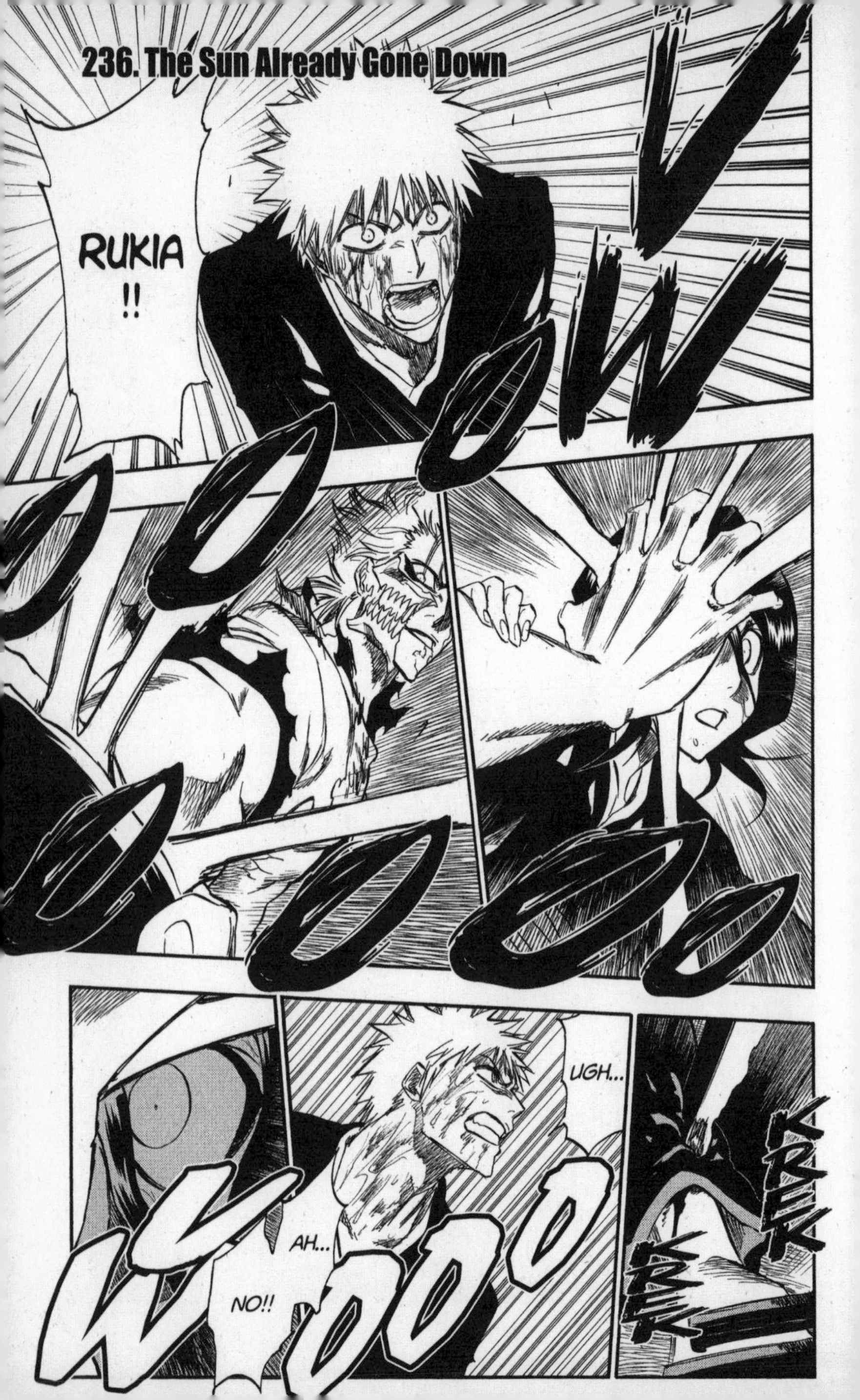
RUKIA !!
KREEK
KREEK
UGH...
AH...
NO!!

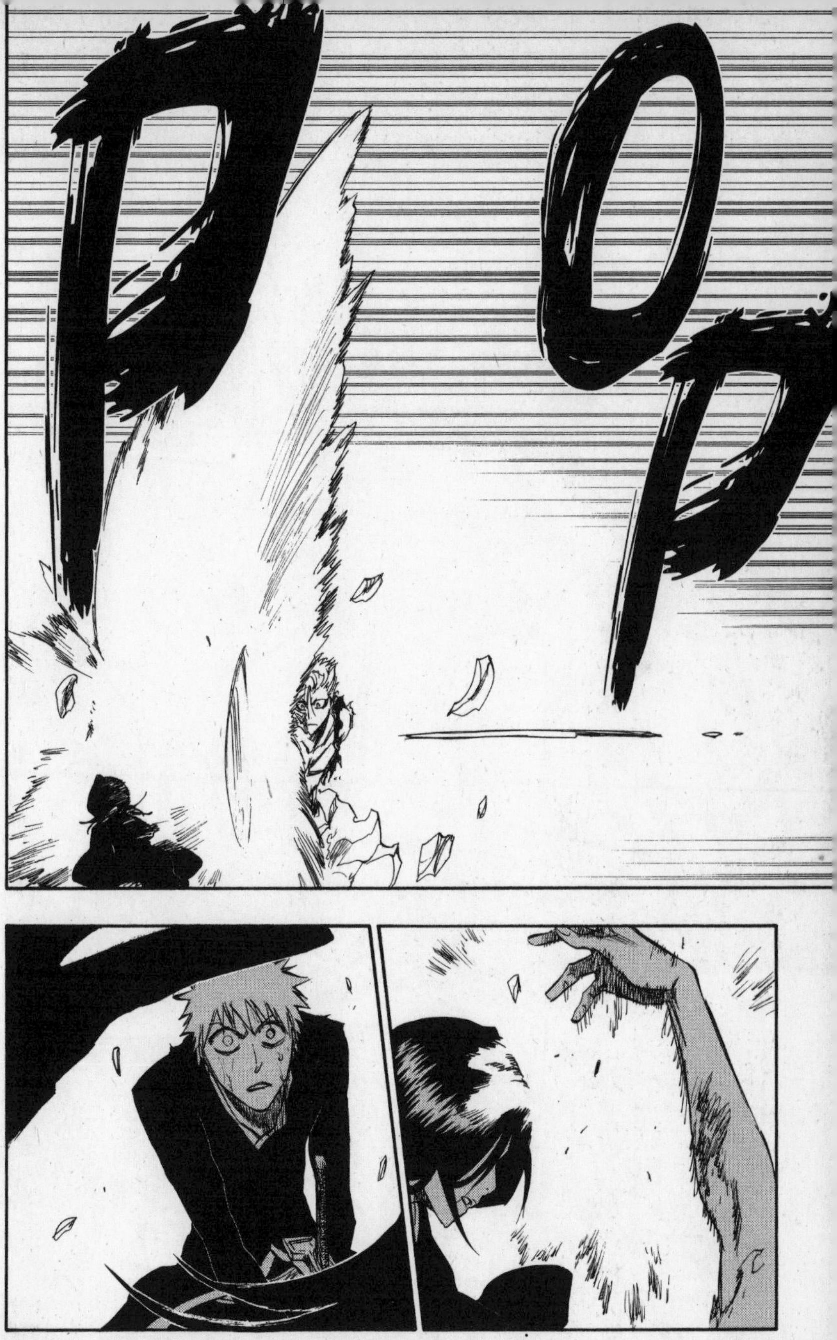

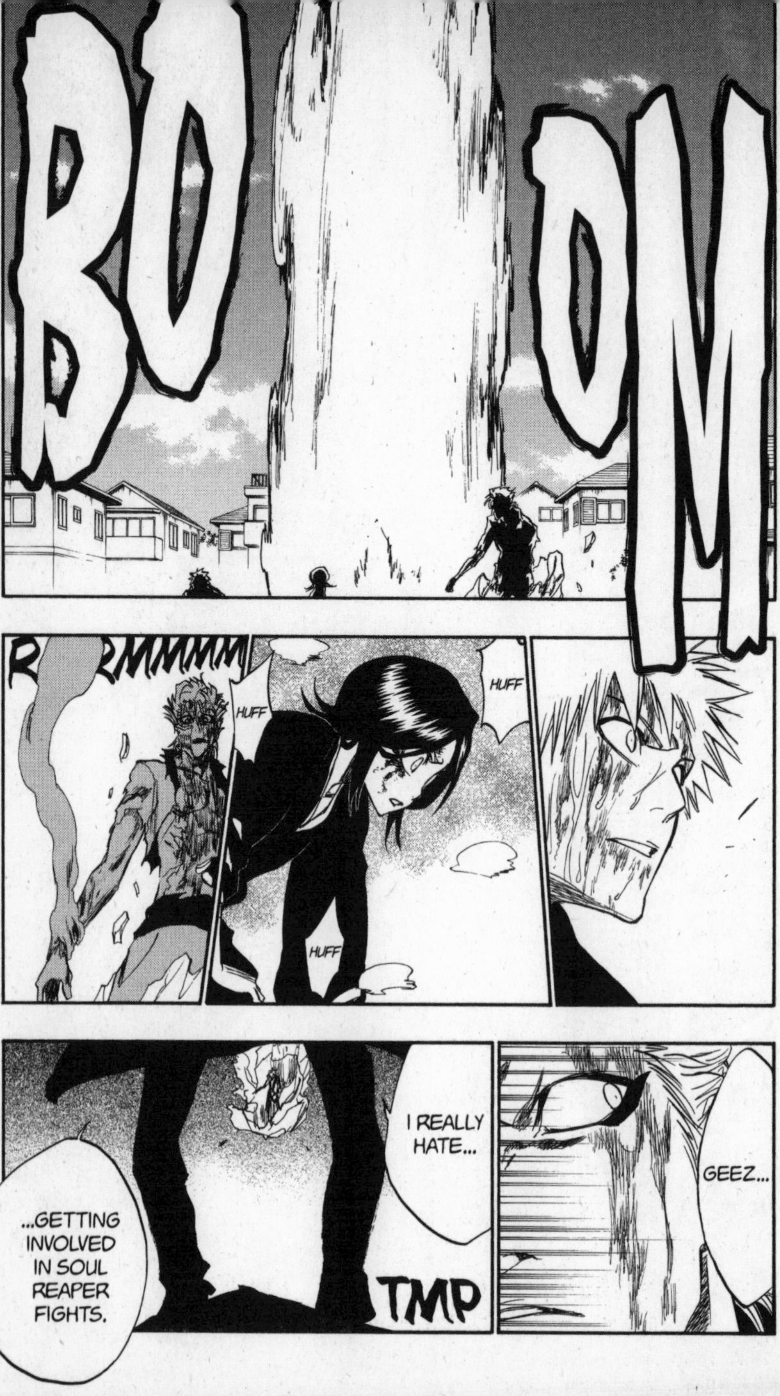
BOOM
HUFF
HUFF
HUFF
GEEZ...
I REALLY HATE...
...GETTING INVOLVED IN SOUL REAPER FIGHTS.
TMP

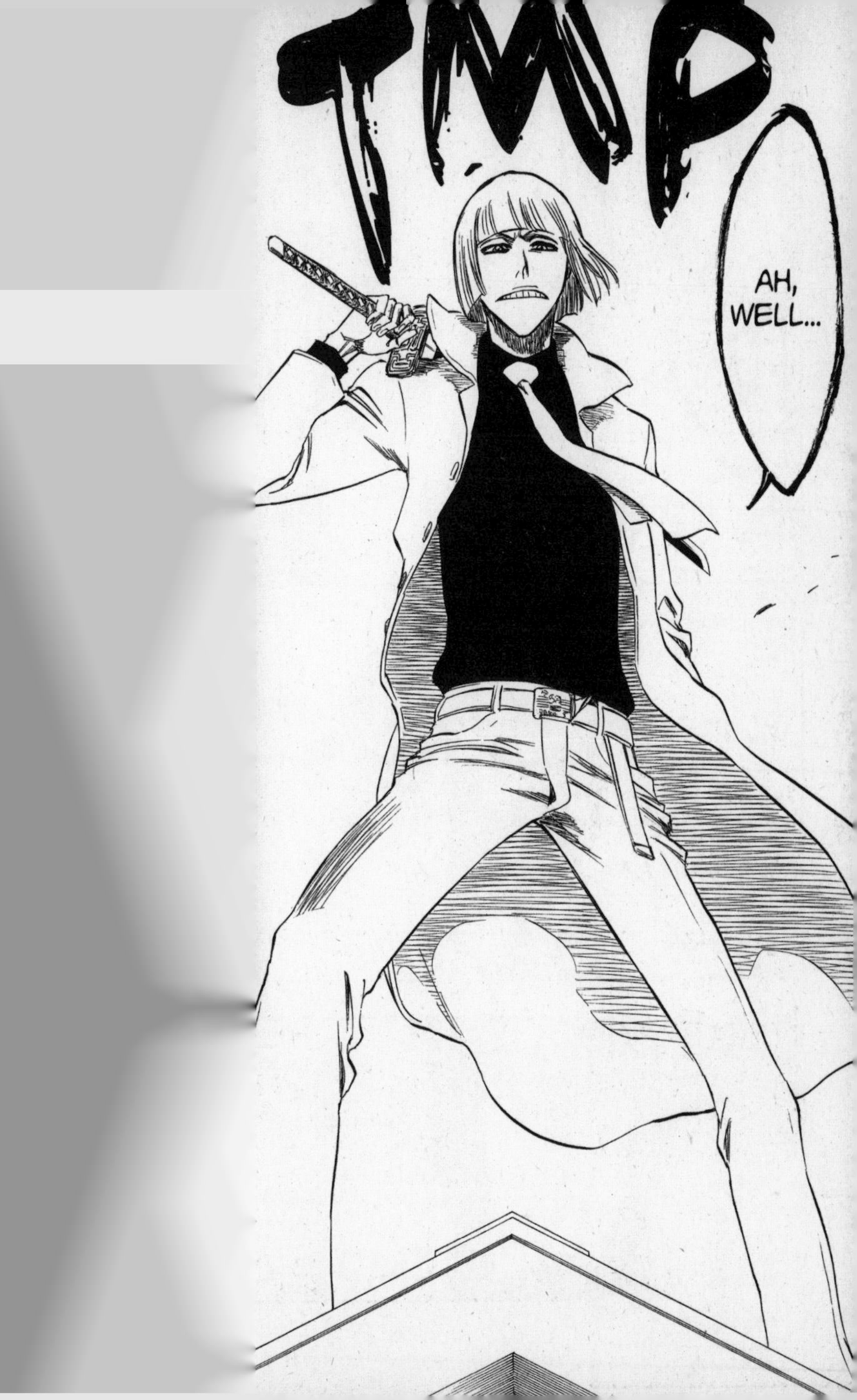
TMP
AH, WELL...

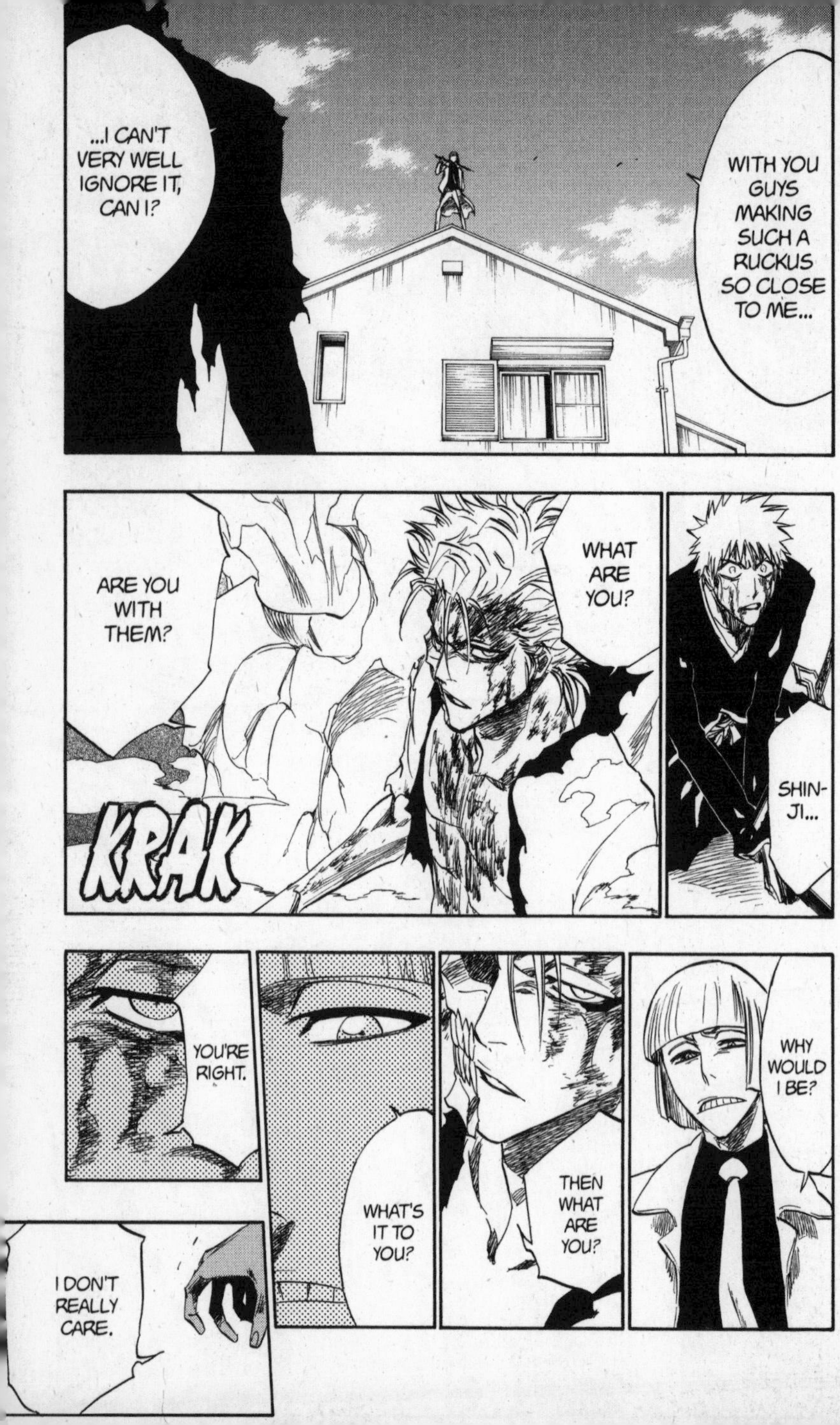
WITH YOU GUYS MAKING SUCH A RUCKUS SO CLOSE TO ME...
...I CAN'T VERY WELL IGNORE IT, CAN I?
SHIN-JI...
WHAT ARE YOU?
ARE YOU WITH THEM?
KRAK
WHY WOULD I BE?
THEN WHAT ARE YOU?
WHAT'S IT TO YOU?
YOU'RE RIGHT.
I DON'T REALLY CARE.

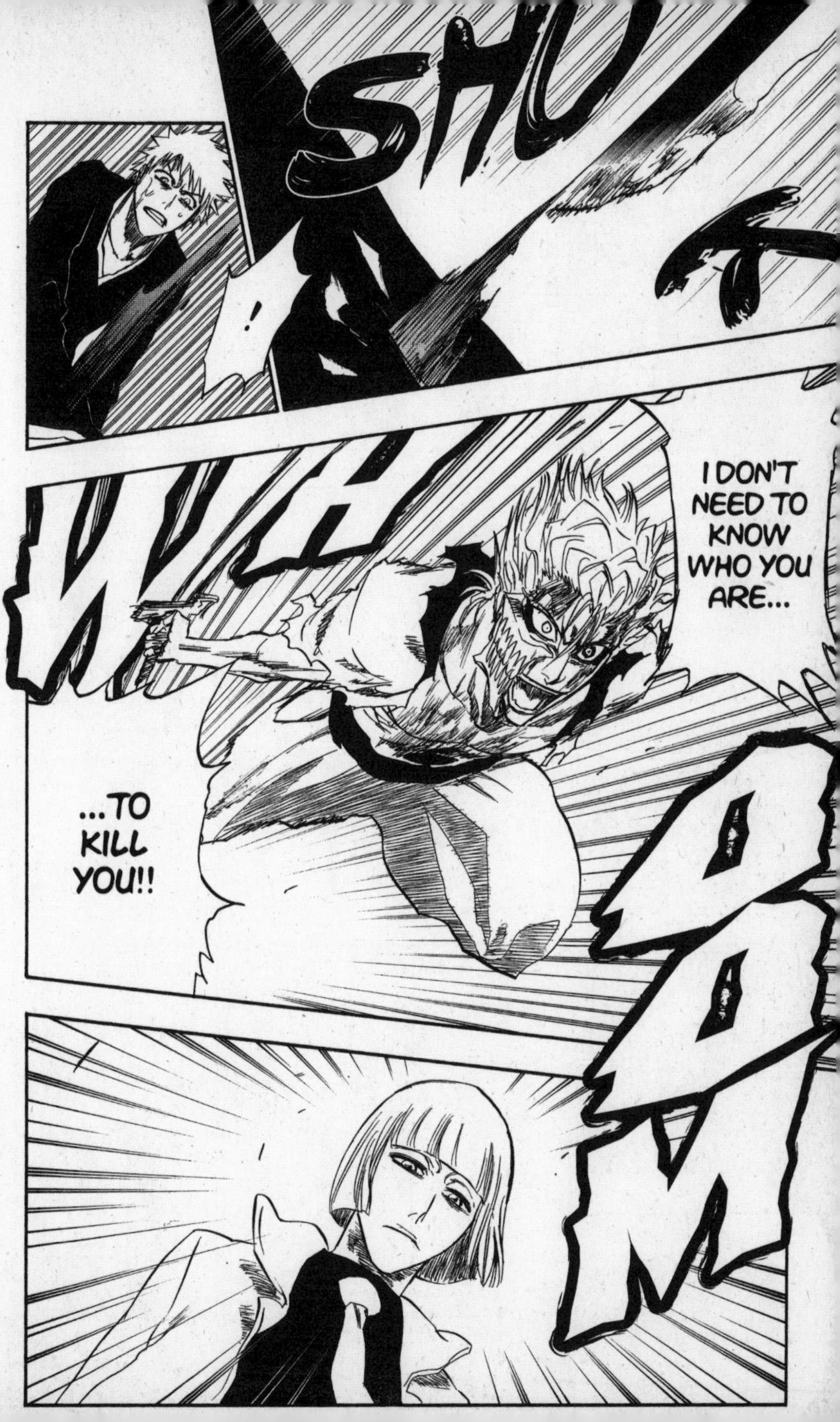
SHU
!
I DON'T NEED TO KNOW WHO YOU ARE...
...TO KILL YOU!!

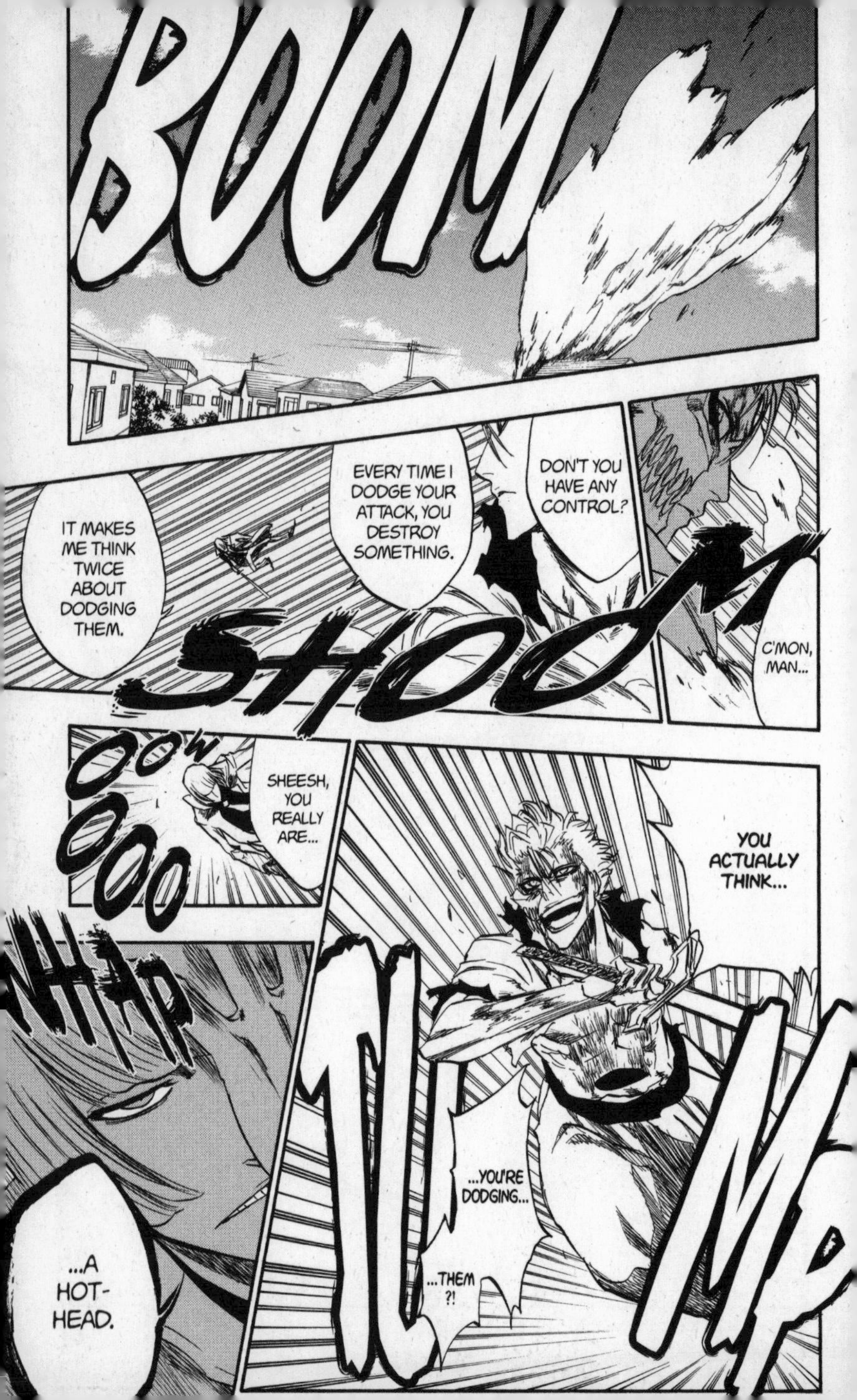
BOOM
C'MON, MAN...
DON'T YOU HAVE ANY CONTROL?
EVERY TIME I DODGE YOUR ATTACK, YOU DESTROY SOMETHING.
IT MAKES ME THINK TWICE ABOUT DODGING THEM.
SHOOM
YOU ACTUALLY THINK...
...YOU'RE DODGING...
...THEM?!
SHEESH, YOU REALLY ARE...
...A HOT-HEAD.

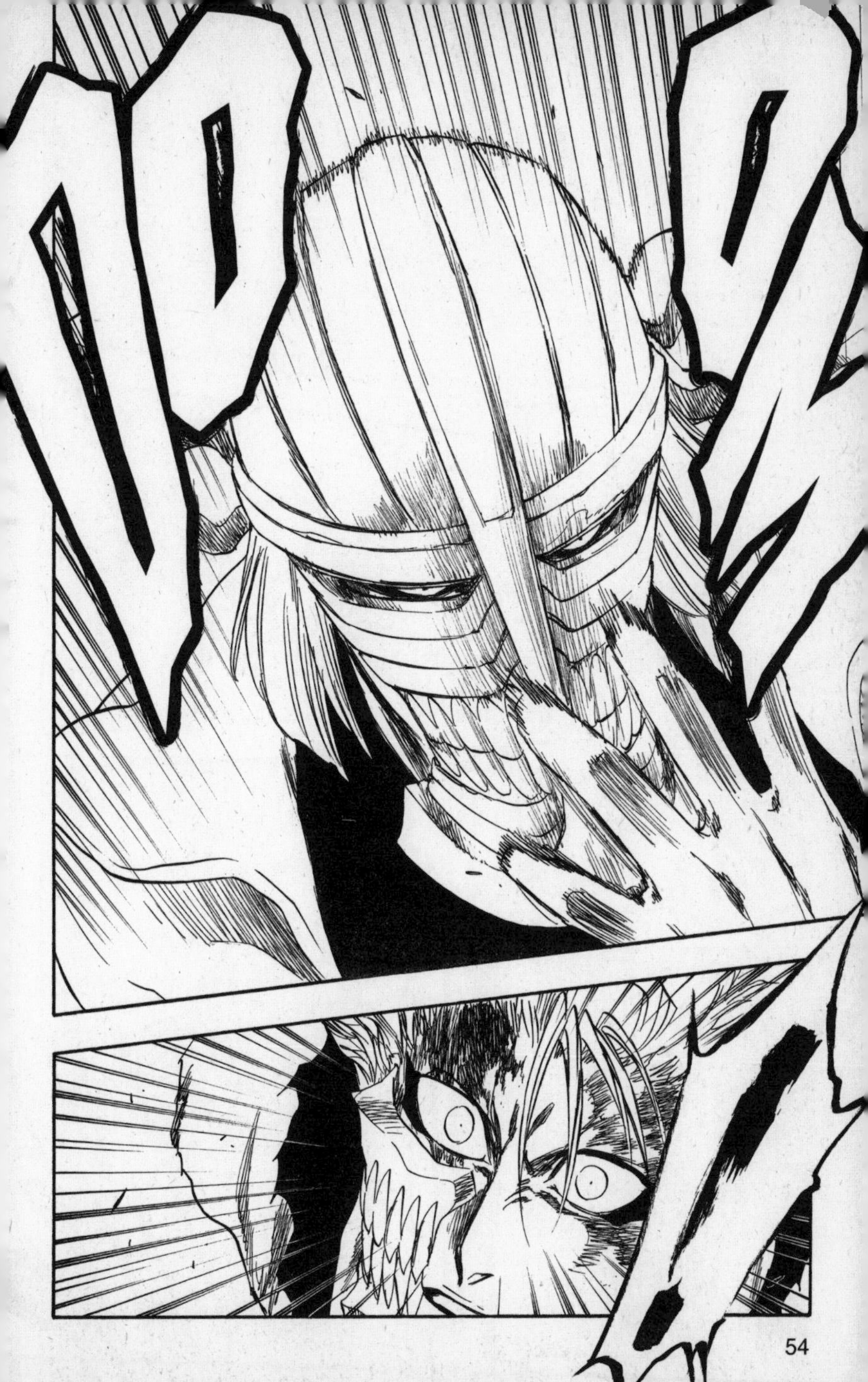

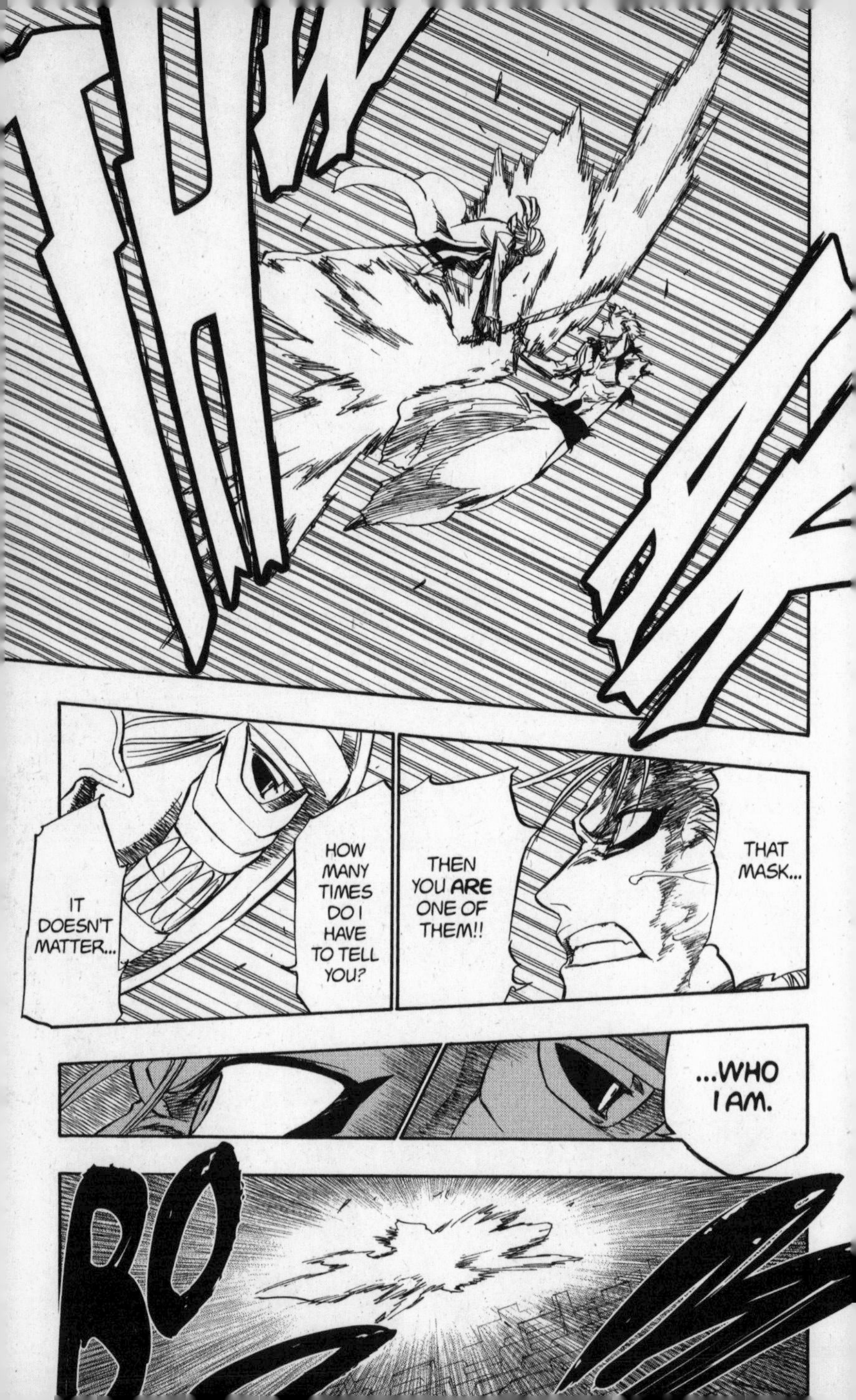
THAT MASK...
THEN YOU **ARE** ONE OF THEM!!
HOW MANY TIMES DO I HAVE TO TELL YOU?
IT DOESN'T MATTER...
...WHO I AM.

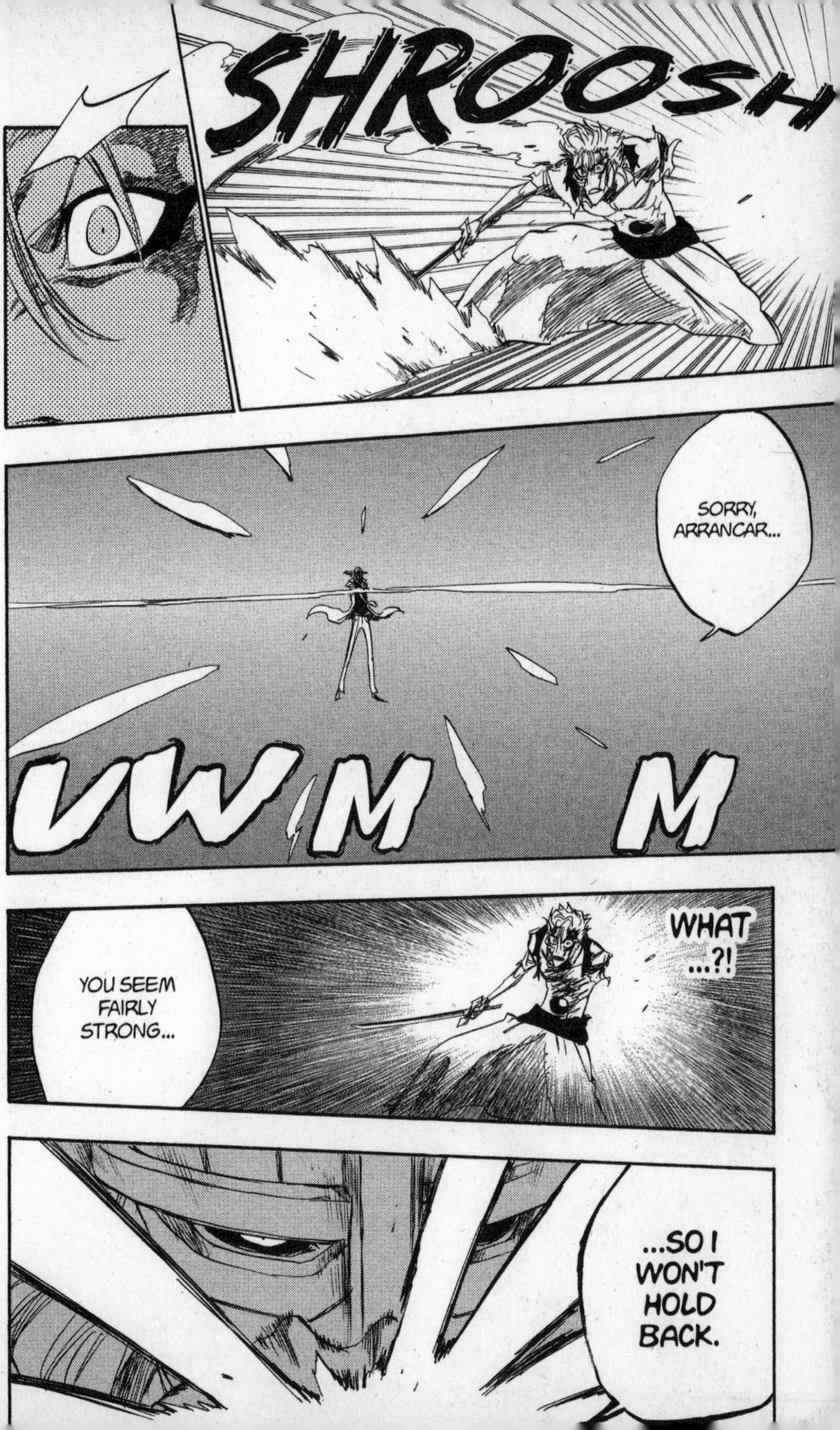
SHROOSH
SORRY, ARRANCAR...
UWM M
WHAT ...?!
YOU SEEM FAIRLY STRONG...
...SO I WON'T HOLD BACK.

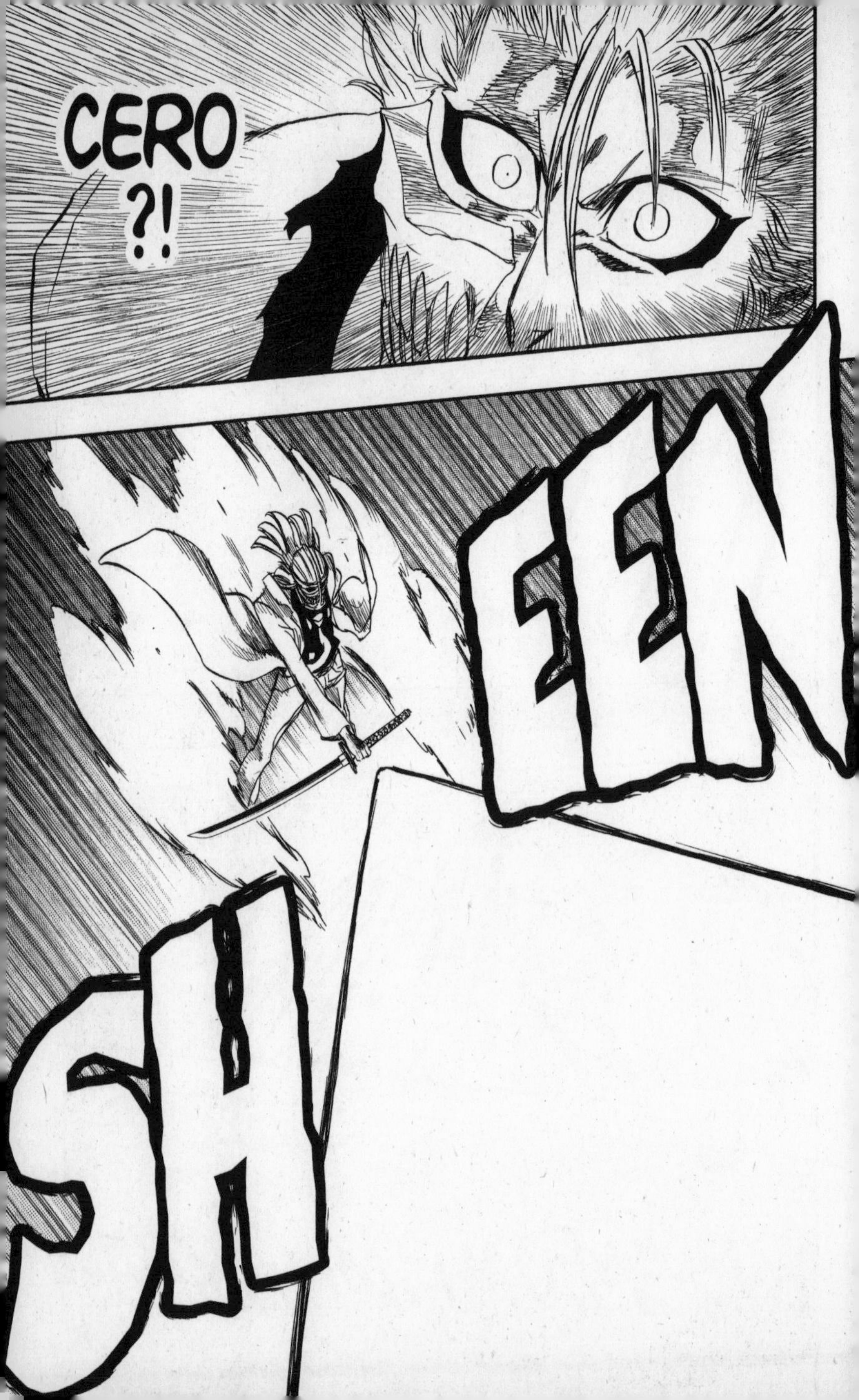
CERO ?!
SHEEN

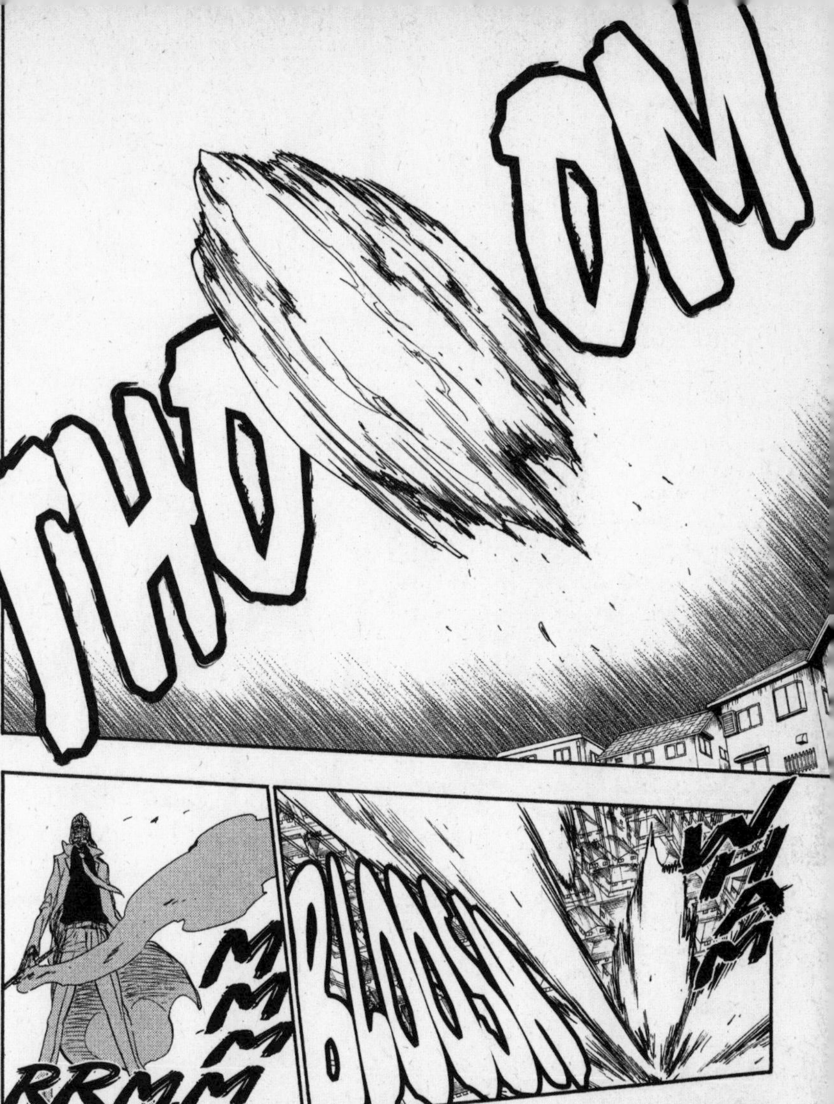
THO
OM
RRMMMMMMM
KOFF
KLAK
KOFF
RRMMMMM
MMMMMMMMM

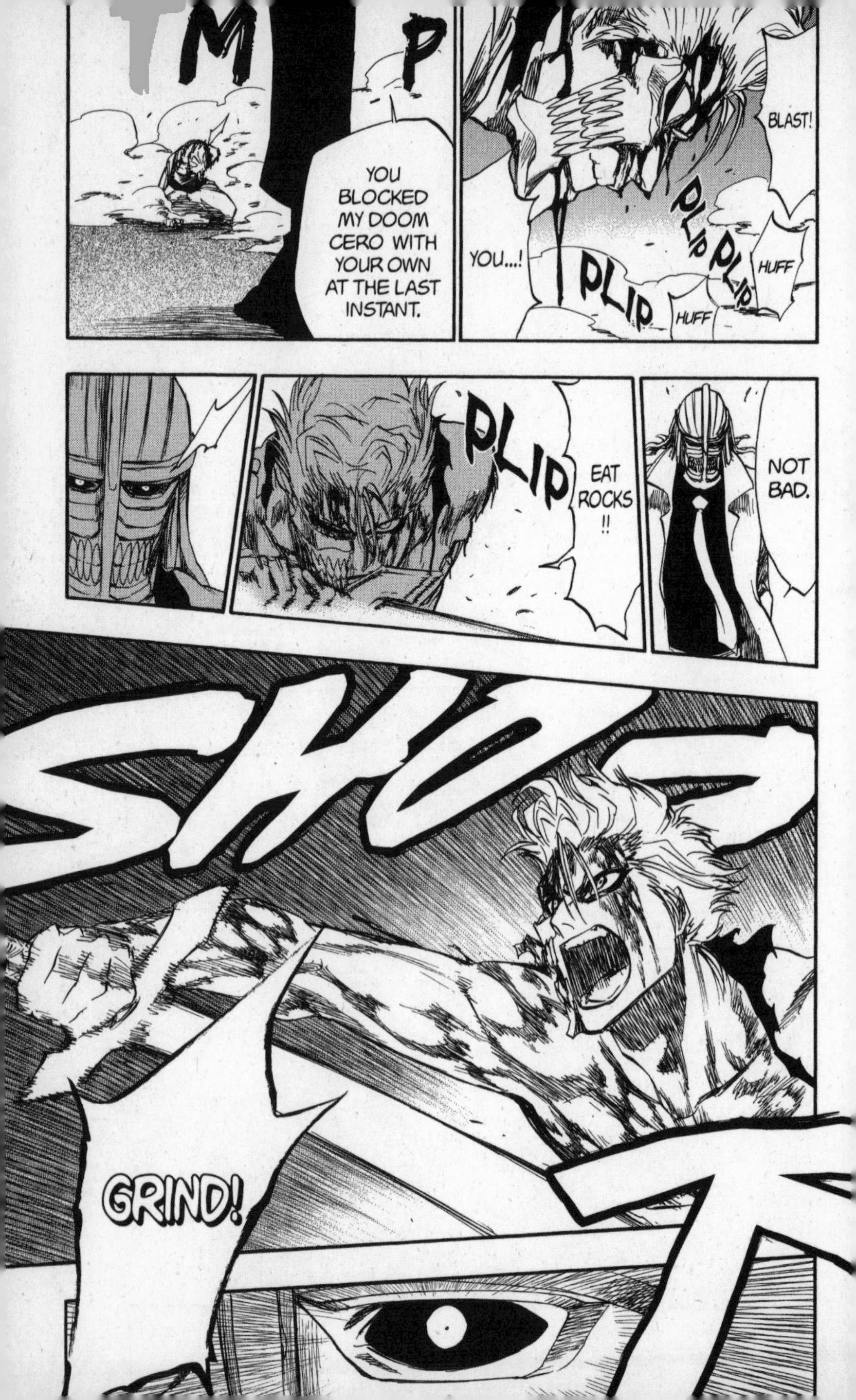
BLAST!
PLIP
PLIP
PLIP
HUFF
HUFF
PLIP
YOU...!
M P
YOU BLOCKED MY DOOM CERO WITH YOUR OWN AT THE LAST INSTANT.
NOT BAD.
EAT ROCKS !!
PLIP
GRIND!

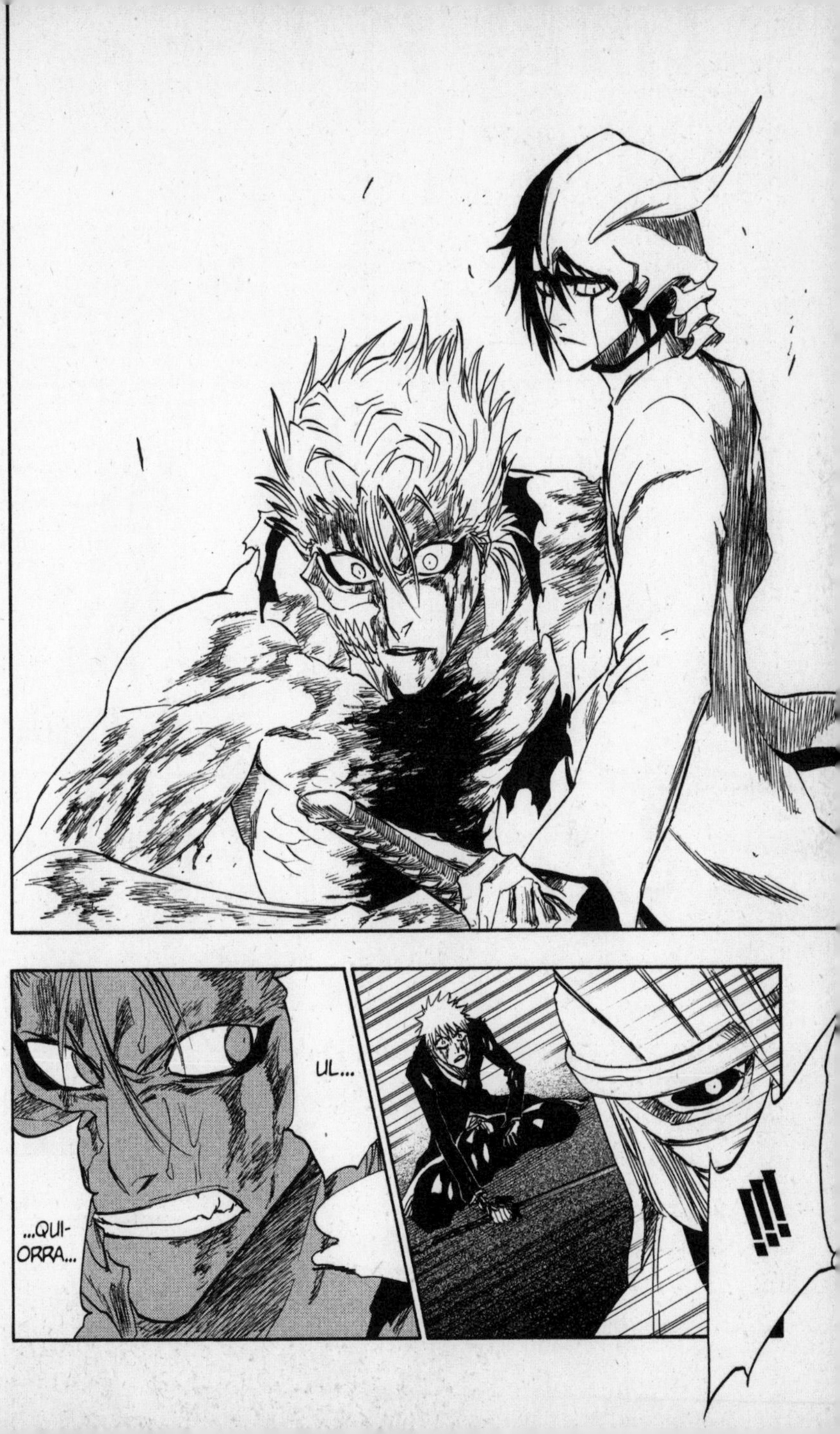
!!!
UL...
...QUI-
ORRA...

READ THIS WAY

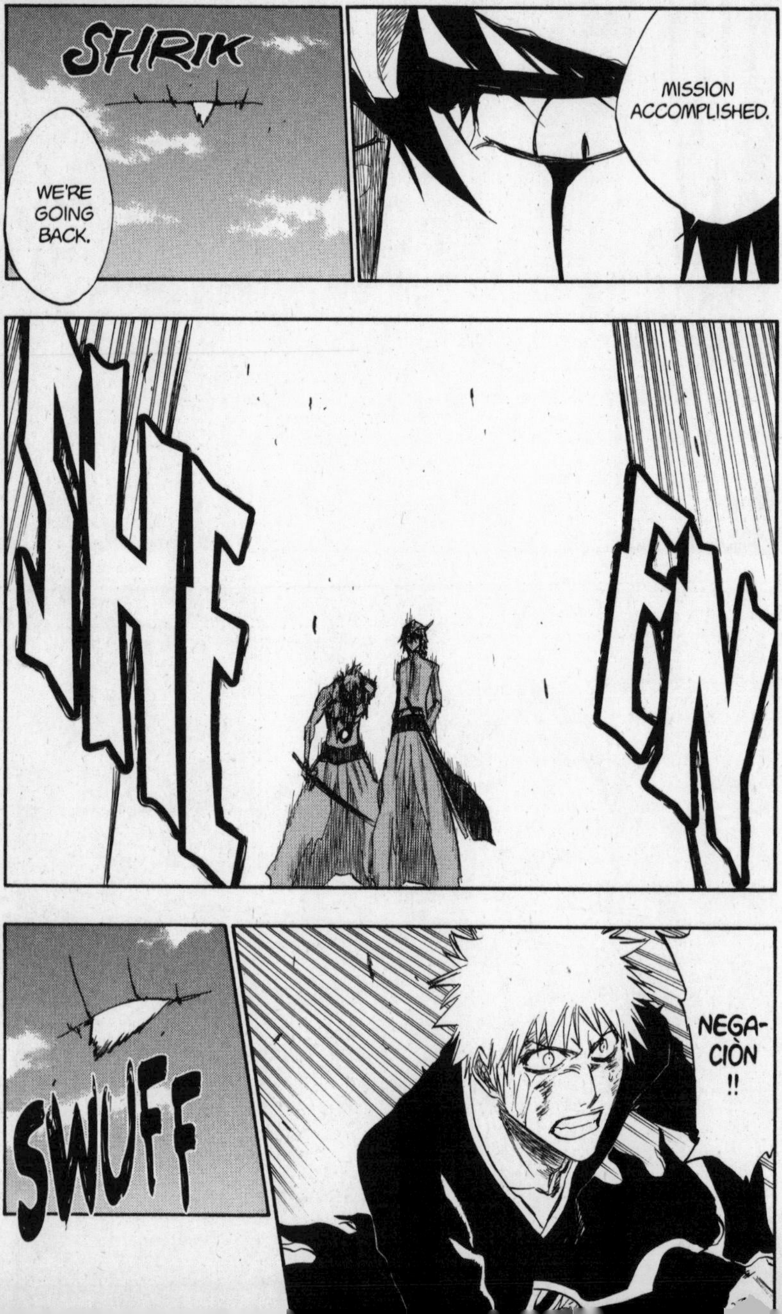
MISSION ACCOMPLISHED.
SHRIK
WE'RE GOING BACK.
NEGA-CIÒN!!
SWUFF

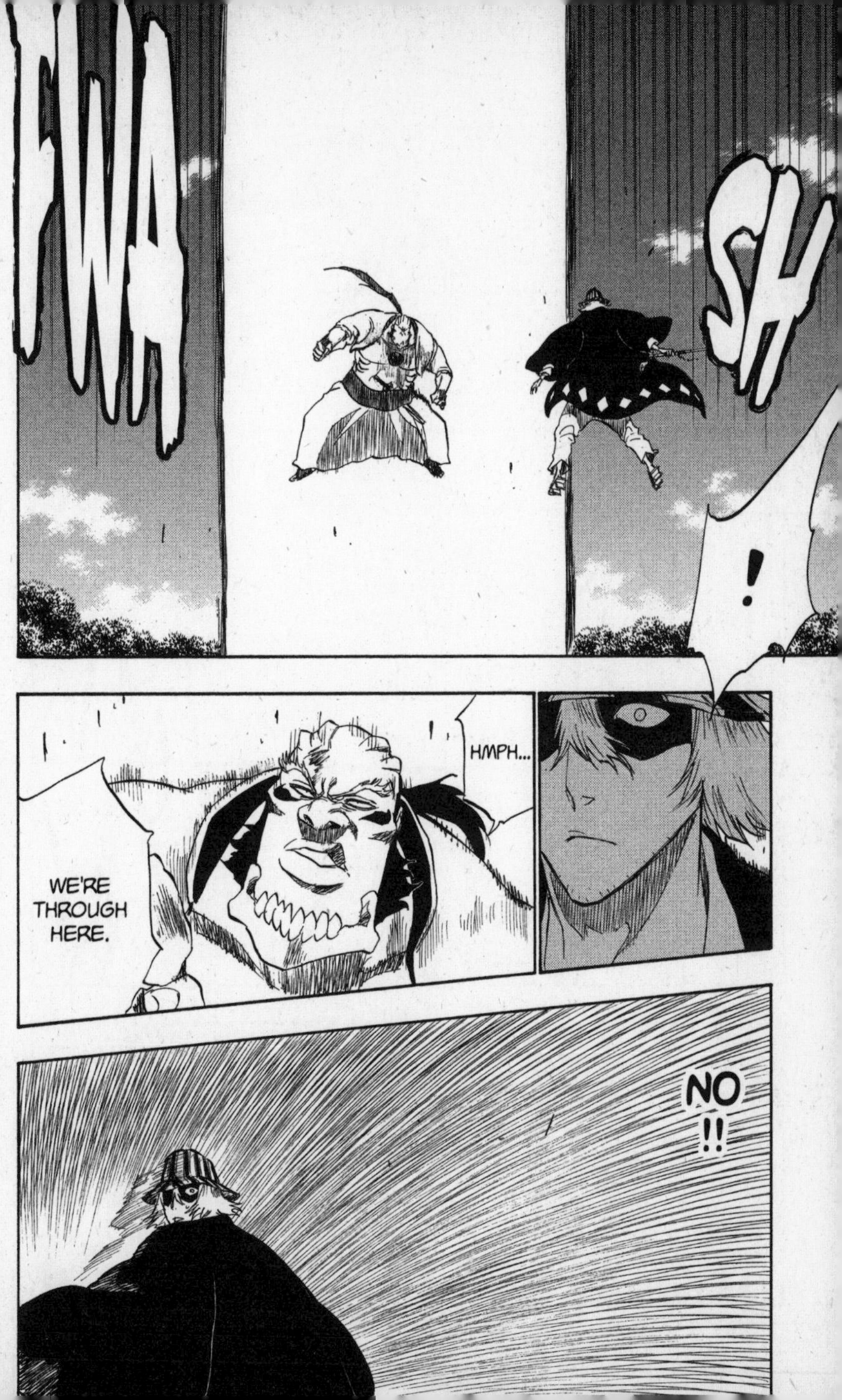
SH
!
FWA
HMPH...
WE'RE THROUGH HERE.
NO !!

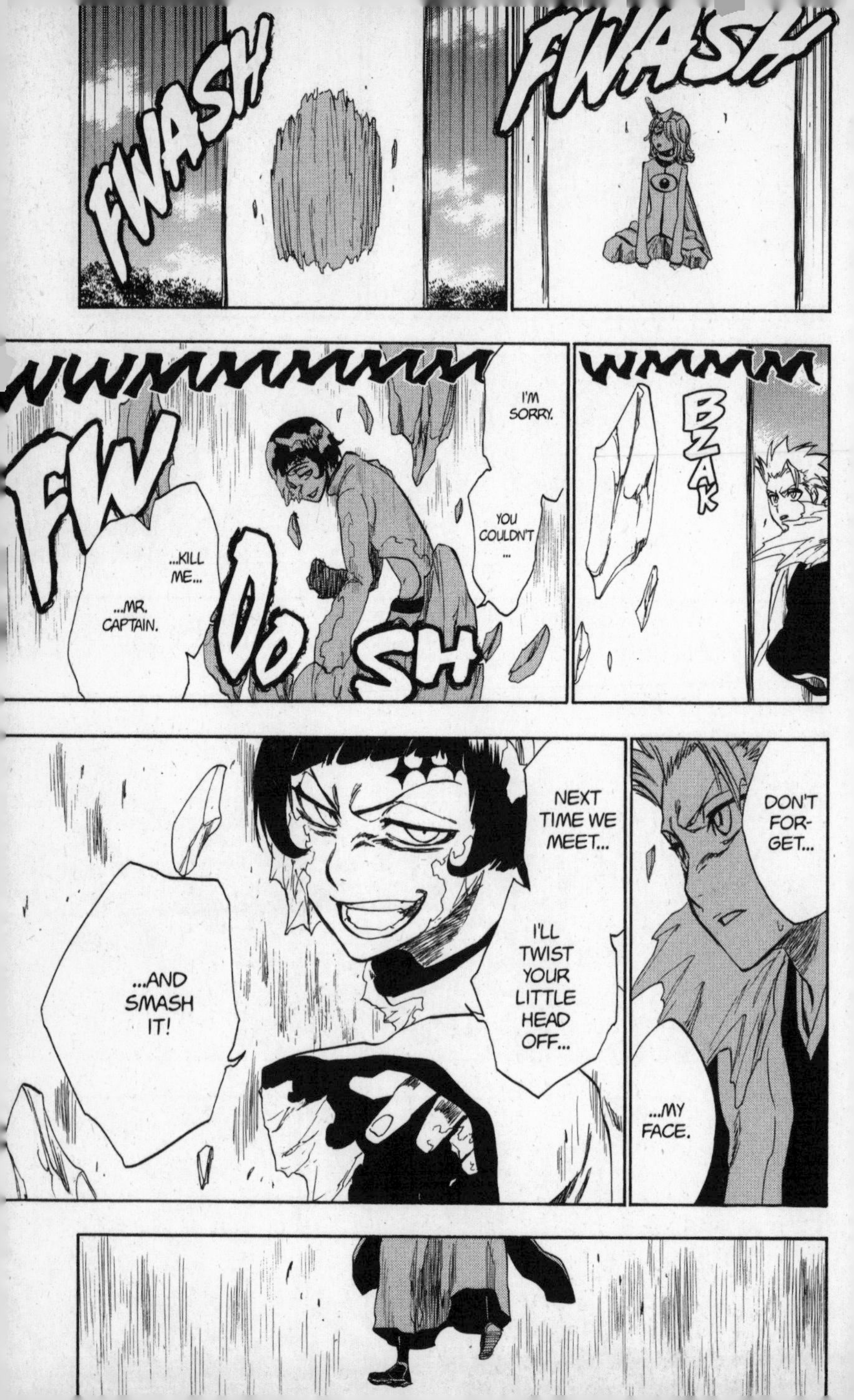
FWASH
FWASH
WMMMM
BZAK
NWMMMMMMMM
I'M SORRY.
YOU COULDN'T ...
...KILL ME...
...MR. CAPTAIN.
FWOOSH
DON'T FOR-GET...
...MY FACE.
NEXT TIME WE MEET...
I'LL TWIST YOUR LITTLE HEAD OFF...
...AND SMASH IT!

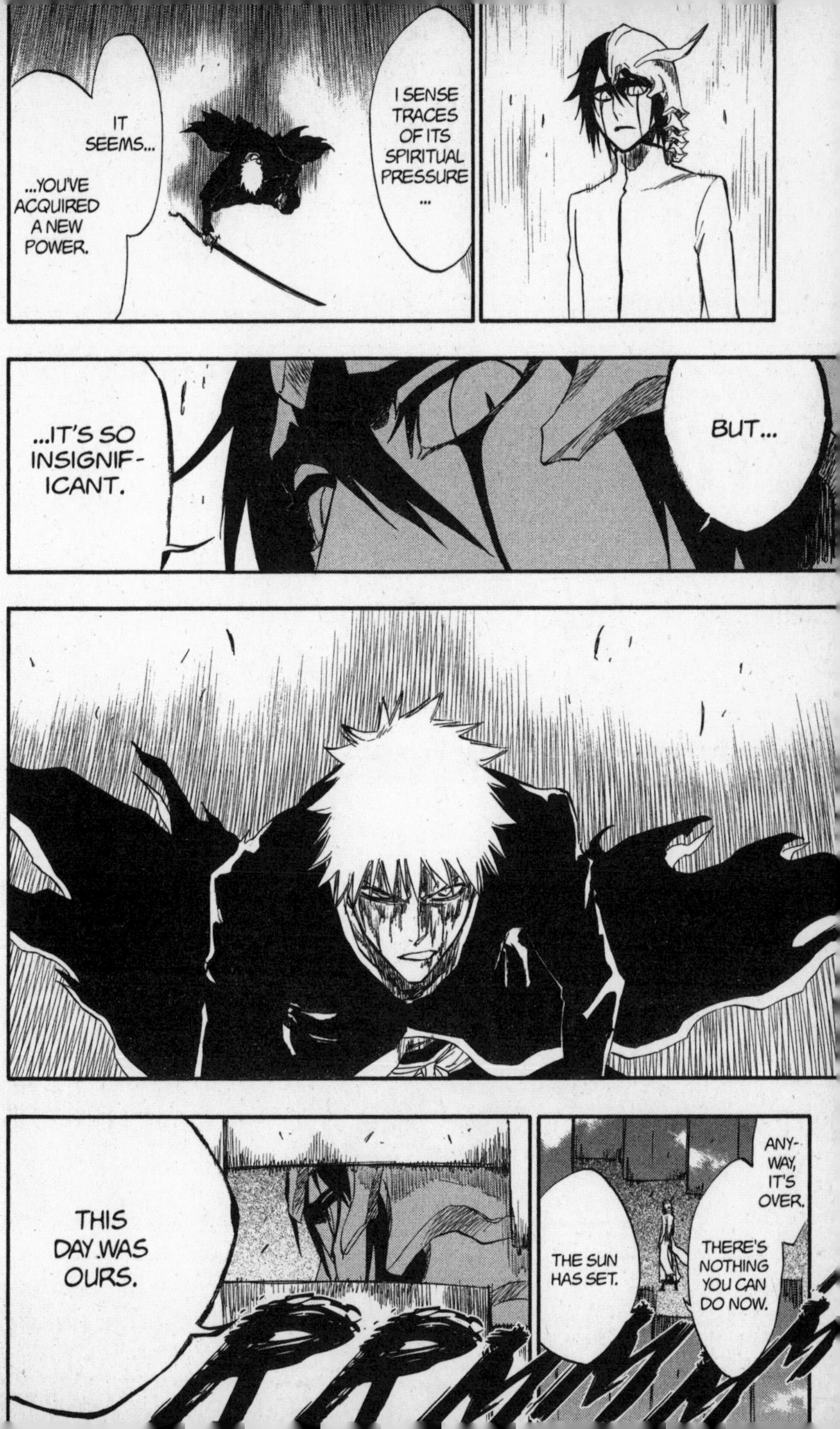
I SENSE TRACES OF ITS SPIRITUAL PRESSURE...
IT SEEMS...
...YOU'VE ACQUIRED A NEW POWER.
BUT...
...IT'S SO INSIGNIFICANT.
ANYWAY, IT'S OVER.
THERE'S NOTHING YOU CAN DO NOW.
THE SUN HAS SET.
THIS DAY WAS OURS.

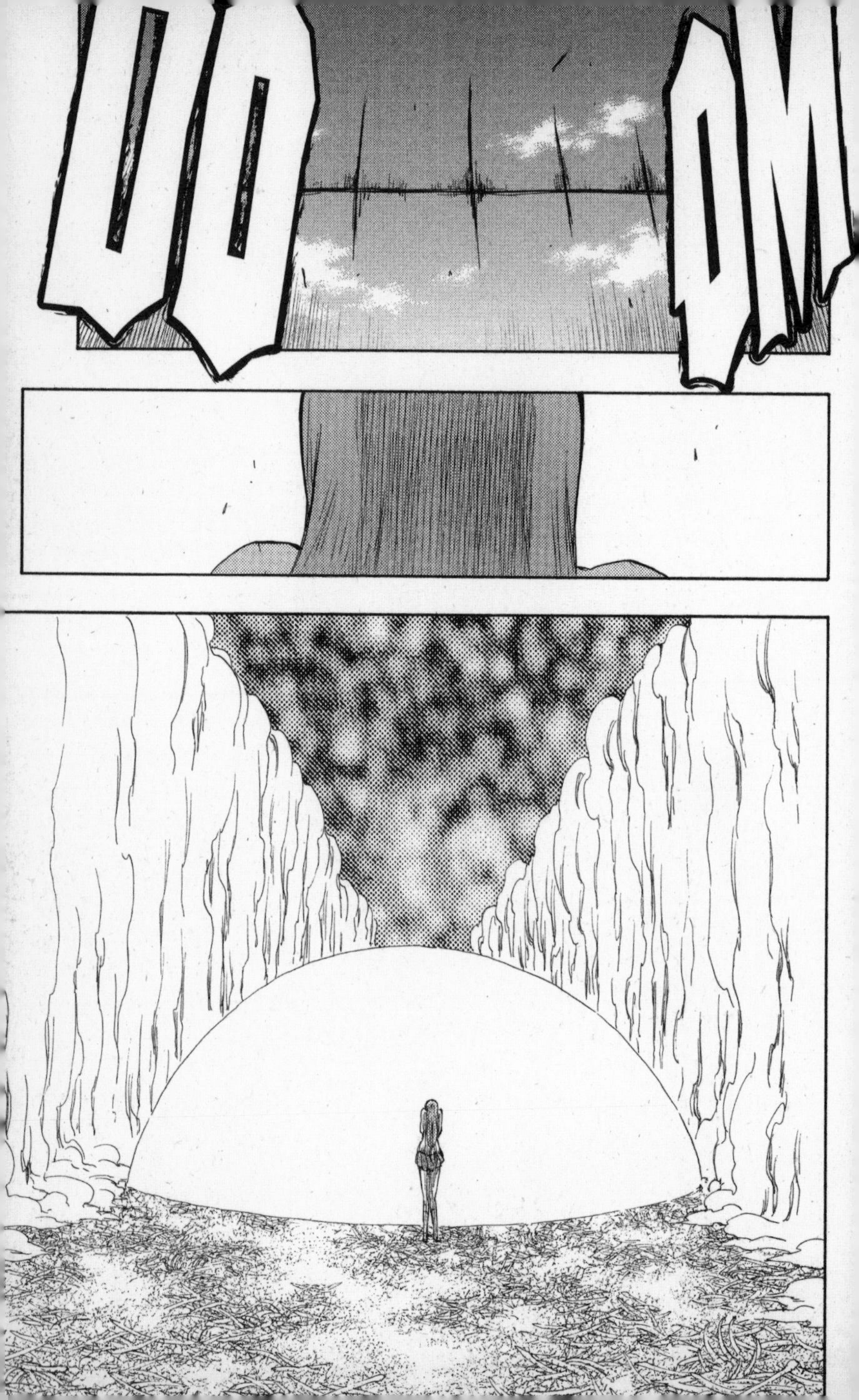

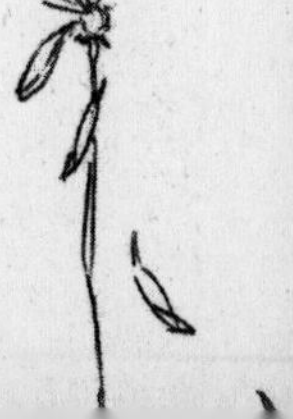

237. goodbye, halcyon days.

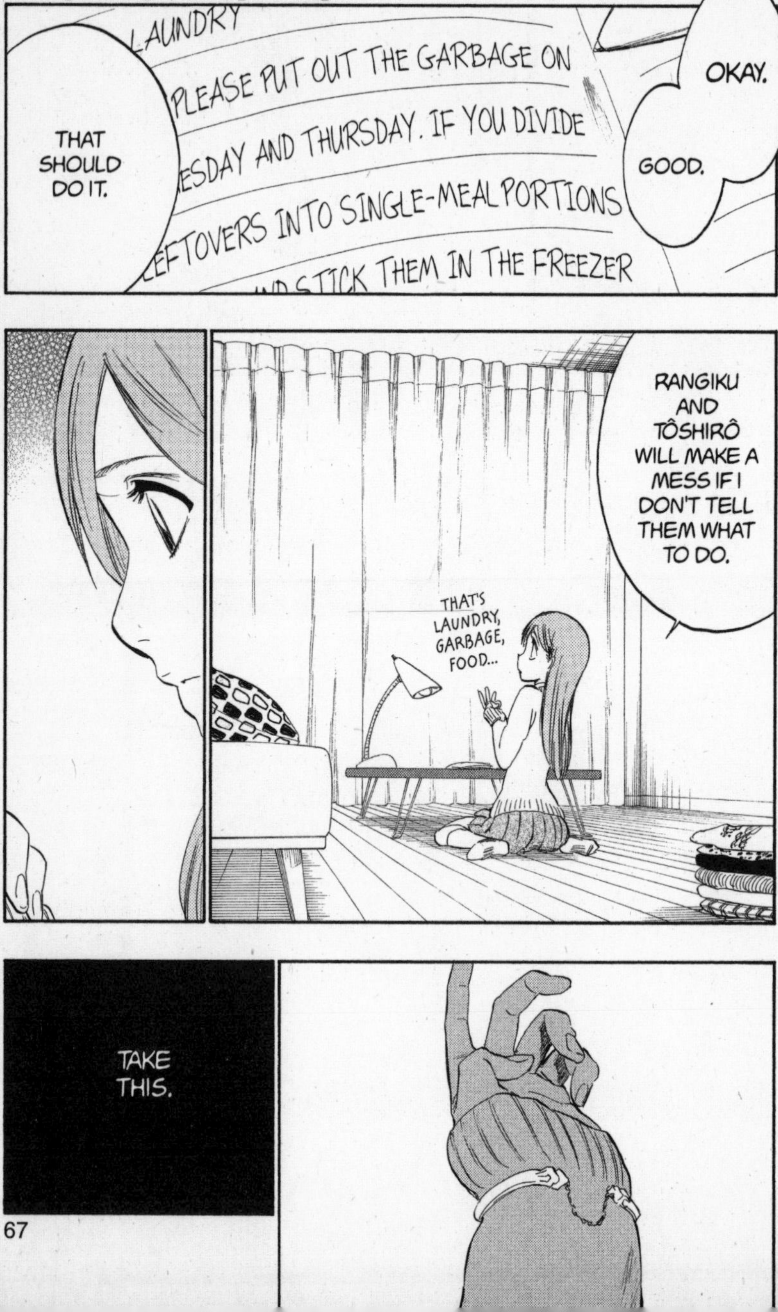
OKAY.
GOOD.
LAUNDRY
PLEASE PUT OUT THE GARBAGE ON
ESDAY AND THURSDAY. IF YOU DIVIDE
EFTOVERS INTO SINGLE-MEAL PORTIONS
STICK THEM IN THE FREEZER
THAT SHOULD DO IT.
RANGIKU AND TÔSHIRÔ WILL MAKE A MESS IF I DON'T TELL THEM WHAT TO DO.
THAT'S LAUNDRY, GARBAGE, FOOD...
TAKE THIS.

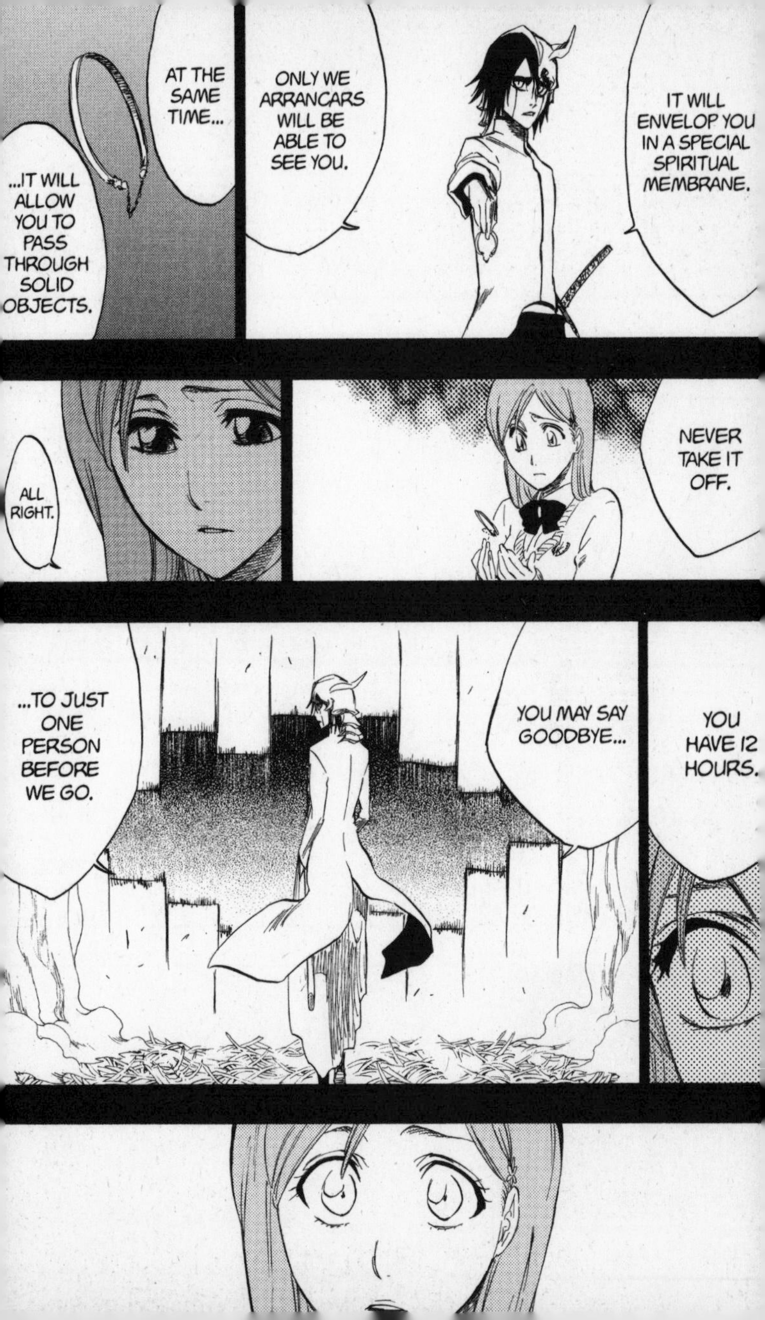
IT WILL ENVELOP YOU IN A SPECIAL SPIRITUAL MEMBRANE.
ONLY WE ARRANCARS WILL BE ABLE TO SEE YOU.
AT THE SAME TIME...
...IT WILL ALLOW YOU TO PASS THROUGH SOLID OBJECTS.
NEVER TAKE IT OFF.
ALL RIGHT.
YOU HAVE 12 HOURS.
YOU MAY SAY GOODBYE...
...TO JUST ONE PERSON BEFORE WE GO.

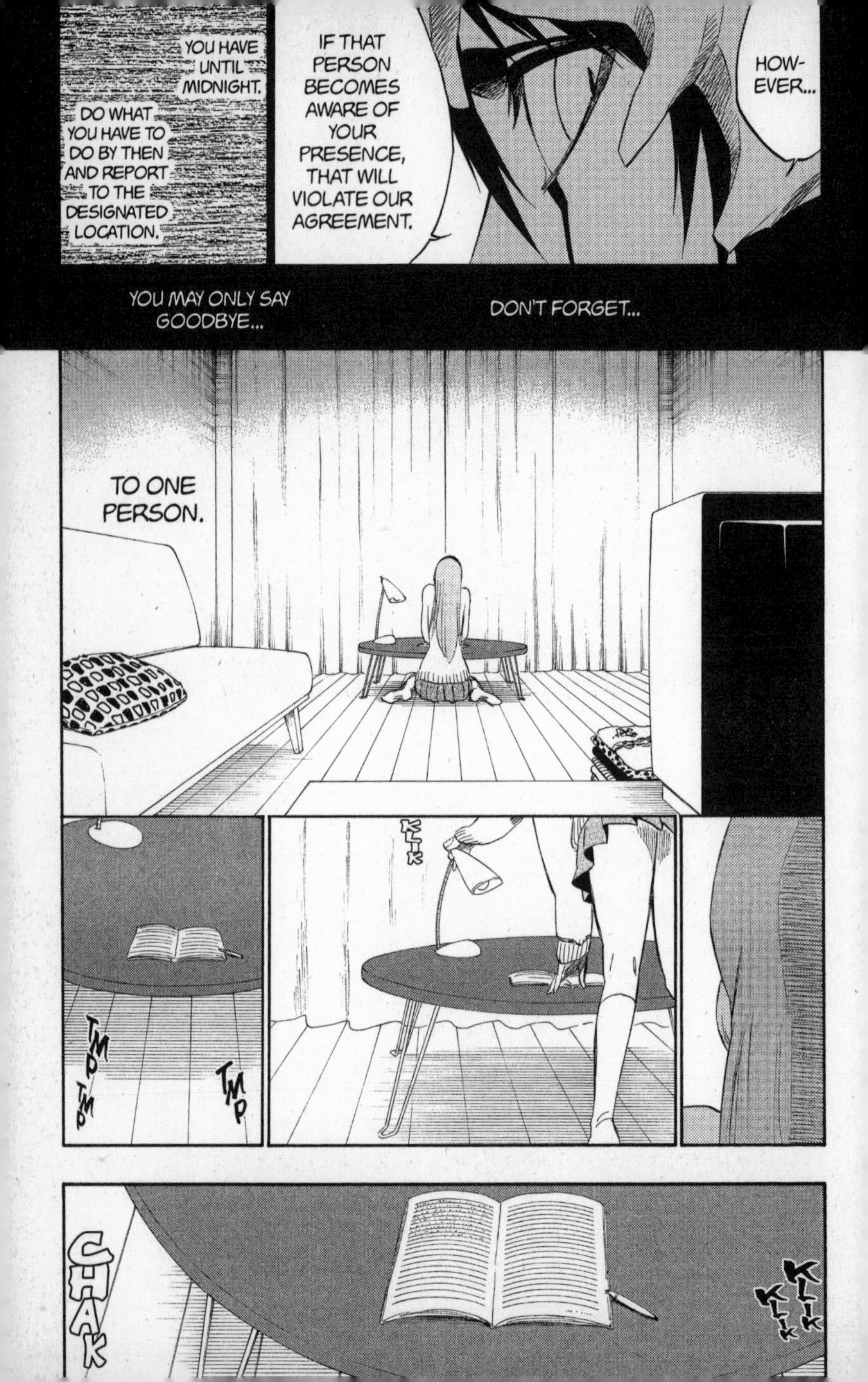
HOW-EVER...
IF THAT PERSON BECOMES AWARE OF YOUR PRESENCE, THAT WILL VIOLATE OUR AGREEMENT.
YOU HAVE UNTIL MIDNIGHT.
DO WHAT YOU HAVE TO DO BY THEN AND REPORT TO THE DESIGNATED LOCATION.
DON'T FORGET...
YOU MAY ONLY SAY GOODBYE...
TO ONE PERSON.
KLIK
TMP
TMP TMP
KLIK KLIK
CHAK

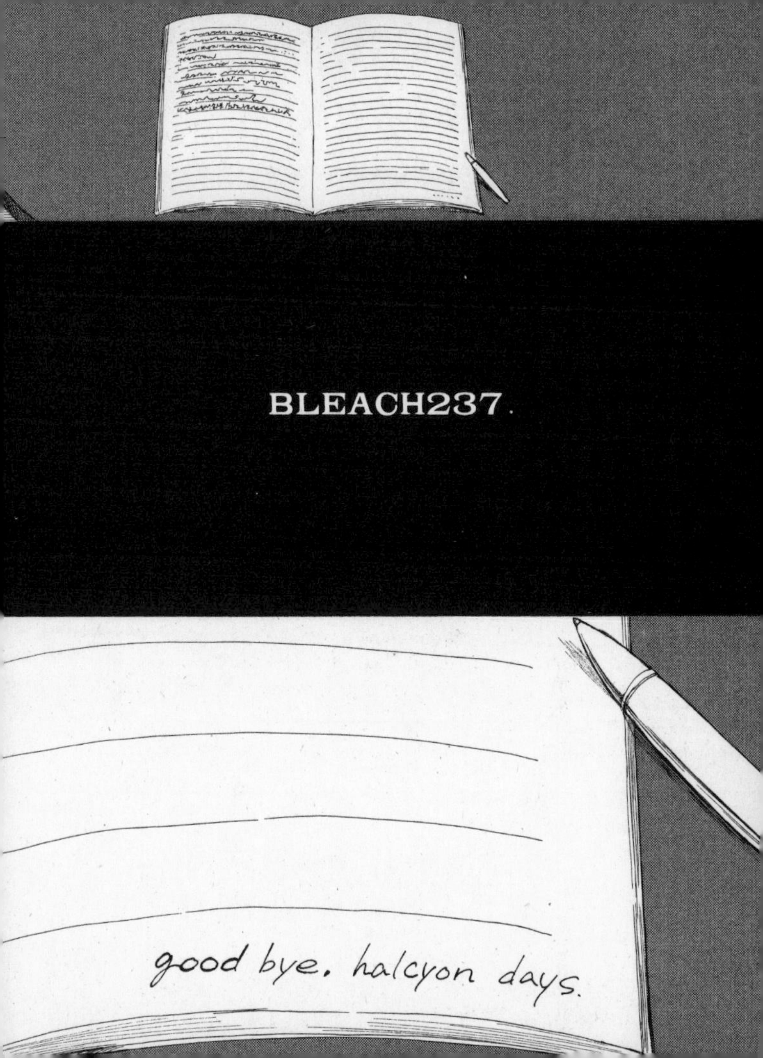
BLEACH237.
good bye. halcyon days.

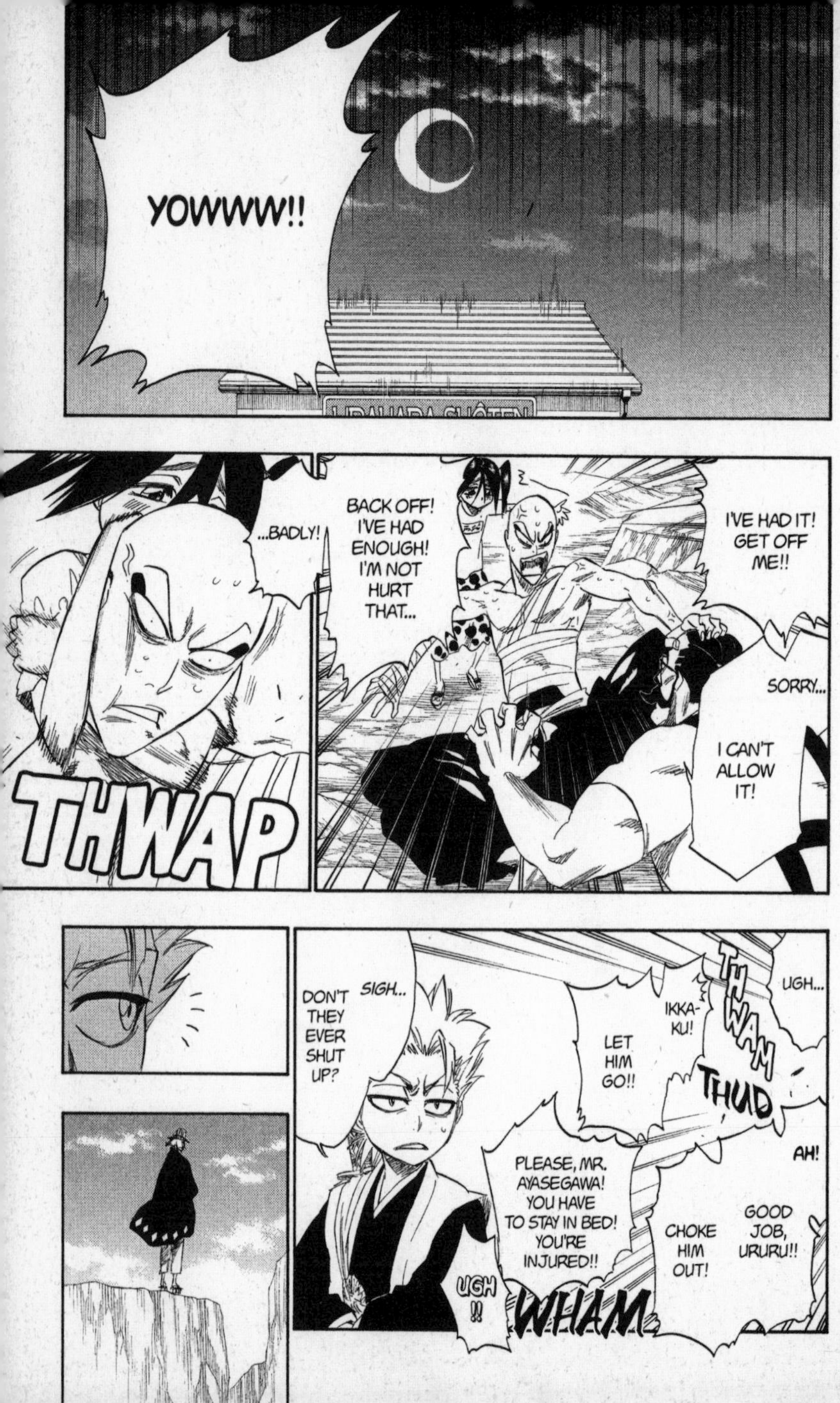
YOWWW!!
I'VE HAD IT! GET OFF ME!!
BACK OFF! I'VE HAD ENOUGH! I'M NOT HURT THAT...
SORRY...
I CAN'T ALLOW IT!
...BADLY!
THWAP
UGH...
THWAM
IKKA-KU!
LET HIM GO!!
THUD
AH!
GOOD JOB, URURU!!
CHOKE HIM OUT!
PLEASE, MR. AYASEGAWA! YOU HAVE TO STAY IN BED! YOU'RE INJURED!!
SIGH...
DON'T THEY EVER SHUT UP?
UGH !!
WHAM

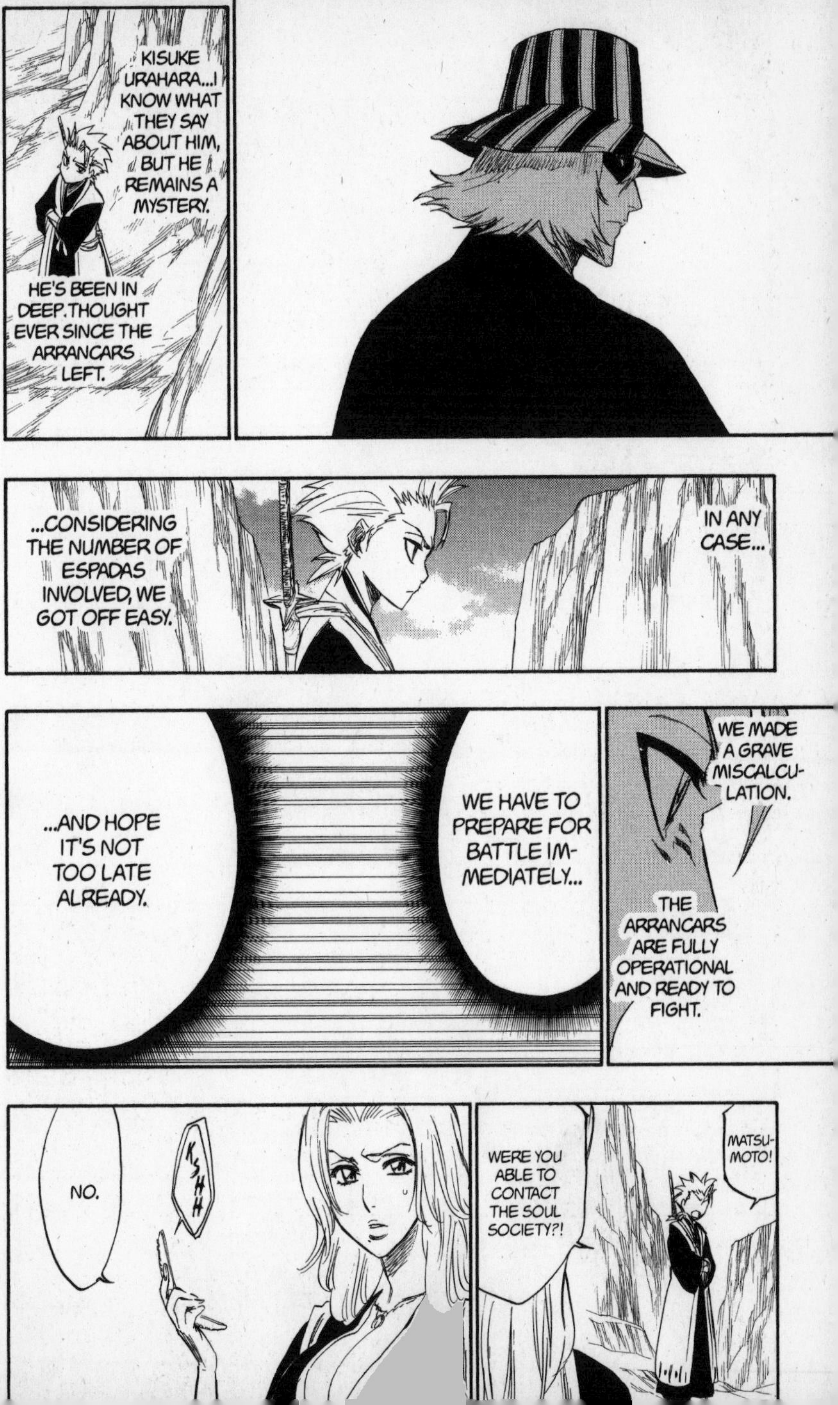
KISUKE URAHARA...I KNOW WHAT THEY SAY ABOUT HIM, BUT HE REMAINS A MYSTERY.
HE'S BEEN IN DEEP THOUGHT EVER SINCE THE ARRANCARS LEFT.
IN ANY CASE...
...CONSIDERING THE NUMBER OF ESPADAS INVOLVED, WE GOT OFF EASY.
WE MADE A GRAVE MISCALCU-LATION.
THE ARRANCARS ARE FULLY OPERATIONAL AND READY TO FIGHT.
WE HAVE TO PREPARE FOR BATTLE IM-MEDIATELY...
...AND HOPE IT'S NOT TOO LATE ALREADY.
MATSU-MOTO!
WERE YOU ABLE TO CONTACT THE SOUL SOCIETY?!
KSHH
NO.

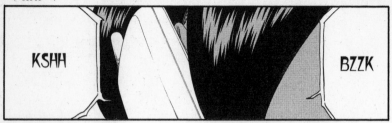

KSHH

BZZK

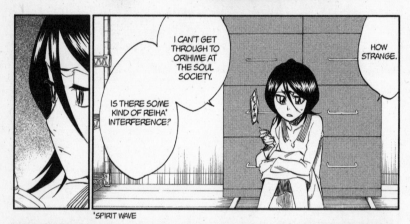

I CAN'T GET THROUGH TO ORIHIME AT THE SOUL SOCIETY.

IS THERE SOME KIND OF REIHA* INTERFERENCE?

HOW STRANGE.

*SPIRIT WAVE

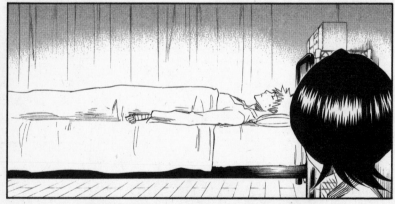

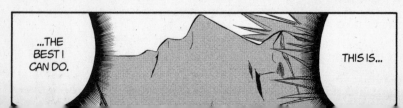

...THE BEST I CAN DO.

THIS IS...

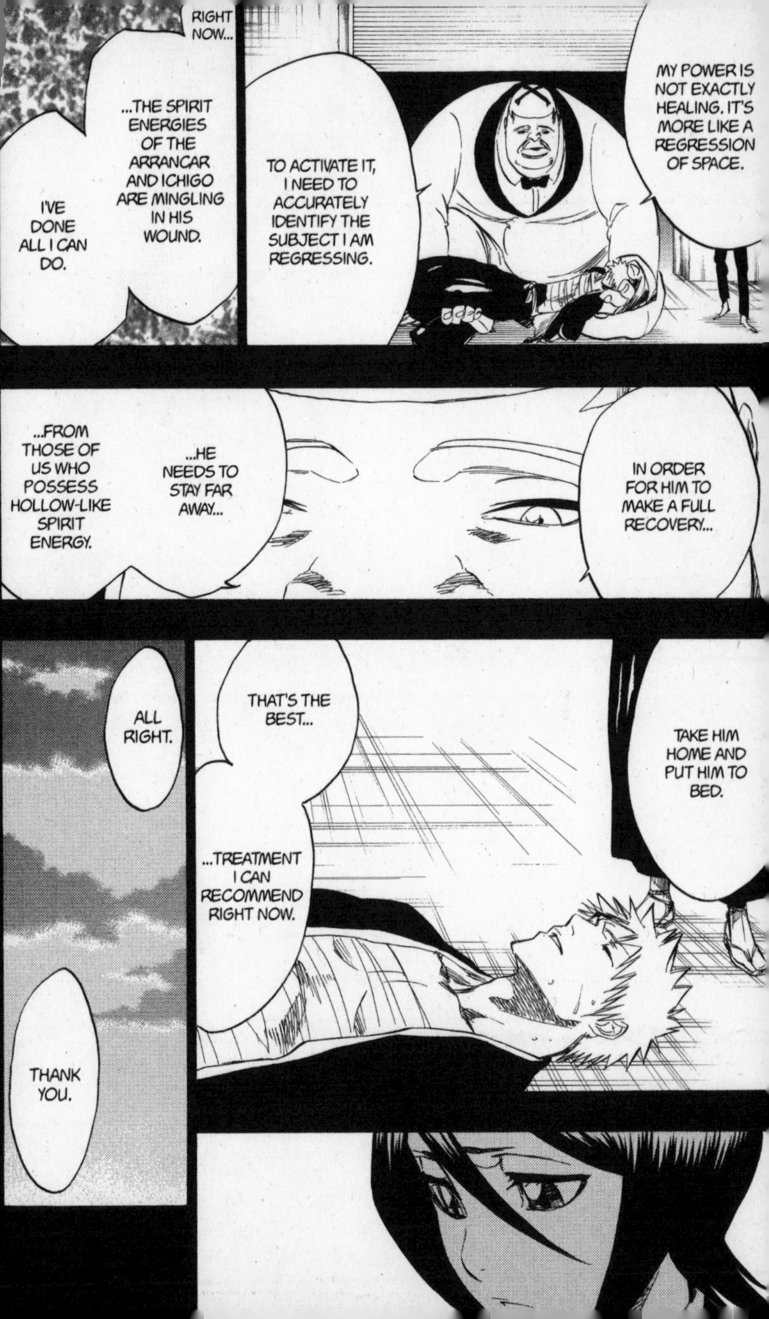
MY POWER IS NOT EXACTLY HEALING. IT'S MORE LIKE A REGRESSION OF SPACE.
TO ACTIVATE IT, I NEED TO ACCURATELY IDENTIFY THE SUBJECT I AM REGRESSING.
RIGHT NOW...
...THE SPIRIT ENERGIES OF THE ARRANCAR AND ICHIGO ARE MINGLING IN HIS WOUND.
I'VE DONE ALL I CAN DO.
IN ORDER FOR HIM TO MAKE A FULL RECOVERY...
...HE NEEDS TO STAY FAR AWAY...
...FROM THOSE OF US WHO POSSESS HOLLOW-LIKE SPIRIT ENERGY.
TAKE HIM HOME AND PUT HIM TO BED.
THAT'S THE BEST...
...TREATMENT I CAN RECOMMEND RIGHT NOW.
ALL RIGHT.
THANK YOU.

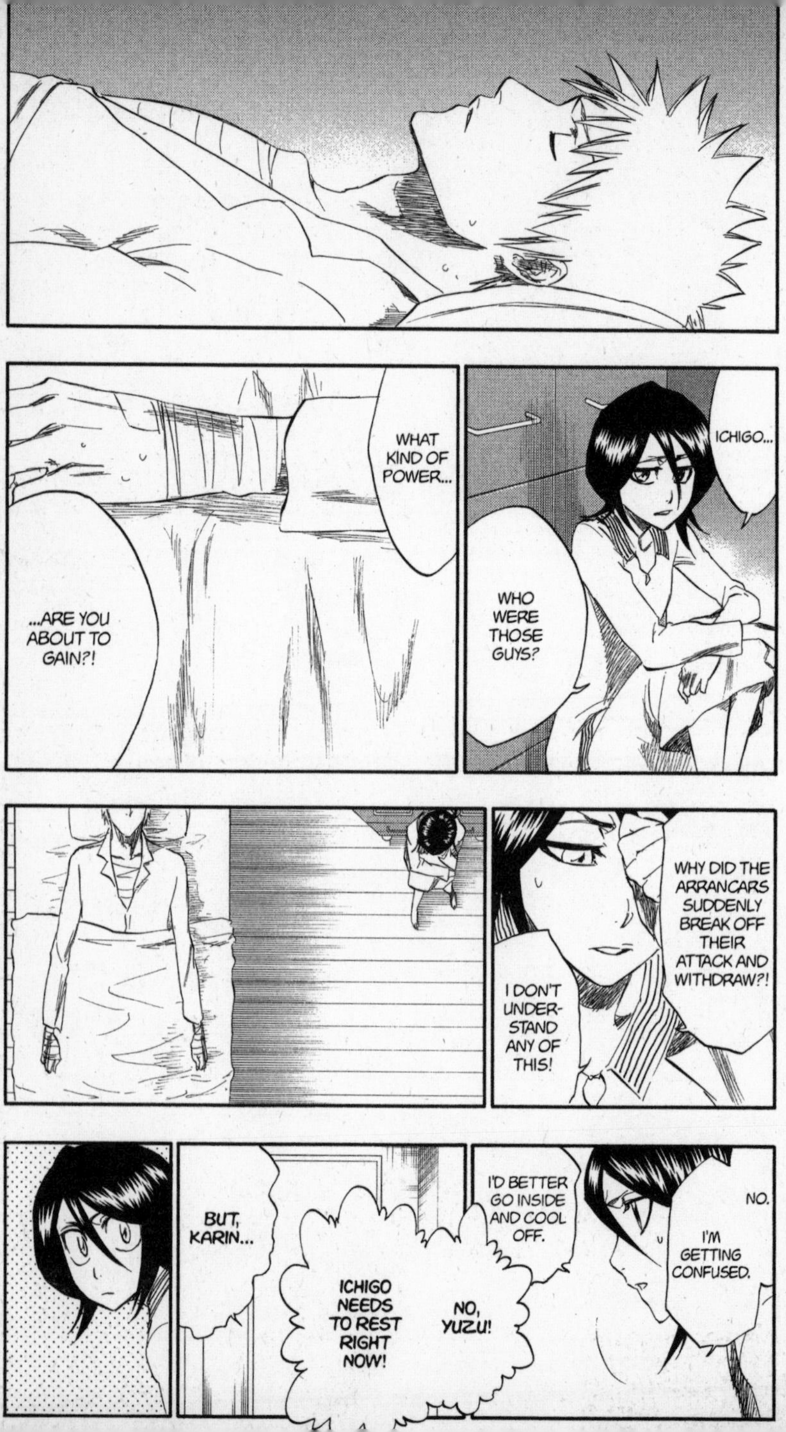
ICHIGO...
WHO WERE THOSE GUYS?
WHAT KIND OF POWER...
...ARE YOU ABOUT TO GAIN?!
WHY DID THE ARRANCARS SUDDENLY BREAK OFF THEIR ATTACK AND WITHDRAW?!
I DON'T UNDER-STAND ANY OF THIS!
NO.
I'M GETTING CONFUSED.
I'D BETTER GO INSIDE AND COOL OFF.
NO, YUZU!
ICHIGO NEEDS TO REST RIGHT NOW!
BUT, KARIN...

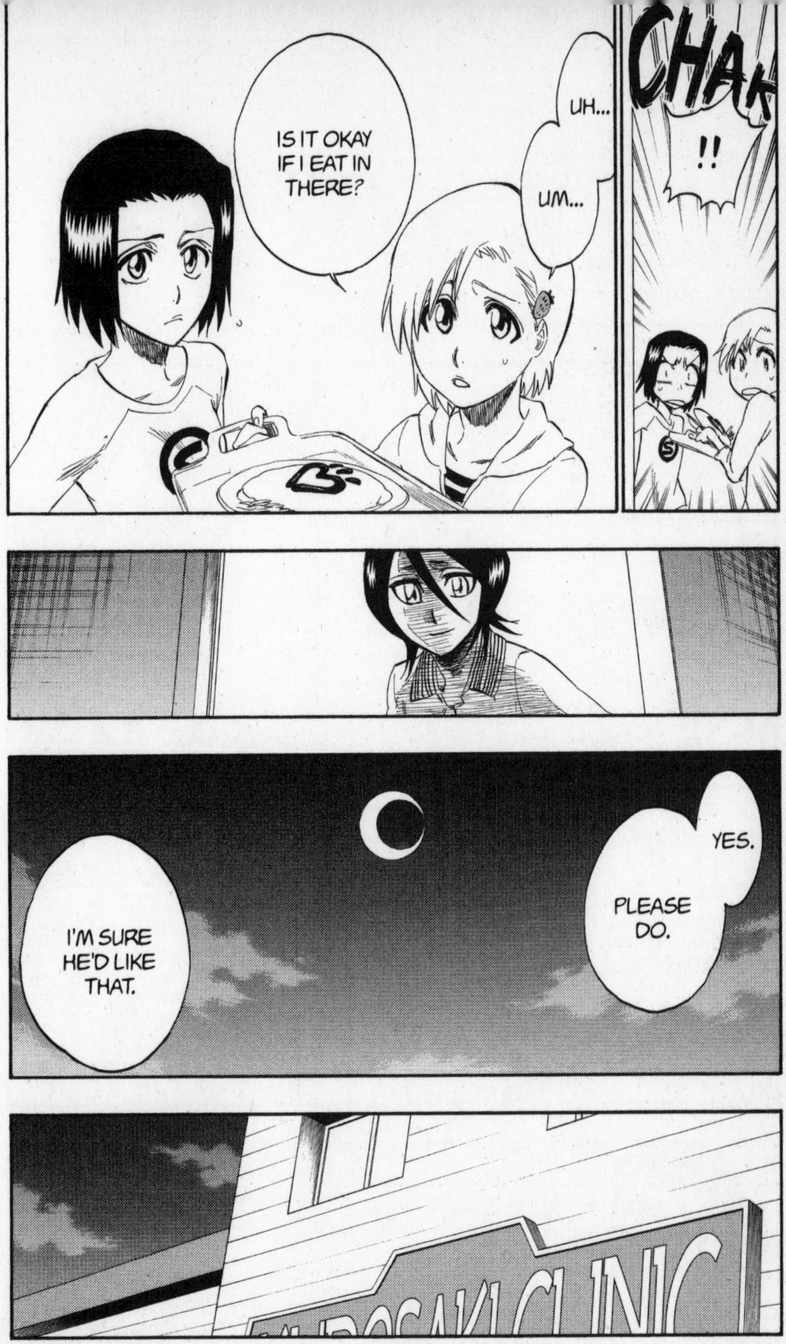
CHAK
!!
UH...
UM...
IS IT OKAY IF I EAT IN THERE?
YES.
PLEASE DO.
I'M SURE HE'D LIKE THAT.
CLINIC

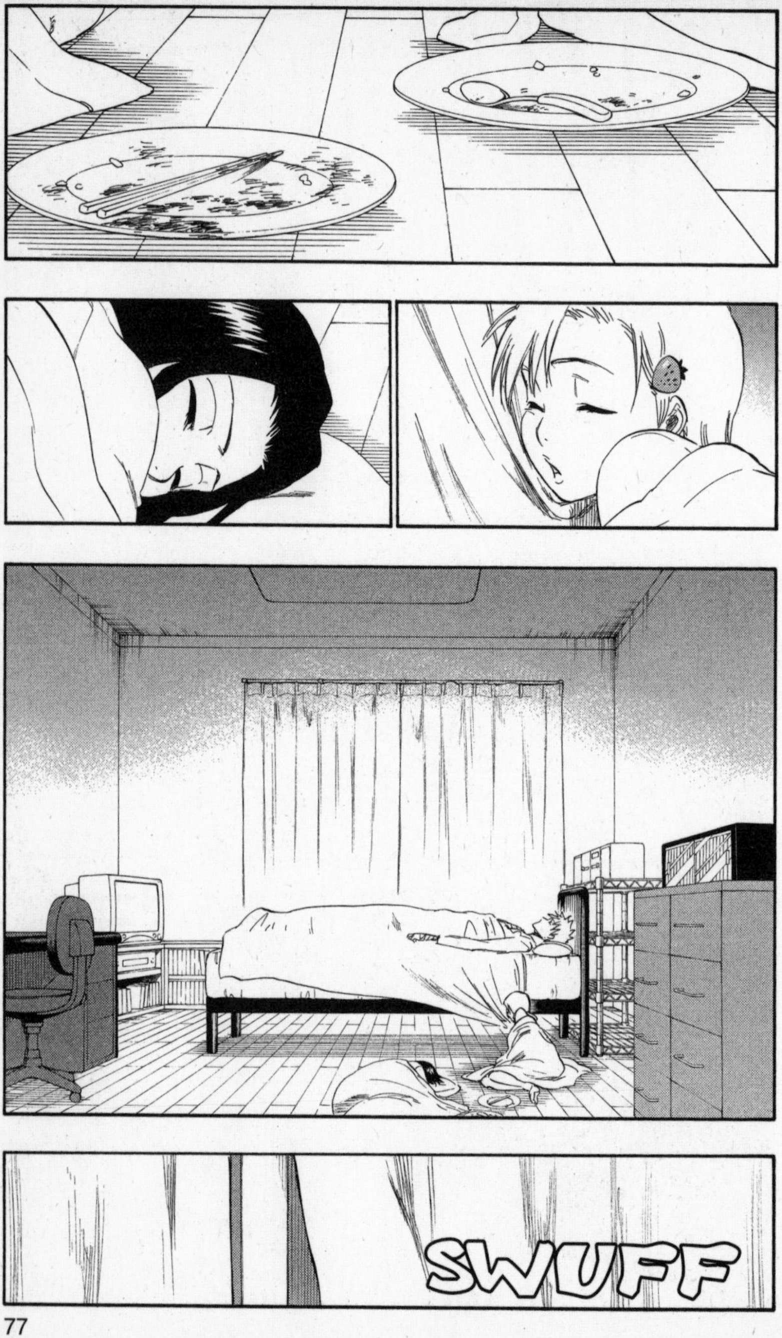
SWUFF

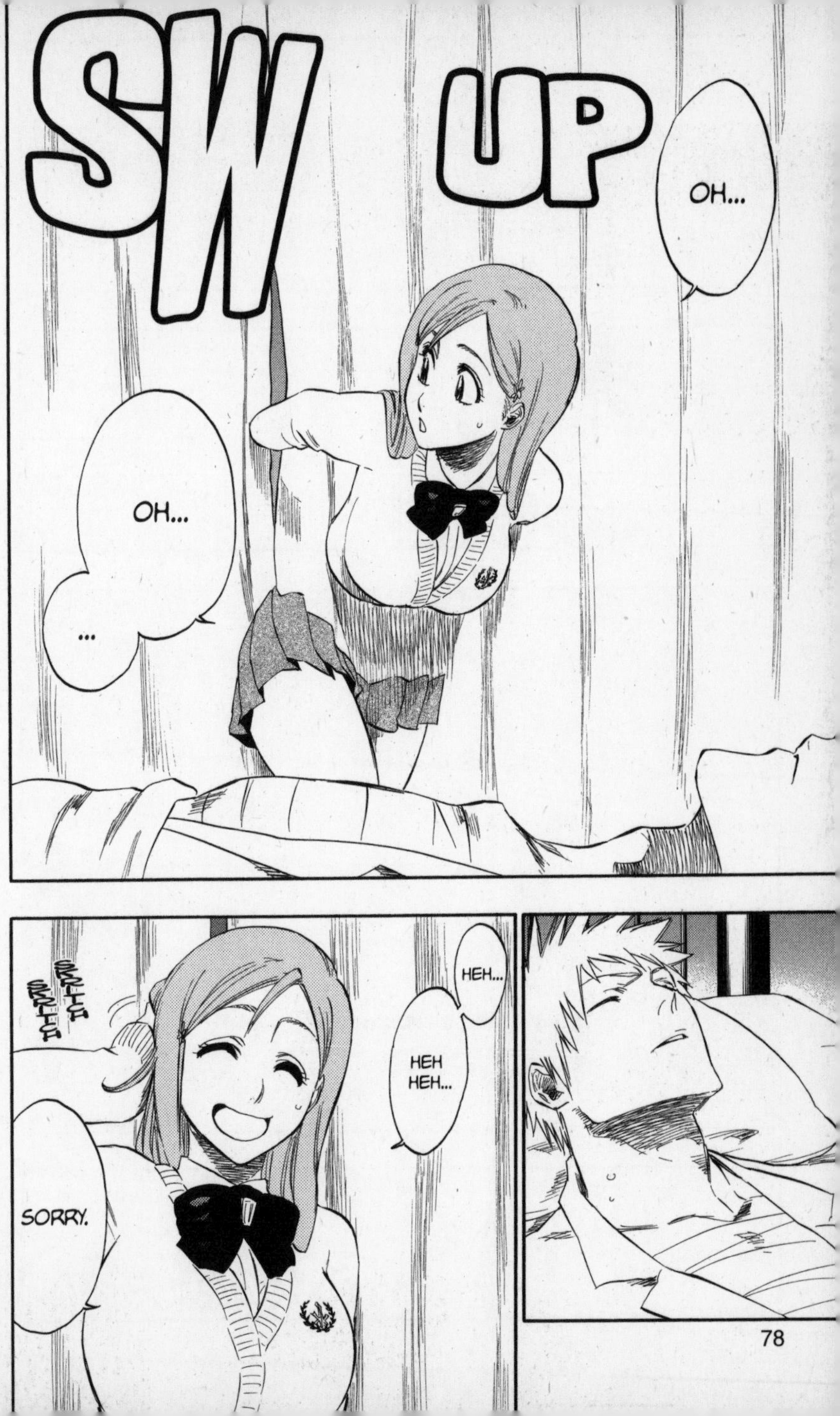
SW UP
OH...
OH...
...
HEH...
HEH
HEH...
SCRITCH
SCRITCH
SORRY.

READ THIS WAY

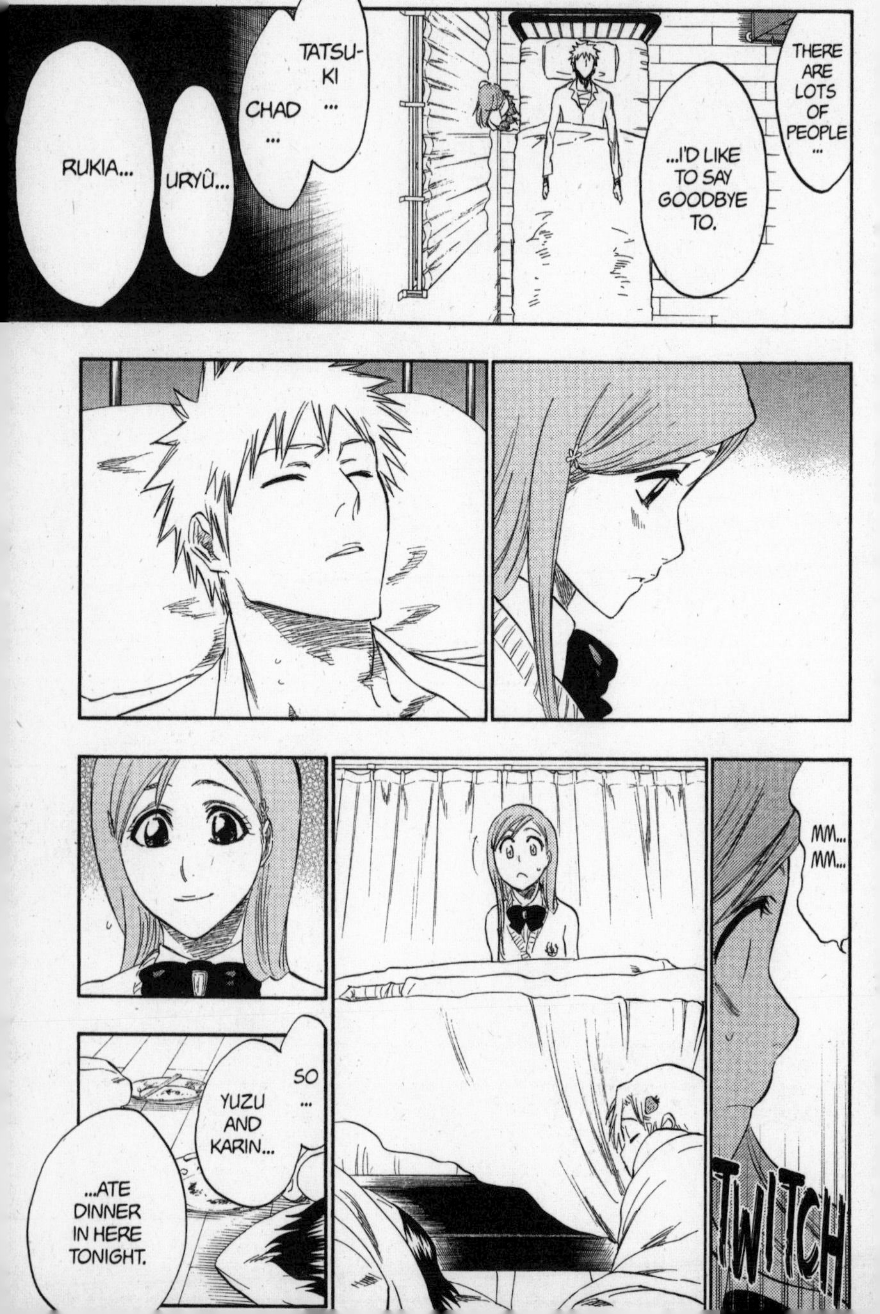
THERE ARE LOTS OF PEOPLE...
...I'D LIKE TO SAY GOODBYE TO.
TATSU-KI...
CHAD...
URYÛ...
RUKIA...
MM... MM...
TWITCH
SO...
YUZU AND KARIN...
...ATE DINNER IN HERE TONIGHT.

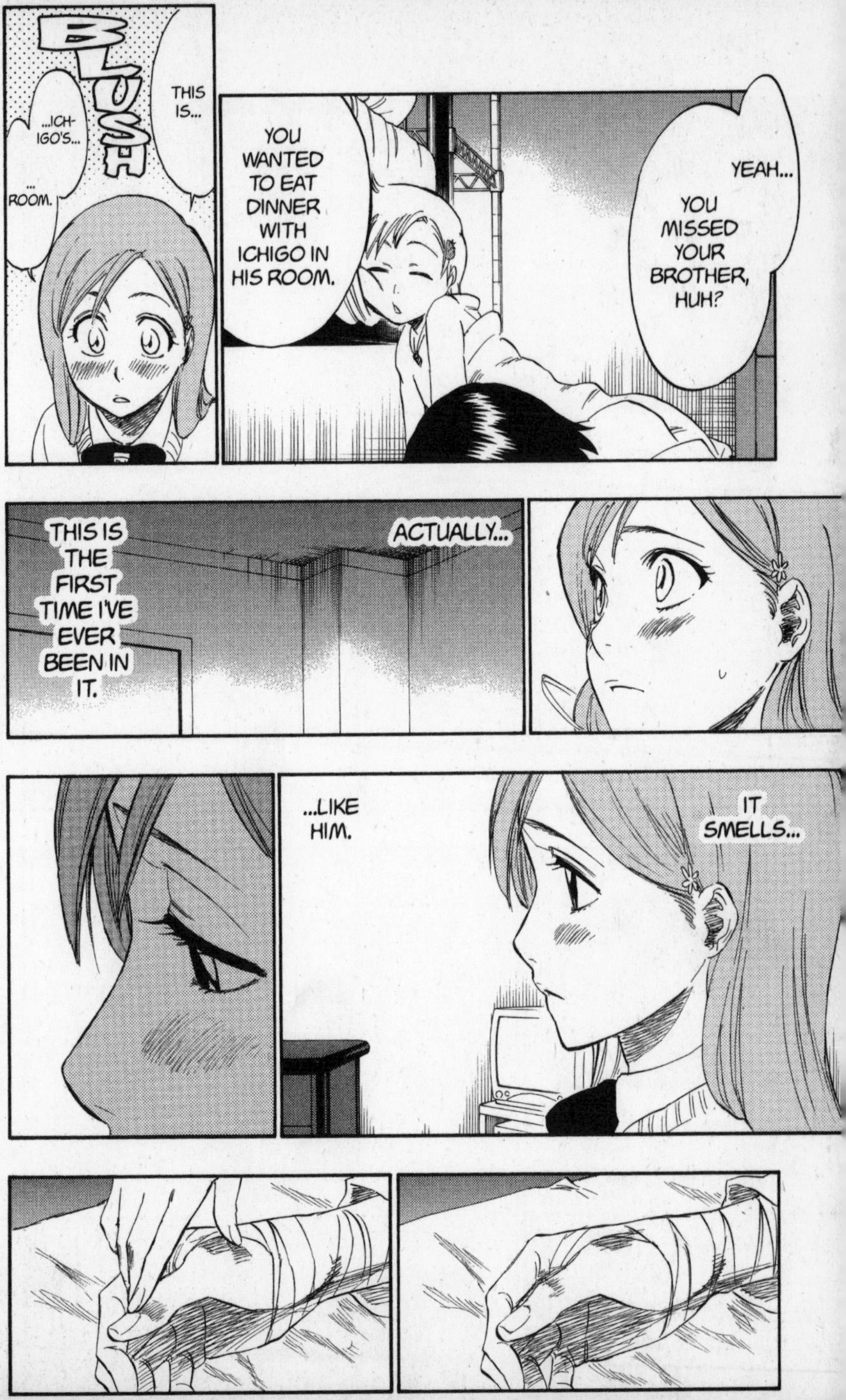
YEAH...
YOU MISSED YOUR BROTHER, HUH?
YOU WANTED TO EAT DINNER WITH ICHIGO IN HIS ROOM.
BLUSH
THIS IS...
...ICH-IGO'S...
... ROOM.
ACTUALLY...
THIS IS THE FIRST TIME I'VE EVER BEEN IN IT.
IT SMELLS...
...LIKE HIM.

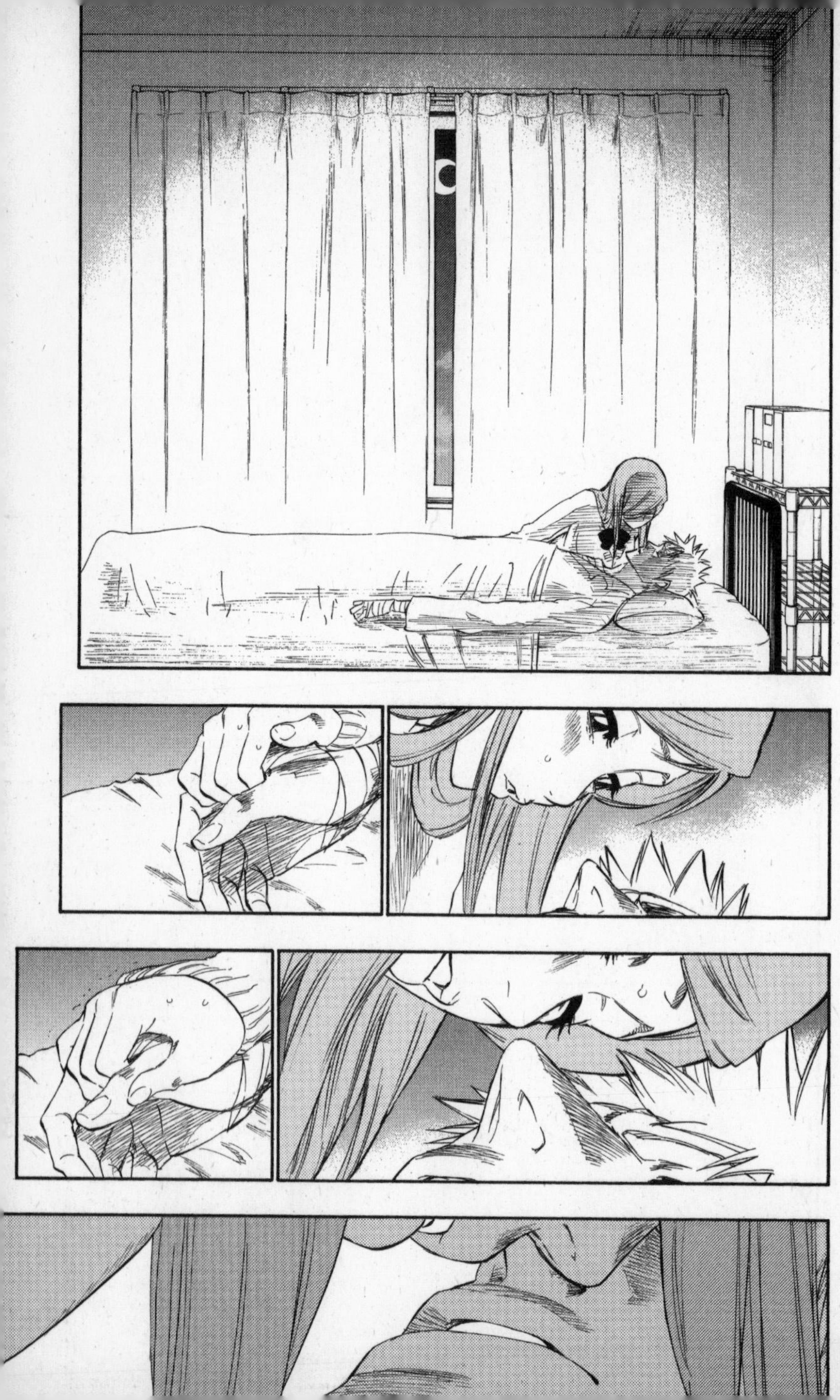

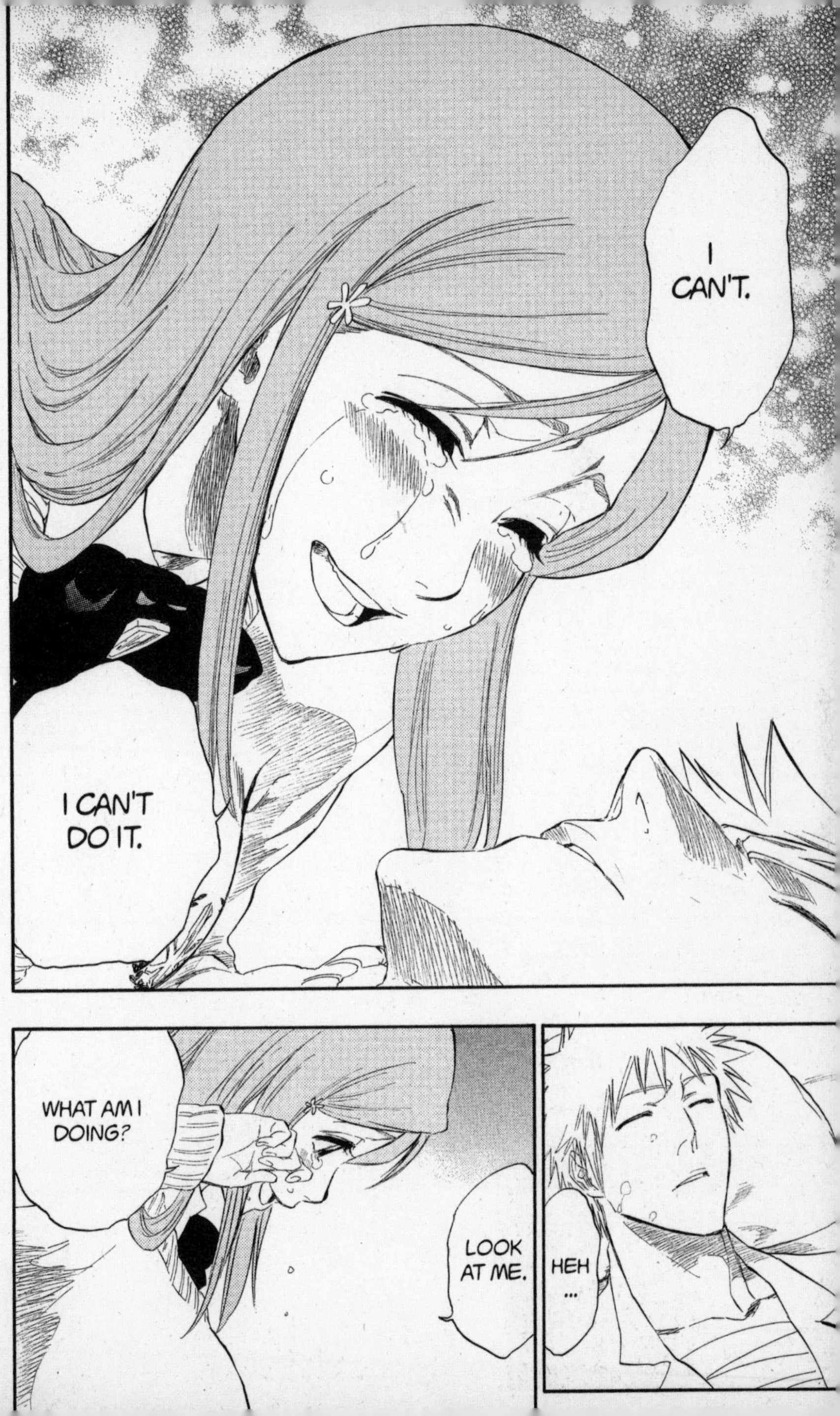

I CAN'T.
I CAN'T DO IT.
HEH ...
WHAT AM I DOING?
LOOK AT ME.

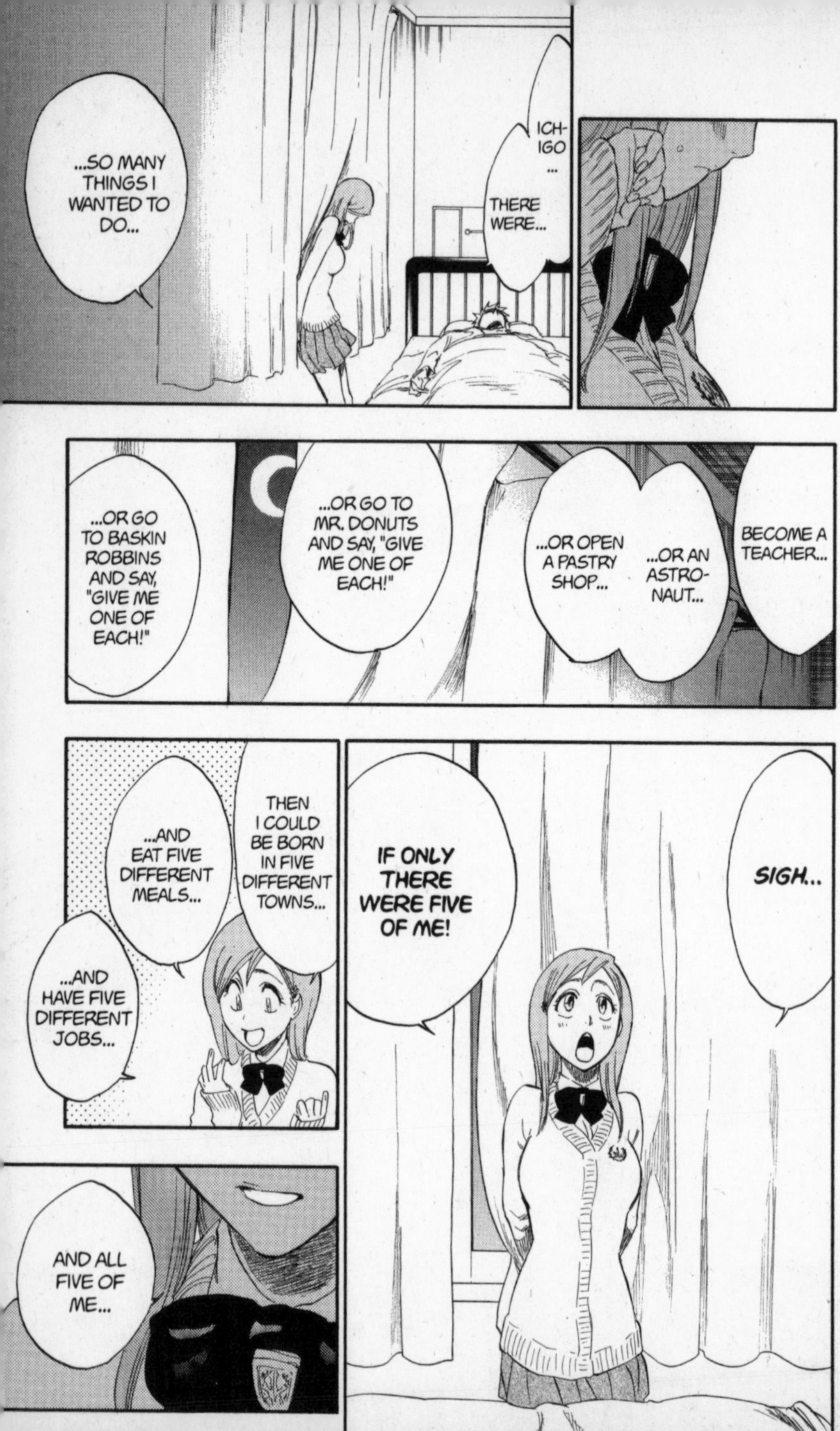
ICH-IGO... THERE WERE...
...SO MANY THINGS I WANTED TO DO...
BECOME A TEACHER...
...OR AN ASTRO-NAUT...
...OR OPEN A PASTRY SHOP...
...OR GO TO MR. DONUTS AND SAY, "GIVE ME ONE OF EACH!"
...OR GO TO BASKIN ROBBINS AND SAY, "GIVE ME ONE OF EACH!"
SIGH...
IF ONLY THERE WERE FIVE OF ME!
THEN I COULD BE BORN IN FIVE DIFFERENT TOWNS...
...AND EAT FIVE DIFFERENT MEALS...
...AND HAVE FIVE DIFFERENT JOBS...
AND ALL FIVE OF ME...

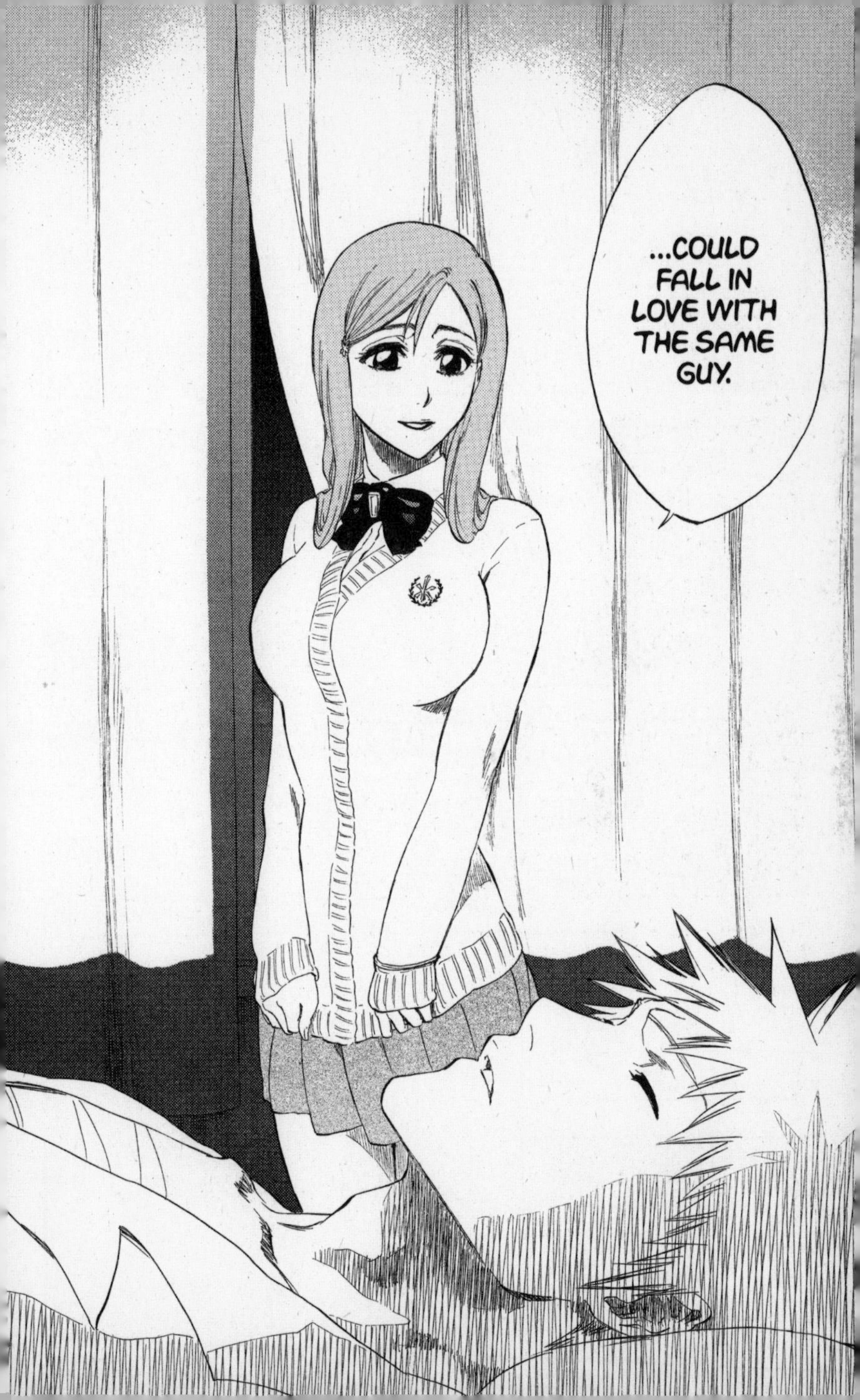
...COULD FALL IN LOVE WITH THE SAME GUY.

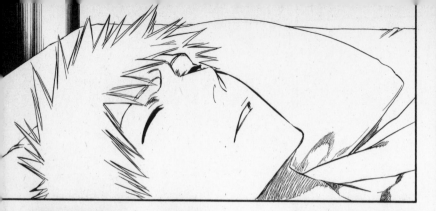

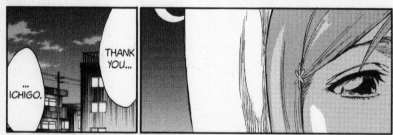

THANK YOU...

...ICHIGO.

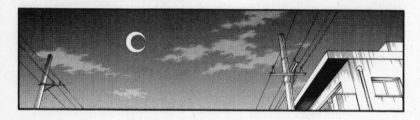

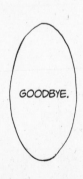

GOODBYE.

238. Eagle Without Wings

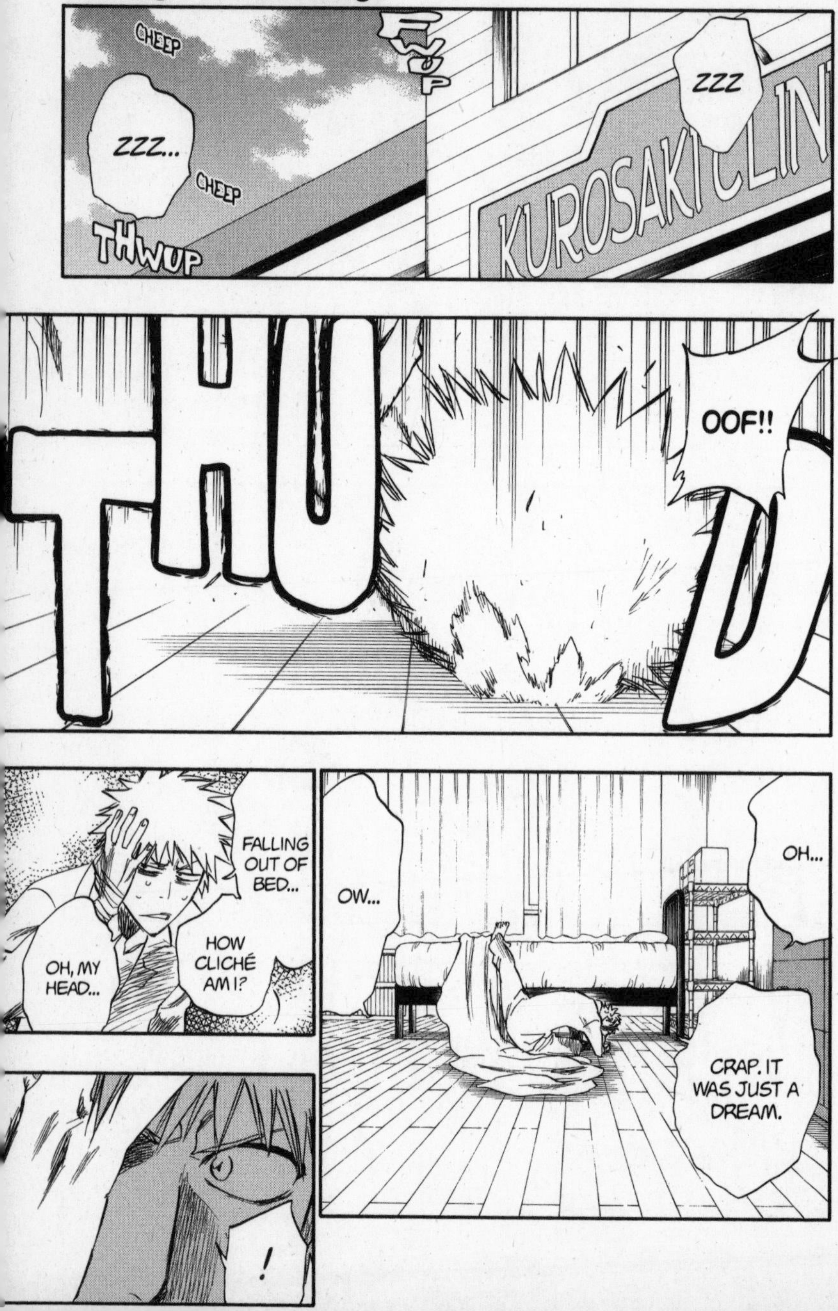
ZZZ
KUROSAKI CLIN
FWOP
CHEEP
ZZZ...
CHEEP
THWUP
OOF!!
THUD
OH...
CRAP. IT WAS JUST A DREAM.
OW...
FALLING OUT OF BED...
HOW CLICHÉ AM I?
OH, MY HEAD...
!

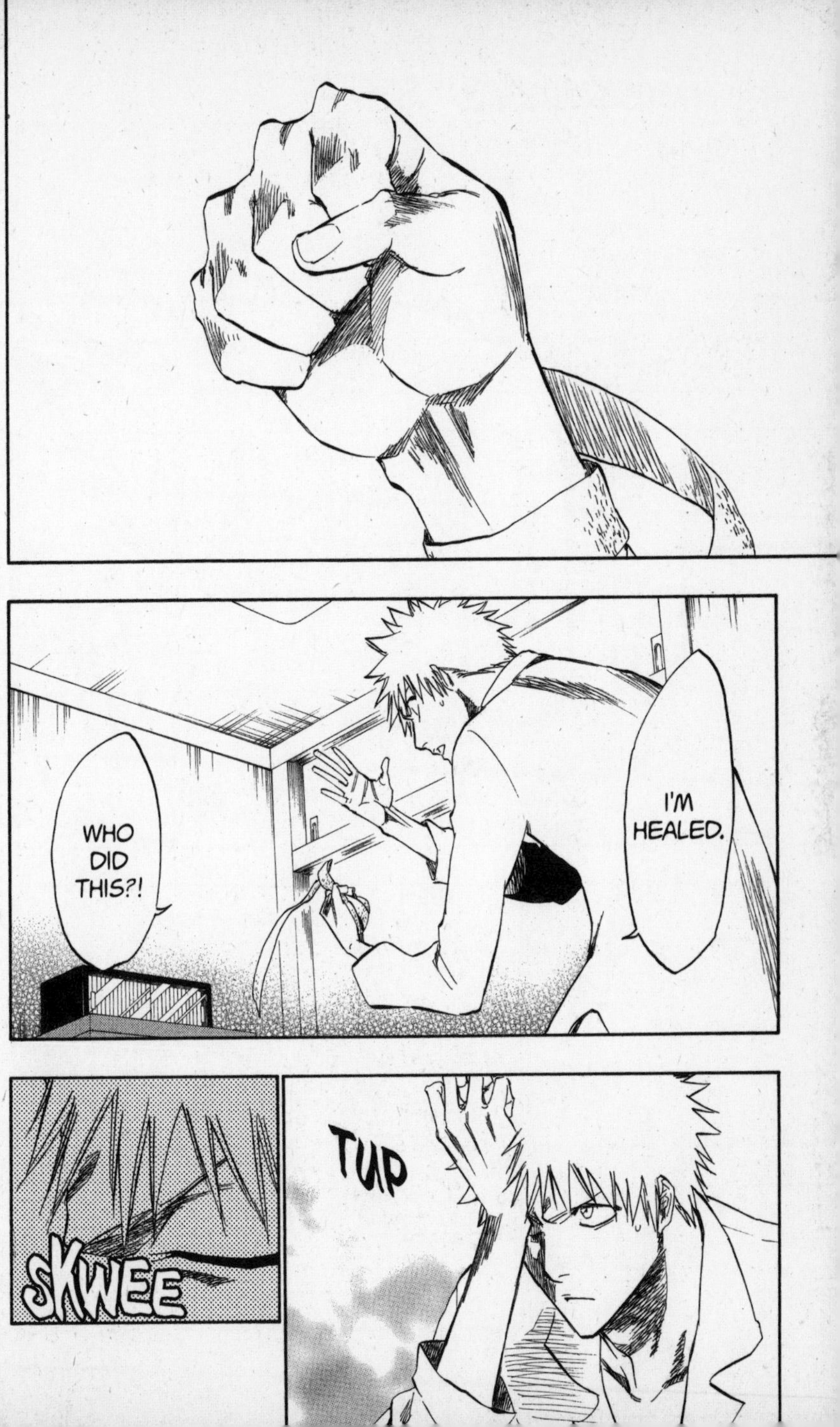
I'M HEALED.
WHO DID THIS?!
TUP
SKWEE

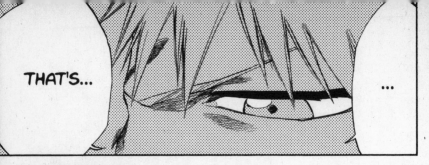

THAT'S...

...

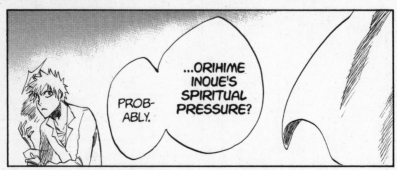

PROB-ABLY.

...ORIHIME INOUE'S SPIRITUAL PRESSURE?

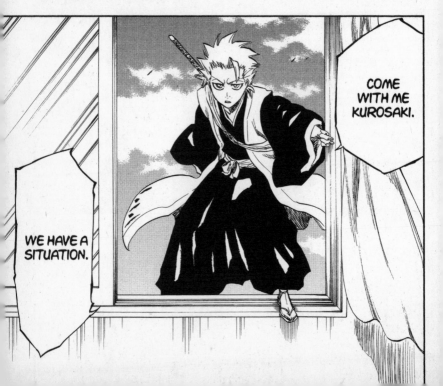

COME WITH ME KUROSAKI.

WE HAVE A SITUATION.

Eagle Without Wings

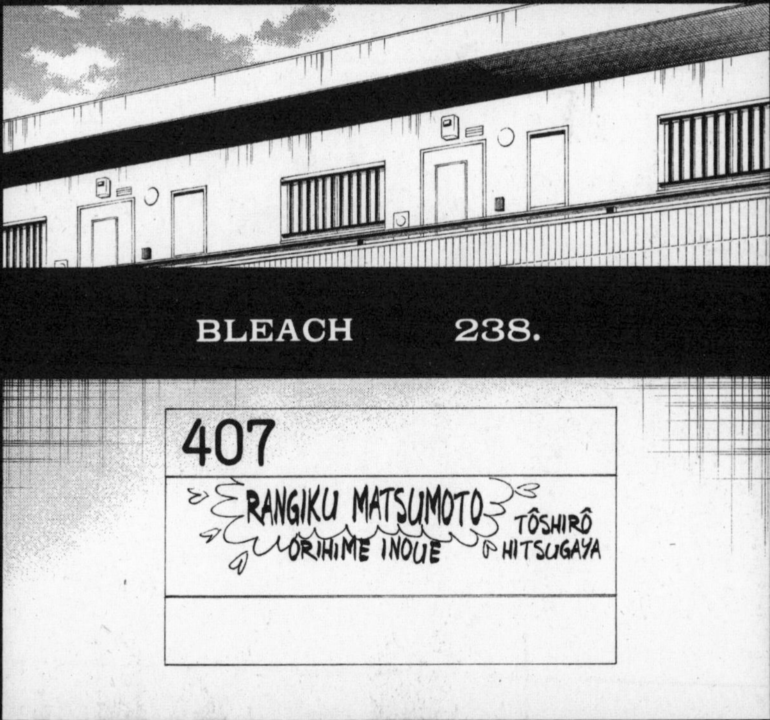

BLEACH 238.
407
RANGIKU MATSUMOTO
ORIHIME INOUE
TÔSHIRÔ HITSUGAYA

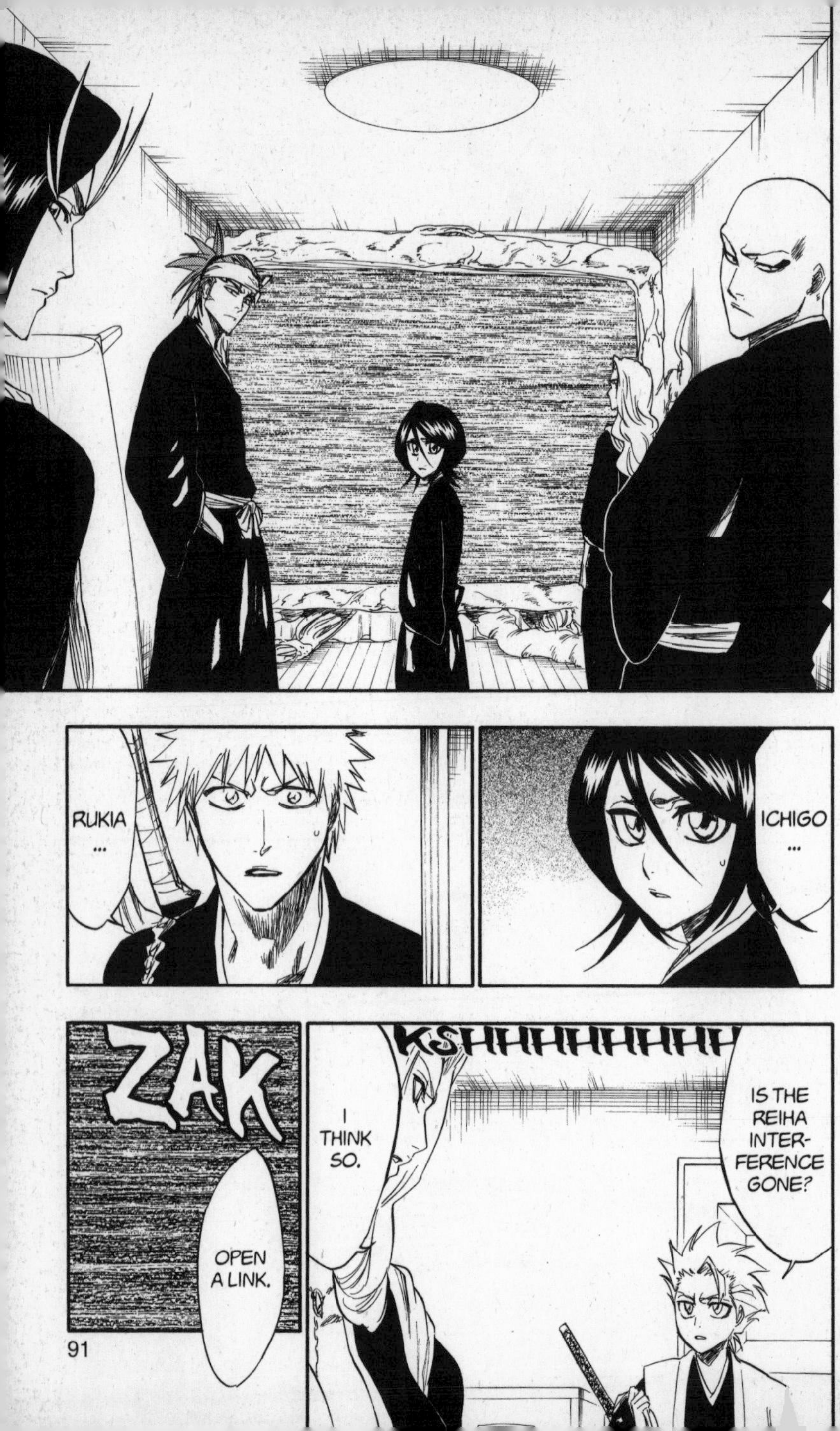
ICHIGO ...
RUKIA ...
KSHHHHHHHHH
IS THE REIHA INTER-FERENCE GONE?
I THINK SO.
ZAK
OPEN A LINK.

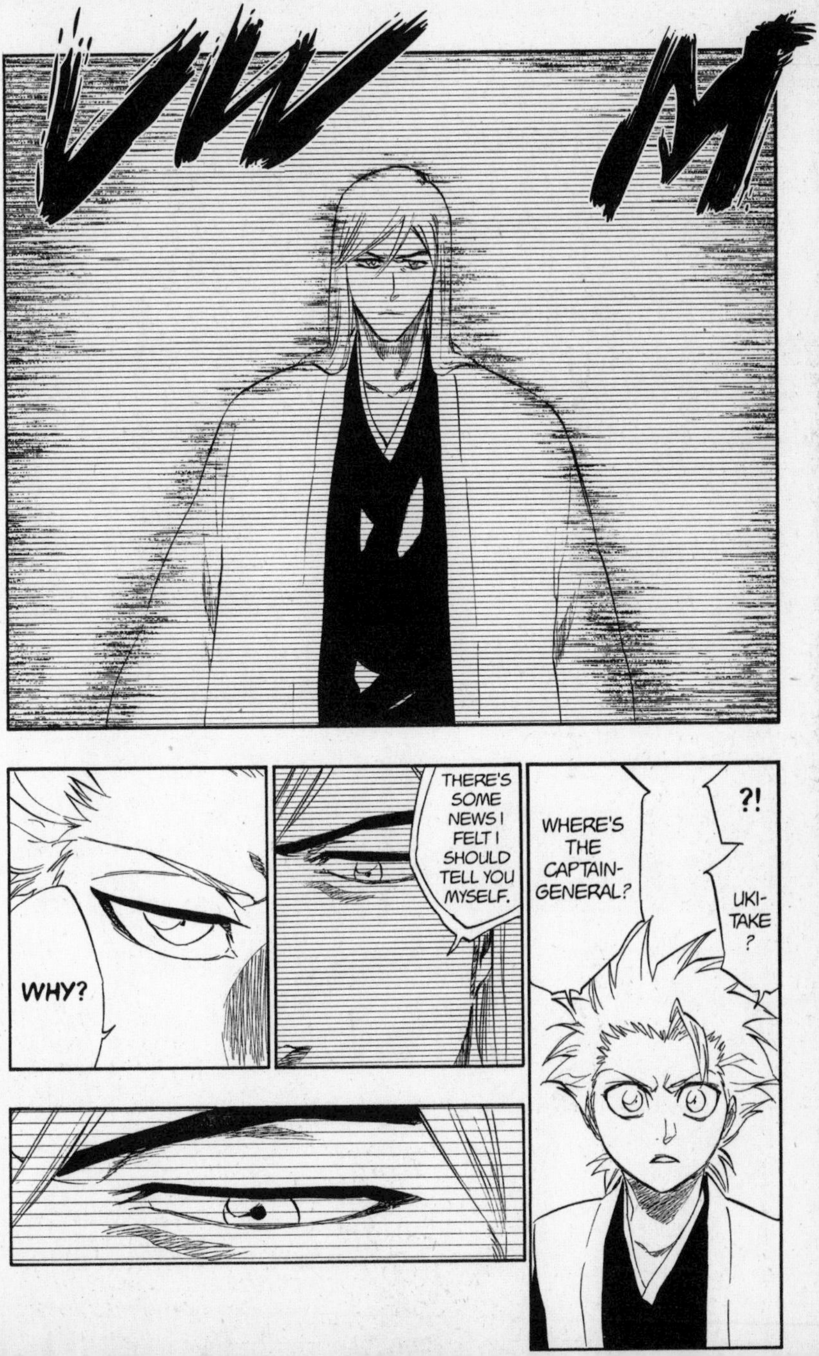
VWMM
?!
UKI-TAKE?
WHERE'S THE CAPTAIN-GENERAL?
THERE'S SOME NEWS I FELT I SHOULD TELL YOU MYSELF.
WHY?

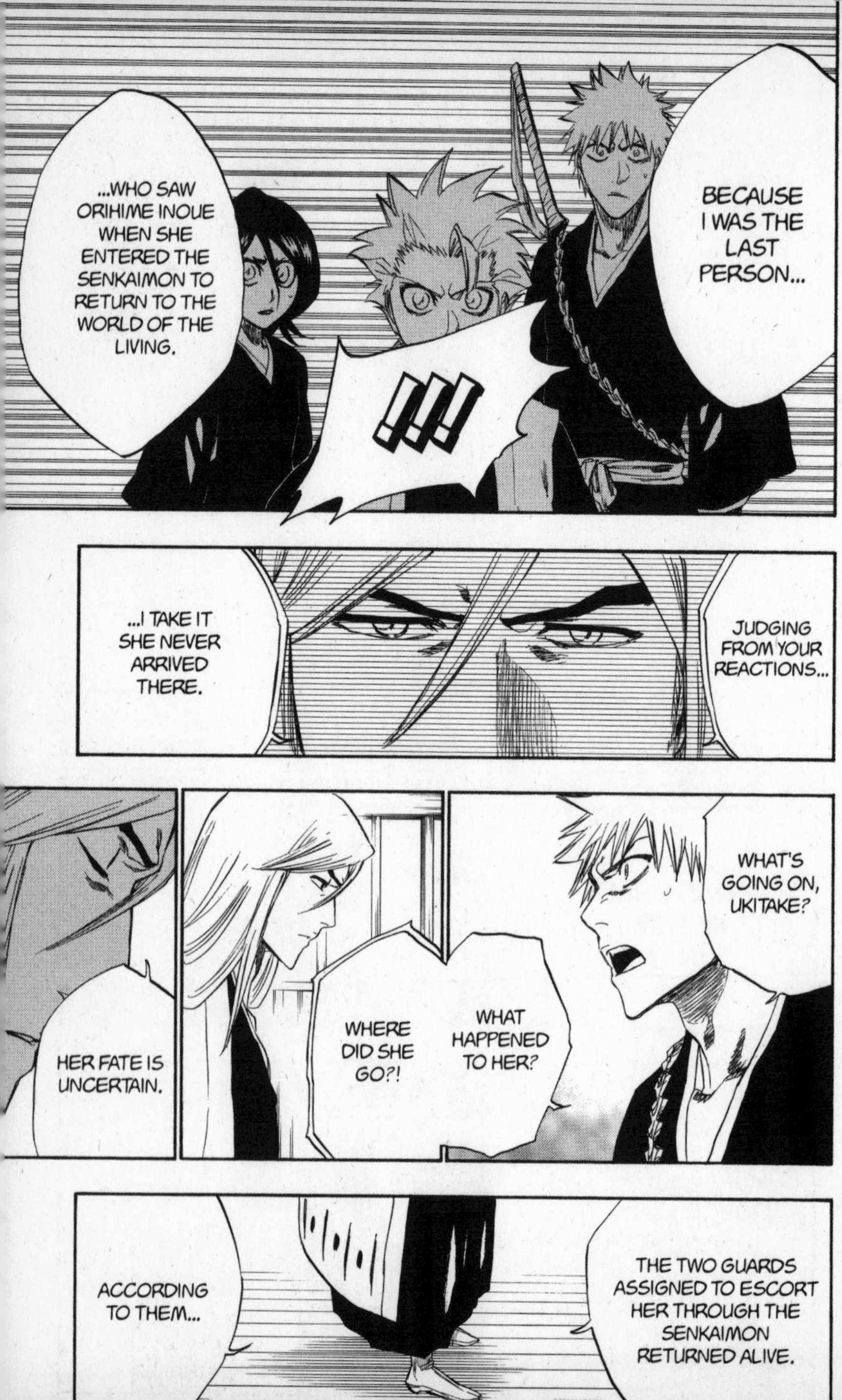
BECAUSE I WAS THE LAST PERSON...
...WHO SAW ORIHIME INOUE WHEN SHE ENTERED THE SENKAIMON TO RETURN TO THE WORLD OF THE LIVING.
!!!
JUDGING FROM YOUR REACTIONS...
...I TAKE IT SHE NEVER ARRIVED THERE.
WHAT'S GOING ON, UKITAKE?
WHAT HAPPENED TO HER?
WHERE DID SHE GO?!
HER FATE IS UNCERTAIN.
THE TWO GUARDS ASSIGNED TO ESCORT HER THROUGH THE SENKAIMON RETURNED ALIVE.
ACCORDING TO THEM...

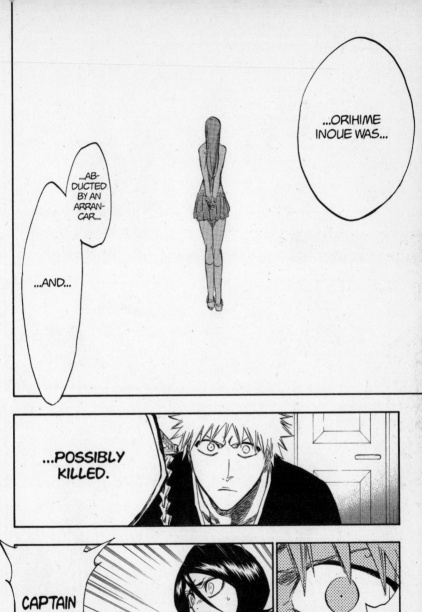

...ORIHIME INOUE WAS...

...AB-DUCTED BY AN ARRAN-CAR...

...AND...

...POSSIBLY KILLED.

CAPTAIN UKITAKE!!

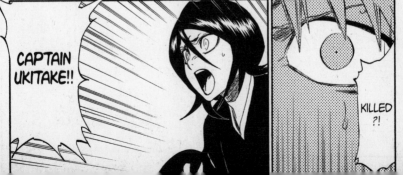

KILLED ?!

READ THIS WAY

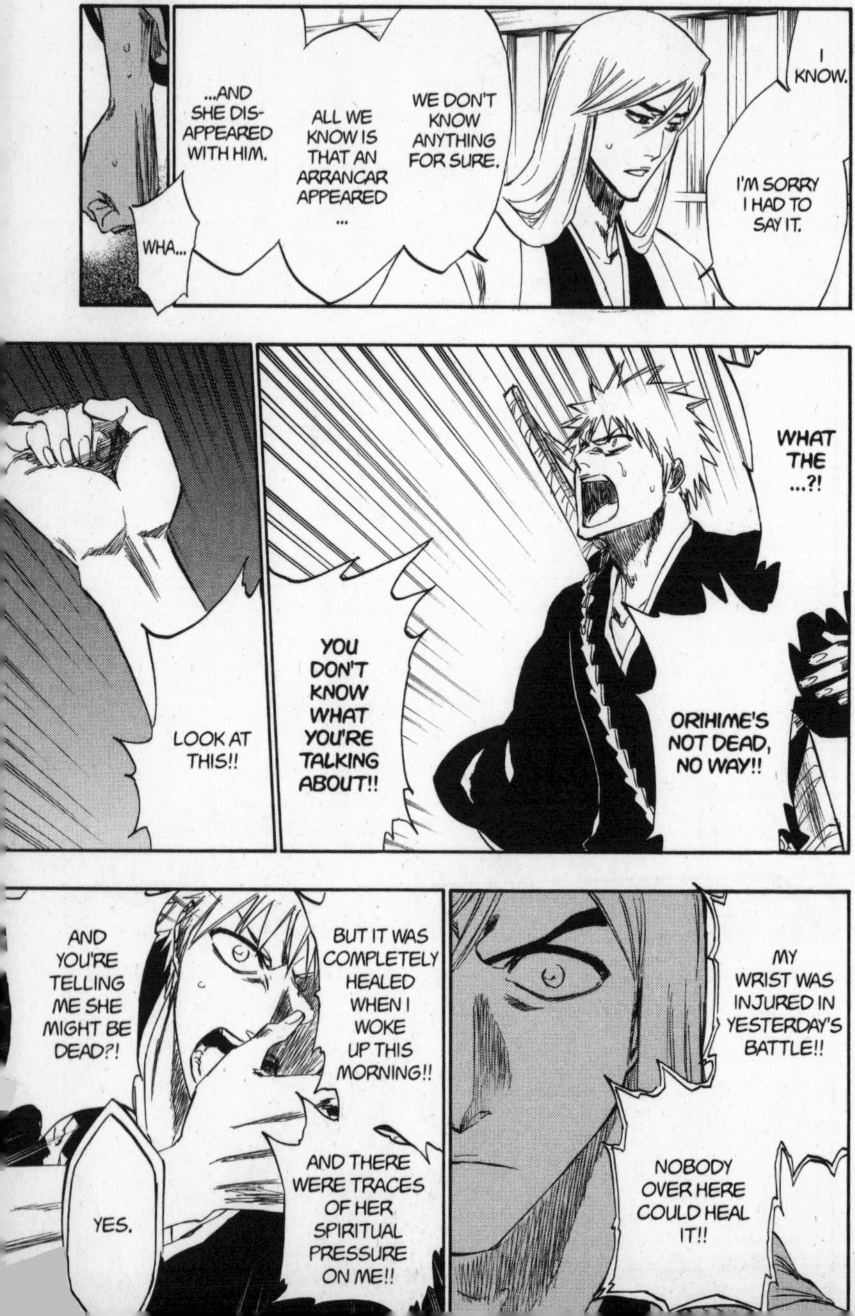
I KNOW.
I'M SORRY I HAD TO SAY IT.
WE DON'T KNOW ANYTHING FOR SURE.
ALL WE KNOW IS THAT AN ARRANCAR APPEARED...
...AND SHE DISAPPEARED WITH HIM.
WHA...
WHAT THE ...?!
ORIHIME'S NOT DEAD, NO WAY!!
YOU DON'T KNOW WHAT YOU'RE TALKING ABOUT!!
LOOK AT THIS!!
MY WRIST WAS INJURED IN YESTERDAY'S BATTLE!!
NOBODY OVER HERE COULD HEAL IT!!
BUT IT WAS COMPLETELY HEALED WHEN I WOKE UP THIS MORNING!!
AND THERE WERE TRACES OF HER SPIRITUAL PRESSURE ON ME!!
AND YOU'RE TELLING ME SHE MIGHT BE DEAD?!
YES.

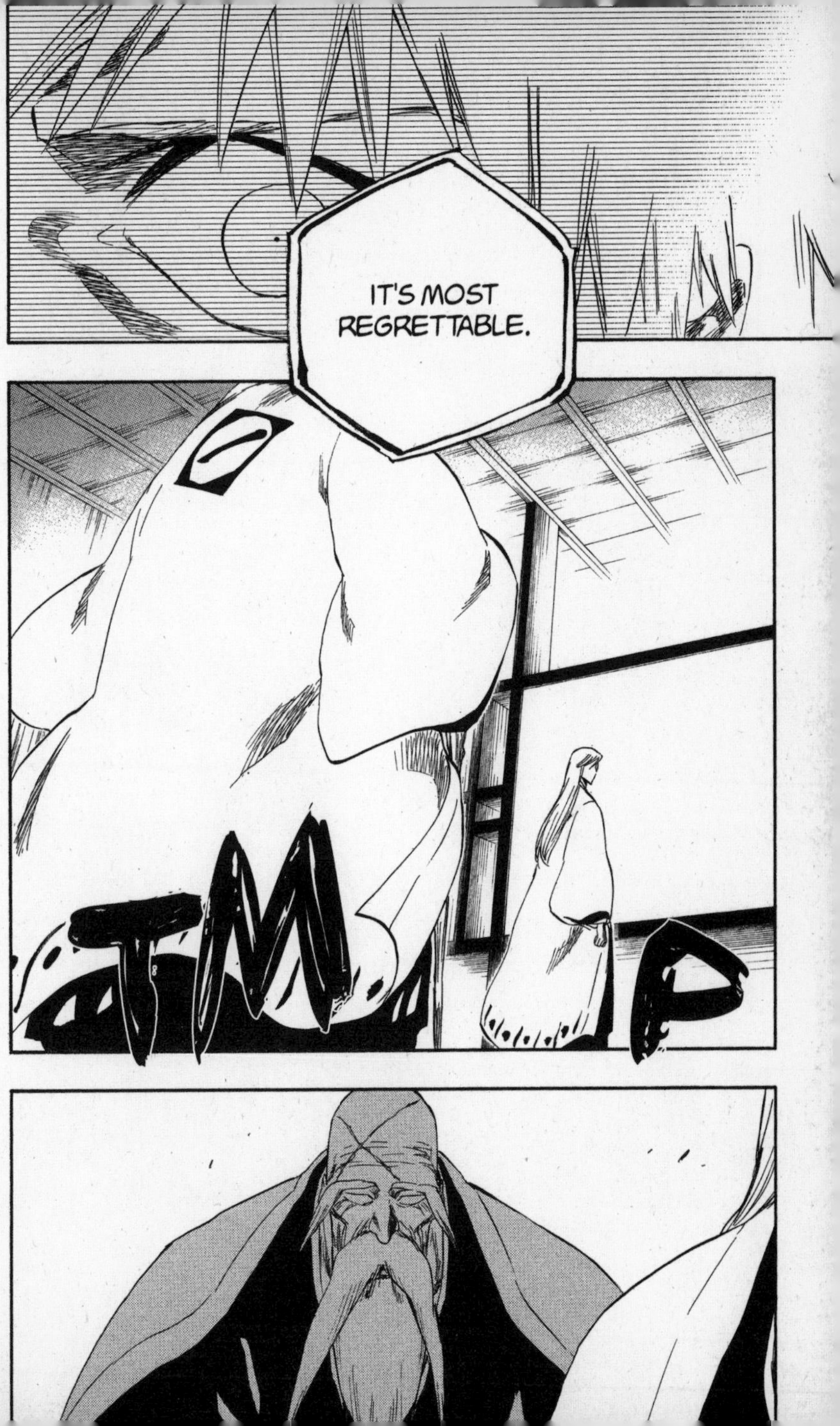
IT'S MOST REGRETTABLE.
TMP

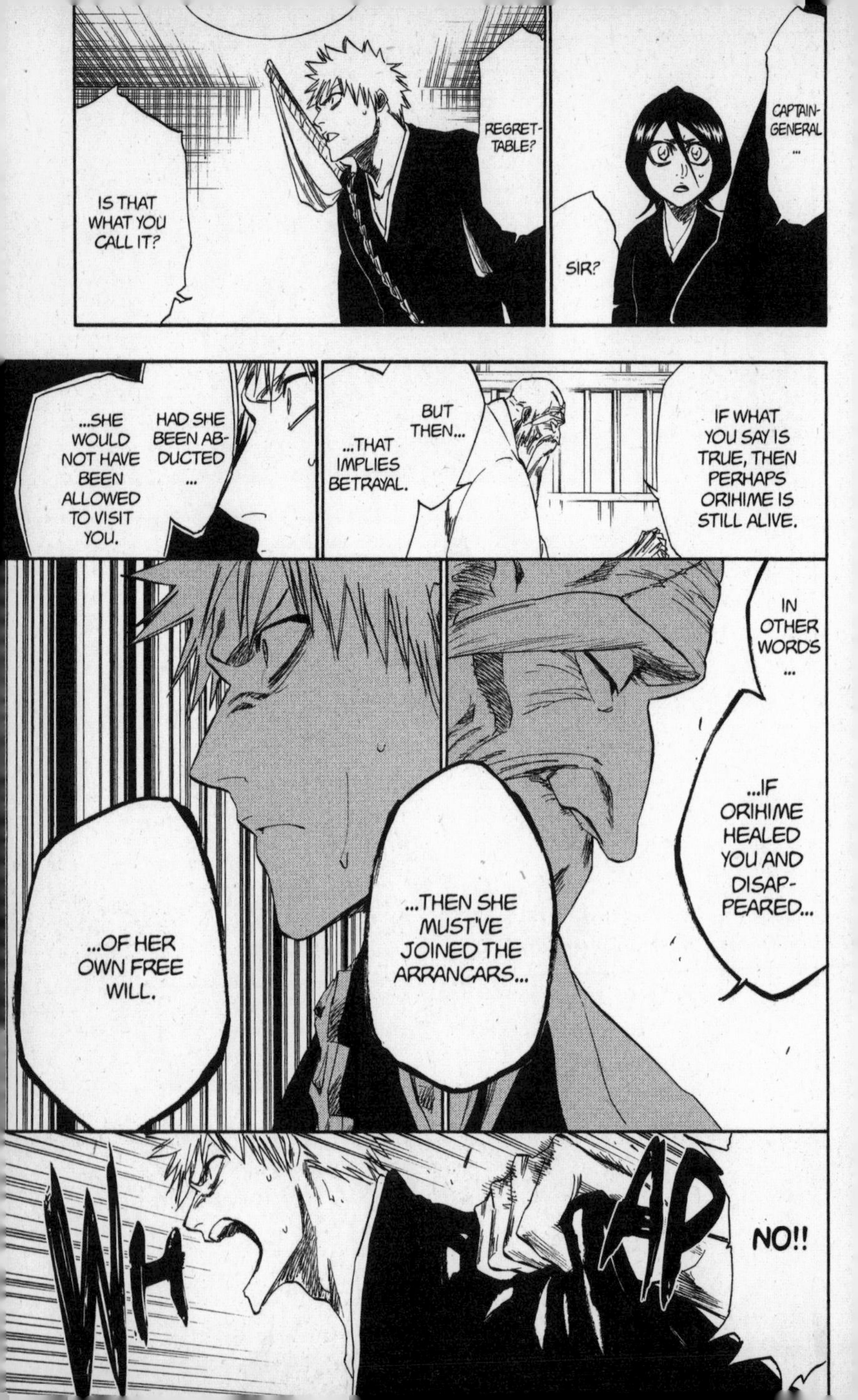
CAPTAIN-GENERAL...
SIR?
REGRET-TABLE?
IS THAT WHAT YOU CALL IT?
IF WHAT YOU SAY IS TRUE, THEN PERHAPS ORIHIME IS STILL ALIVE.
BUT THEN...
...THAT IMPLIES BETRAYAL.
HAD SHE BEEN AB-DUCTED...
...SHE WOULD NOT HAVE BEEN ALLOWED TO VISIT YOU.
IN OTHER WORDS...
...IF ORIHIME HEALED YOU AND DISAP-PEARED...
...THEN SHE MUST'VE JOINED THE ARRANCARS...
...OF HER OWN FREE WILL.
NO!!
WHAP

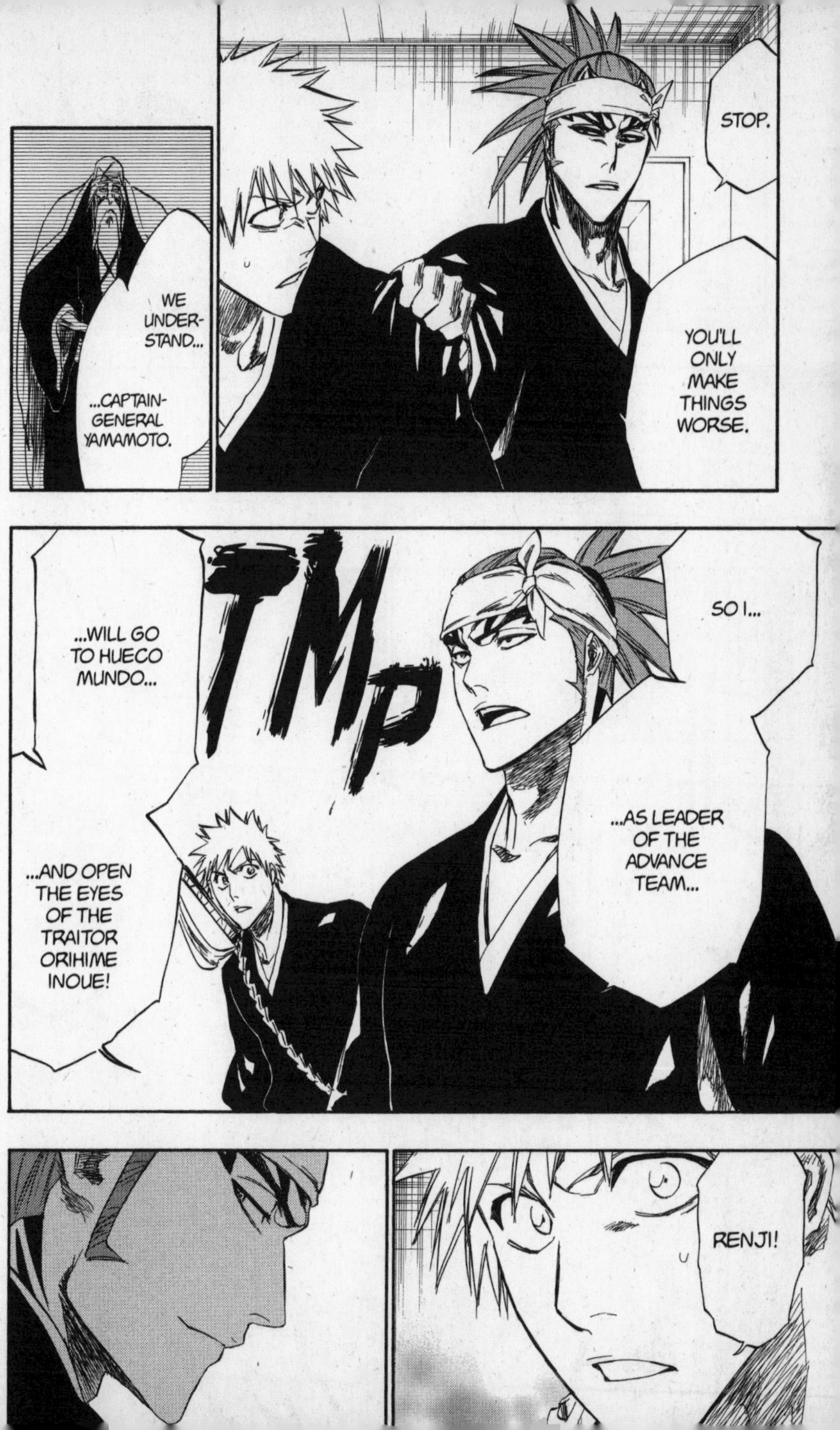
STOP.
YOU'LL ONLY MAKE THINGS WORSE.
WE UNDER-STAND...
...CAPTAIN-GENERAL YAMAMOTO.
SO I...
...AS LEADER OF THE ADVANCE TEAM...
TMP
...WILL GO TO HUECO MUNDO...
...AND OPEN THE EYES OF THE TRAITOR ORIHIME INOUE!
RENJI!

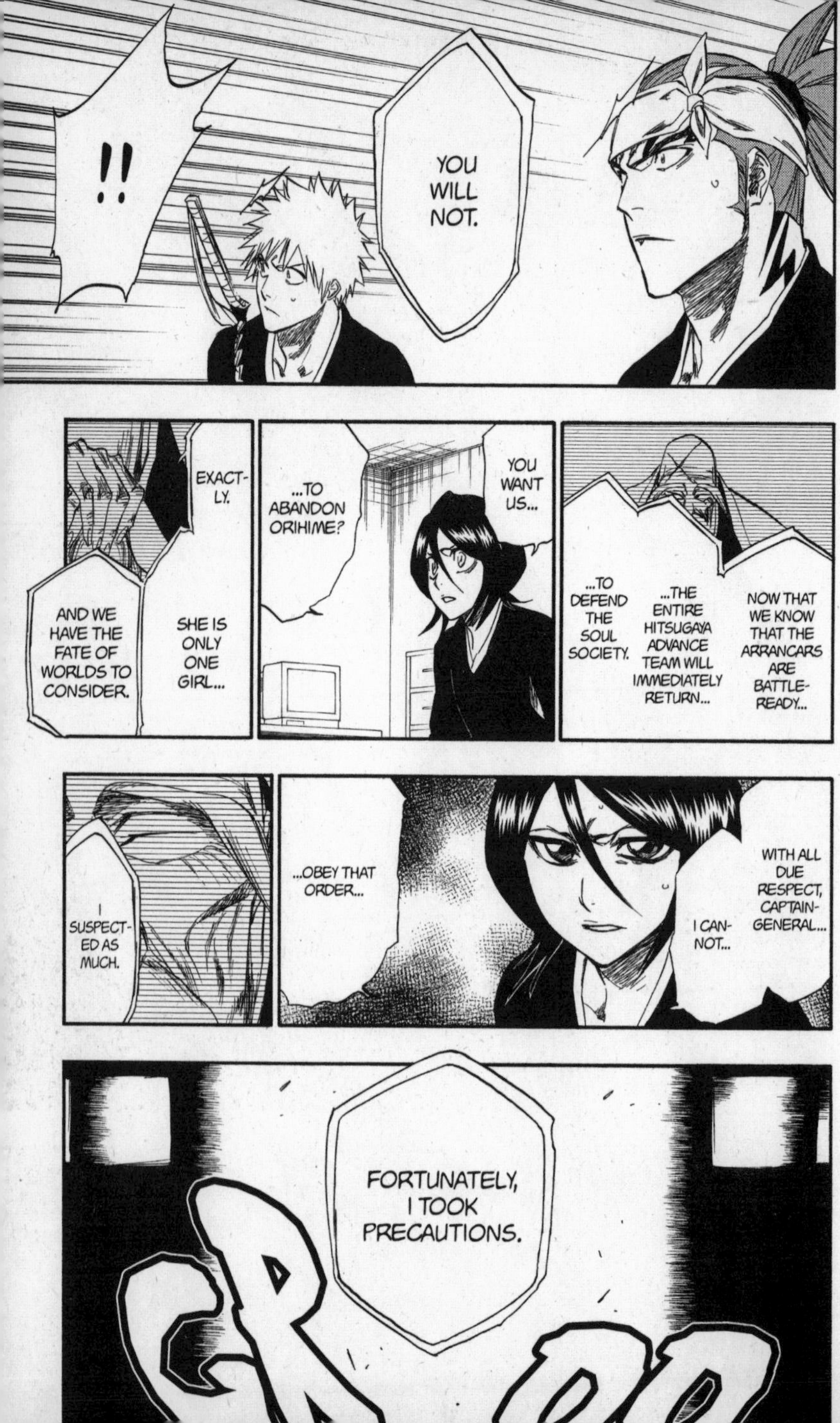
YOU WILL NOT.
!!
NOW THAT WE KNOW THAT THE ARRANCARS ARE BATTLE-READY...
...THE ENTIRE HITSUGAYA ADVANCE TEAM WILL IMMEDIATELY RETURN...
...TO DEFEND THE SOUL SOCIETY.
YOU WANT US...
...TO ABANDON ORIHIME?
EXACT-LY.
SHE IS ONLY ONE GIRL...
AND WE HAVE THE FATE OF WORLDS TO CONSIDER.
WITH ALL DUE RESPECT, CAPTAIN-GENERAL...
I CAN-NOT...
...OBEY THAT ORDER...
I SUSPECT-ED AS MUCH.
FORTUNATELY, I TOOK PRECAUTIONS.

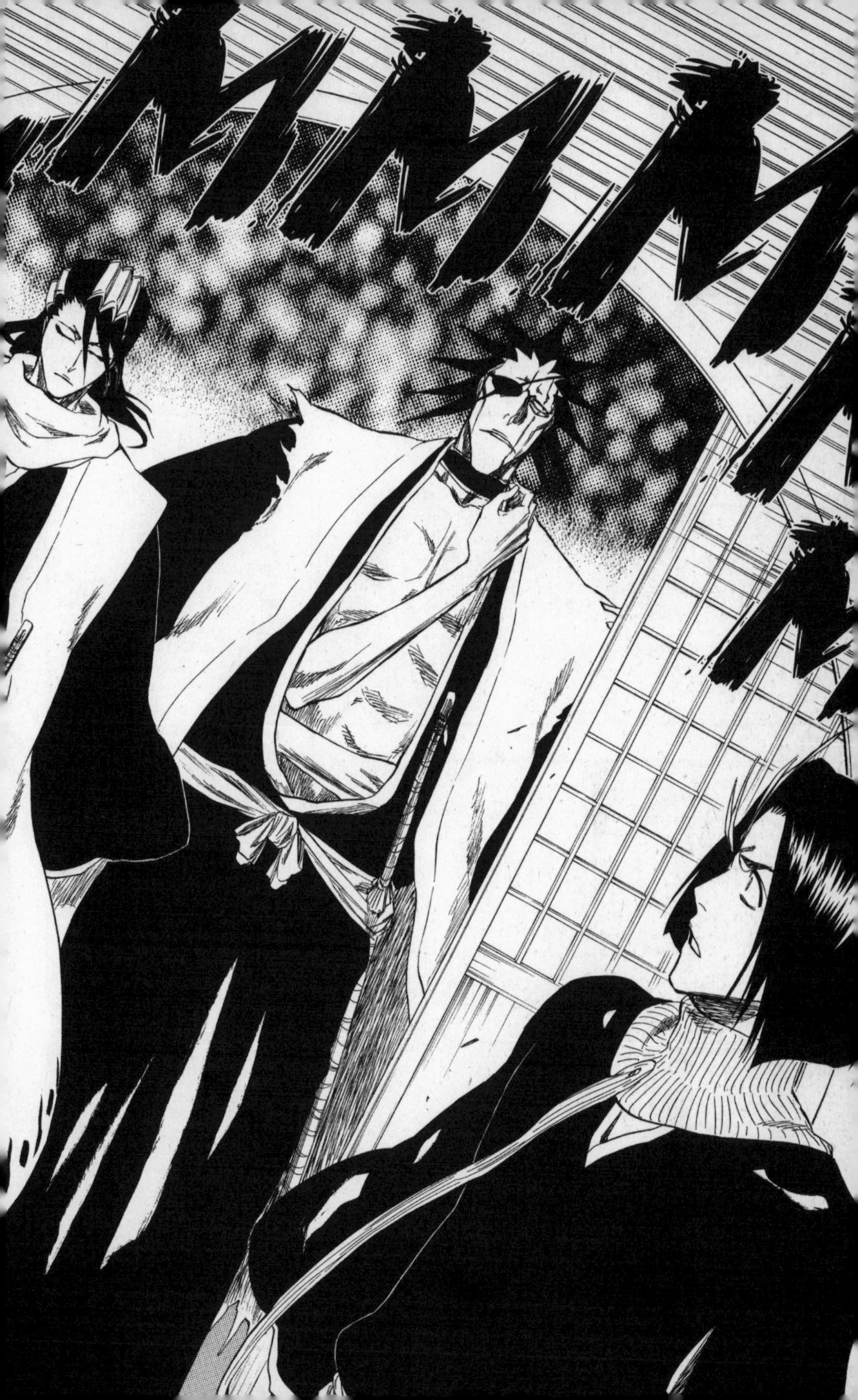

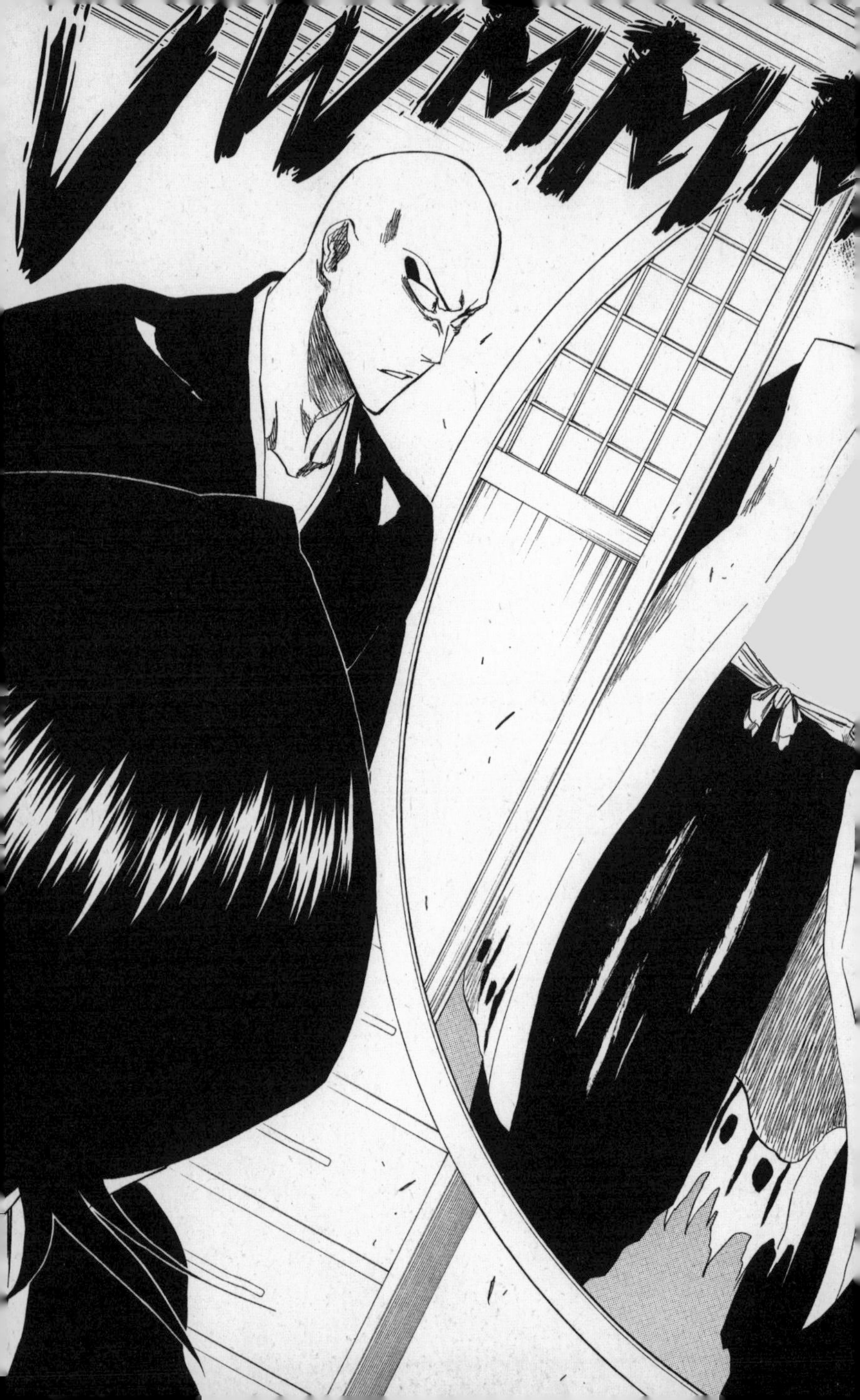
VWMMM

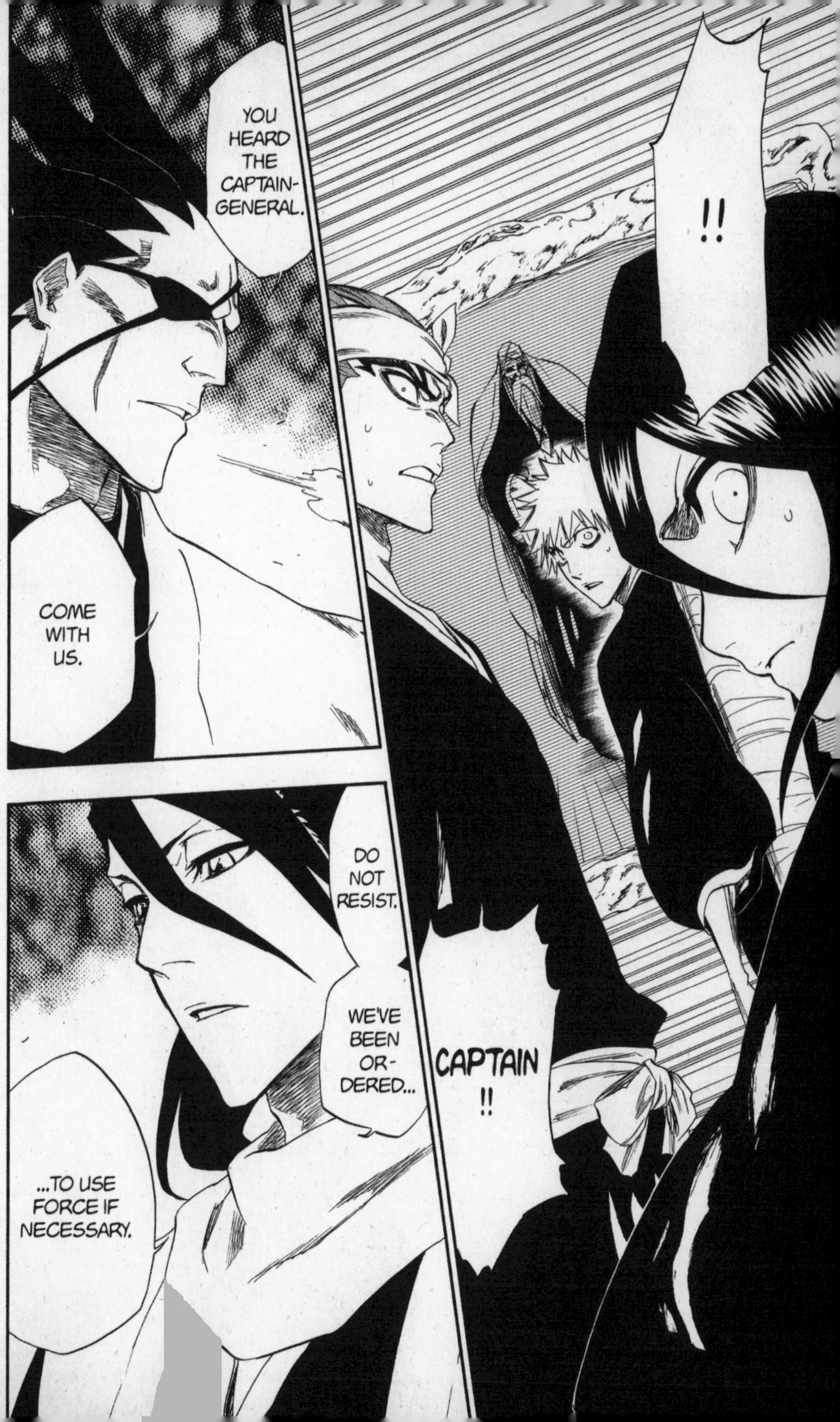
!!
CAPTAIN!!
YOU HEARD THE CAPTAIN-GENERAL.
COME WITH US.
DO NOT RESIST.
WE'VE BEEN ORDERED...
...TO USE FORCE IF NECESSARY.

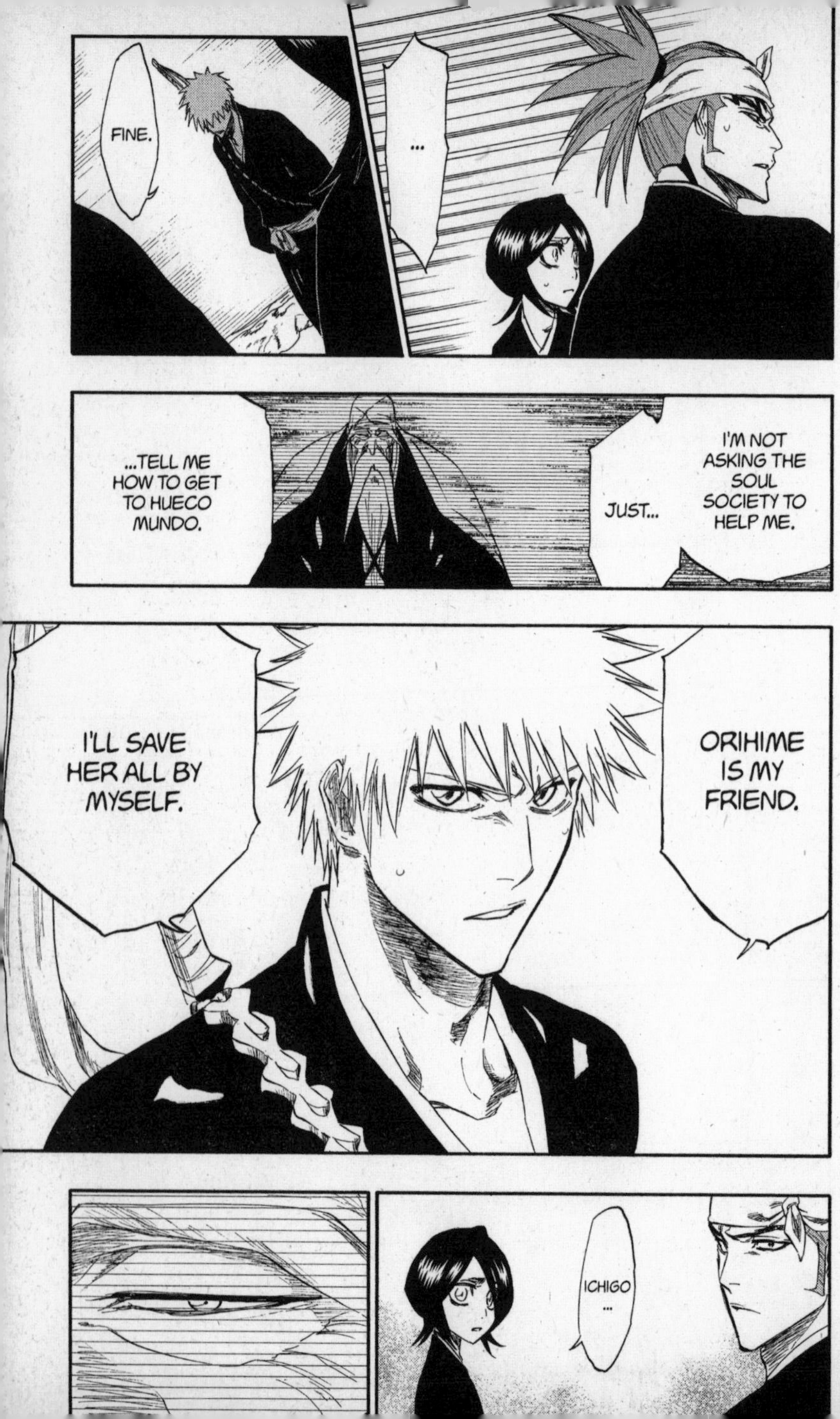
...
FINE.
I'M NOT ASKING THE SOUL SOCIETY TO HELP ME.
JUST...
...TELL ME HOW TO GET TO HUECO MUNDO.
ORIHIME IS MY FRIEND.
I'LL SAVE HER ALL BY MYSELF.
ICHIGO ...

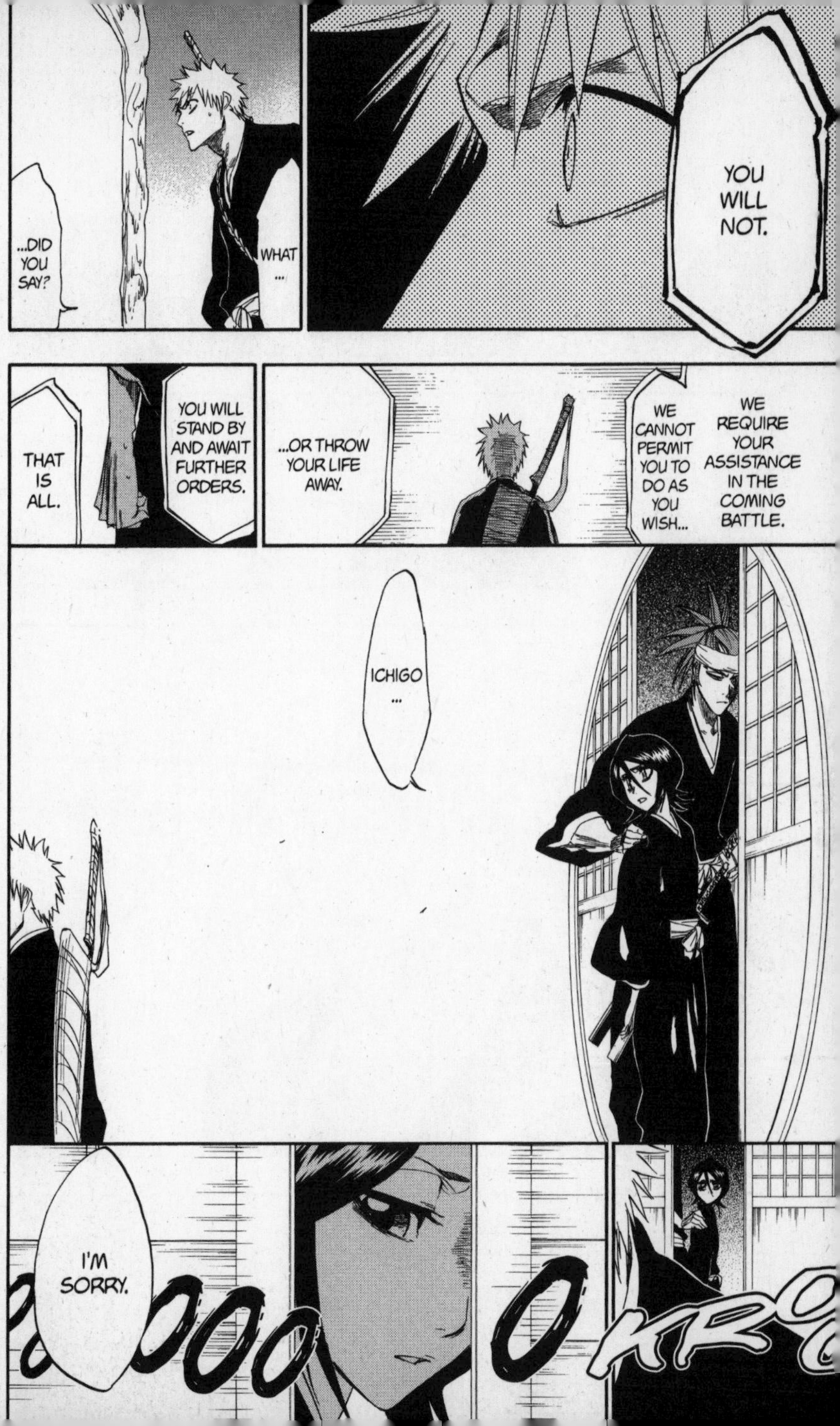
YOU WILL NOT.
WHAT ...
...DID YOU SAY?
WE REQUIRE YOUR ASSISTANCE IN THE COMING BATTLE.
WE CANNOT PERMIT YOU TO DO AS YOU WISH...
...OR THROW YOUR LIFE AWAY.
YOU WILL STAND BY AND AWAIT FURTHER ORDERS.
THAT IS ALL.
ICHIGO ...
KRO
OOOOO
I'M SORRY.

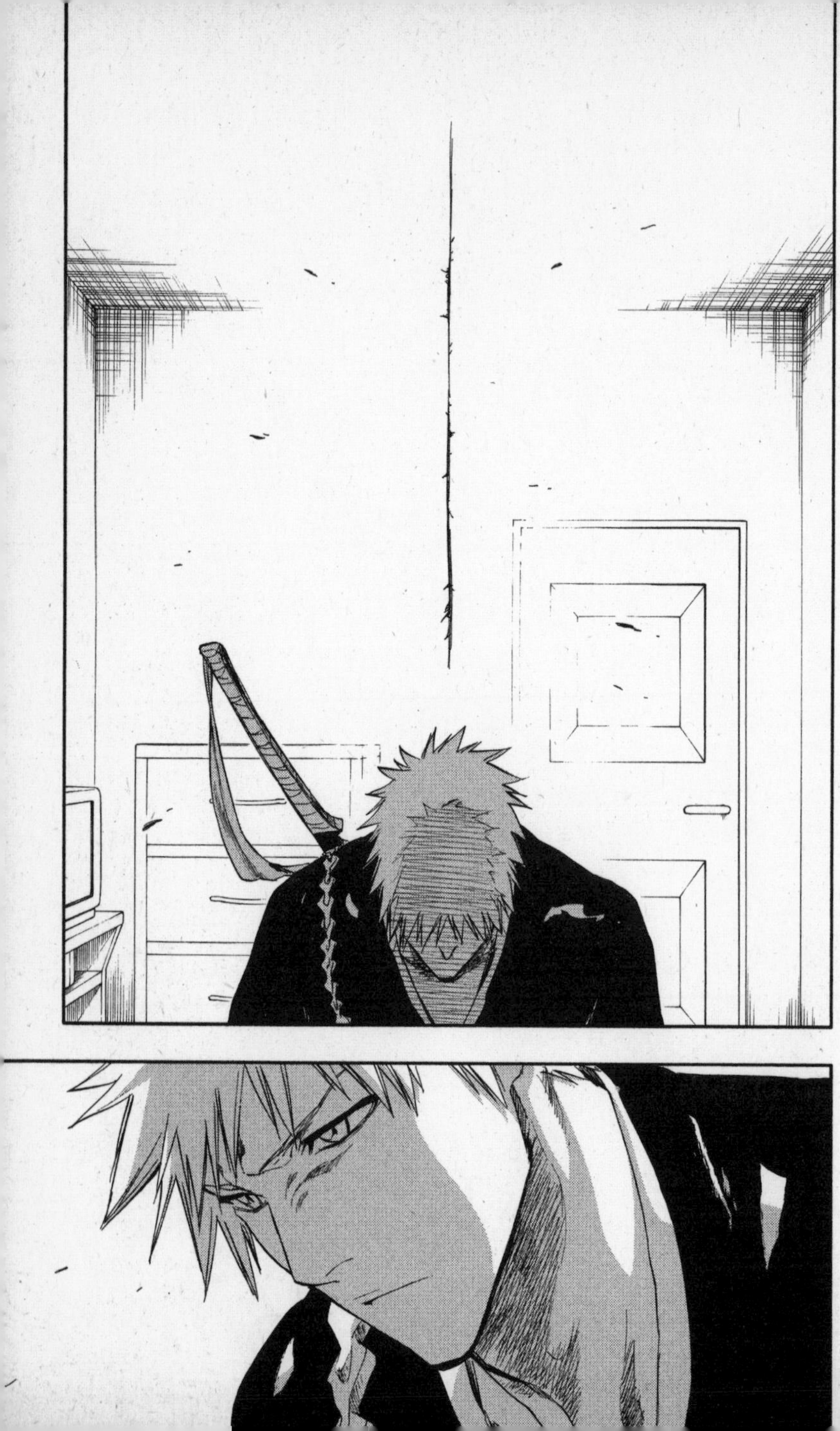

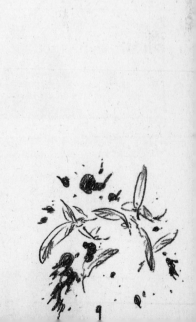

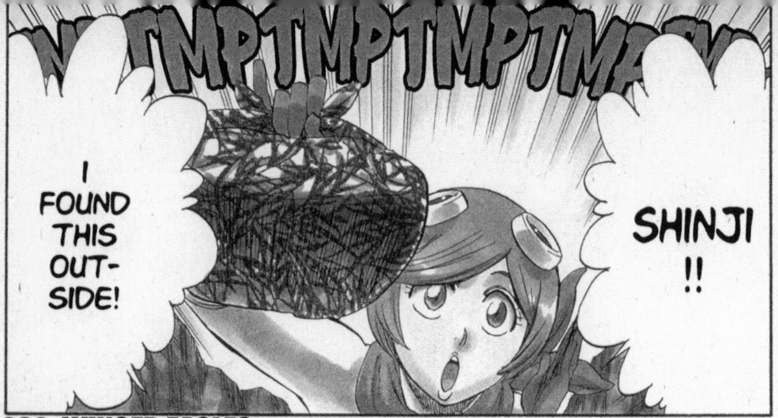
TMPTMPTMPTM
SHINJI !!
I FOUND THIS OUT-SIDE!

239. WINGED EAGLES

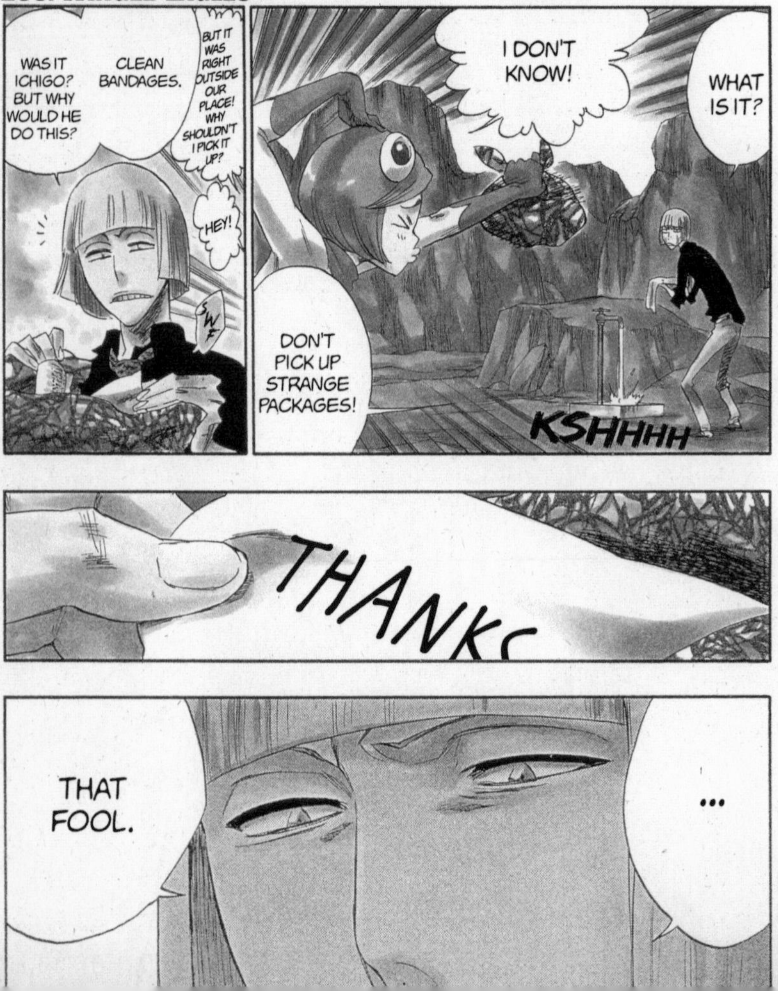
WHAT IS IT?
I DON'T KNOW!
DON'T PICK UP STRANGE PACKAGES!
KSHHHH
BUT IT WAS RIGHT OUTSIDE OUR PLACE! WHY SHOULDN'T I PICK IT UP?
CLEAN BANDAGES.
WAS IT ICHIGO? BUT WHY WOULD HE DO THIS?
HEY!
THANKS
...
THAT FOOL.

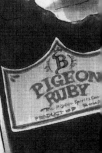

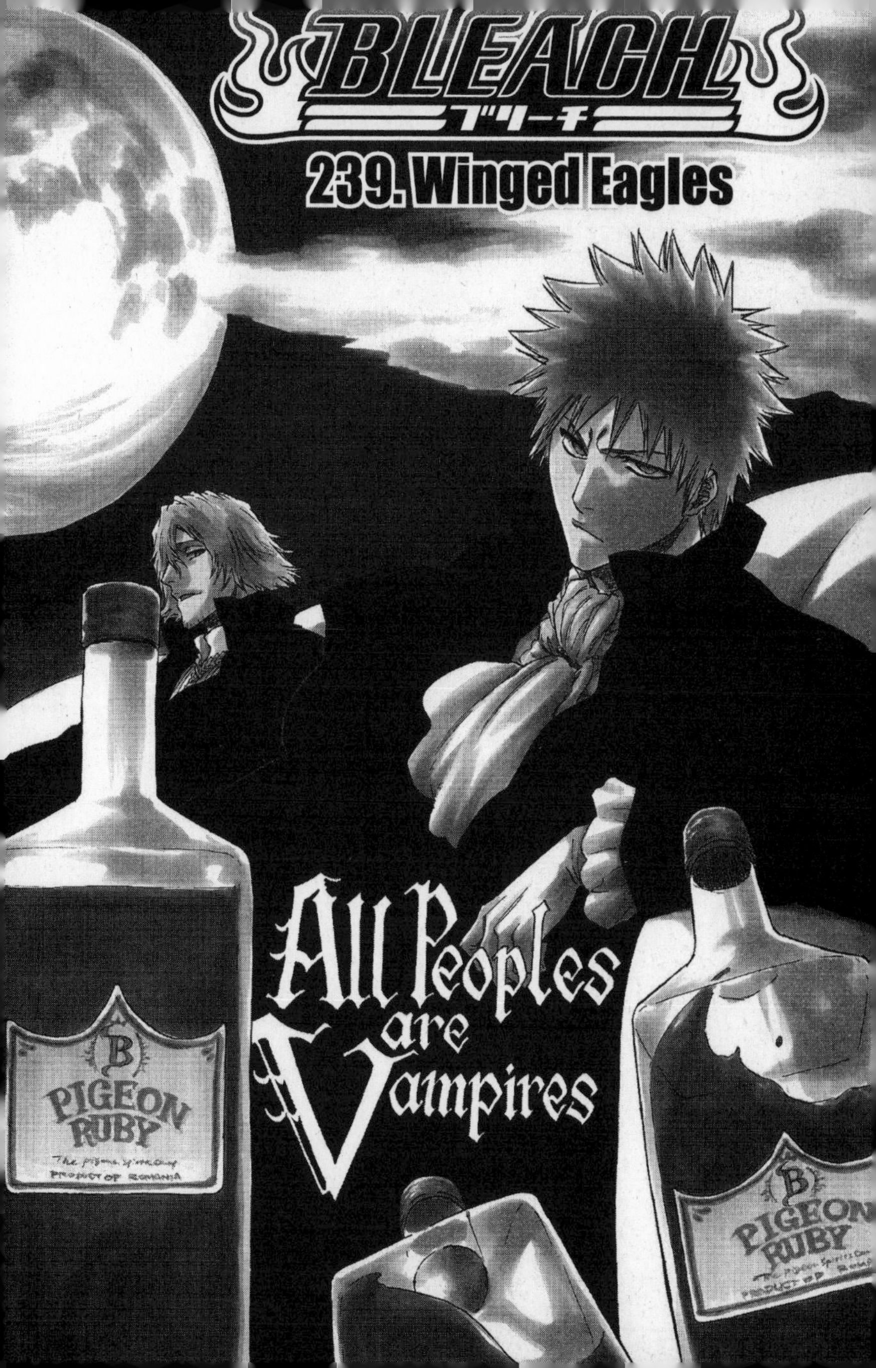

BLEACH
ブリーチ

239. Winged Eagles

All Peoples are Vampires

PIGEON RUBY
The Pigeon Spirit of
PRODUCT OF ROMANIA

PIGEON RUBY
The Pigeon Spirit of
PRODUCT OF ROMANIA

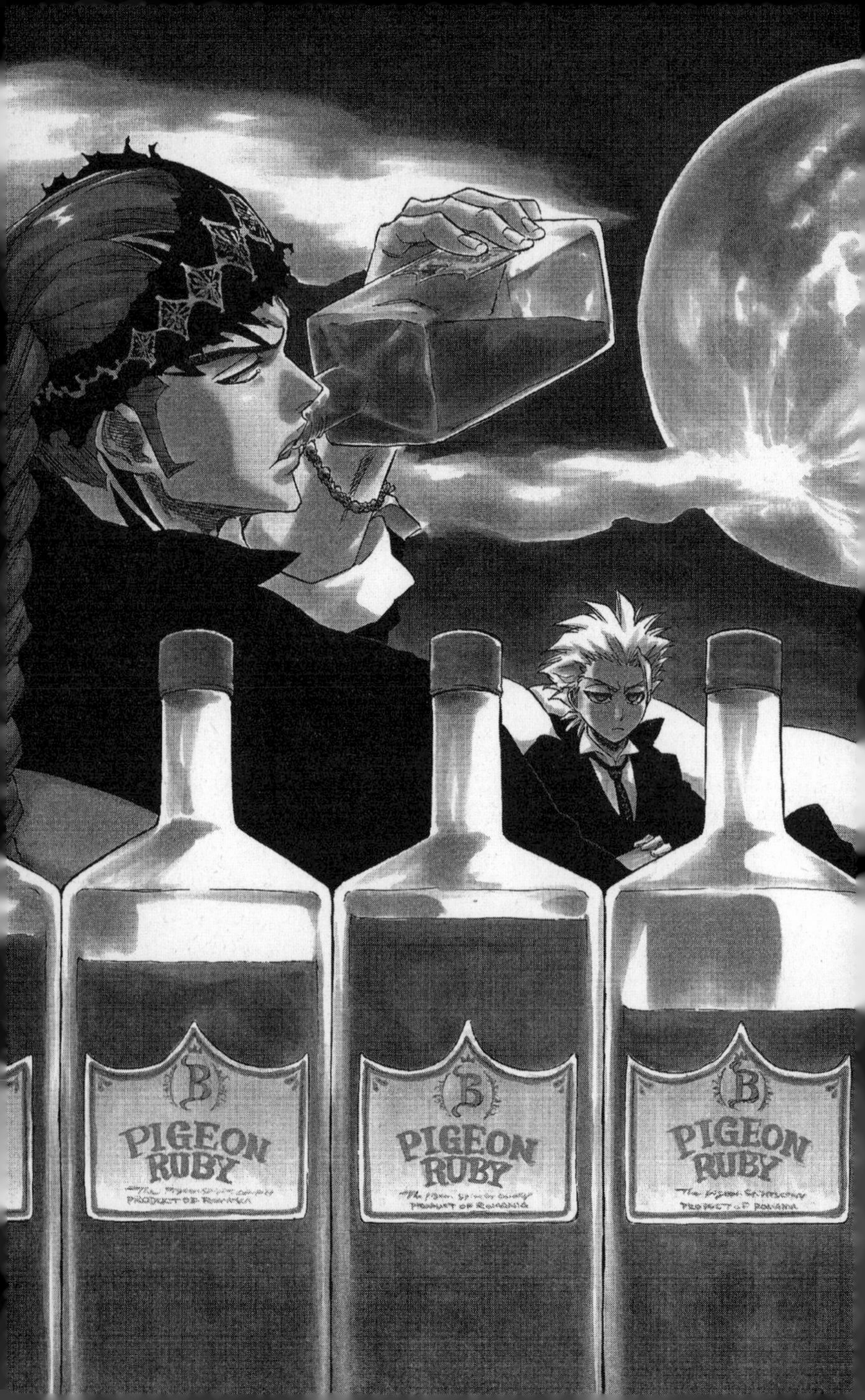
PIGEON RUBY
PIGEON RUBY
PIGEON RUBY

BLEACH
ブリーチ

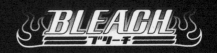

READ THIS WAY

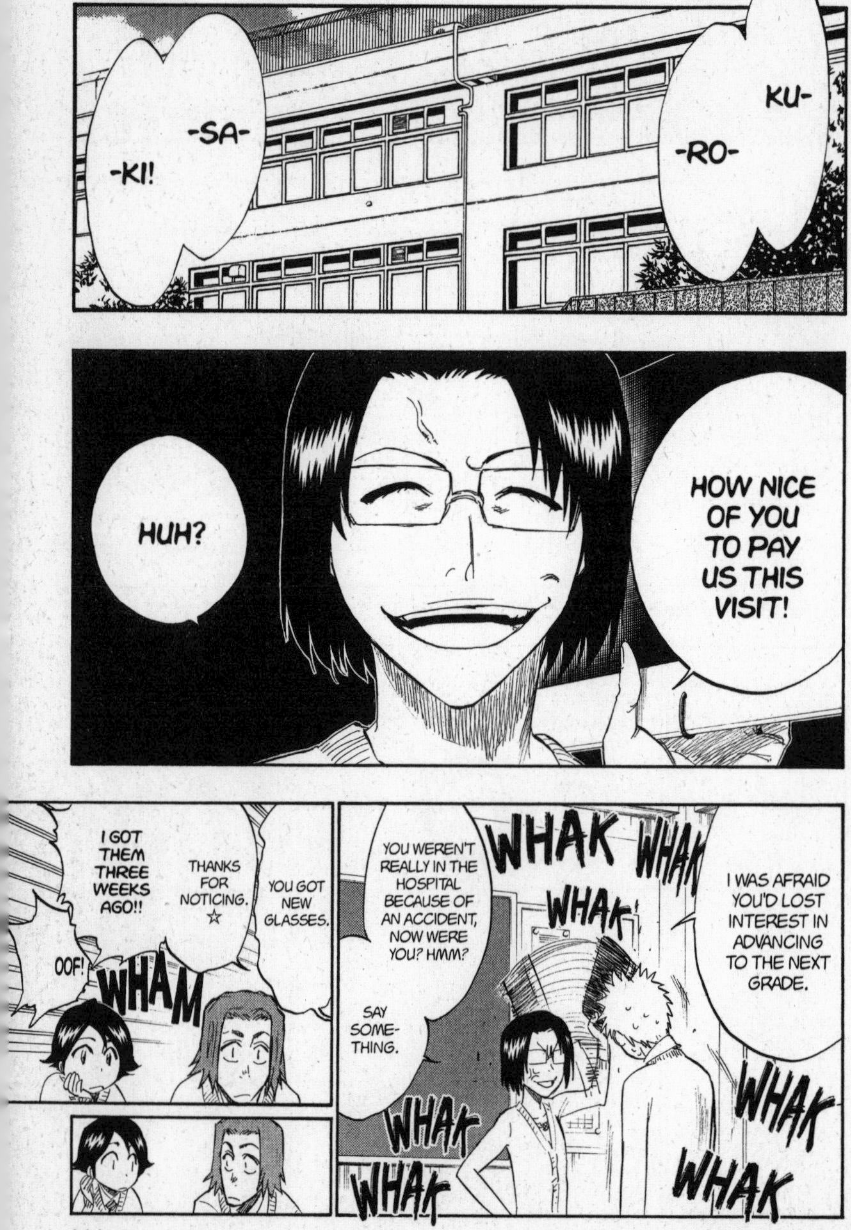

KU- -RO-
-SA- -KI!
HOW NICE OF YOU TO PAY US THIS VISIT!
HUH?
I WAS AFRAID YOU'D LOST INTEREST IN ADVANCING TO THE NEXT GRADE.
WHAK WHAK
WHAK
WHAK
WHAK
YOU WEREN'T REALLY IN THE HOSPITAL BECAUSE OF AN ACCIDENT, NOW WERE YOU? HMM?
SAY SOME-THING.
WHAK
WHAK
YOU GOT NEW GLASSES.
THANKS FOR NOTICING. ☆
I GOT THEM THREE WEEKS AGO!!
WHAM
OOF!

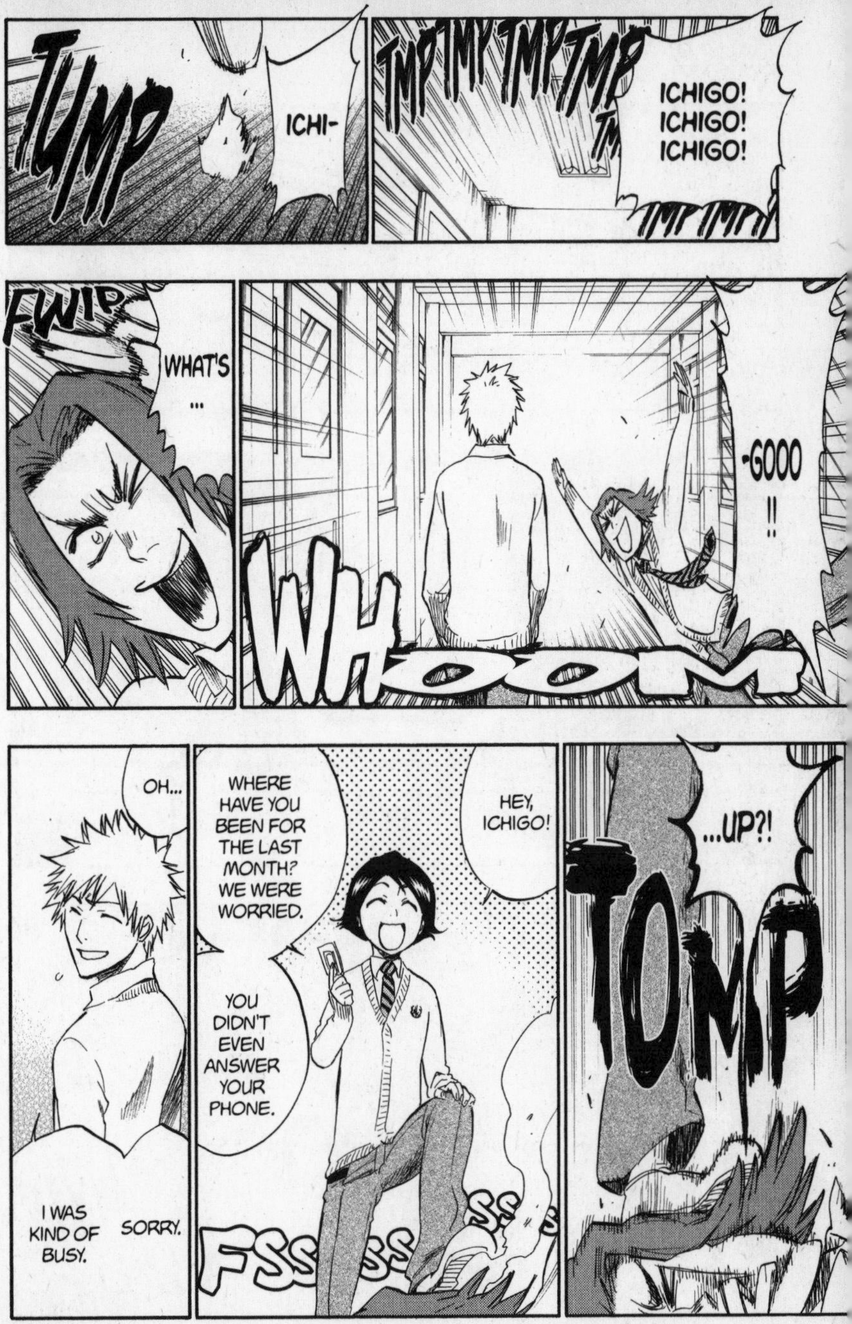
TMP TMP TMP TMP
ICHIGO! ICHIGO! ICHIGO!
TMP TMP
TUMP
ICHI-
-GOOO!!
WHOOM
FWIP
WHAT'S ...
...UP?!
TOMP
HEY, ICHIGO!
WHERE HAVE YOU BEEN FOR THE LAST MONTH? WE WERE WORRIED.
YOU DIDN'T EVEN ANSWER YOUR PHONE.
FSSSSS
OH...
SORRY.
I WAS KIND OF BUSY.

READ THIS WAY

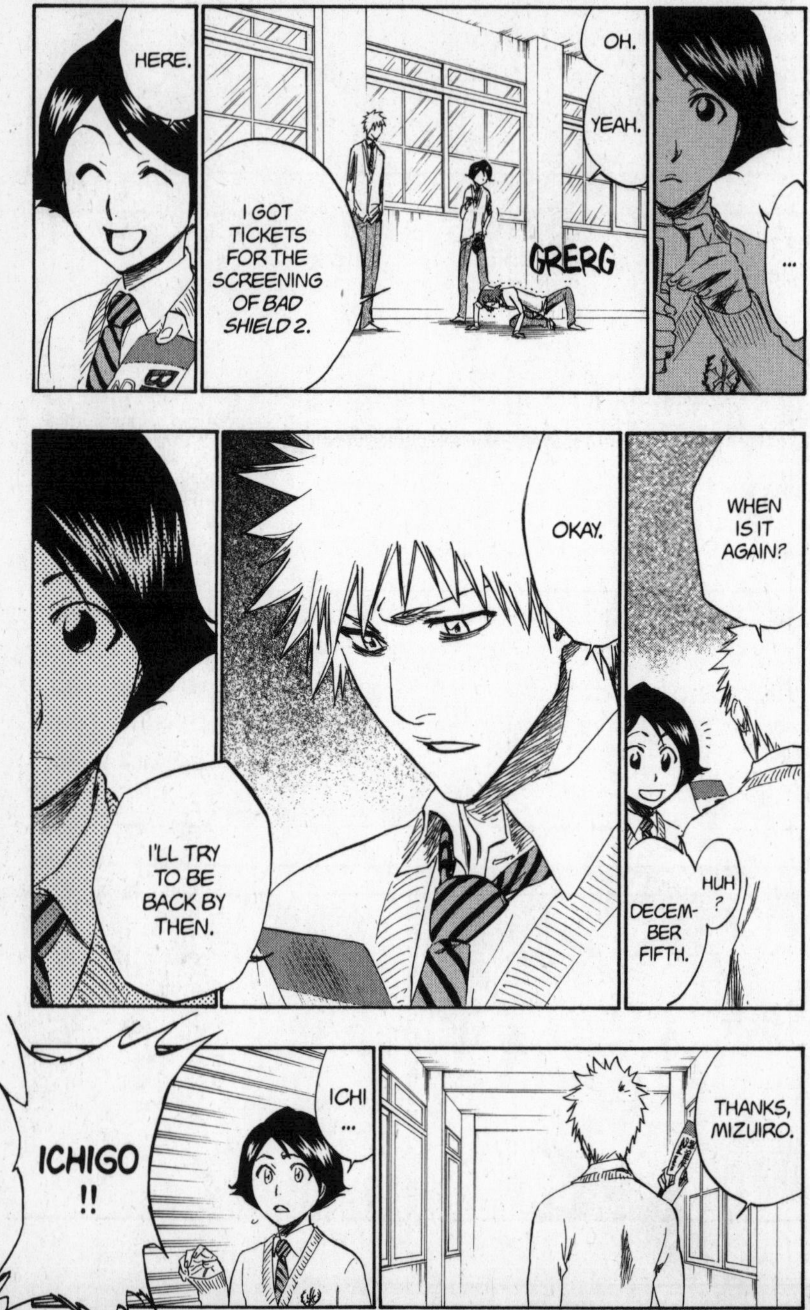
...
OH.
YEAH.
GRERG
I GOT TICKETS FOR THE SCREENING OF BAD SHIELD 2.
HERE.
WHEN IS IT AGAIN?
HUH?
DECEM-BER FIFTH.
OKAY.
I'LL TRY TO BE BACK BY THEN.
THANKS, MIZUIRO.
ICHI...
ICHIGO!!

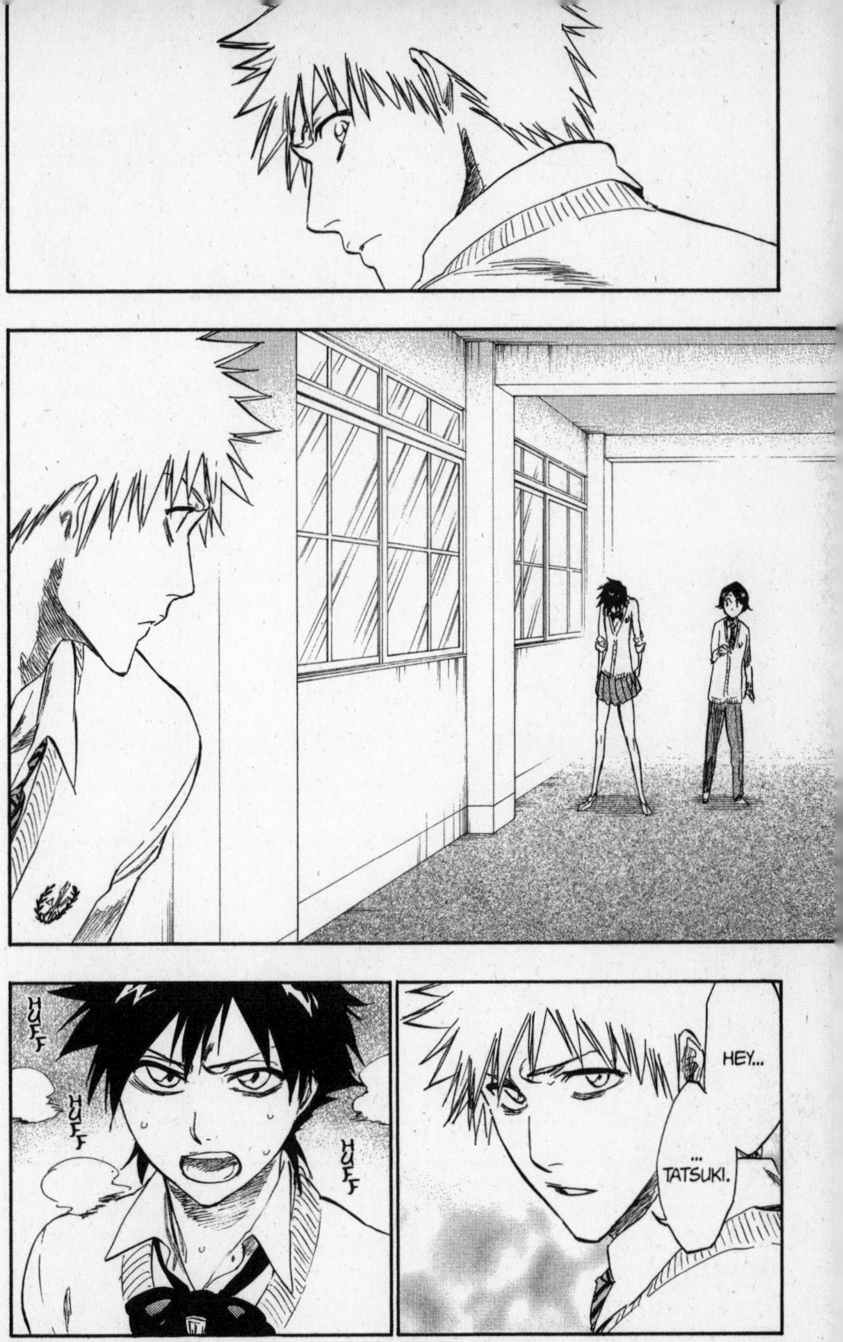
HEY...
...TATSUKI.
HUFF
HUFF
HUFF

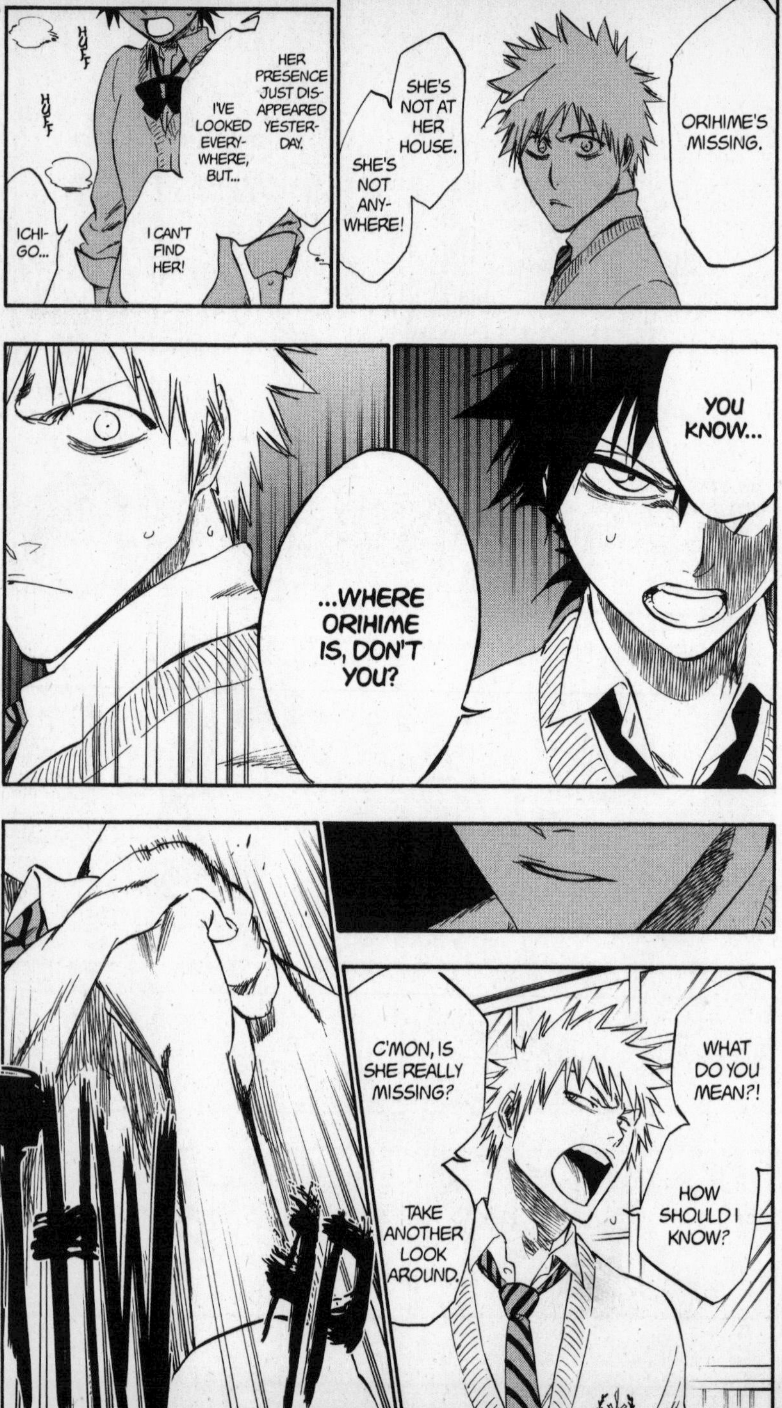
ORIHIME'S MISSING.
SHE'S NOT AT HER HOUSE.
SHE'S NOT ANYWHERE!
HER PRESENCE JUST DIS-APPEARED YESTER-DAY.
I'VE LOOKED EVERY-WHERE, BUT...
HUFF
HUFF
I CAN'T FIND HER!
ICHI-GO...
YOU KNOW...
...WHERE ORIHIME IS, DON'T YOU?
WHAT DO YOU MEAN?!
HOW SHOULD I KNOW?
C'MON, IS SHE REALLY MISSING?
TAKE ANOTHER LOOK AROUND.

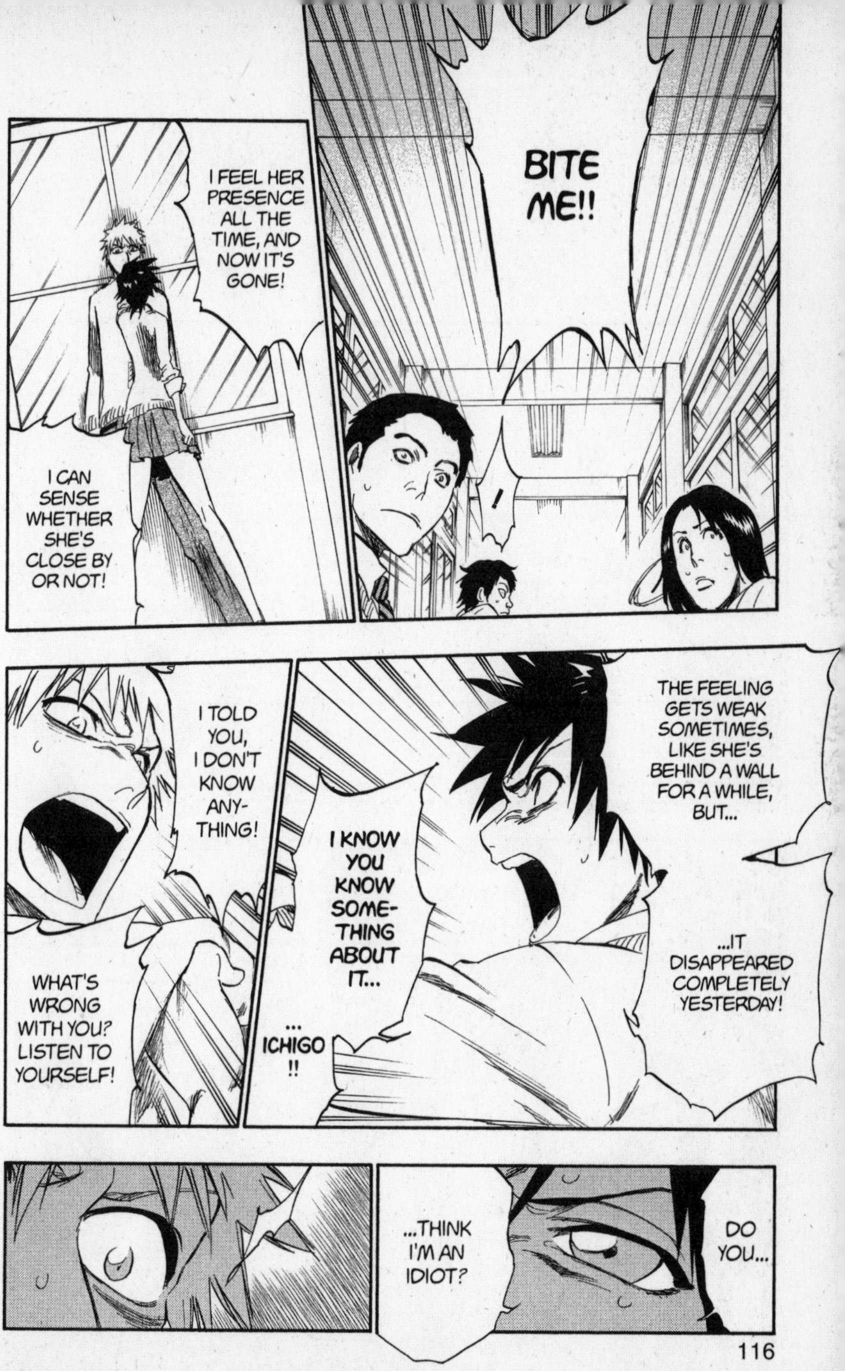
BITE ME!!
!
I FEEL HER PRESENCE ALL THE TIME, AND NOW IT'S GONE!
I CAN SENSE WHETHER SHE'S CLOSE BY OR NOT!
THE FEELING GETS WEAK SOMETIMES, LIKE SHE'S BEHIND A WALL FOR A WHILE, BUT...
...IT DISAPPEARED COMPLETELY YESTERDAY!
I KNOW YOU KNOW SOMETHING ABOUT IT...
...ICHIGO!!
I TOLD YOU, I DON'T KNOW ANYTHING!
WHAT'S WRONG WITH YOU? LISTEN TO YOURSELF!
DO YOU...
...THINK I'M AN IDIOT?

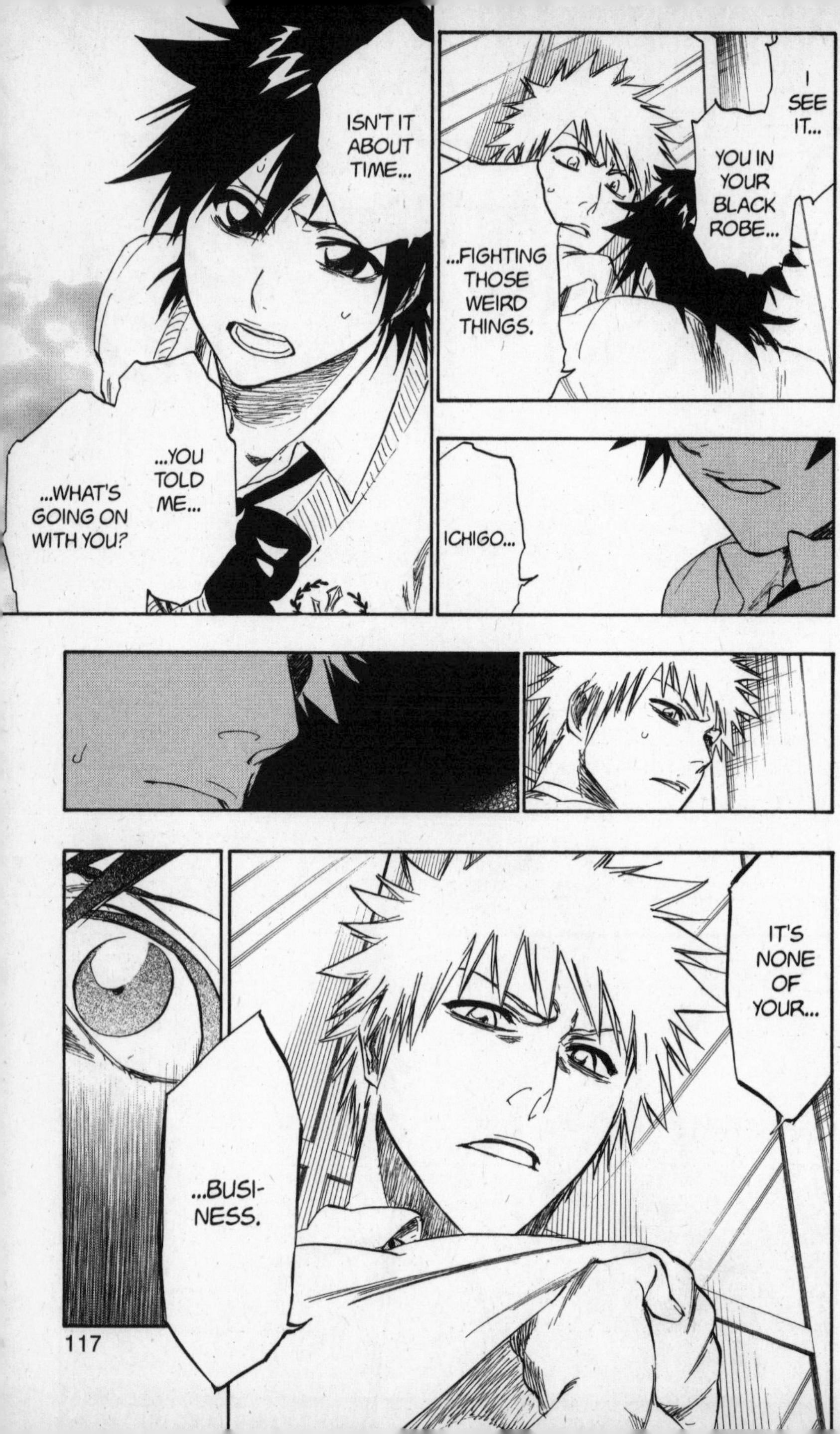
I SEE IT...
YOU IN YOUR BLACK ROBE...
...FIGHTING THOSE WEIRD THINGS.
ICHIGO...
ISN'T IT ABOUT TIME...
...YOU TOLD ME...
...WHAT'S GOING ON WITH YOU?
IT'S NONE OF YOUR...
...BUSI-NESS.

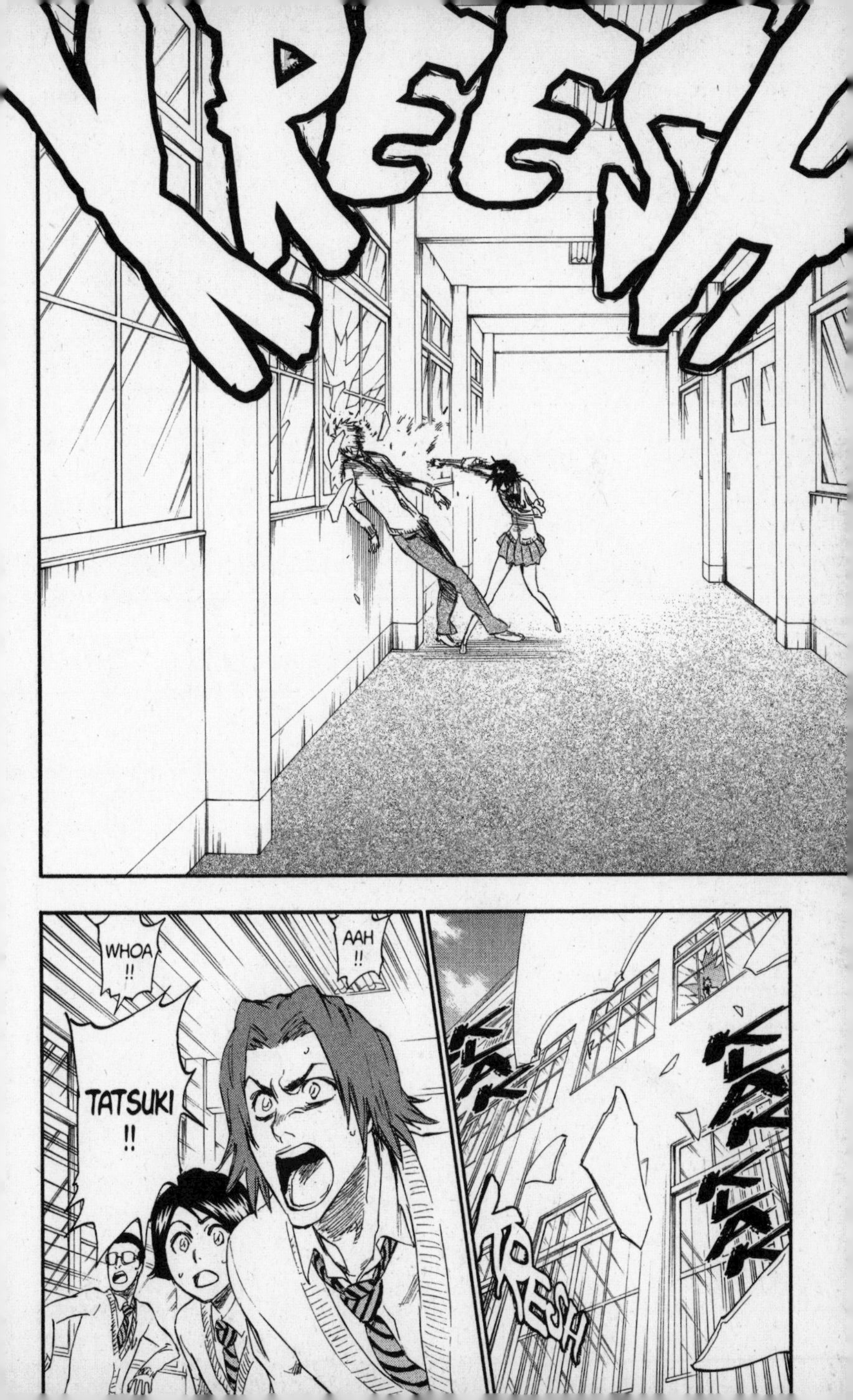
KLAK KLAK KLAK
KLAK
TRESH
AAH !!
WHOA !!
TATSUKI !!

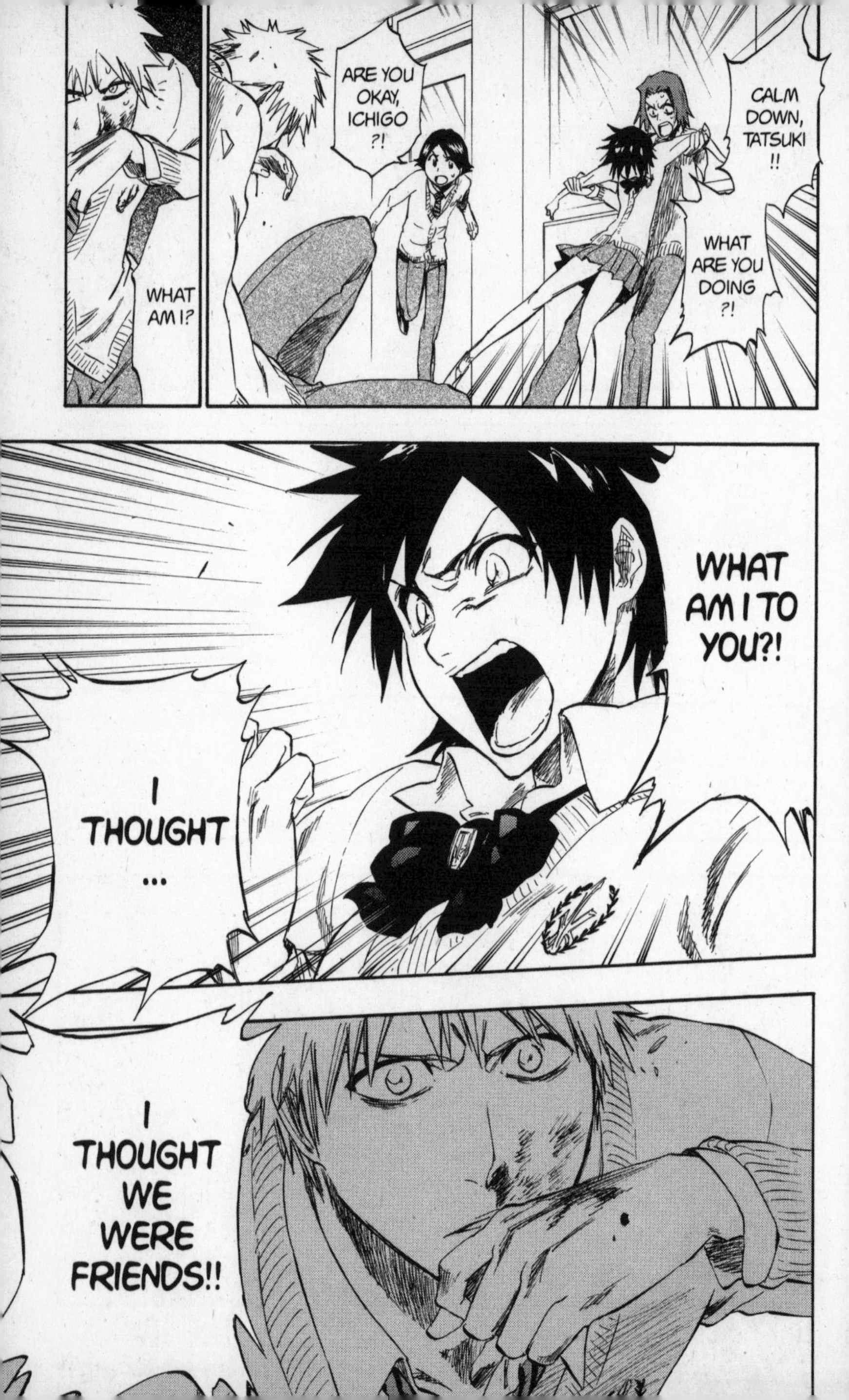
CALM DOWN, TATSUKI!!
WHAT ARE YOU DOING?!
ARE YOU OKAY, ICHIGO?!
WHAT AM I?
WHAT AM I TO YOU?!
I THOUGHT...
I THOUGHT WE WERE FRIENDS!!

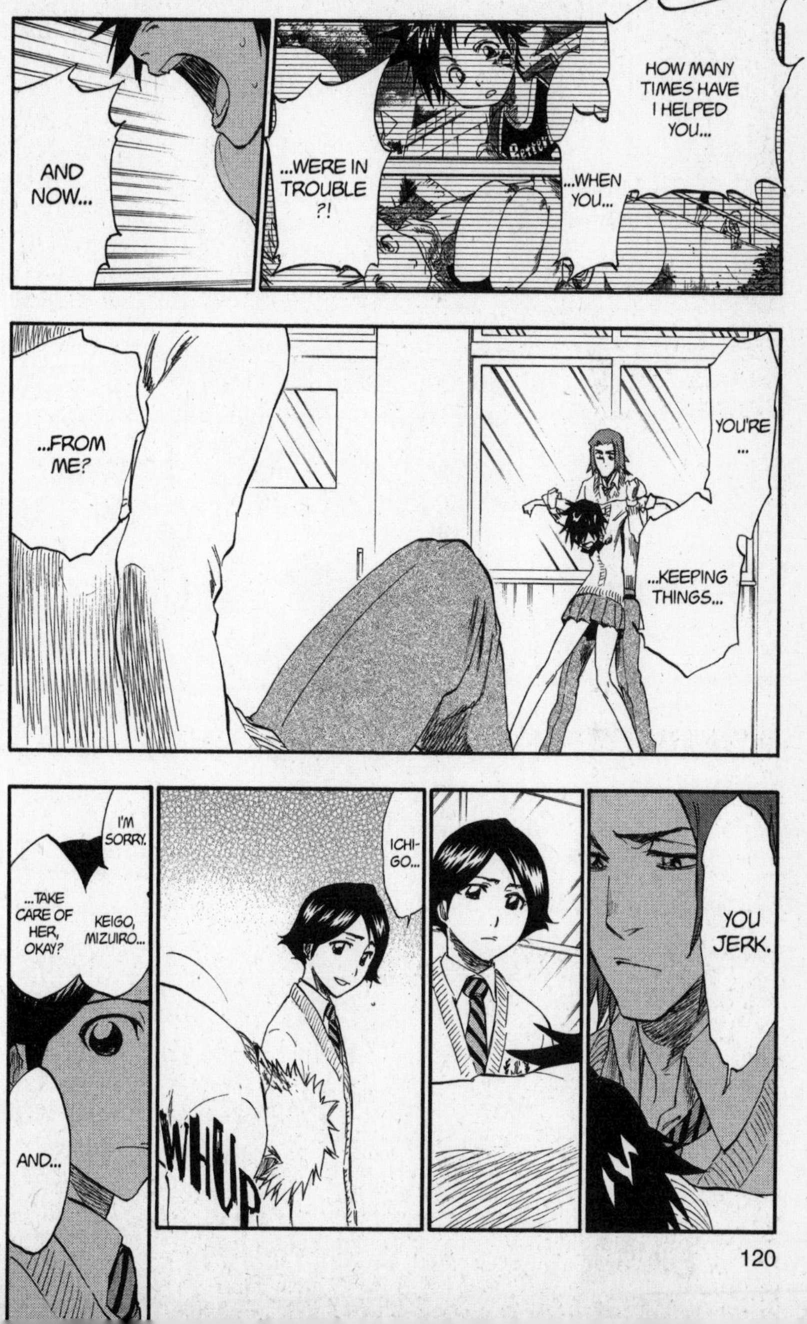
HOW MANY TIMES HAVE I HELPED YOU...
...WHEN YOU...
...WERE IN TROUBLE ?!
AND NOW...
YOU'RE ...
...KEEPING THINGS...
...FROM ME?
YOU JERK.
ICHI-GO...
WHUP
I'M SORRY.
KEIGO, MIZUIRO...
...TAKE CARE OF HER, OKAY?
AND...

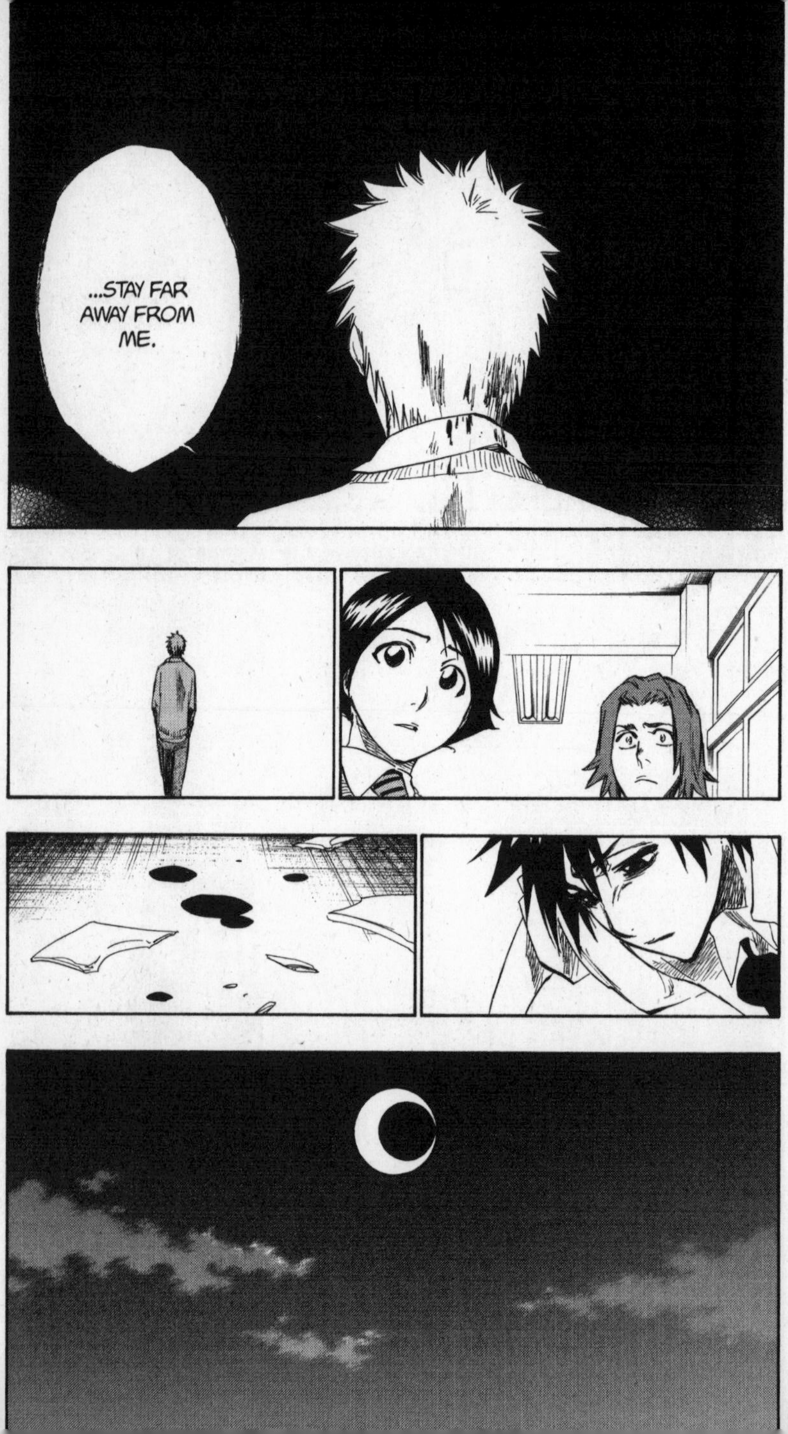
...STAY FAR AWAY FROM ME.

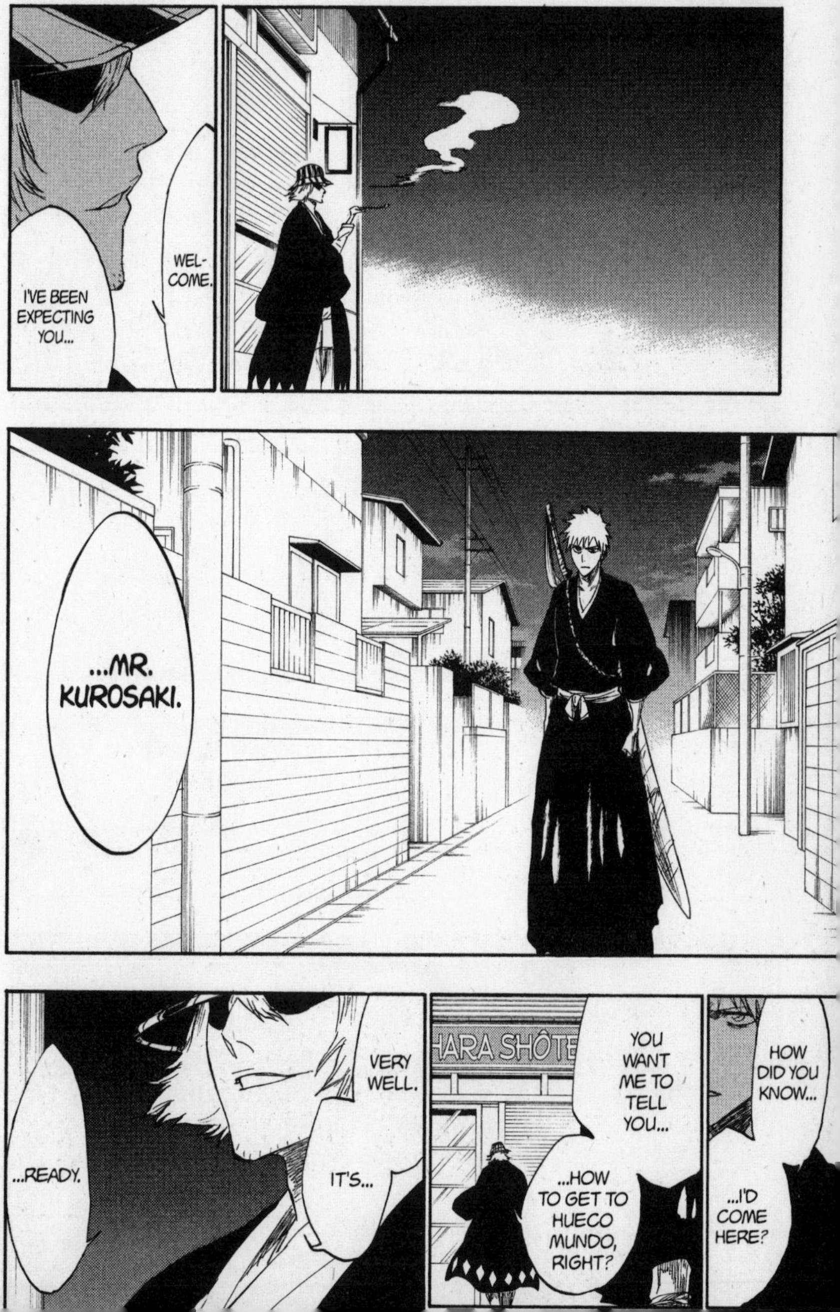
WEL-COME.
I'VE BEEN EXPECTING YOU...
...MR. KUROSAKI.
HOW DID YOU KNOW...
...I'D COME HERE?
HARA SHÔTE
YOU WANT ME TO TELL YOU...
...HOW TO GET TO HUECO MUNDO, RIGHT?
VERY WELL.
IT'S...
...READY.

READ THIS WAY

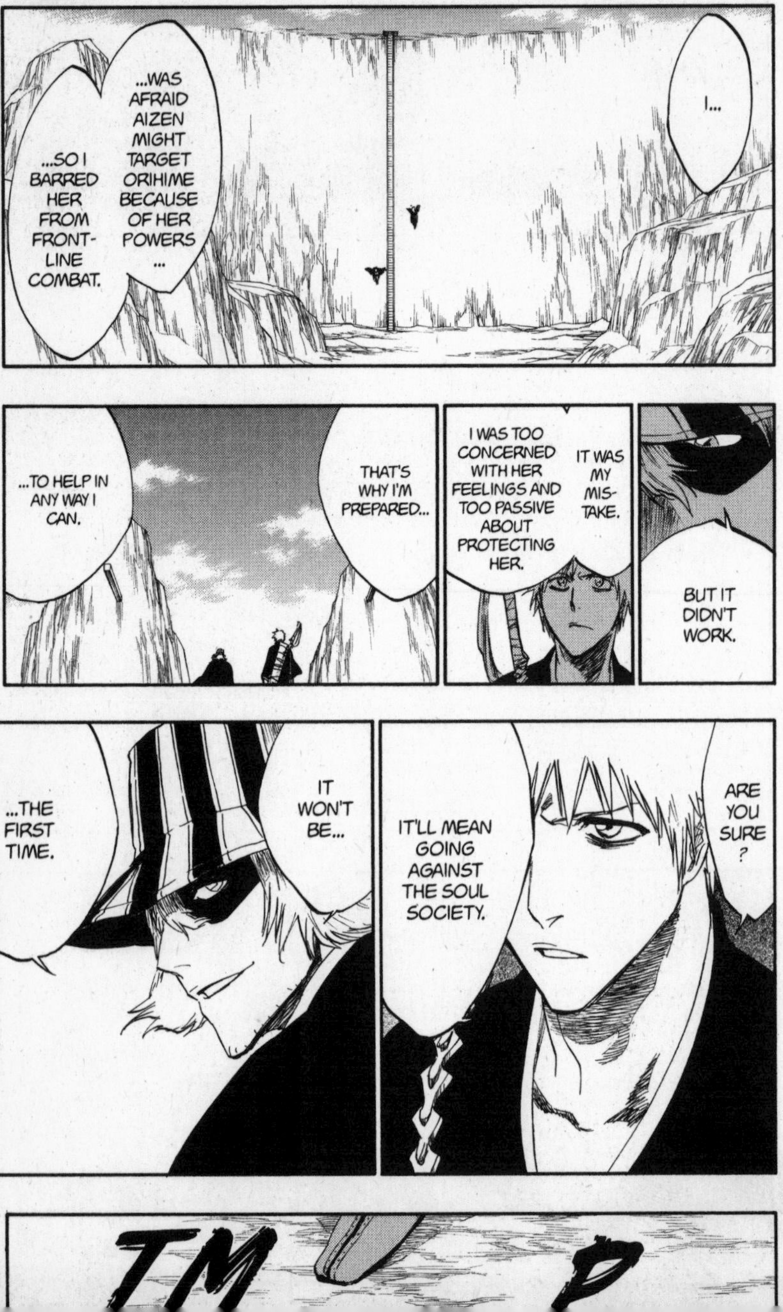
I...
...WAS AFRAID AIZEN MIGHT TARGET ORIHIME BECAUSE OF HER POWERS...
...SO I BARRED HER FROM FRONT-LINE COMBAT.
BUT IT DIDN'T WORK.
IT WAS MY MIS-TAKE.
I WAS TOO CONCERNED WITH HER FEELINGS AND TOO PASSIVE ABOUT PROTECTING HER.
THAT'S WHY I'M PREPARED...
...TO HELP IN ANY WAY I CAN.
ARE YOU SURE?
IT'LL MEAN GOING AGAINST THE SOUL SOCIETY.
IT WON'T BE...
...THE FIRST TIME.
TMP

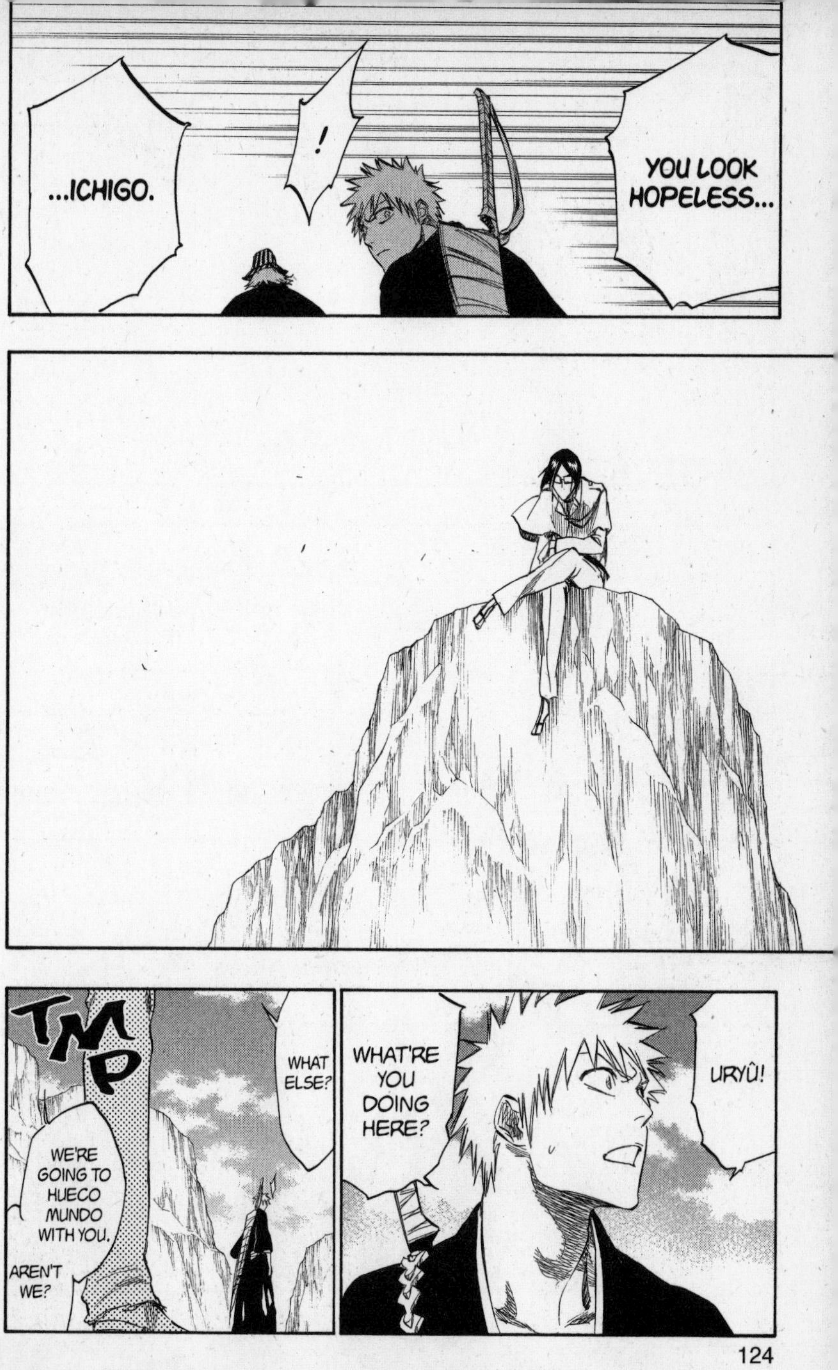
YOU LOOK HOPELESS...
!
...ICHIGO.
URYÛ!
WHAT'RE YOU DOING HERE?
WHAT ELSE?
TMP
WE'RE GOING TO HUECO MUNDO WITH YOU.
AREN'T WE?

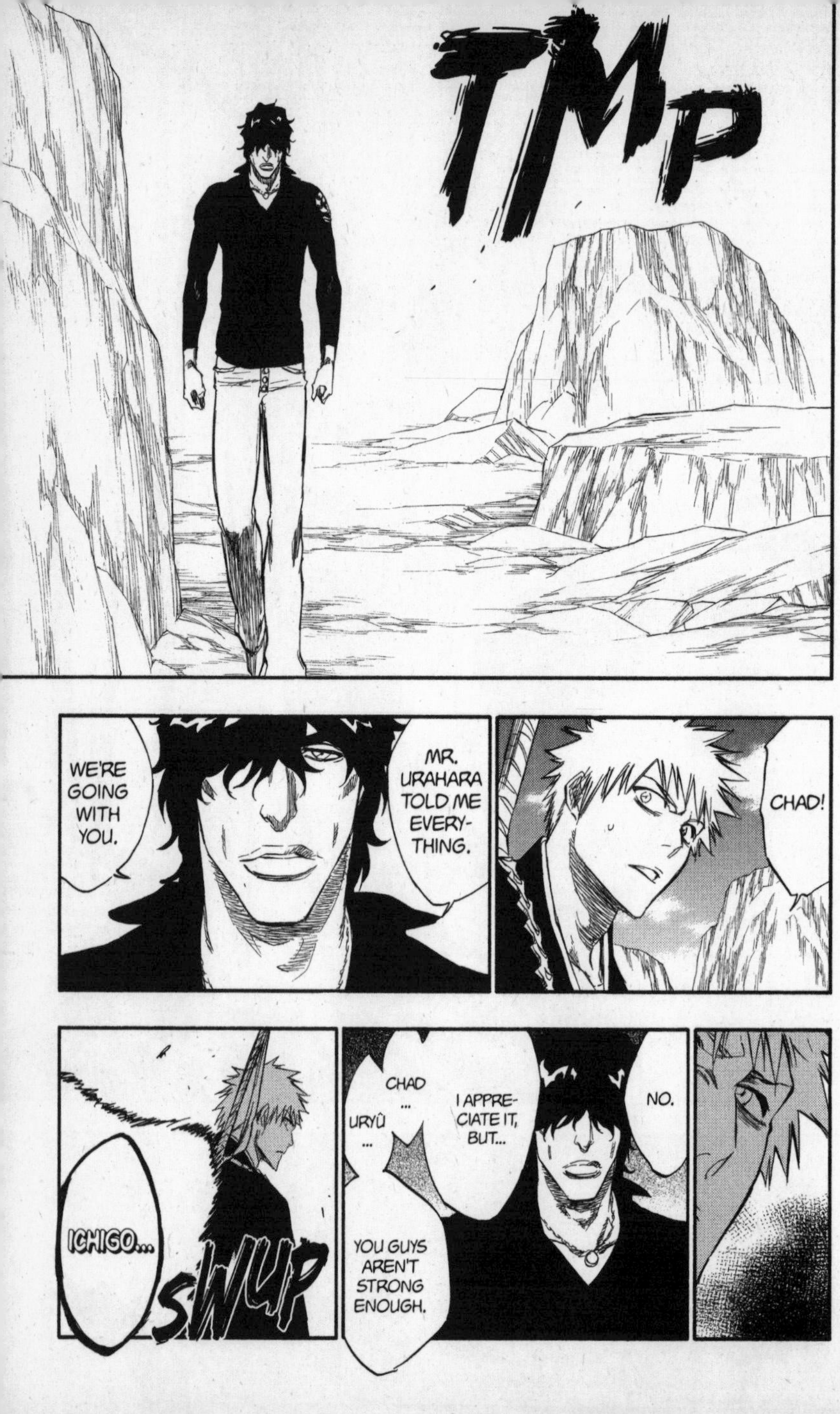
TMP
CHAD!
MR. URAHARA TOLD ME EVERY-THING.
WE'RE GOING WITH YOU.
NO.
I APPRE-CIATE IT, BUT...
CHAD ...
URYÛ ...
YOU GUYS AREN'T STRONG ENOUGH.
ICHIGO...
SWUP

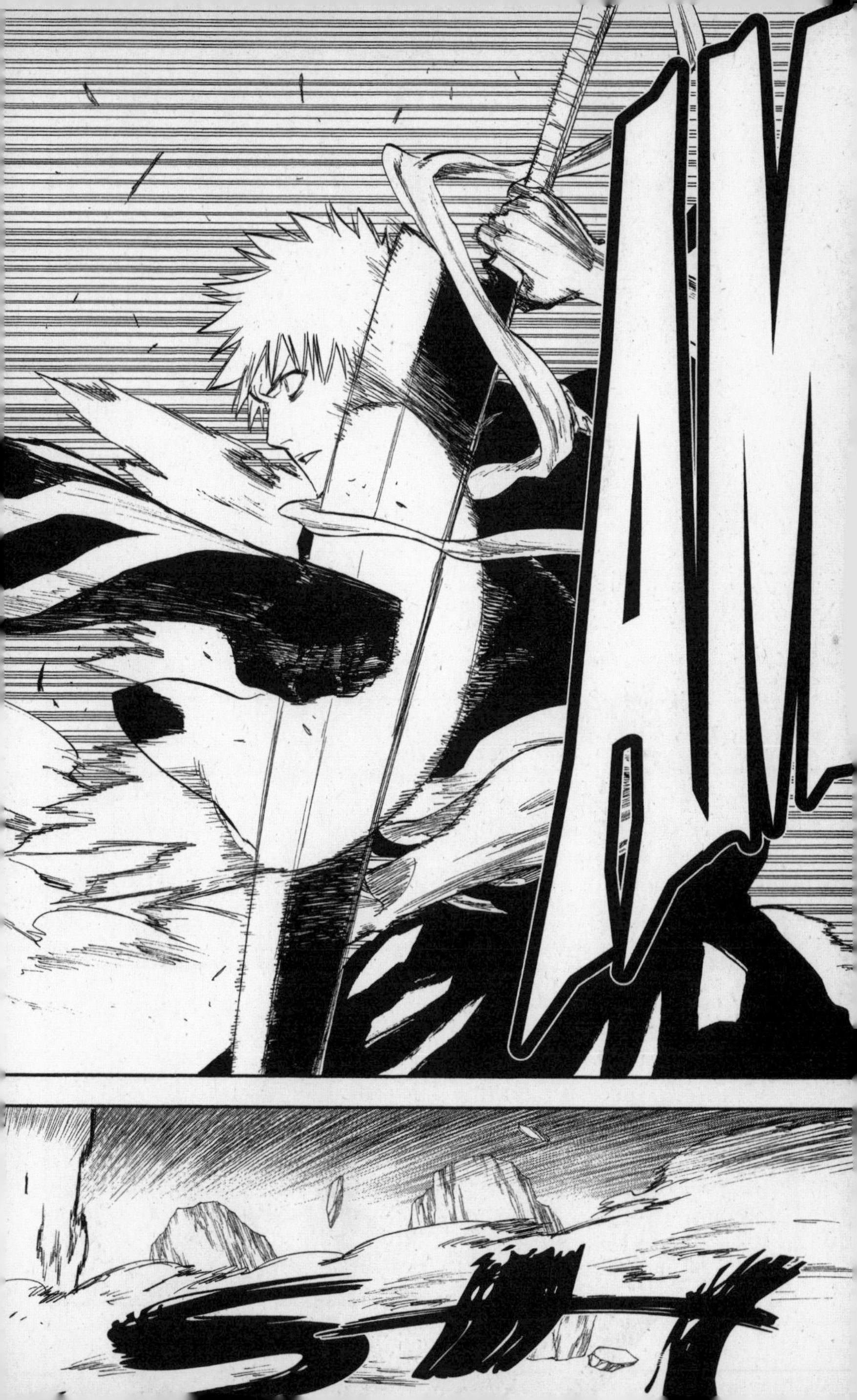

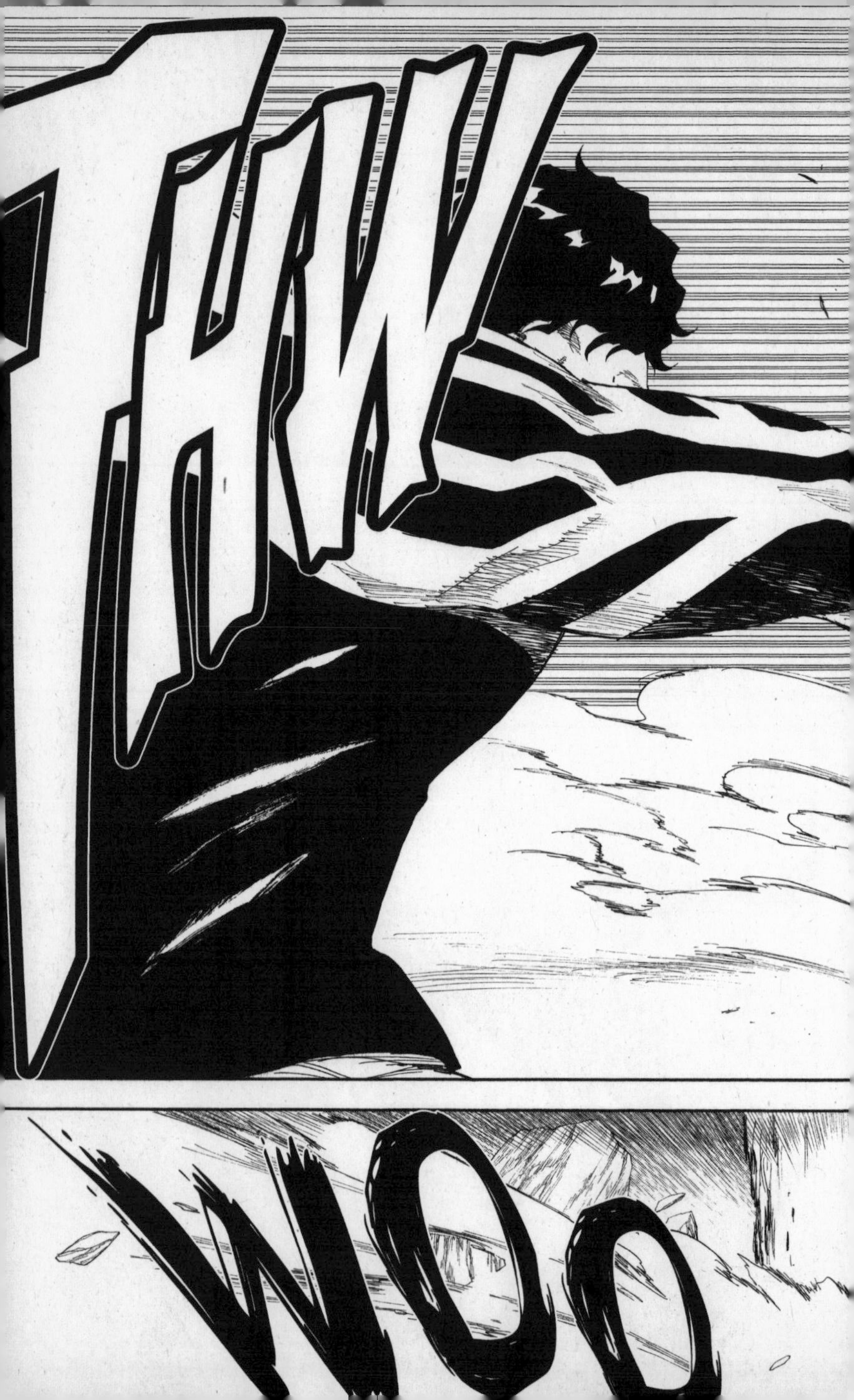
TAW
WOO

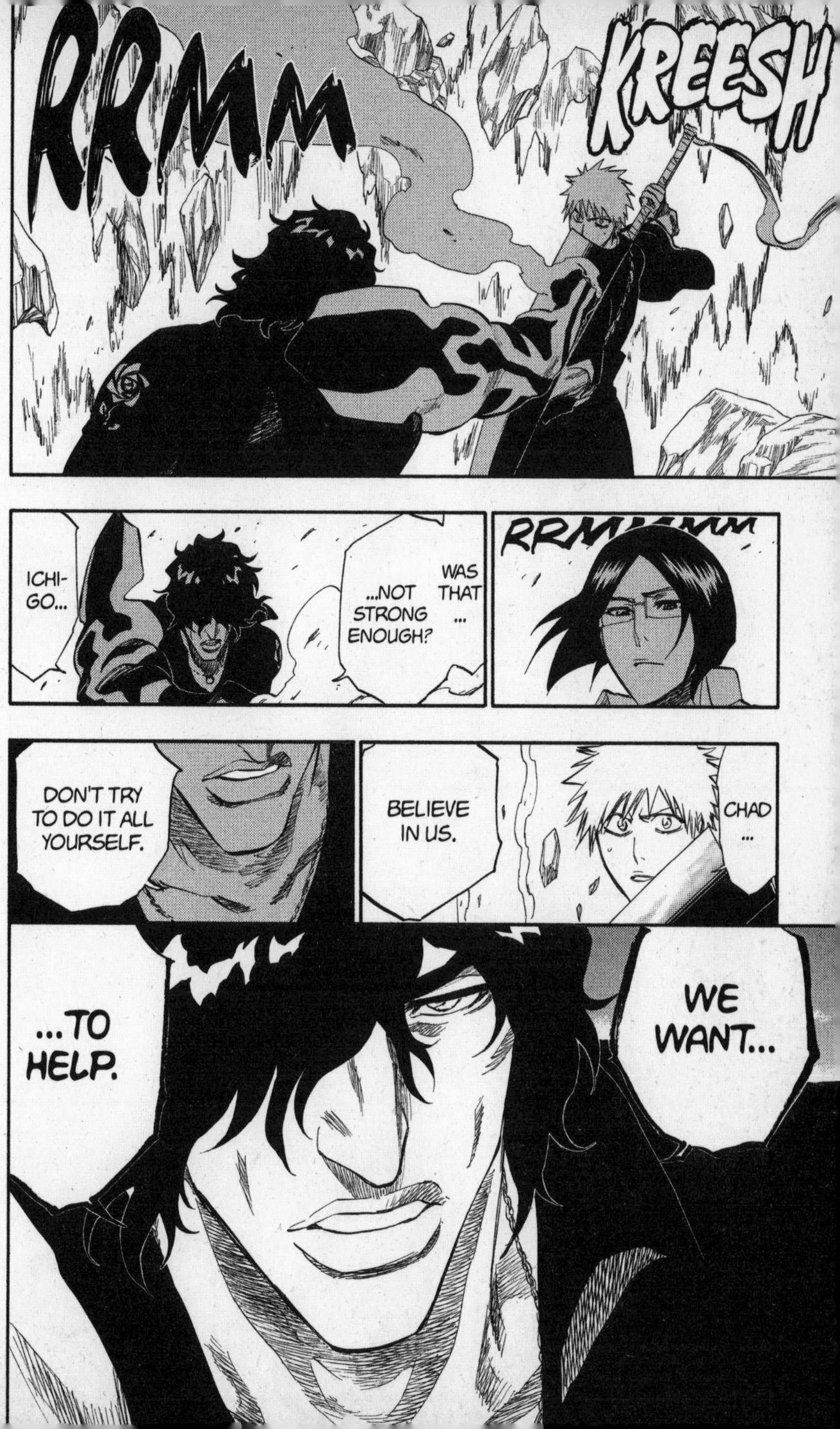
KREESH
RRMM
RRMMMMM
WAS THAT ...
...NOT STRONG ENOUGH?
ICHI-GO...
CHAD ...
BELIEVE IN US.
DON'T TRY TO DO IT ALL YOURSELF.
WE WANT...
...TO HELP.

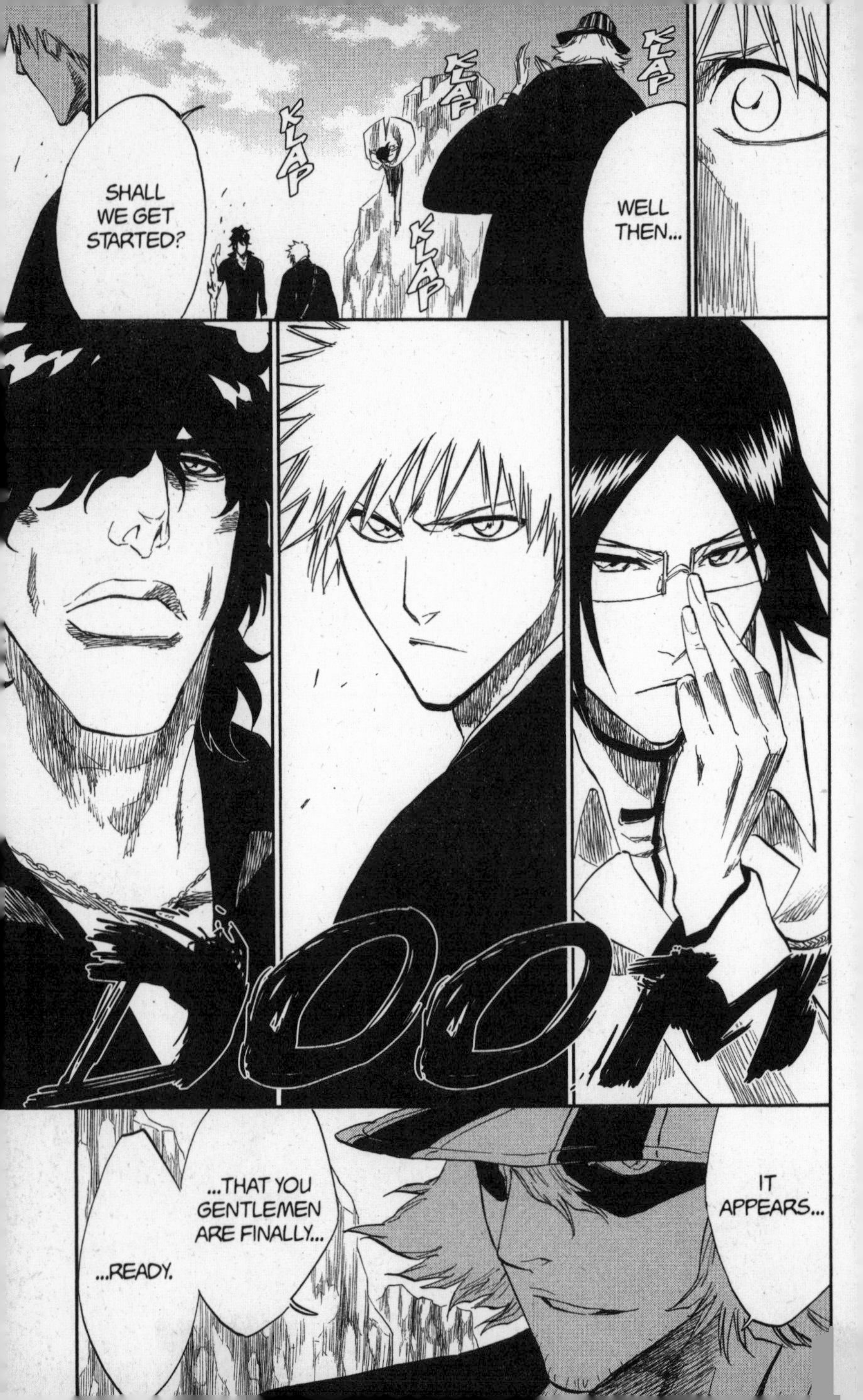
WELL THEN...
KLAP
KLAP
KLAP
KLAP
SHALL WE GET STARTED?
DOOM
IT APPEARS...
...THAT YOU GENTLEMEN ARE FINALLY...
...READY.

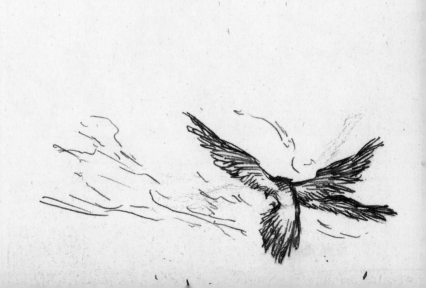

240. regeneration.

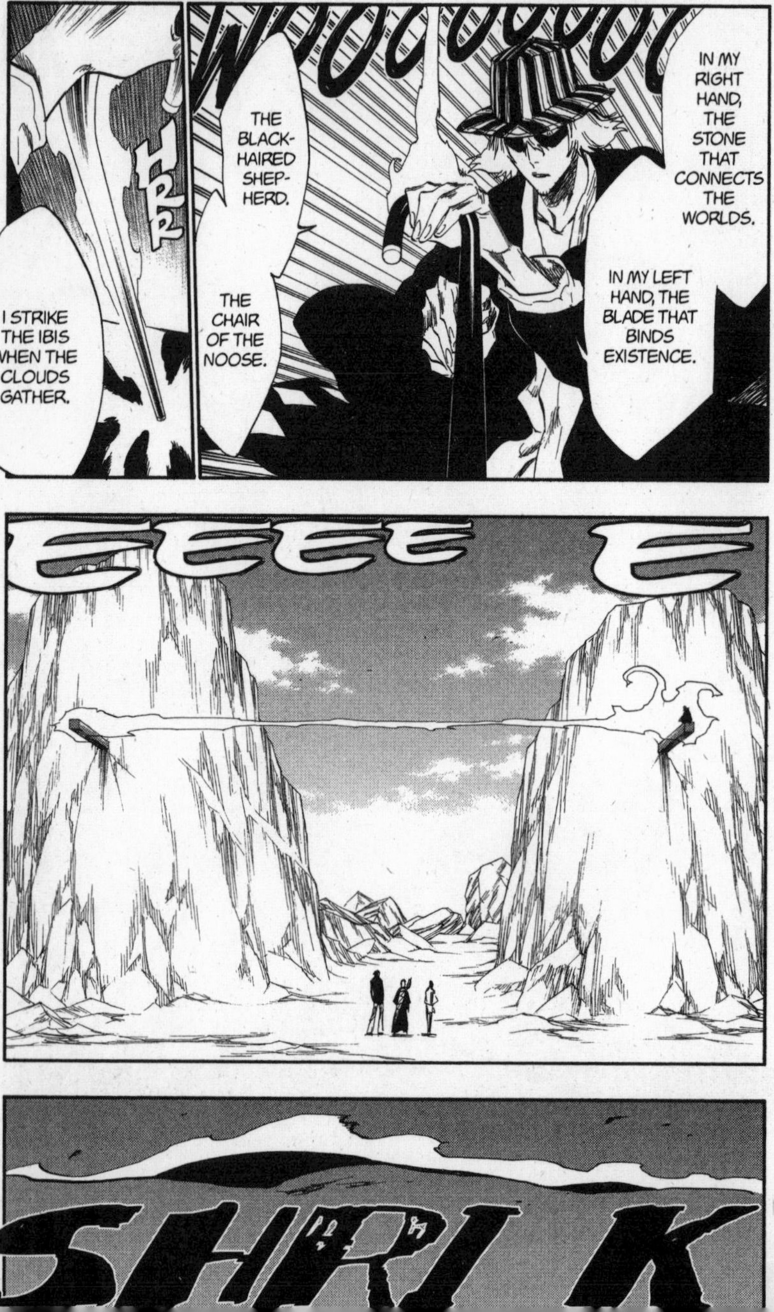
IN MY RIGHT HAND, THE STONE THAT CONNECTS THE WORLDS.
IN MY LEFT HAND, THE BLADE THAT BINDS EXISTENCE.
THE BLACK-HAIRED SHEP-HERD.
THE CHAIR OF THE NOOSE.
HRR
I STRIKE THE IBIS WHEN THE CLOUDS GATHER.
EEEE E
SHRI K

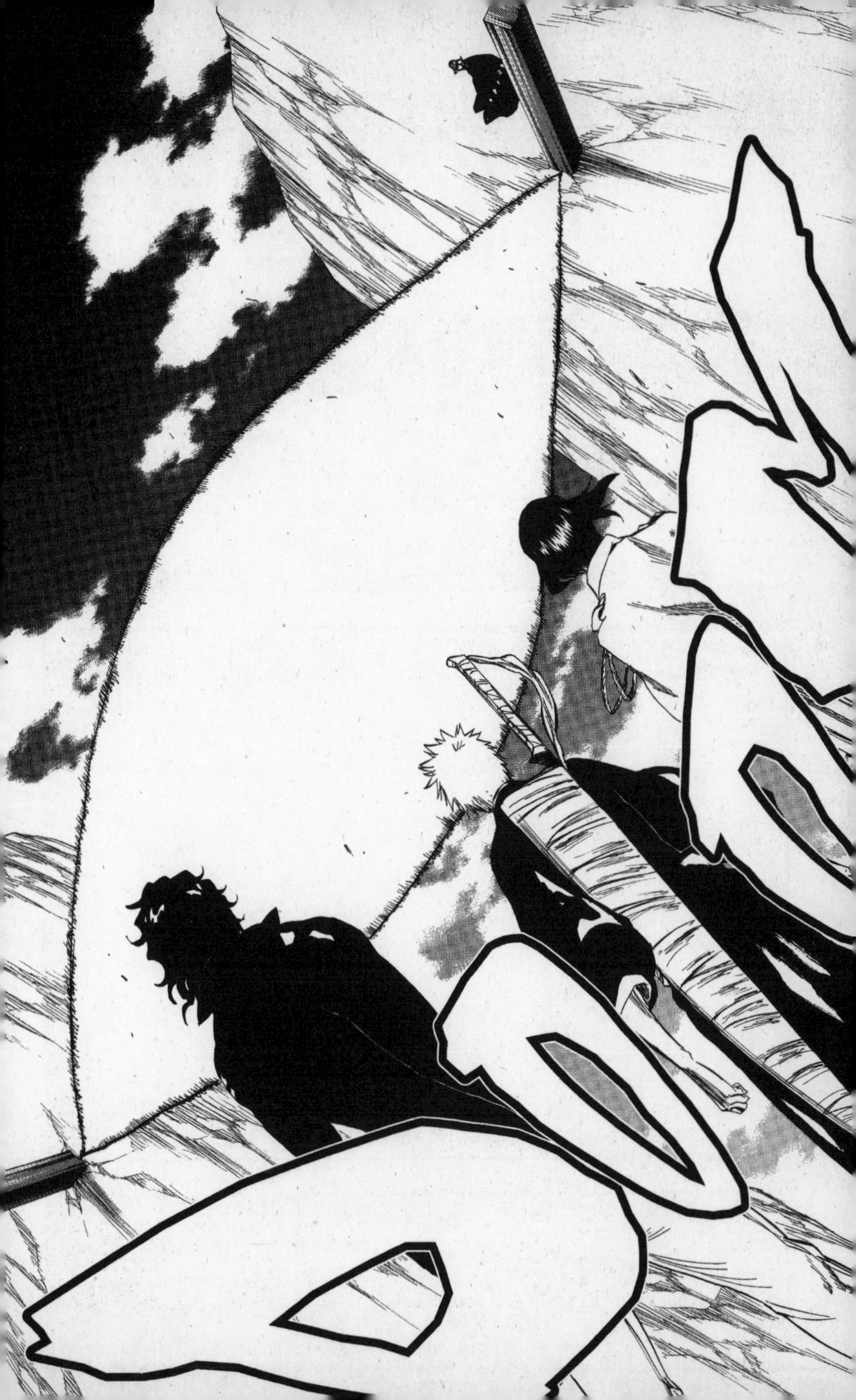

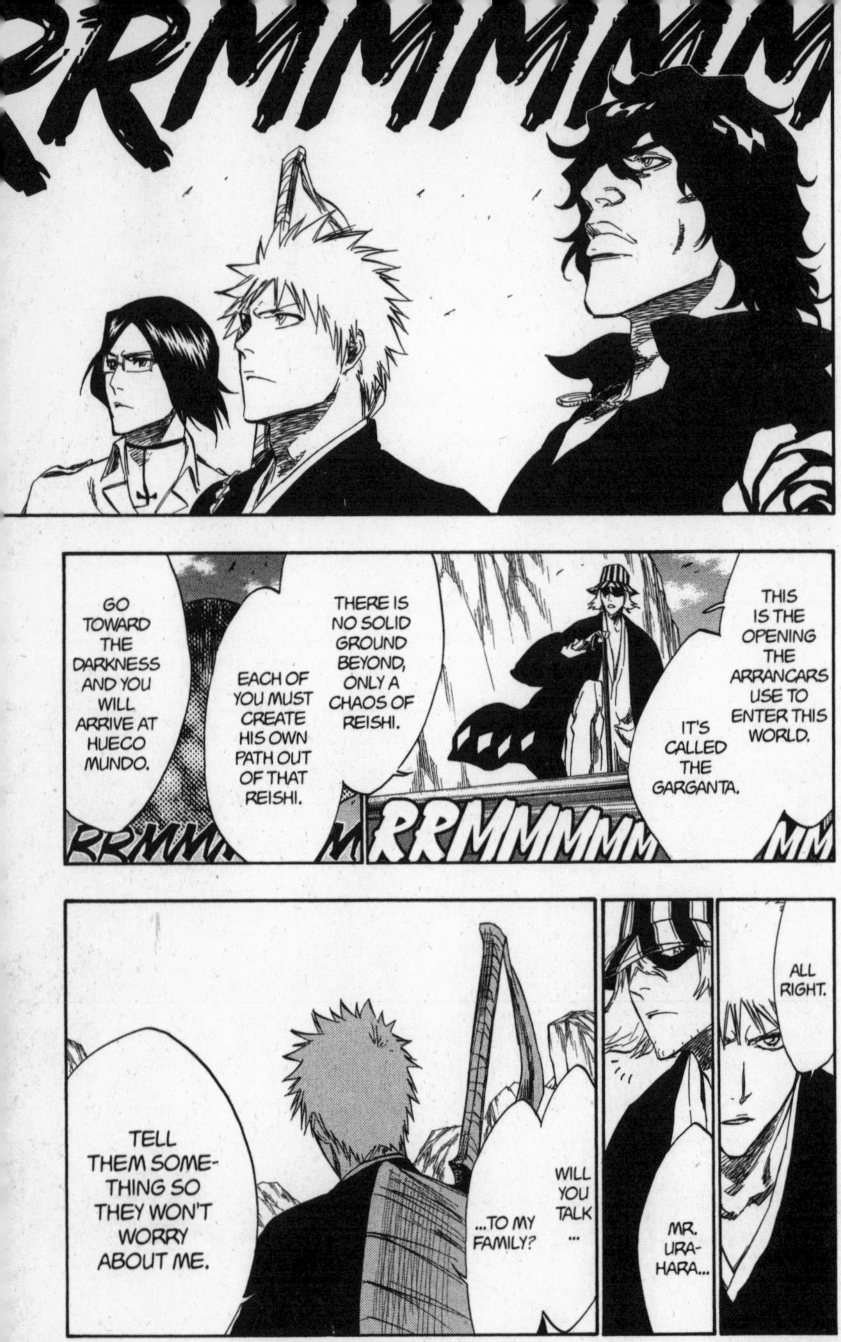
RRMMMMM
THIS IS THE OPENING THE ARRANCARS USE TO ENTER THIS WORLD.
IT'S CALLED THE GARGANTA.
RRMMMMMM
MM
THERE IS NO SOLID GROUND BEYOND, ONLY A CHAOS OF REISHI.
EACH OF YOU MUST CREATE HIS OWN PATH OUT OF THAT REISHI.
GO TOWARD THE DARKNESS AND YOU WILL ARRIVE AT HUECO MUNDO.
ALL RIGHT.
MR. URAHARA...
WILL YOU TALK...
...TO MY FAMILY?
TELL THEM SOME-THING SO THEY WON'T WORRY ABOUT ME.

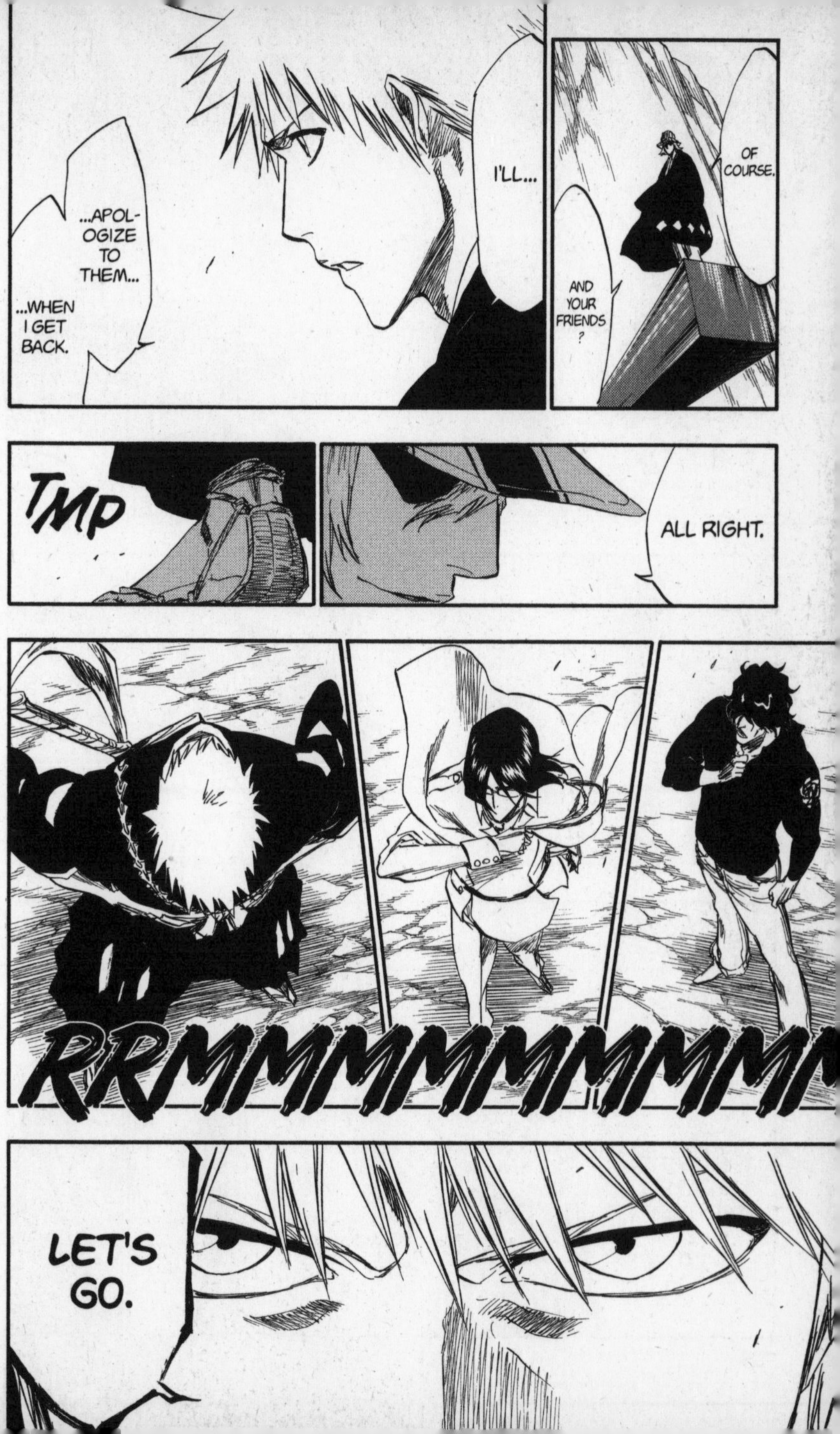
OF COURSE.
AND YOUR FRIENDS?
I'LL...
...APOLOGIZE TO THEM...
...WHEN I GET BACK.
ALL RIGHT.
TMP
RRMMMMMMMMMM
LET'S GO.

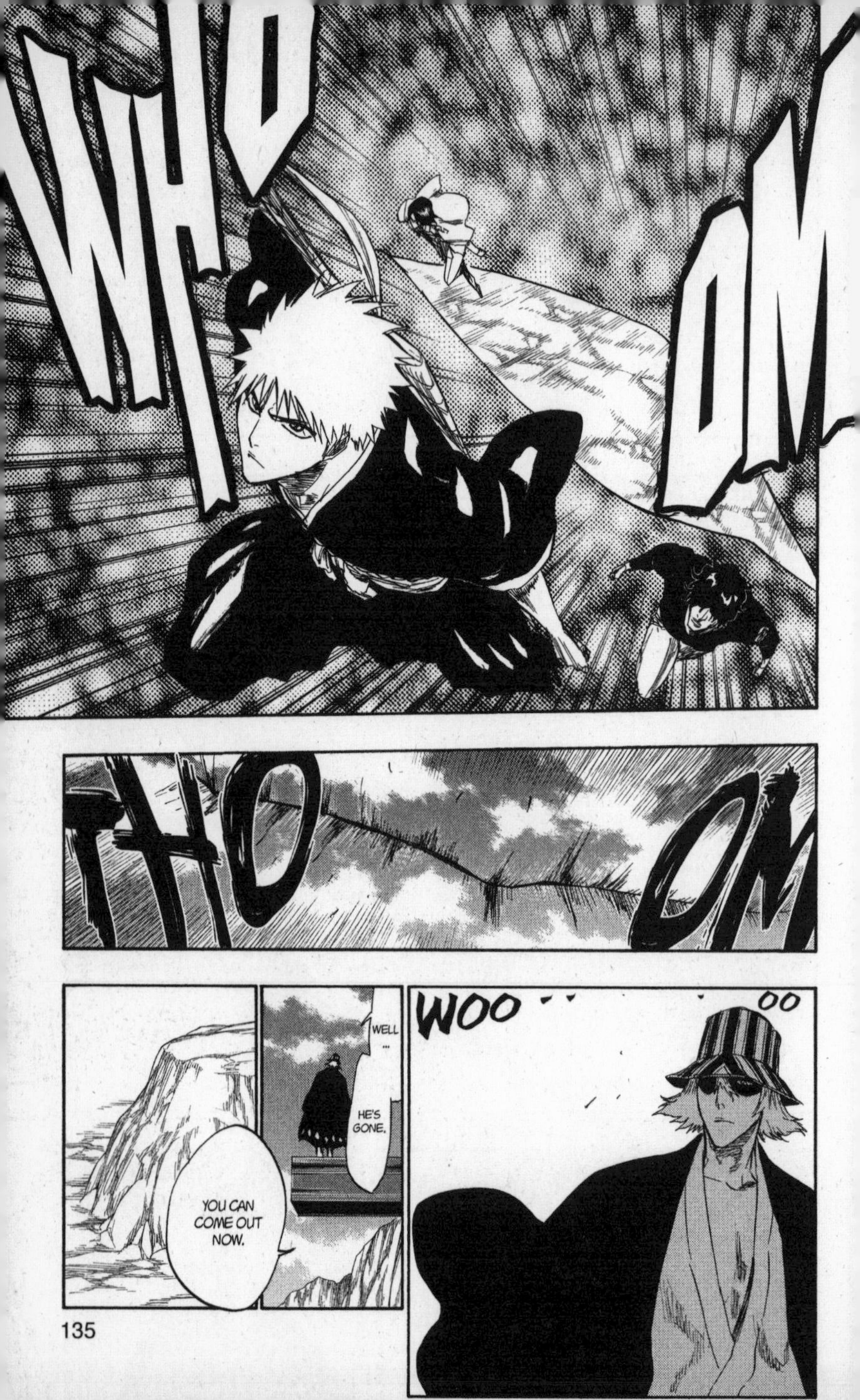
WHOOM
THOOM
WOO . . . OO
WELL ...
HE'S GONE.
YOU CAN COME OUT NOW.

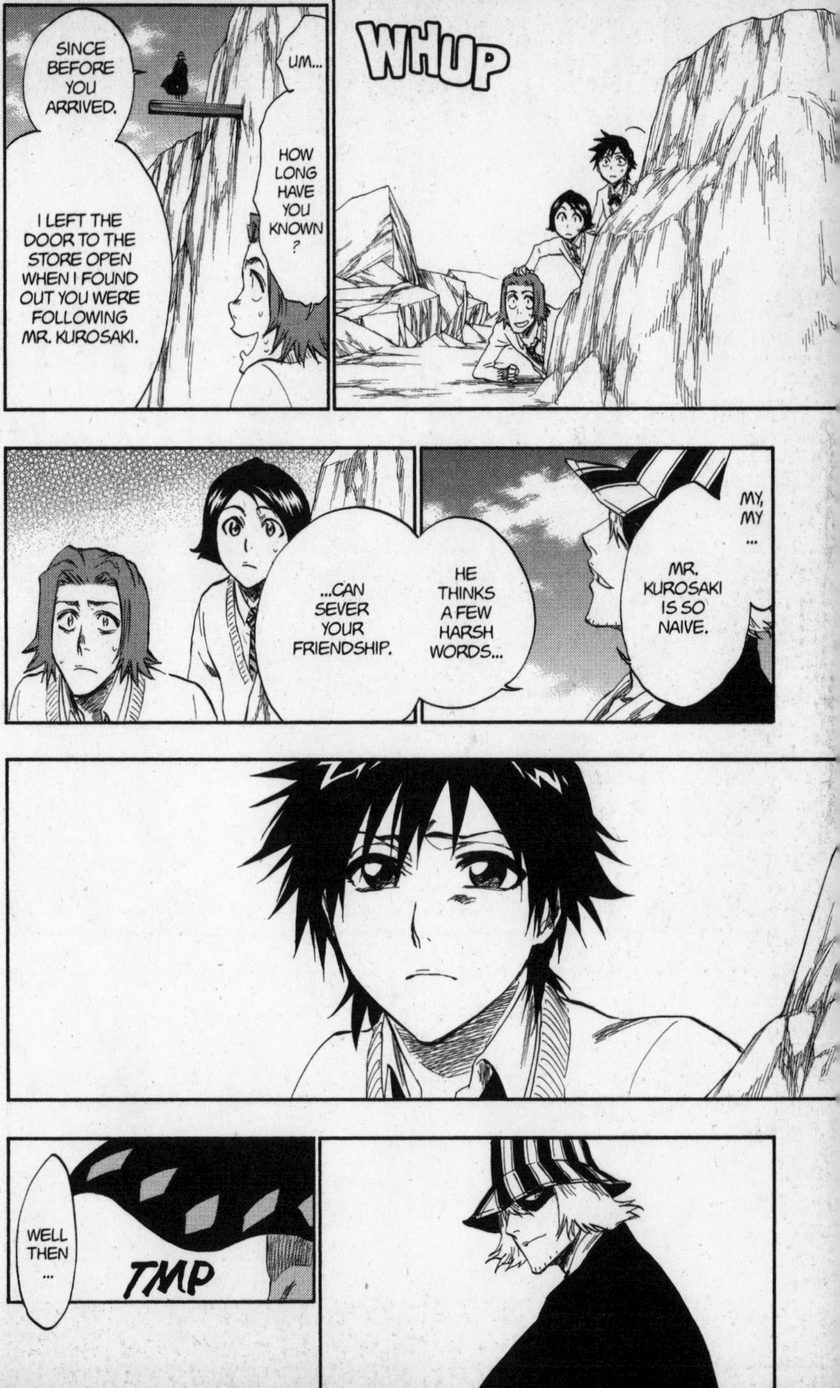
WHUP
UM...
HOW LONG HAVE YOU KNOWN?
SINCE BEFORE YOU ARRIVED.
I LEFT THE DOOR TO THE STORE OPEN WHEN I FOUND OUT YOU WERE FOLLOWING MR. KUROSAKI.
MY, MY...
MR. KUROSAKI IS SO NAIVE.
HE THINKS A FEW HARSH WORDS...
...CAN SEVER YOUR FRIENDSHIP.
WELL THEN...
TMP

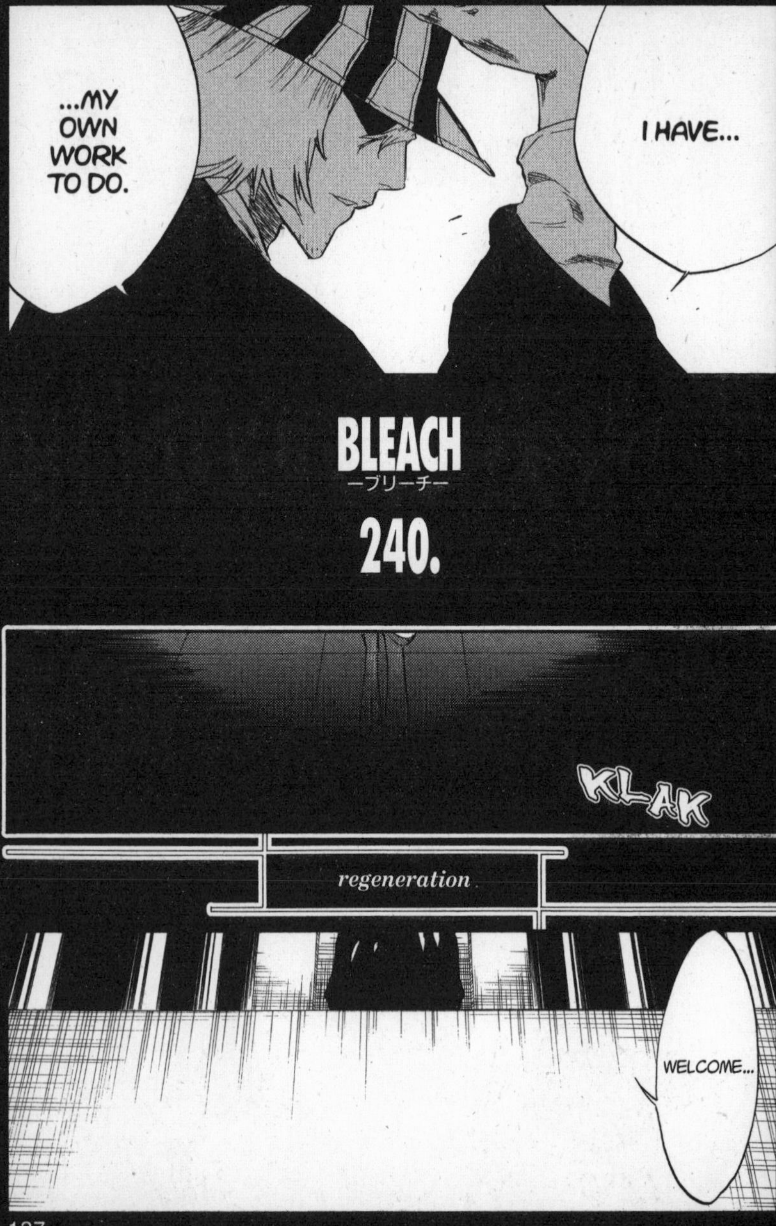
I HAVE...
...MY OWN WORK TO DO.
BLEACH
ーブリーチー
240.
KLAK
regeneration
WELCOME...

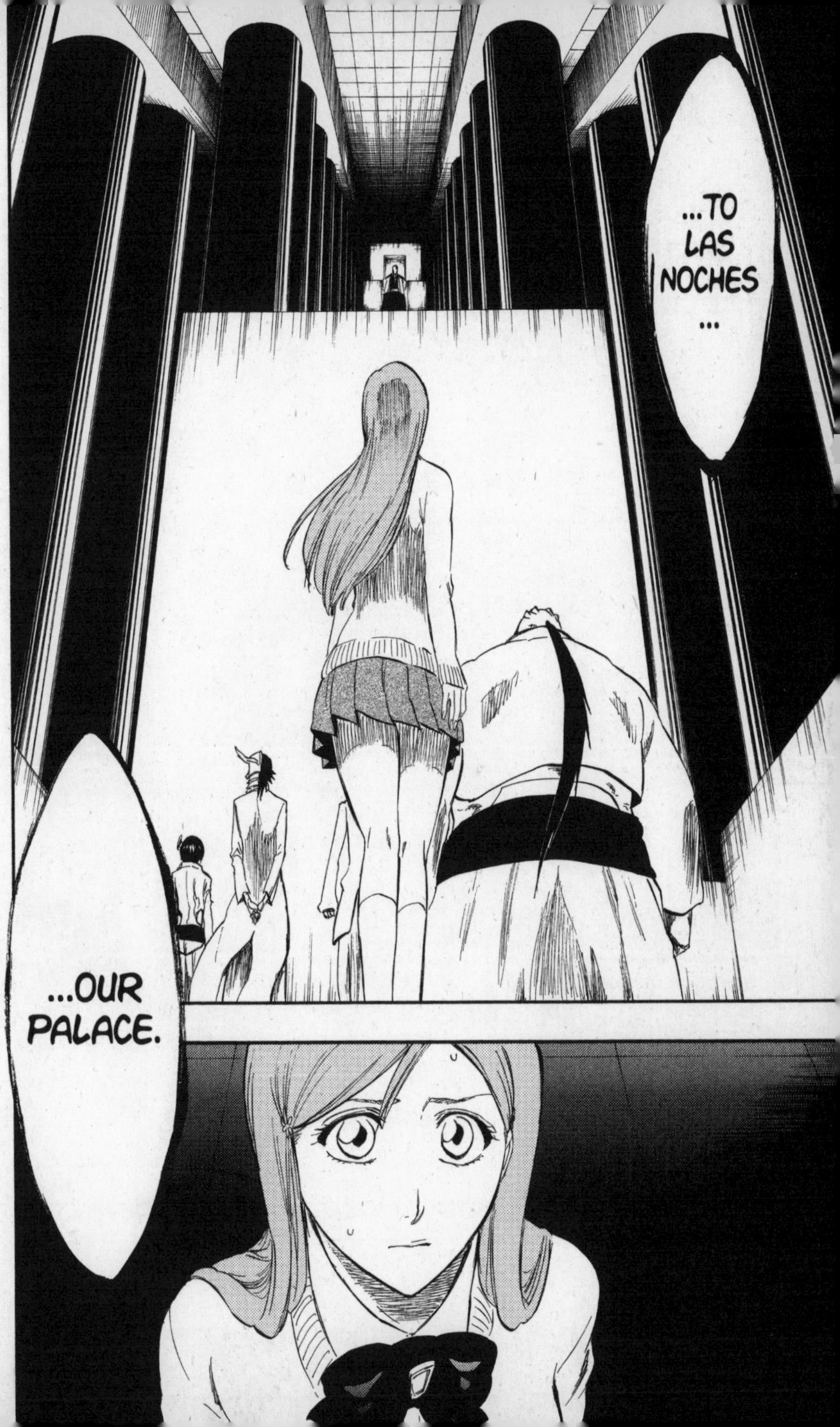
...TO LAS NOCHES ...
...OUR PALACE.

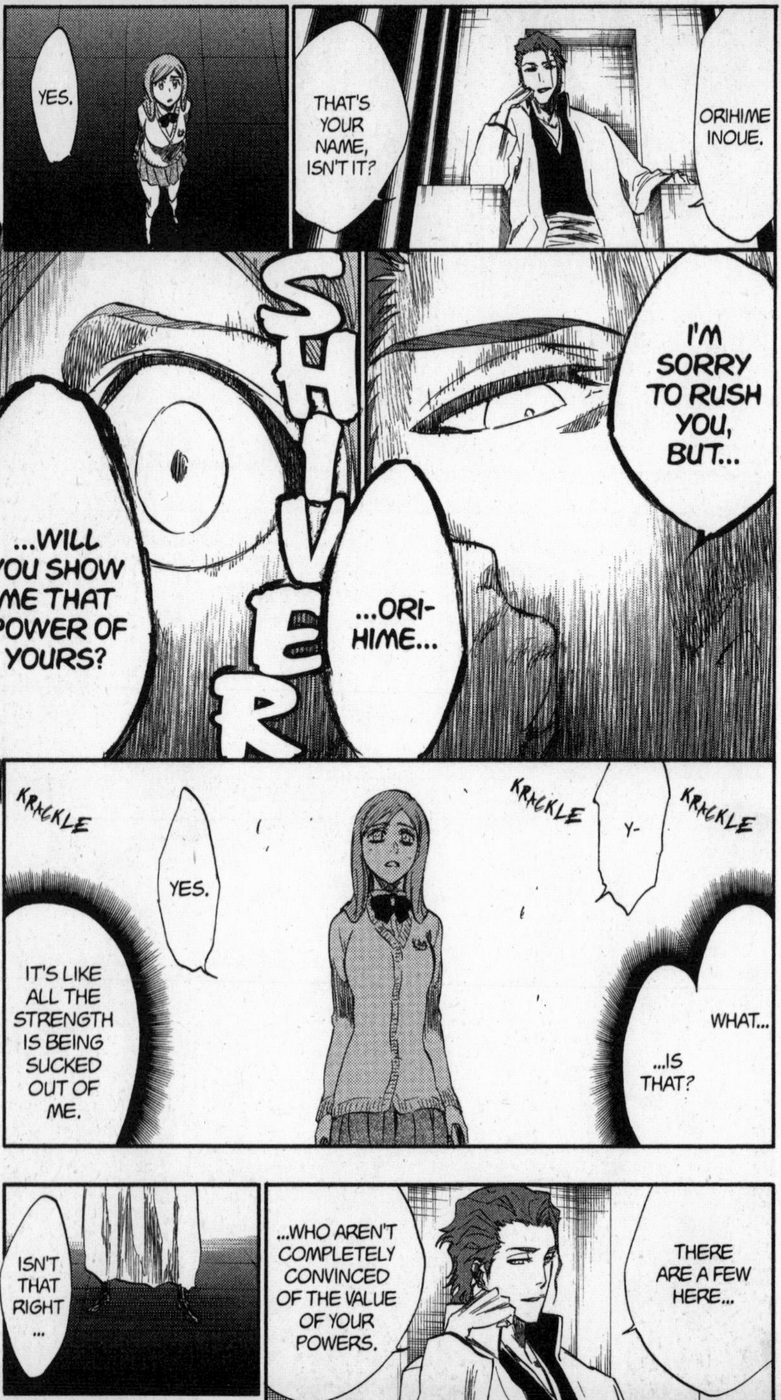
ORIHIME INOUE.
THAT'S YOUR NAME, ISN'T IT?
YES.
I'M SORRY TO RUSH YOU, BUT...
...ORI-HIME...
...WILL YOU SHOW ME THAT POWER OF YOURS?
SHIVER
KRACKLE
Y-
KRACKLE
WHAT...
...IS THAT?
YES.
IT'S LIKE ALL THE STRENGTH IS BEING SUCKED OUT OF ME.
KRACKLE
THERE ARE A FEW HERE...
...WHO AREN'T COMPLETELY CONVINCED OF THE VALUE OF YOUR POWERS.
ISN'T THAT RIGHT ...

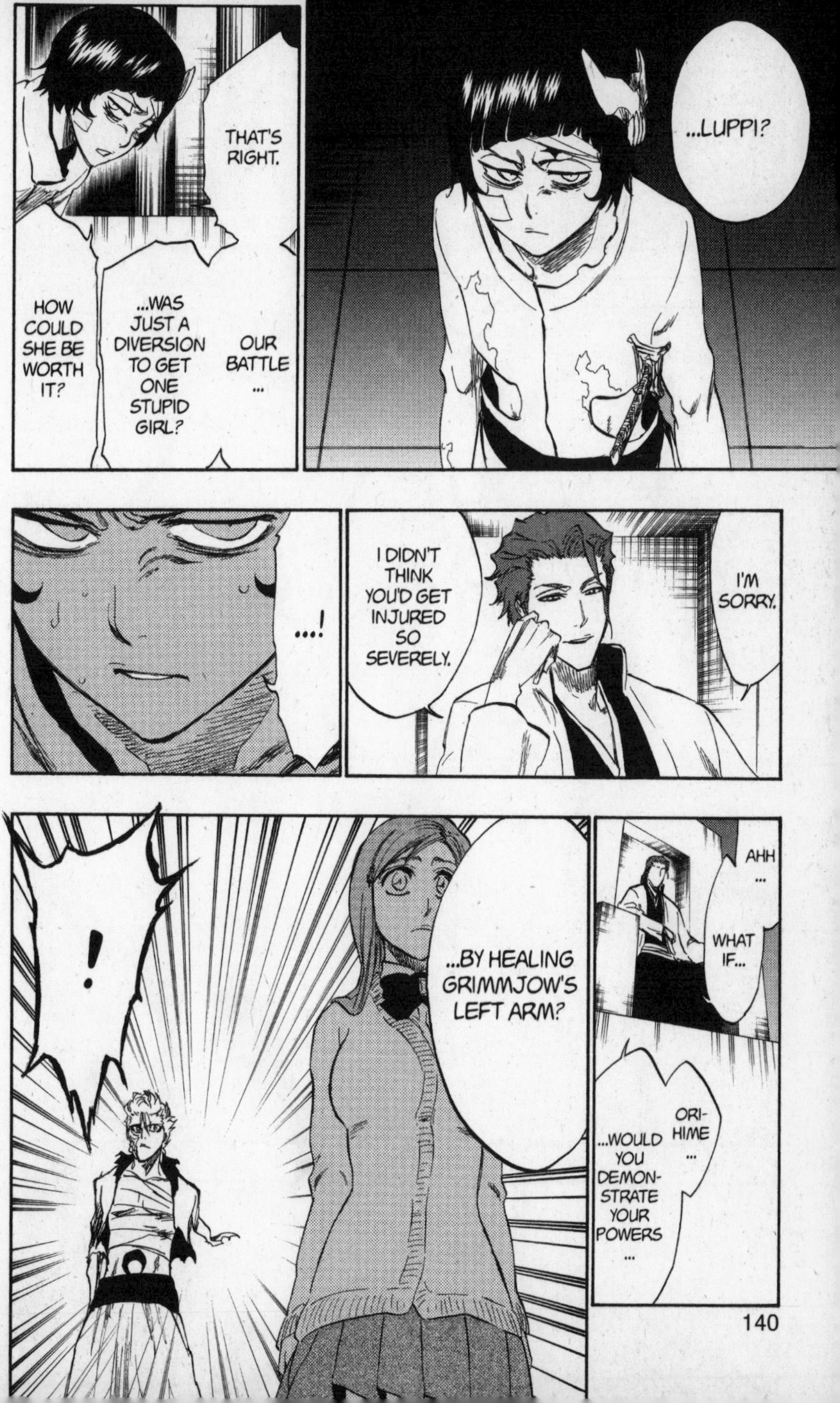

...LUPPI?
THAT'S RIGHT.
OUR BATTLE ...
...WAS JUST A DIVERSION TO GET ONE STUPID GIRL?
HOW COULD SHE BE WORTH IT?
I'M SORRY.
I DIDN'T THINK YOU'D GET INJURED SO SEVERELY.
...!
AHH ...
WHAT IF...
ORI-HIME ...
...WOULD YOU DEMON-STRATE YOUR POWERS ...
...BY HEALING GRIMMJOW'S LEFT ARM?
!

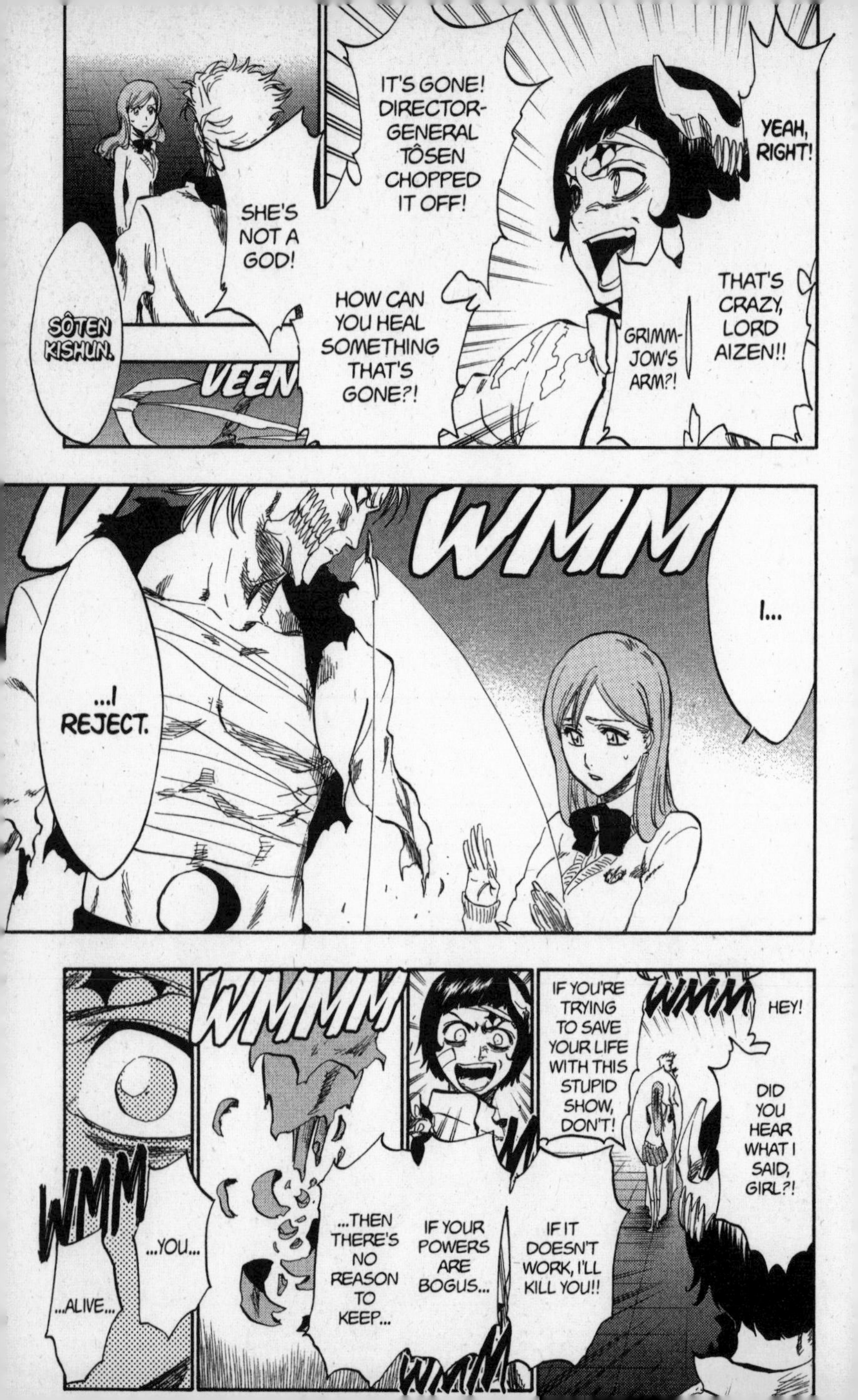
YEAH, RIGHT!
THAT'S CRAZY, LORD AIZEN!!
GRIMM-JOW'S ARM?!
IT'S GONE! DIRECTOR-GENERAL TÔSEN CHOPPED IT OFF!
HOW CAN YOU HEAL SOMETHING THAT'S GONE?!
SHE'S NOT A GOD!
SÔTEN KISHUN.
VEEN
WMM
I...
...I REJECT.
HEY!
WMM
DID YOU HEAR WHAT I SAID, GIRL?!
IF YOU'RE TRYING TO SAVE YOUR LIFE WITH THIS STUPID SHOW, DON'T!
IF IT DOESN'T WORK, I'LL KILL YOU!!
IF YOUR POWERS ARE BOGUS...
...THEN THERE'S NO REASON TO KEEP...
WMMM
...YOU...
...ALIVE...
WMM

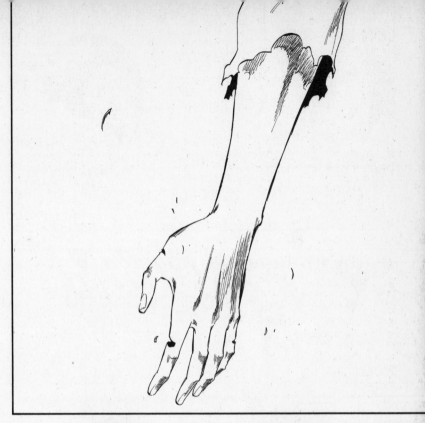

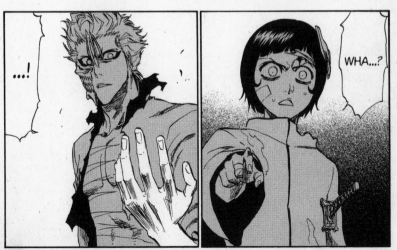

…!

WHA…?

READ THIS WAY

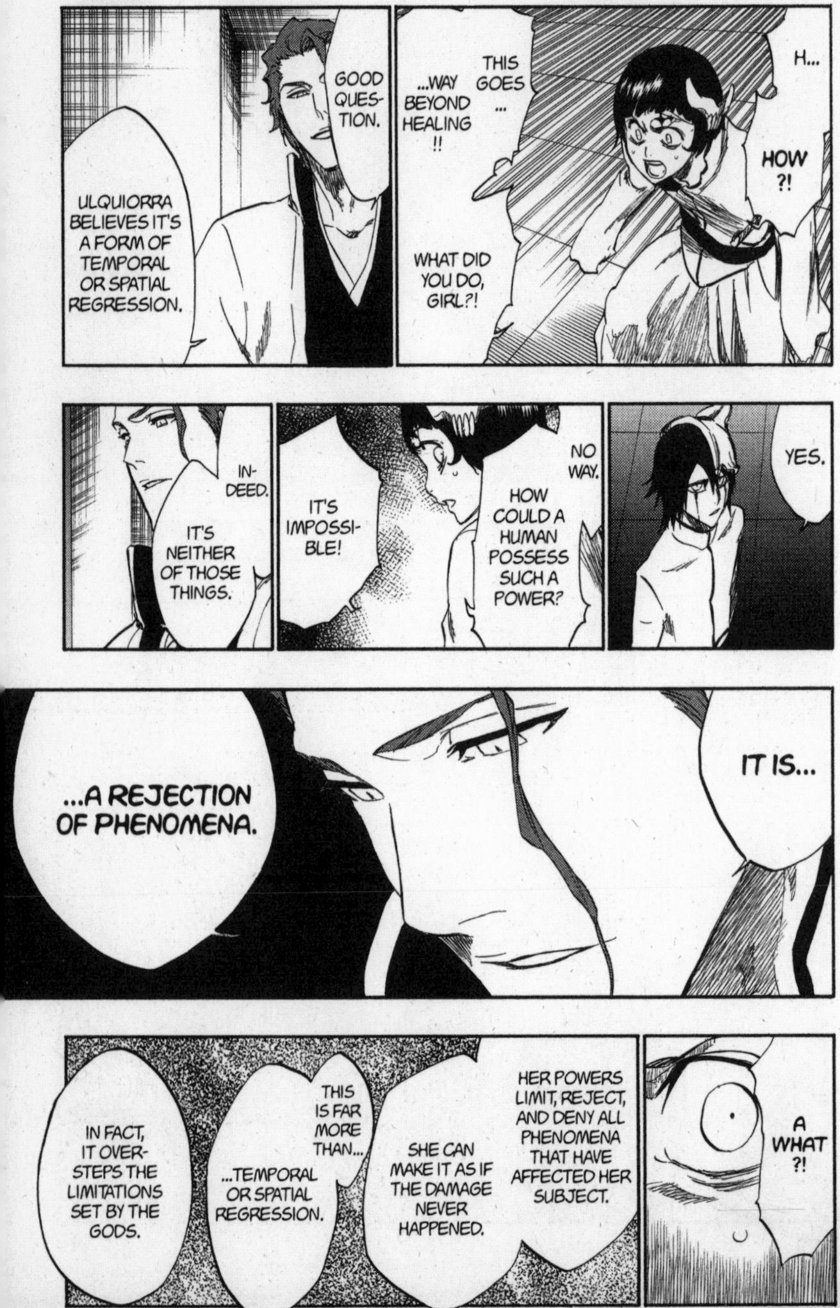
H...
HOW ?!
THIS GOES ...
...WAY BEYOND HEALING !!
WHAT DID YOU DO, GIRL?!
GOOD QUES-TION.
ULQUIORRA BELIEVES IT'S A FORM OF TEMPORAL OR SPATIAL REGRESSION.
YES.
NO WAY.
HOW COULD A HUMAN POSSESS SUCH A POWER?
IT'S IMPOSSI-BLE!
IN-DEED.
IT'S NEITHER OF THOSE THINGS.
IT IS...
...A REJECTION OF PHENOMENA.
A WHAT ?!
HER POWERS LIMIT, REJECT, AND DENY ALL PHENOMENA THAT HAVE AFFECTED HER SUBJECT.
SHE CAN MAKE IT AS IF THE DAMAGE NEVER HAPPENED.
THIS IS FAR MORE THAN...
...TEMPORAL OR SPATIAL REGRESSION.
IN FACT, IT OVER-STEPS THE LIMITATIONS SET BY THE GODS.

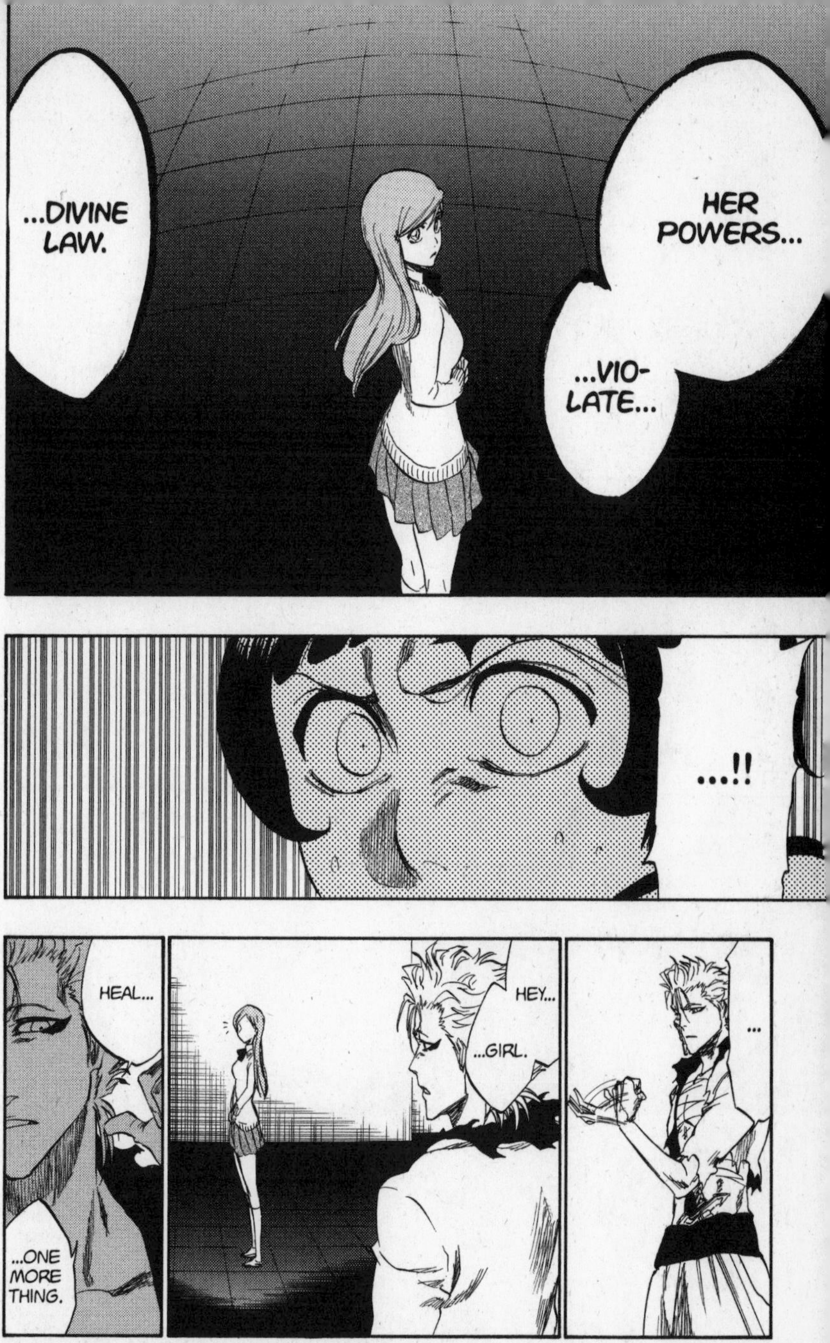
HER POWERS...
...VIO-LATE...
...DIVINE LAW.
...!!
...
HEY...
...GIRL.
HEAL...
...ONE MORE THING.

READ THIS WAY

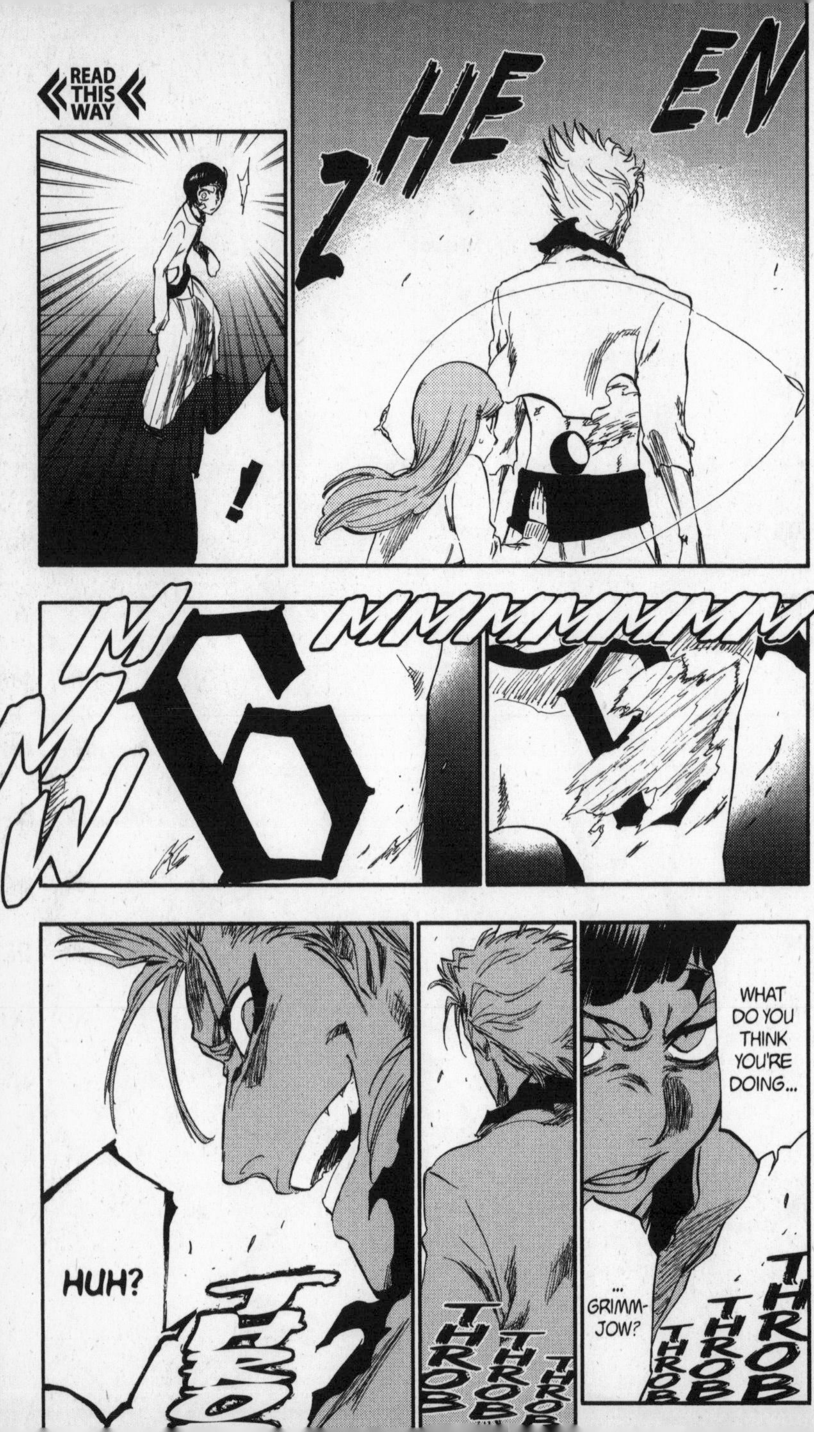
ZHE EN
!
MMMMMMMMM
MMW
WHAT DO YOU THINK YOU'RE DOING...
... GRIMM-JOW?
THROB THROB THROB
THROB THROB THRO
HUH?

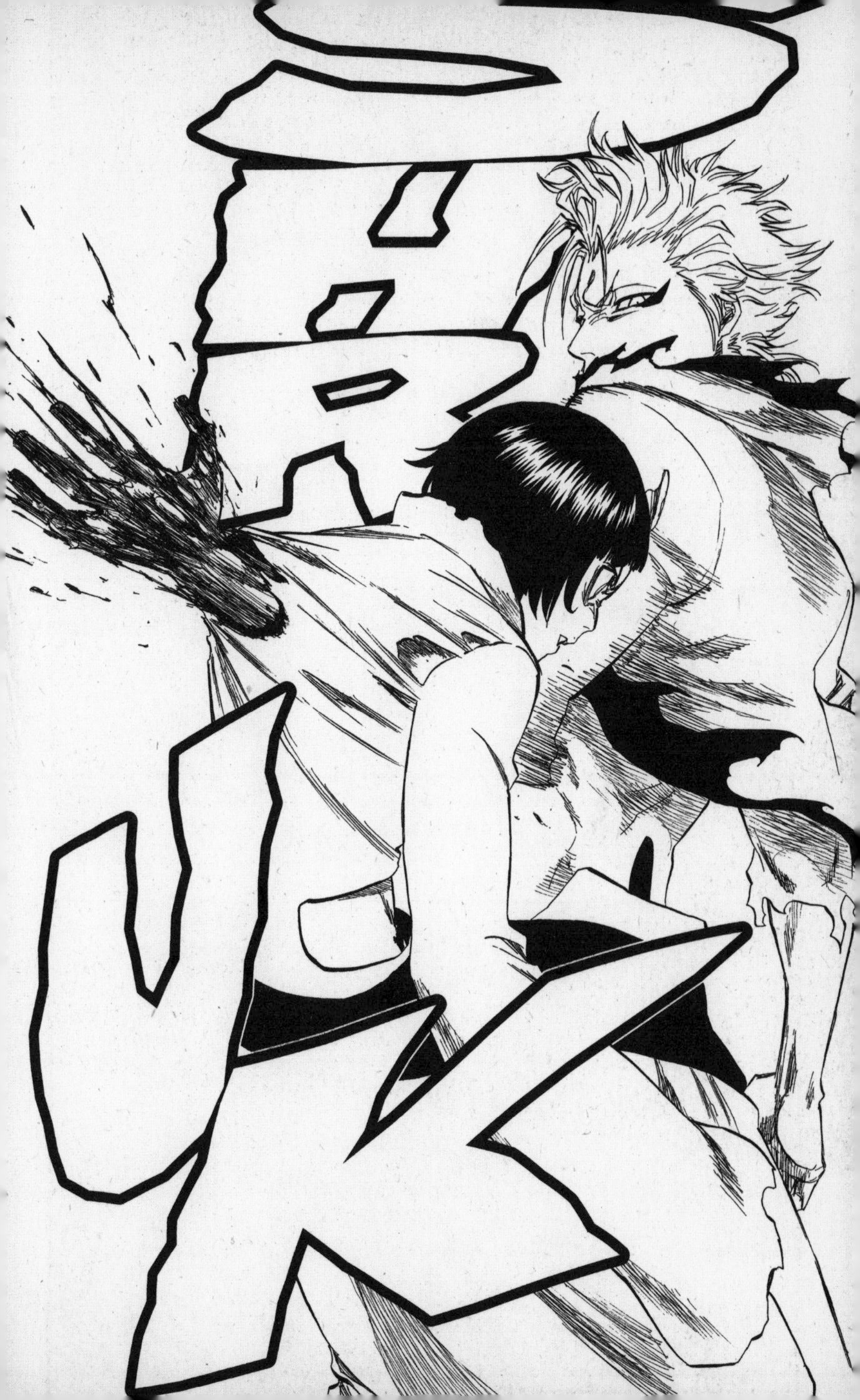

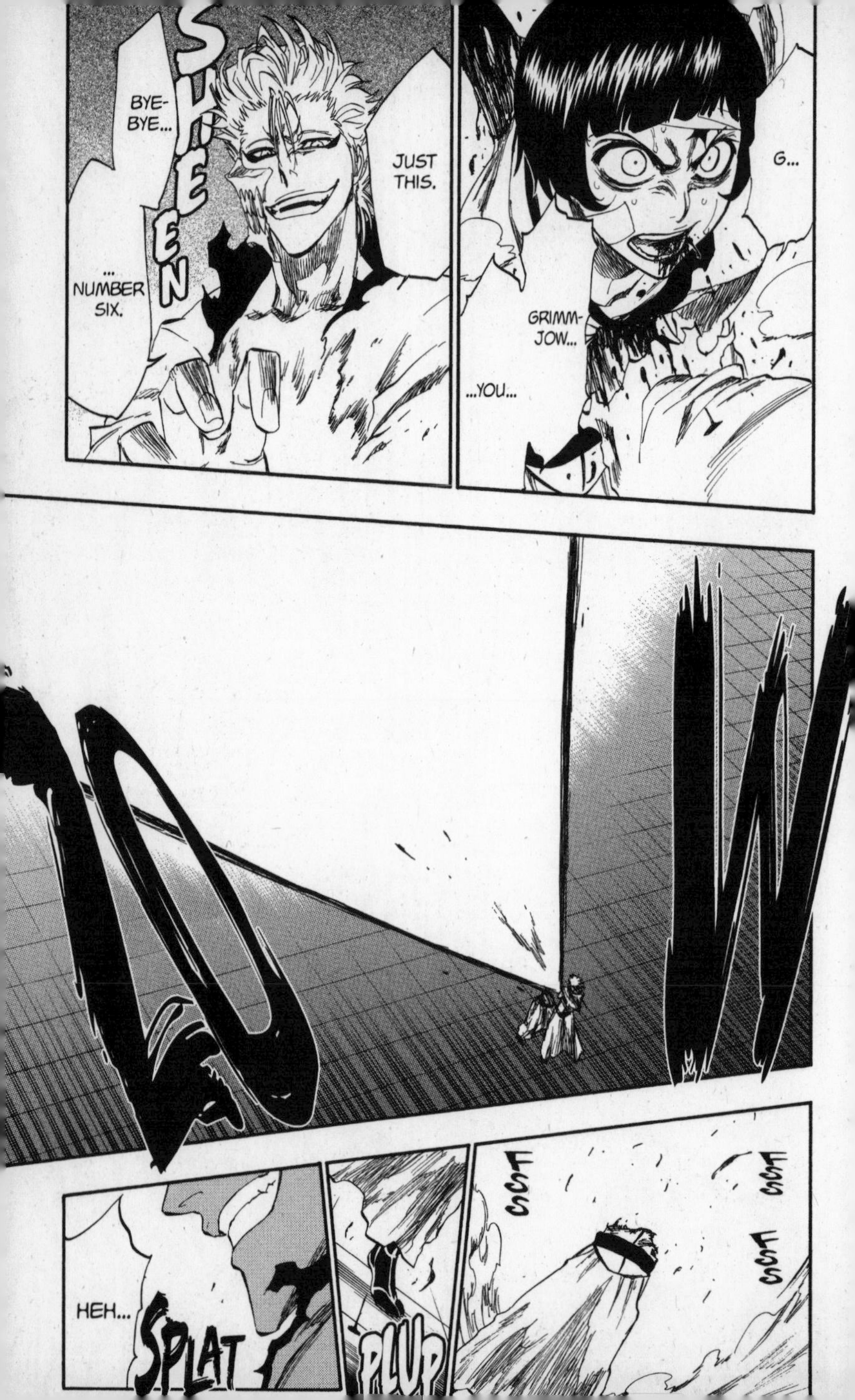
G...
GRIMMJOW...
...YOU...
JUST THIS.
BYE-BYE...
SHEEN
...NUMBER SIX.
FSS
FSS
PLUP
HEH...
SPLAT

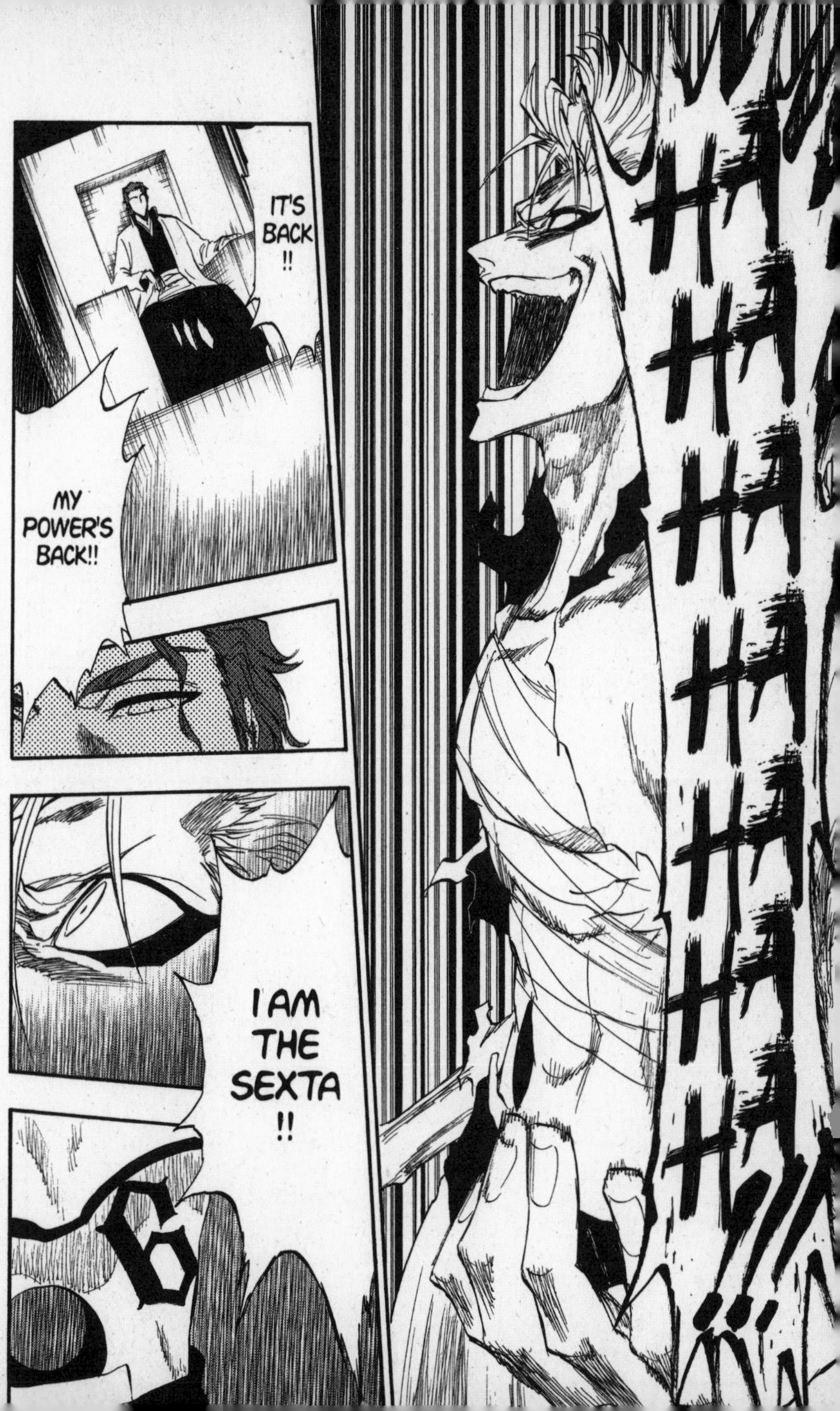
HAHAHAHAHAHAHA!!
IT'S BACK!!
MY POWER'S BACK!!
I AM THE SEXTA!!

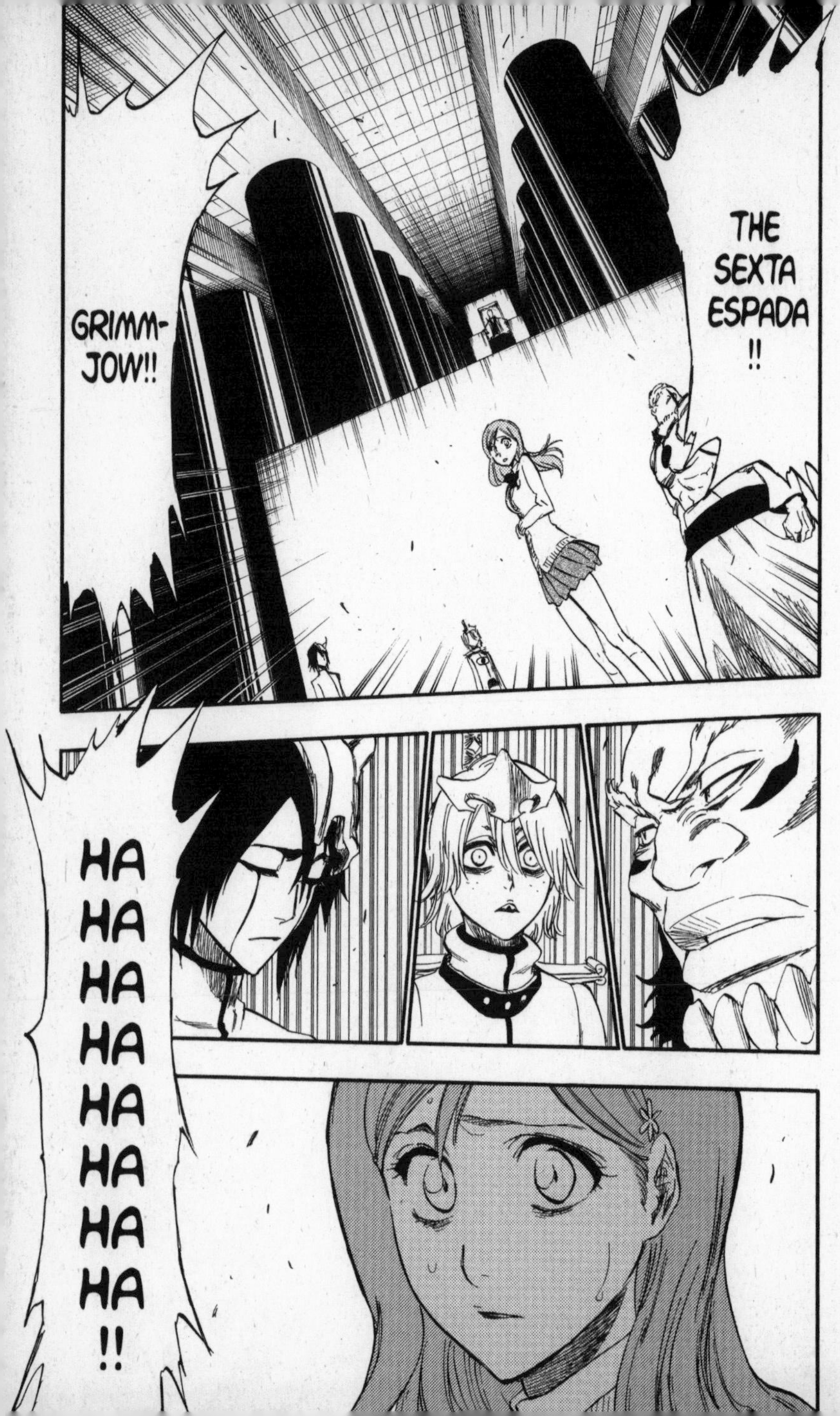
THE SEXTA ESPADA!!
GRIMM-JOW!!
HA HA HA HA HA HA HA HA!!

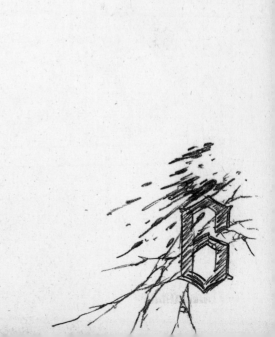

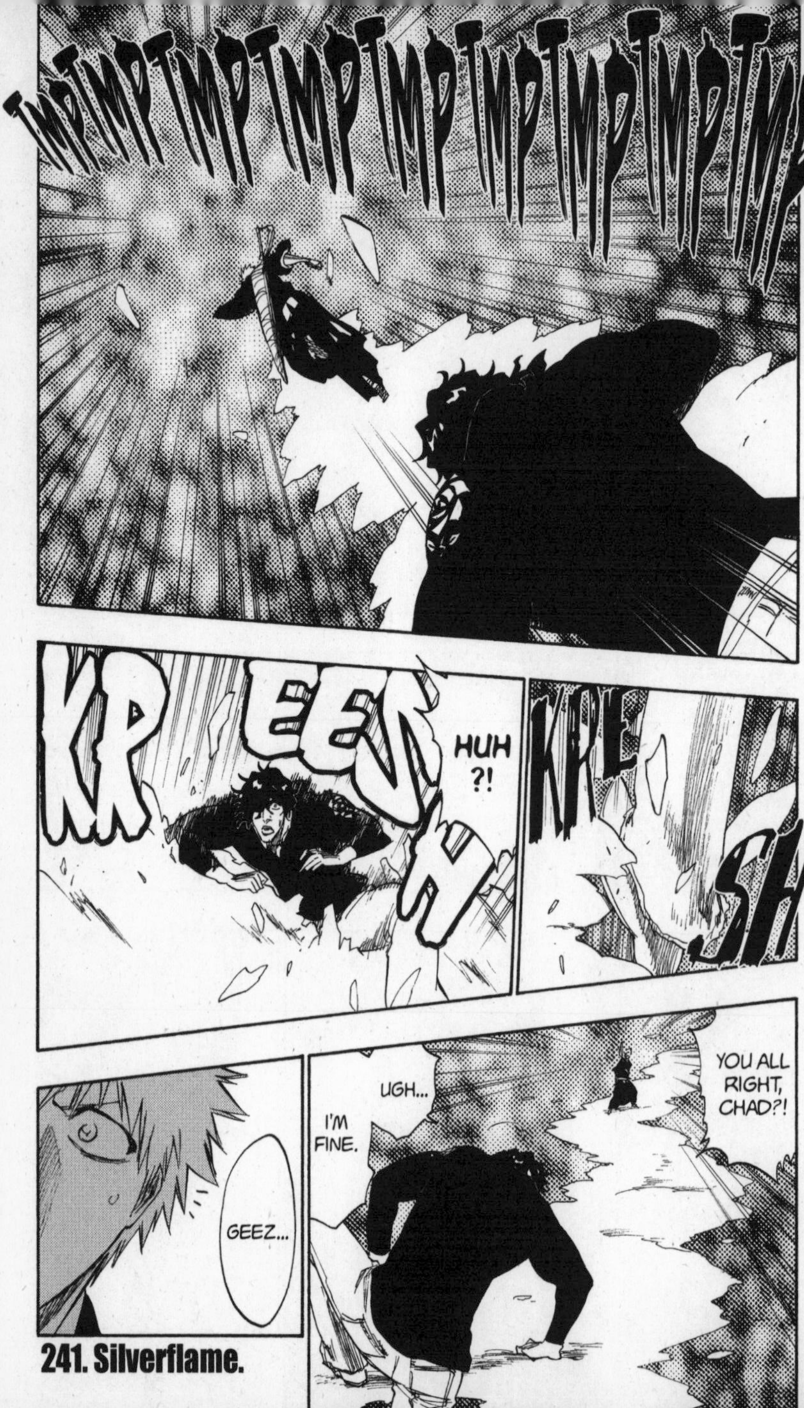
TMP TMP TMP TMP TMP TMP TMP TMP TMP
KRESH
KREESH
HUH ?!
YOU ALL RIGHT, CHAD?!
UGH...
I'M FINE.
GEEZ...

241. Silverflame.

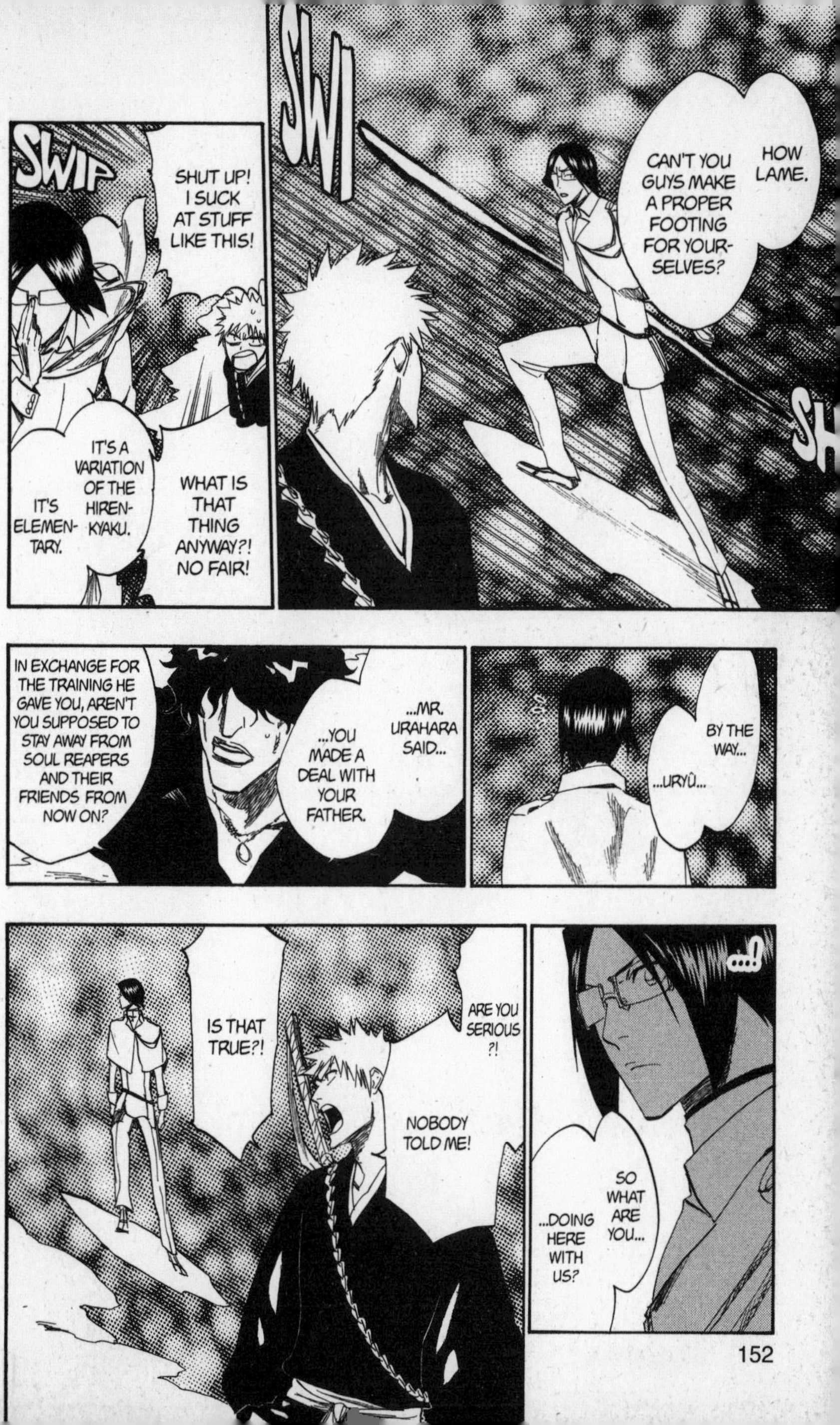
SWI
HOW LAME.
CAN'T YOU GUYS MAKE A PROPER FOOTING FOR YOURSELVES?
SH
SWIP
SHUT UP! I SUCK AT STUFF LIKE THIS!
WHAT IS THAT THING ANYWAY?! NO FAIR!
IT'S A VARIATION OF THE HIREN-KYAKU.
IT'S ELEMENTARY.
BY THE WAY...
...URYŪ...
...MR. URAHARA SAID...
...YOU MADE A DEAL WITH YOUR FATHER.
IN EXCHANGE FOR THE TRAINING HE GAVE YOU, AREN'T YOU SUPPOSED TO STAY AWAY FROM SOUL REAPERS AND THEIR FRIENDS FROM NOW ON?
...!
SO WHAT ARE YOU...
...DOING HERE WITH US?
ARE YOU SERIOUS?!
IS THAT TRUE?!
NOBODY TOLD ME!

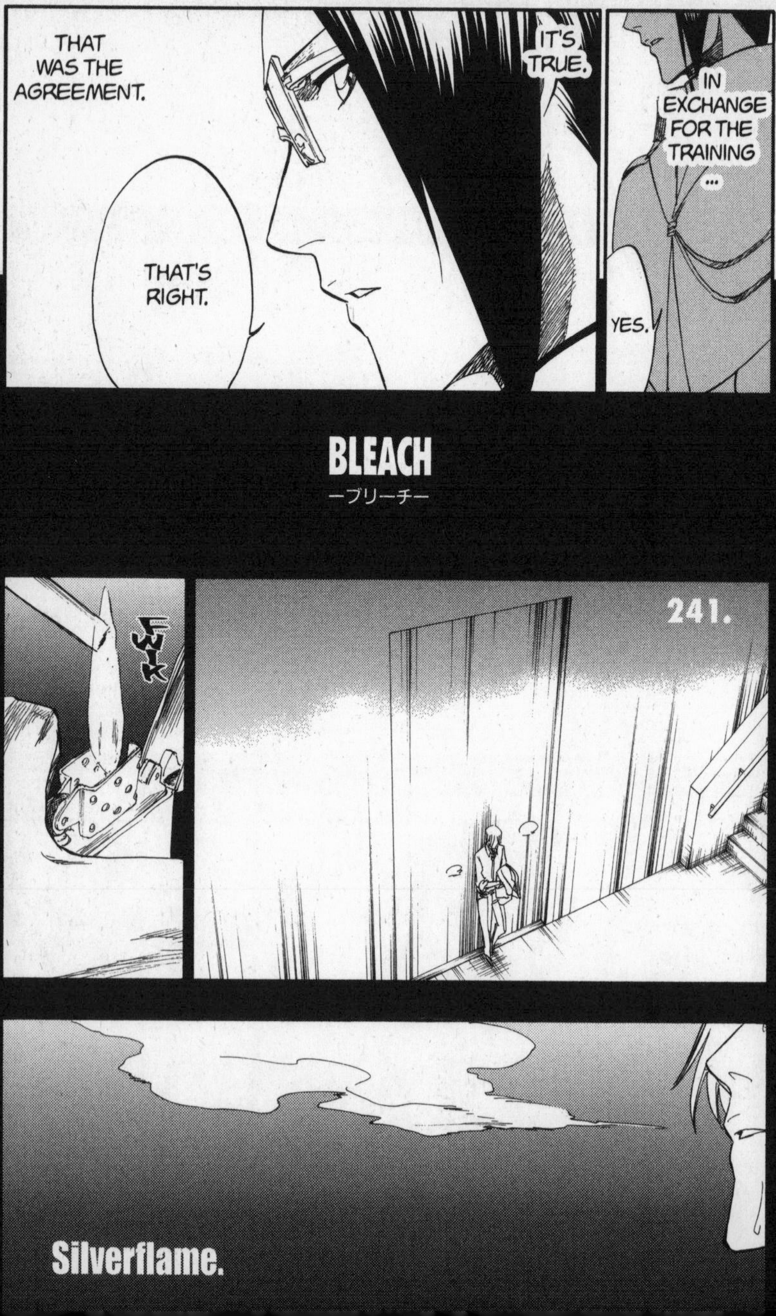
IN EXCHANGE FOR THE TRAINING ...
YES.
IT'S TRUE.
THAT WAS THE AGREEMENT.
THAT'S RIGHT.
BLEACH
ーブリーチー
241.
FWIK
Silverflame.

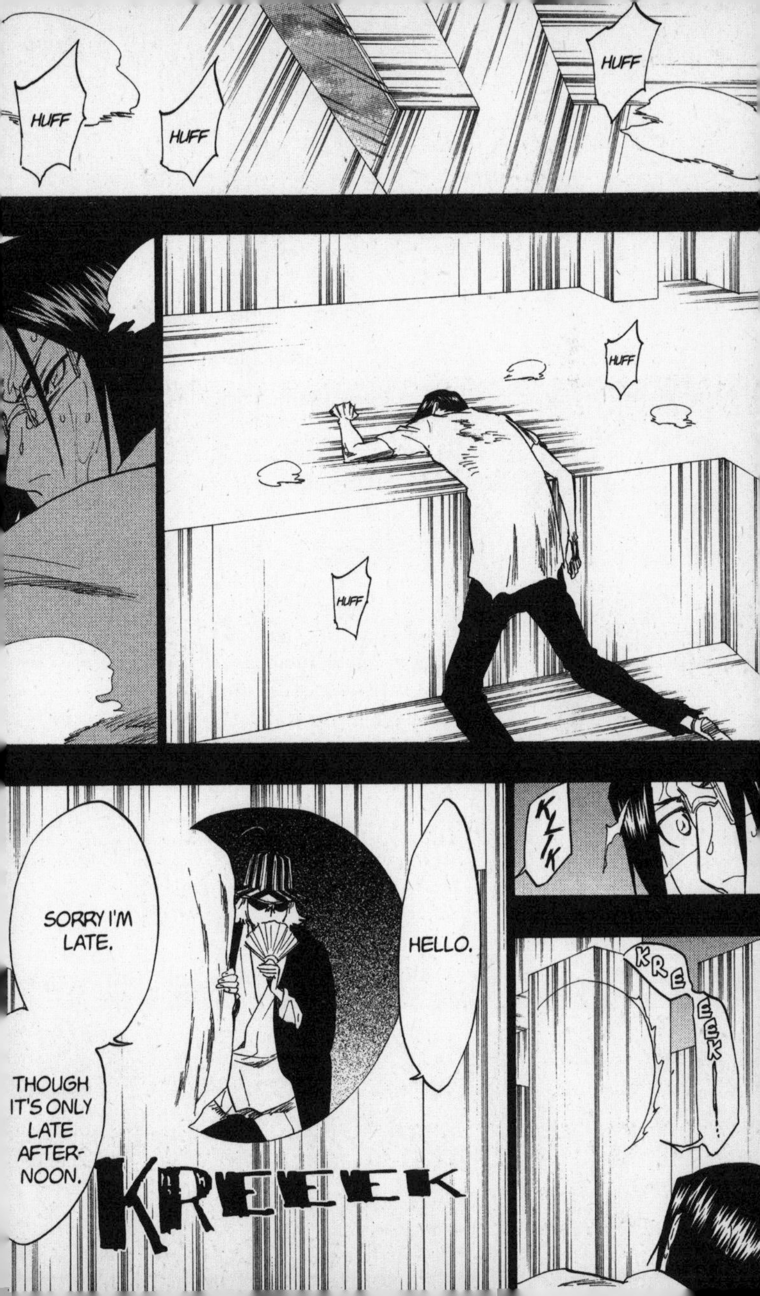
HUFF
HUFF
HUFF
HUFF
HUFF
KLIK
KREEEK—!...
HELLO.
SORRY I'M LATE.
THOUGH IT'S ONLY LATE AFTERNOON.
KREEEK

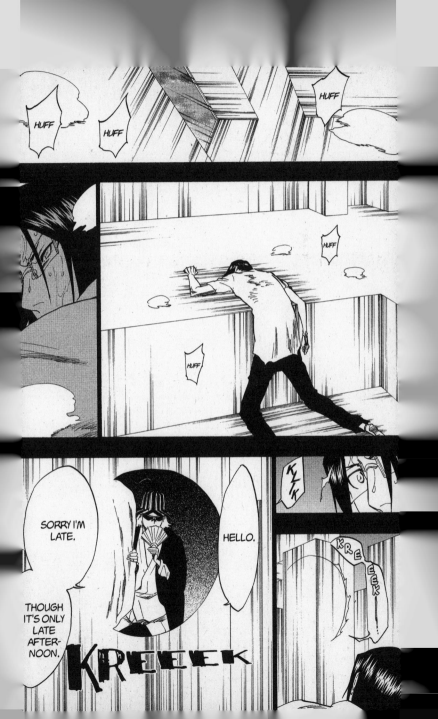

READ THIS WAY

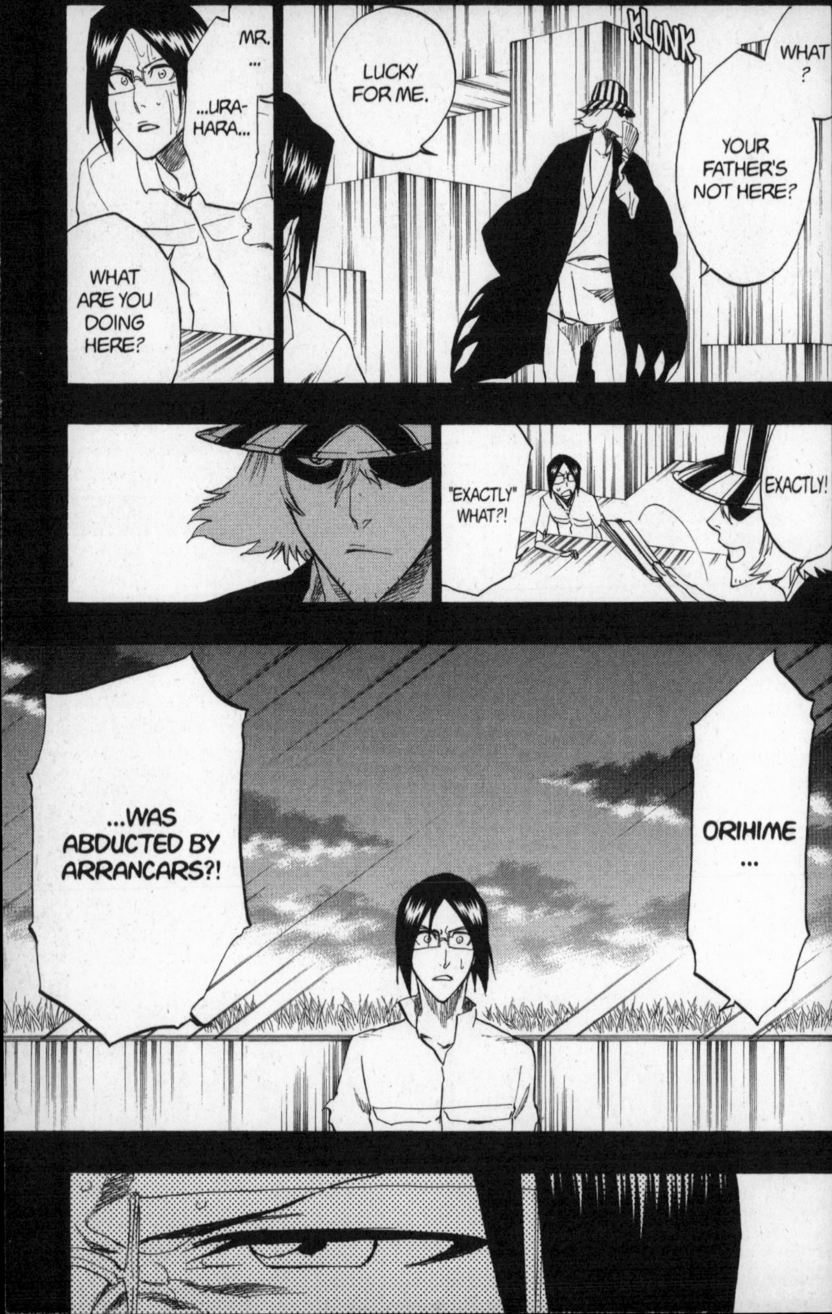

WHAT ?
KLUNK
YOUR FATHER'S NOT HERE?
LUCKY FOR ME.
MR. ...
...URA-HARA...
WHAT ARE YOU DOING HERE?
EXACTLY!
"EXACTLY" WHAT?!
ORIHIME ...
...WAS ABDUCTED BY ARRANCARS?!

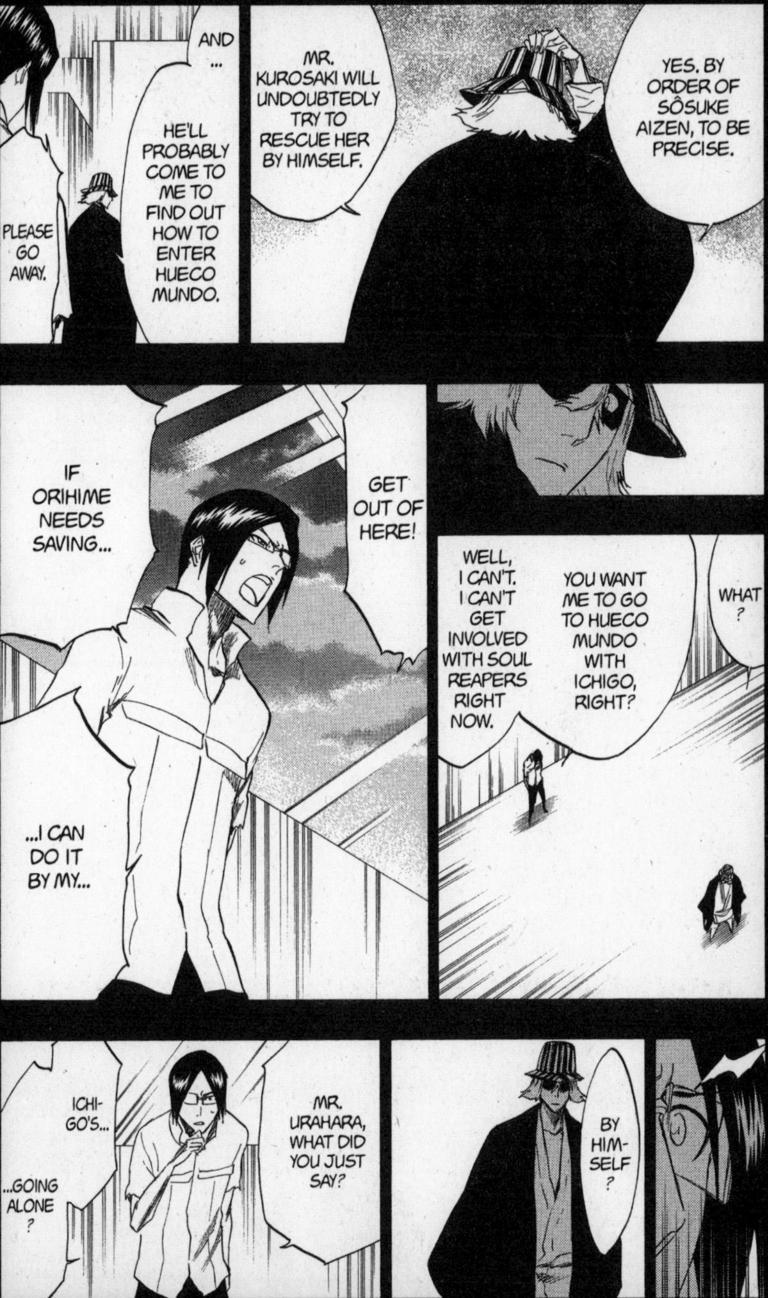
YES. BY ORDER OF SÔSUKE AIZEN, TO BE PRECISE.
MR. KUROSAKI WILL UNDOUBTEDLY TRY TO RESCUE HER BY HIMSELF.
AND ...
HE'LL PROBABLY COME TO ME TO FIND OUT HOW TO ENTER HUECO MUNDO.
PLEASE GO AWAY.
WHAT?
YOU WANT ME TO GO TO HUECO MUNDO WITH ICHIGO, RIGHT?
WELL, I CAN'T. I CAN'T GET INVOLVED WITH SOUL REAPERS RIGHT NOW.
GET OUT OF HERE!
IF ORIHIME NEEDS SAVING...
...I CAN DO IT BY MY...
BY HIM-SELF?
MR. URAHARA, WHAT DID YOU JUST SAY?
ICHI-GO'S...
...GOING ALONE?

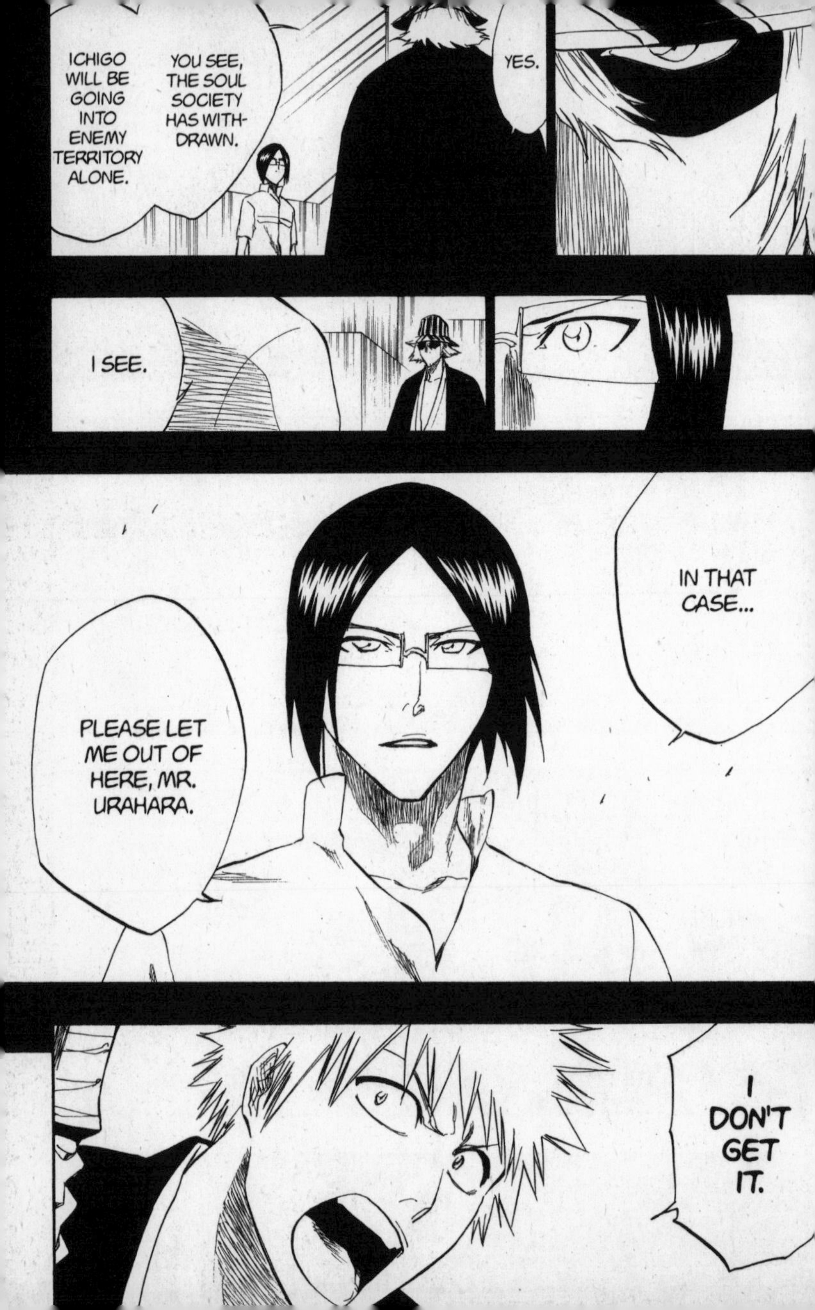
YES.
YOU SEE, THE SOUL SOCIETY HAS WITHDRAWN.
ICHIGO WILL BE GOING INTO ENEMY TERRITORY ALONE.
I SEE.
IN THAT CASE...
PLEASE LET ME OUT OF HERE, MR. URAHARA.
I DON'T GET IT.

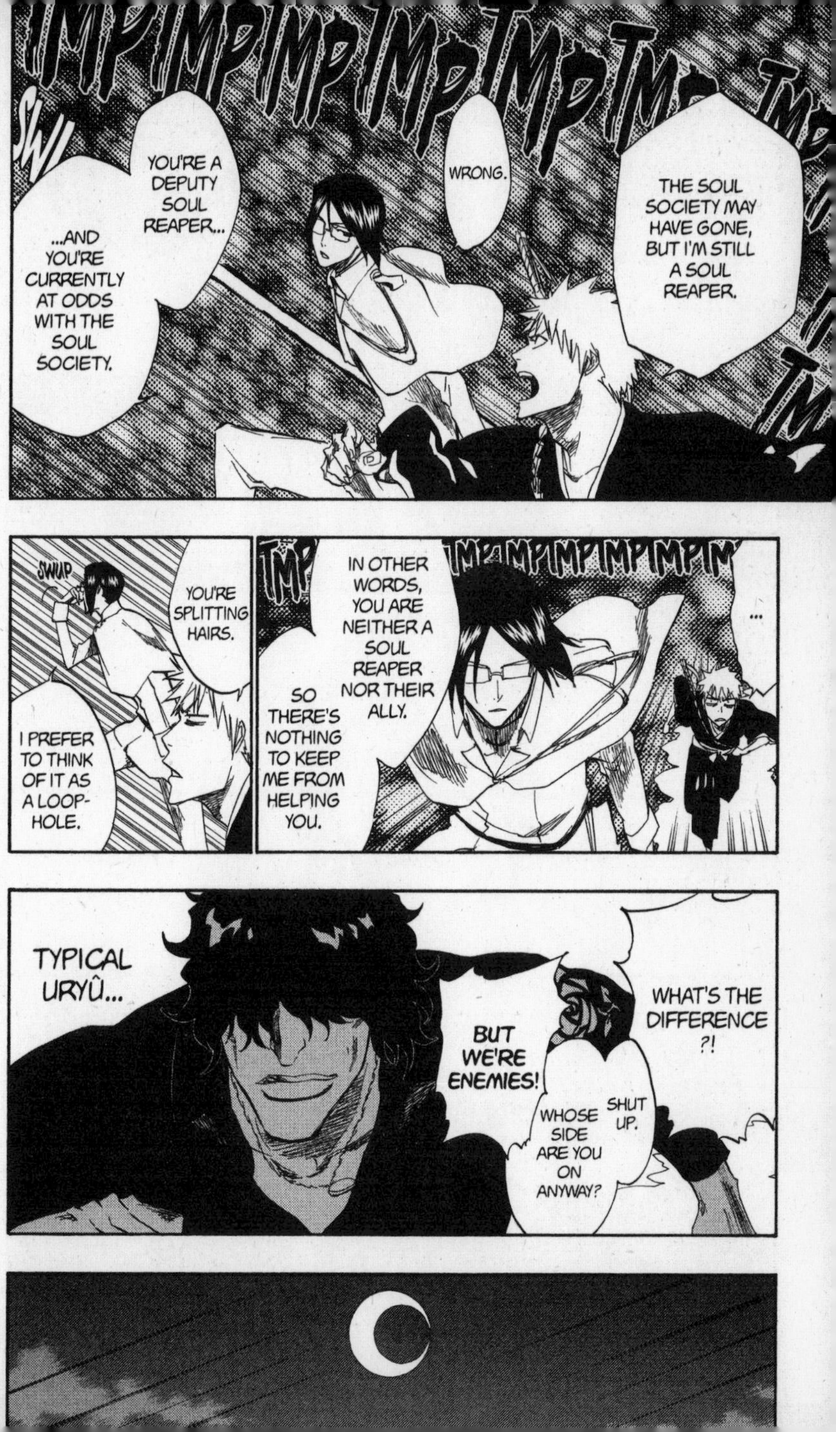

TMP TMP TMP TMP TMP TMP TMP
SWI
THE SOUL SOCIETY MAY HAVE GONE, BUT I'M STILL A SOUL REAPER.
WRONG.
YOU'RE A DEPUTY SOUL REAPER...
...AND YOU'RE CURRENTLY AT ODDS WITH THE SOUL SOCIETY.
TMP TMP TMP TMP TMP
...
IN OTHER WORDS, YOU ARE NEITHER A SOUL REAPER NOR THEIR ALLY.
SO THERE'S NOTHING TO KEEP ME FROM HELPING YOU.
SWUP
YOU'RE SPLITTING HAIRS.
I PREFER TO THINK OF IT AS A LOOP-HOLE.
WHAT'S THE DIFFERENCE ?!
SHUT UP.
BUT WE'RE ENEMIES!
WHOSE SIDE ARE YOU ON ANYWAY?
TYPICAL URYÛ...

READ THIS WAY

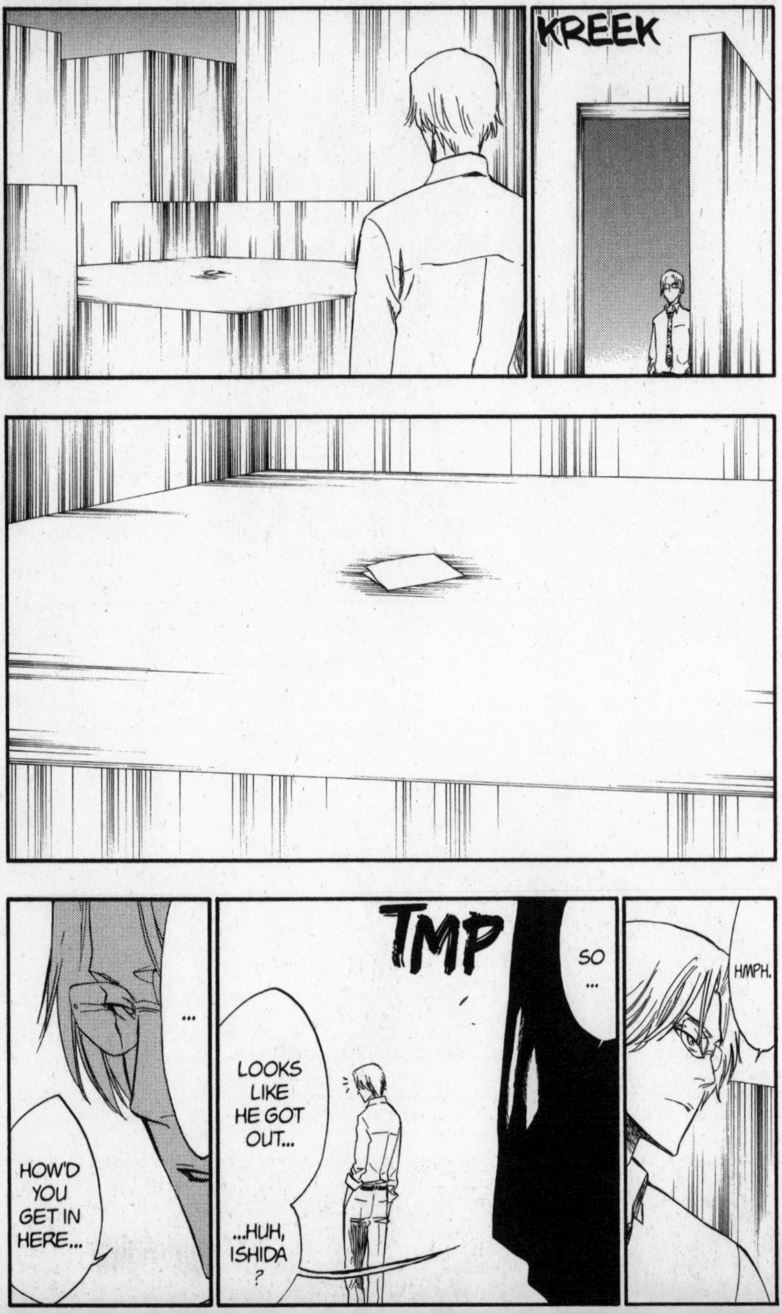
KREEK
HMPH.
TMP
SO ...
LOOKS LIKE HE GOT OUT...
...HUH, ISHIDA ?
...
HOW'D YOU GET IN HERE...

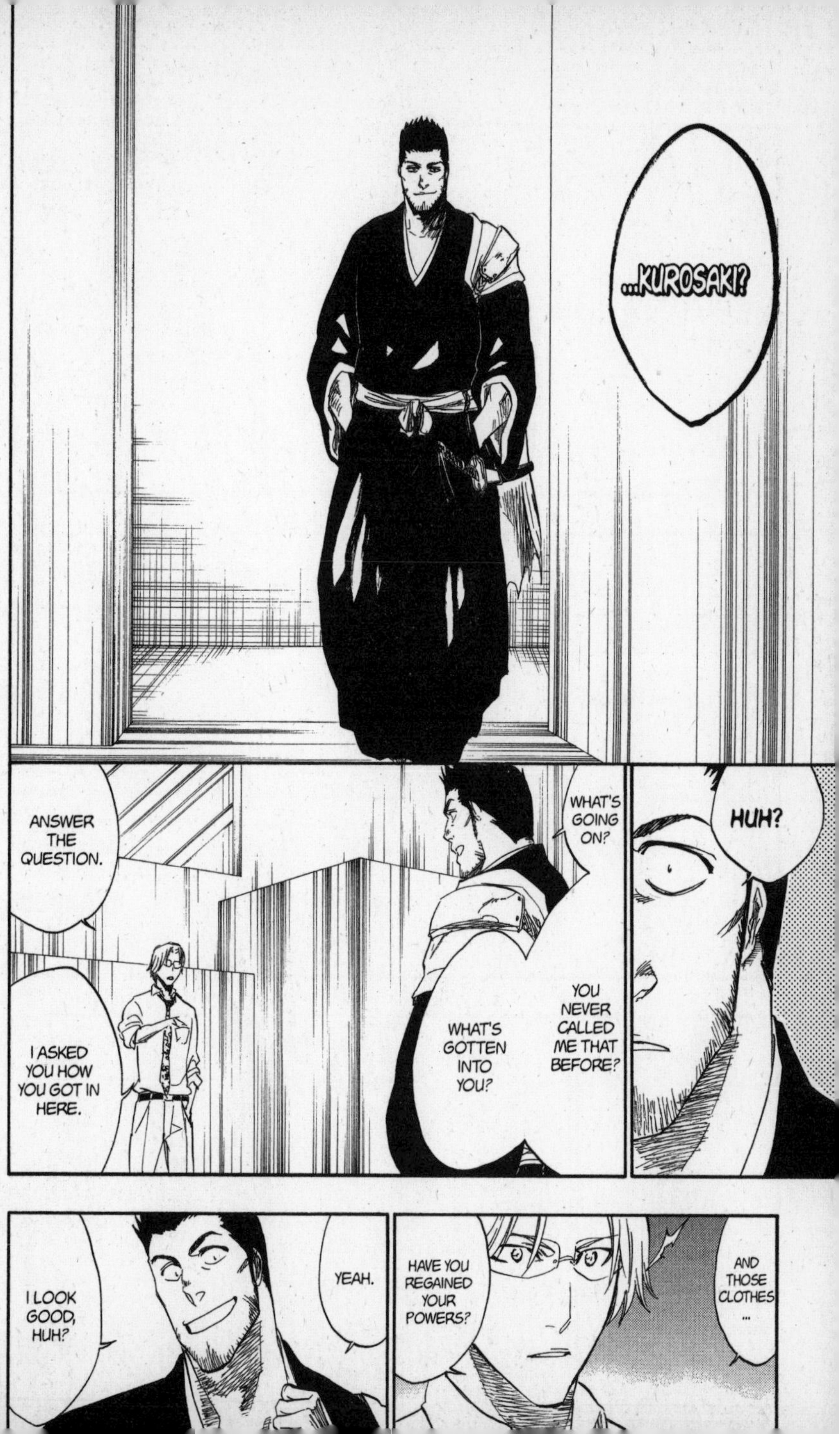
...KUROSAKI?
HUH?
WHAT'S GOING ON?
YOU NEVER CALLED ME THAT BEFORE?
WHAT'S GOTTEN INTO YOU?
ANSWER THE QUESTION.
I ASKED YOU HOW YOU GOT IN HERE.
AND THOSE CLOTHES...
HAVE YOU REGAINED YOUR POWERS?
YEAH.
I LOOK GOOD, HUH?

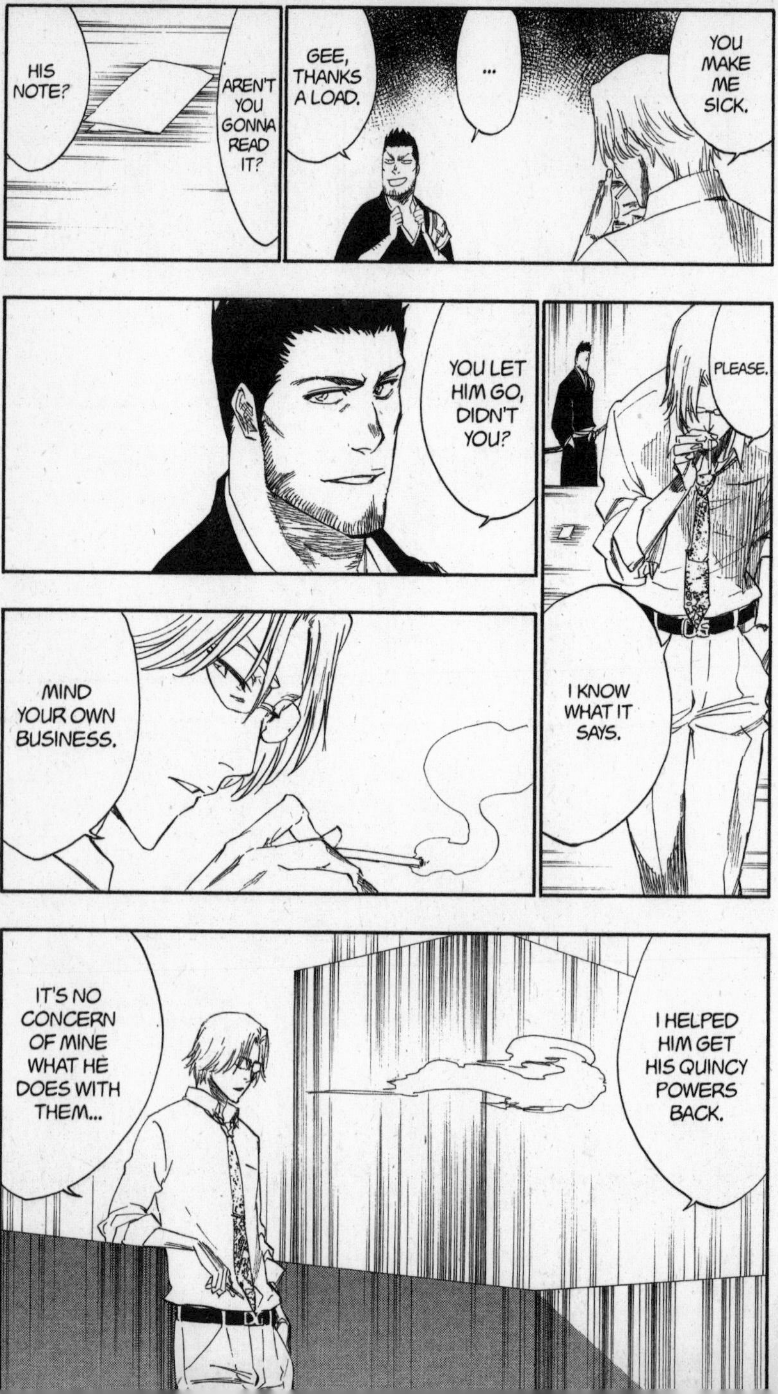
YOU MAKE ME SICK.
...
GEE, THANKS A LOAD.
AREN'T YOU GONNA READ IT?
HIS NOTE?
PLEASE.
I KNOW WHAT IT SAYS.
YOU LET HIM GO, DIDN'T YOU?
MIND YOUR OWN BUSINESS.
I HELPED HIM GET HIS QUINCY POWERS BACK.
IT'S NO CONCERN OF MINE WHAT HE DOES WITH THEM...

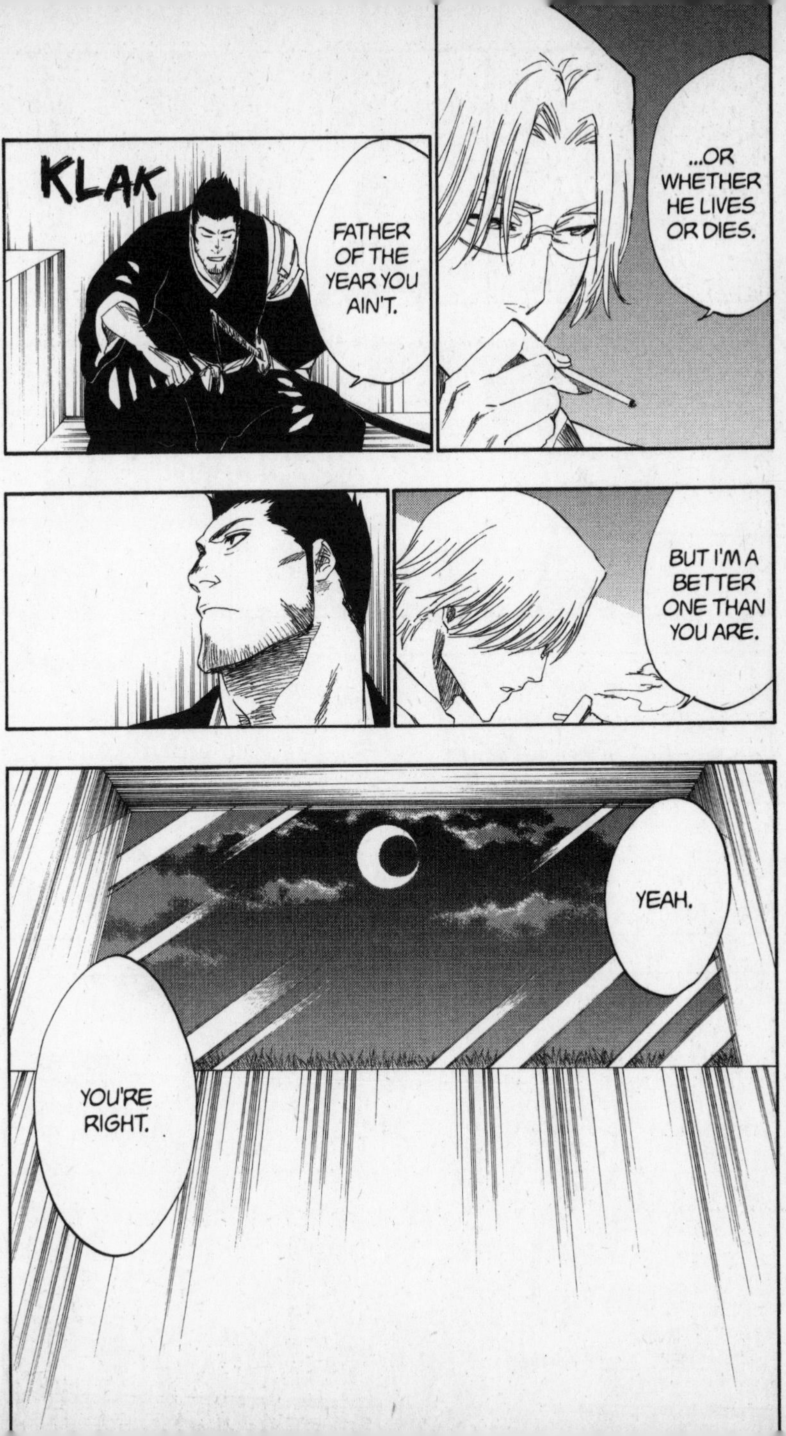
...OR WHETHER HE LIVES OR DIES.
KLAK
FATHER OF THE YEAR YOU AIN'T.
BUT I'M A BETTER ONE THAN YOU ARE.
YEAH.
YOU'RE RIGHT.

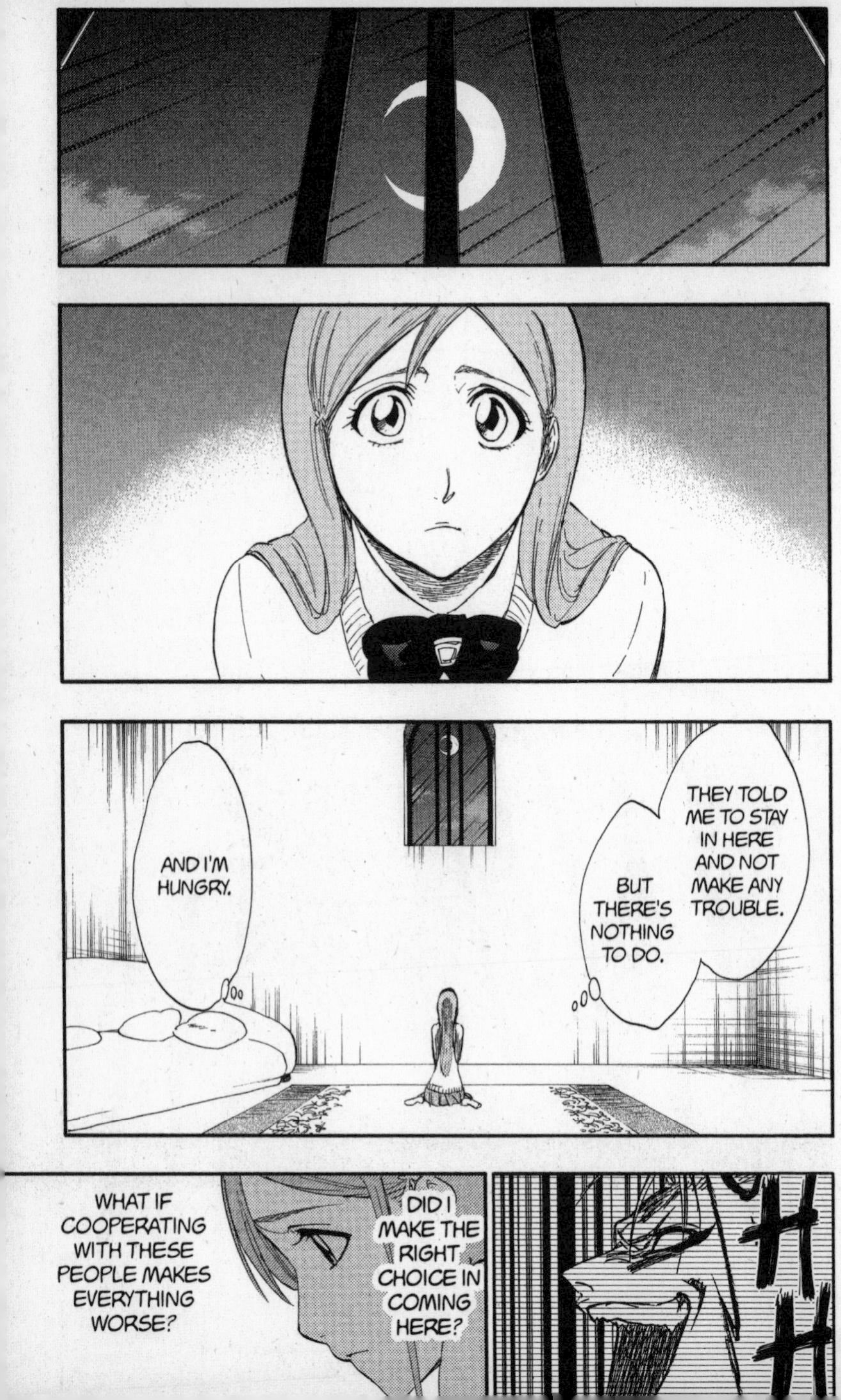
THEY TOLD ME TO STAY IN HERE AND NOT MAKE ANY TROUBLE.
BUT THERE'S NOTHING TO DO.
AND I'M HUNGRY.
DID I MAKE THE RIGHT CHOICE IN COMING HERE?
WHAT IF COOPERATING WITH THESE PEOPLE MAKES EVERYTHING WORSE?

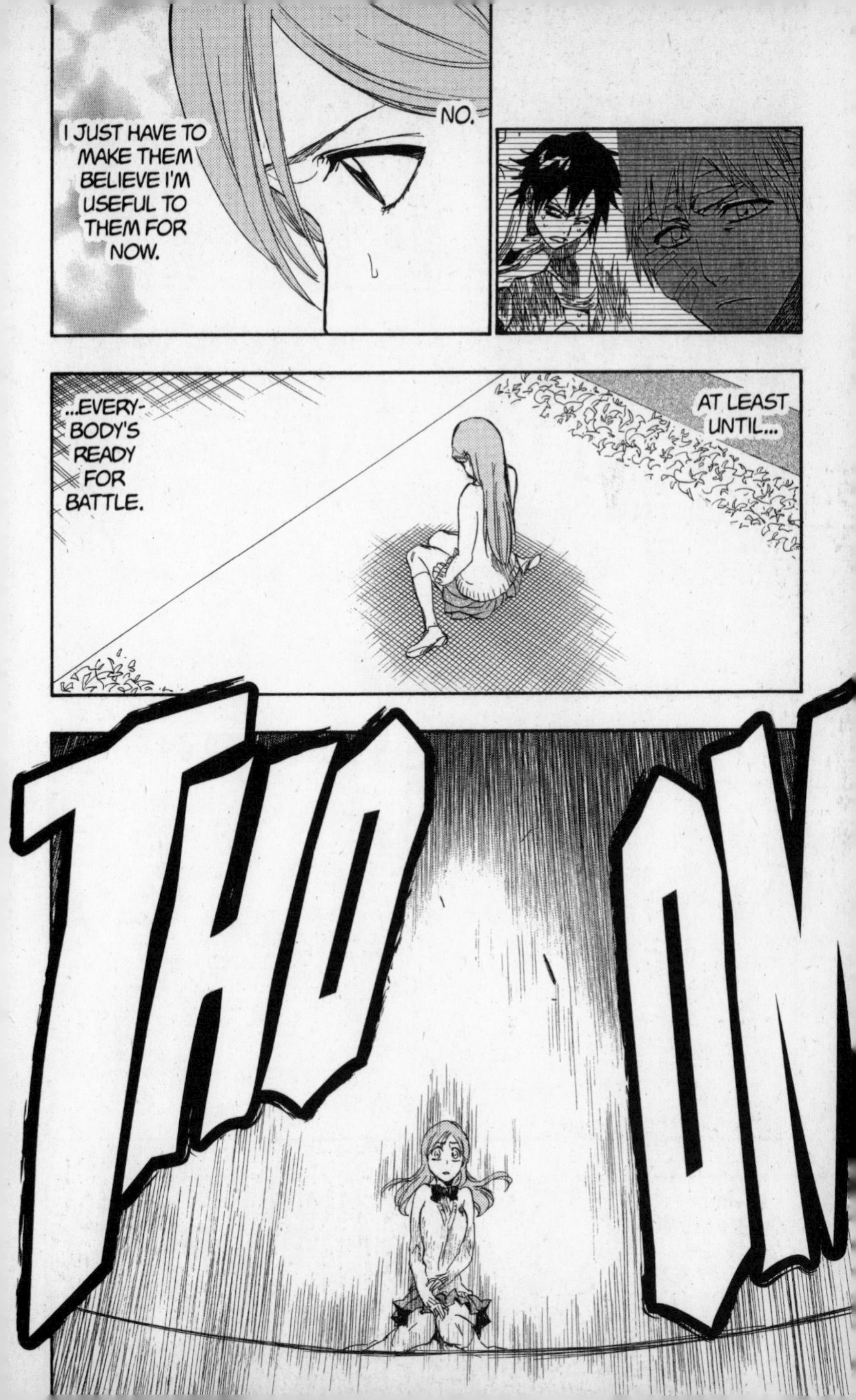
NO.
I JUST HAVE TO MAKE THEM BELIEVE I'M USEFUL TO THEM FOR NOW.
AT LEAST UNTIL...
...EVERY-BODY'S READY FOR BATTLE.
THOOM

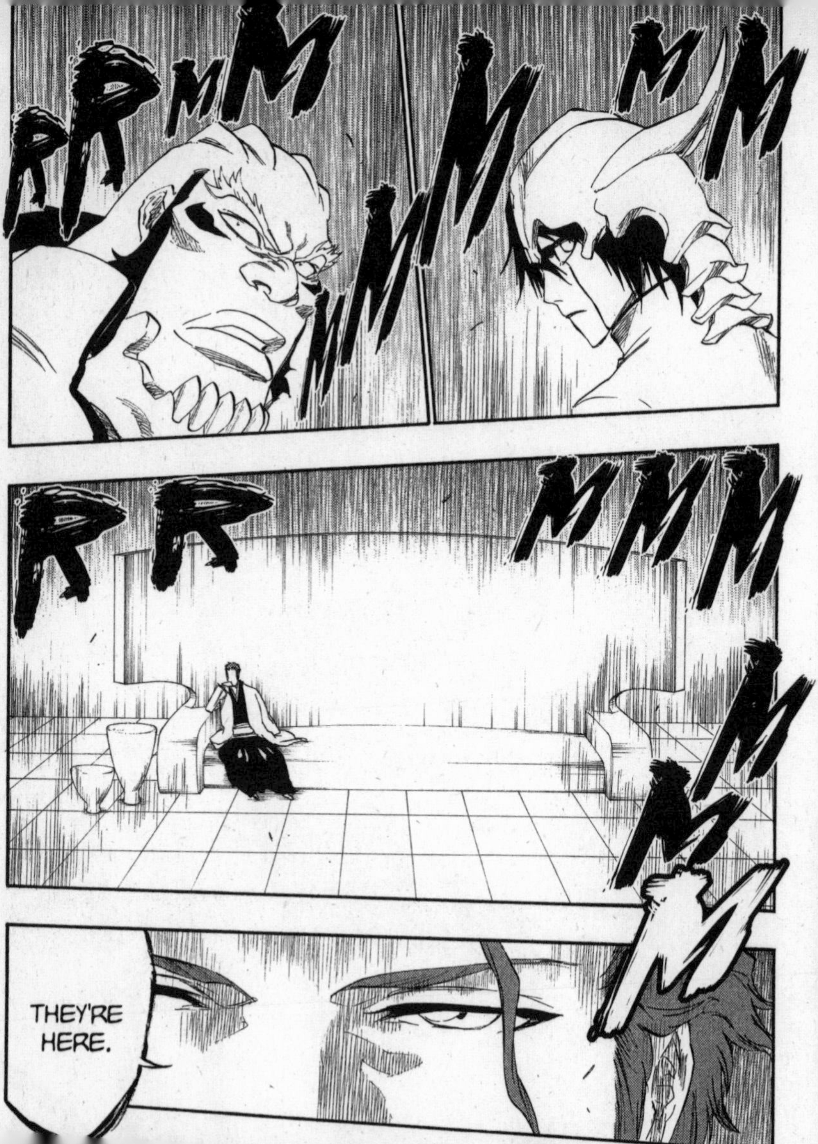
RRMMMMMMMM
RRMMMMMMM
THEY'RE HERE.

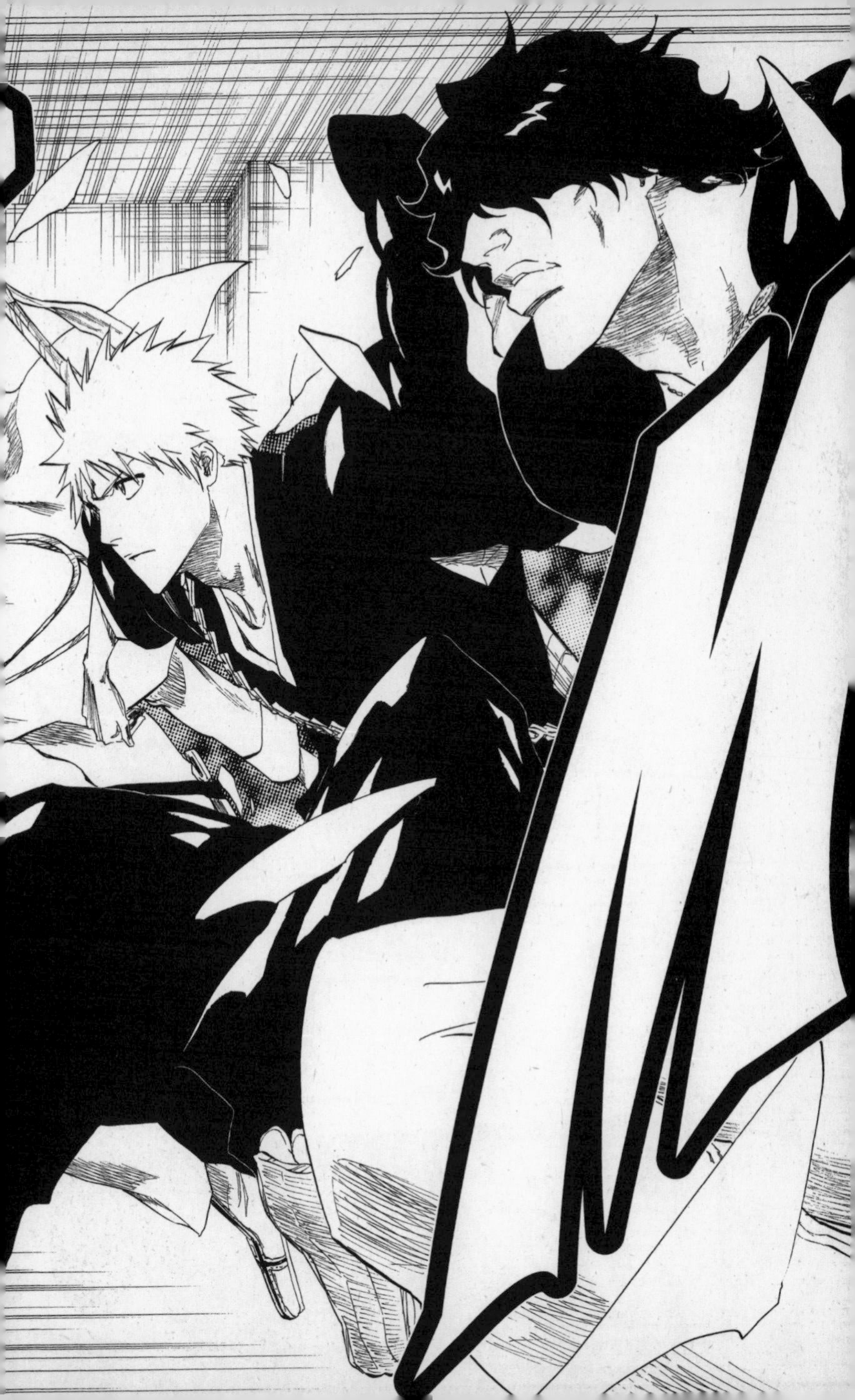

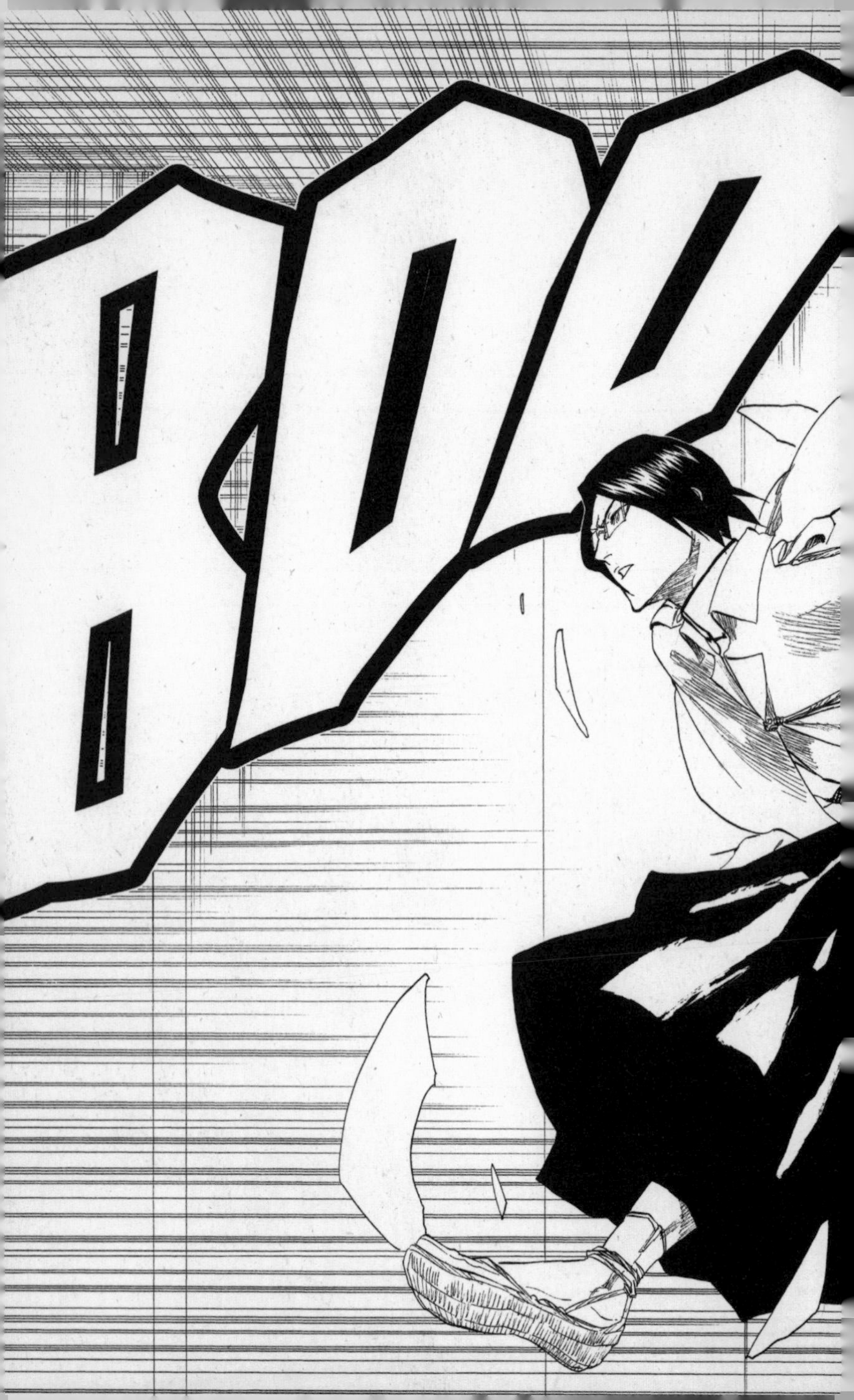

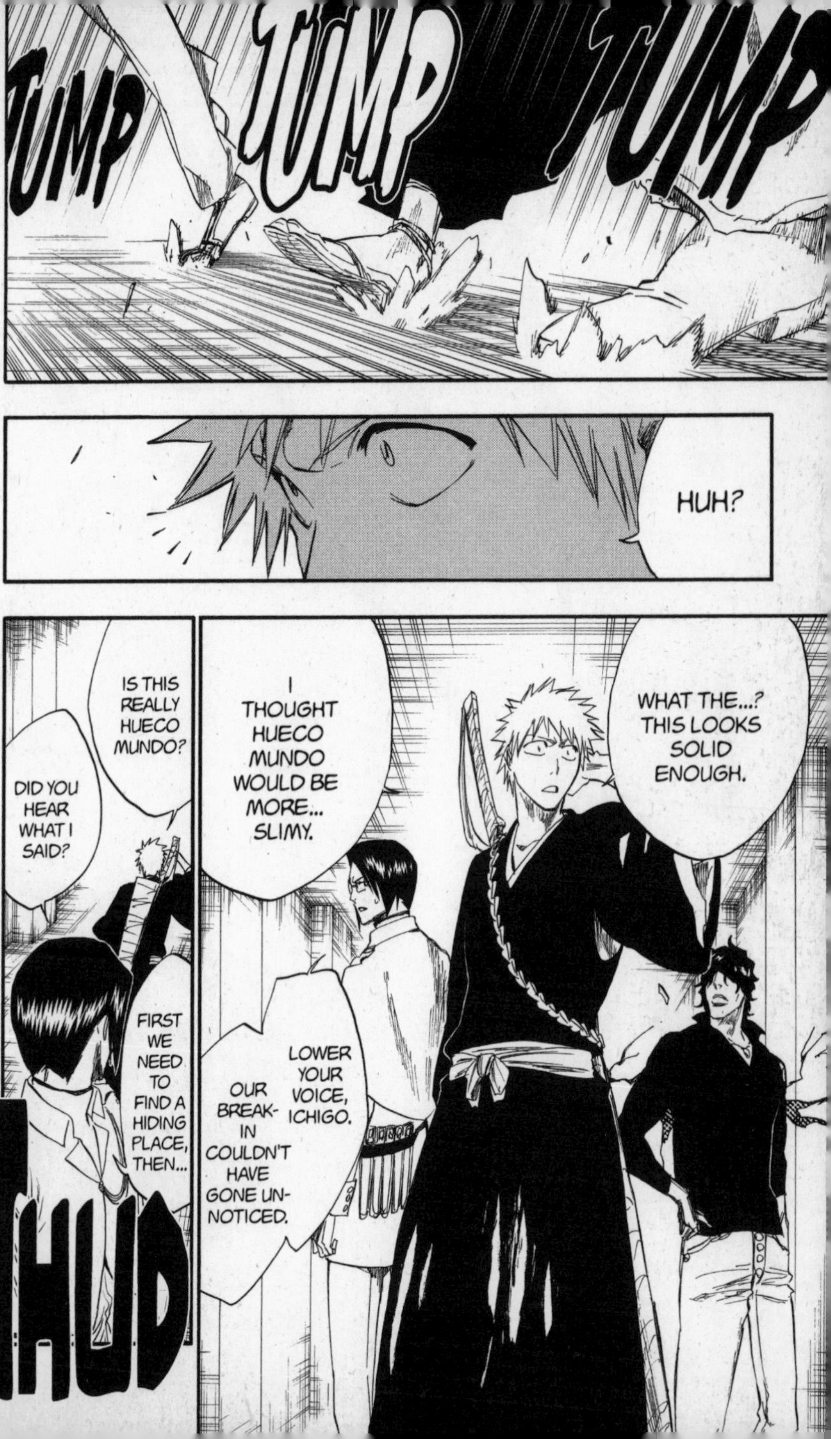
TUMP
TUMP
TUMP
HUH?
WHAT THE...? THIS LOOKS SOLID ENOUGH.
I THOUGHT HUECO MUNDO WOULD BE MORE... SLIMY.
LOWER YOUR VOICE, ICHIGO.
OUR BREAK-IN COULDN'T HAVE GONE UN-NOTICED.
IS THIS REALLY HUECO MUNDO?
DID YOU HEAR WHAT I SAID?
FIRST WE NEED TO FIND A HIDING PLACE, THEN...
THUD

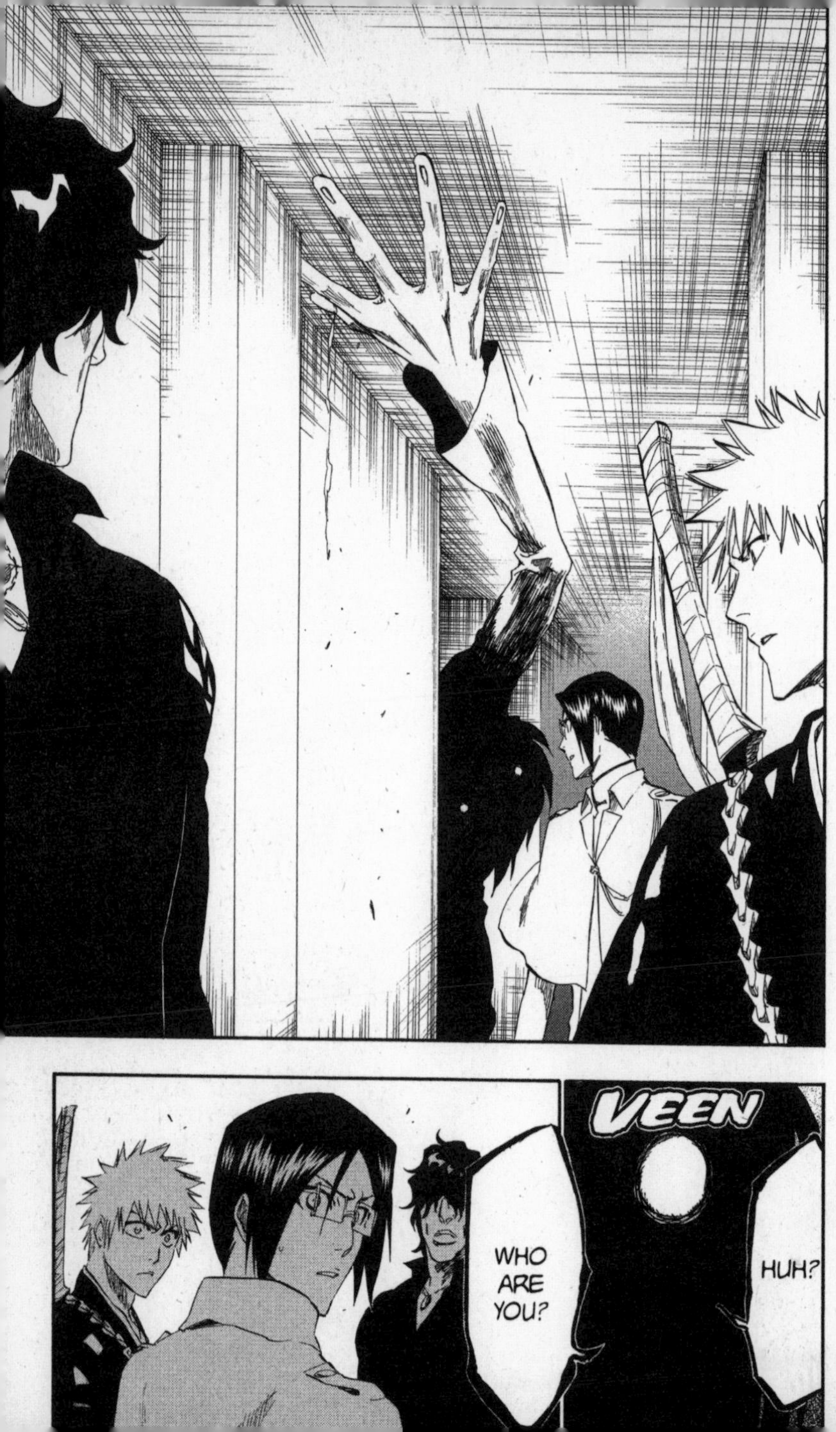
VEEN
HUH?
WHO ARE YOU?

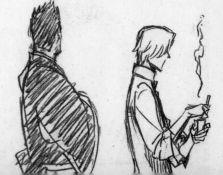

NO SMOKING

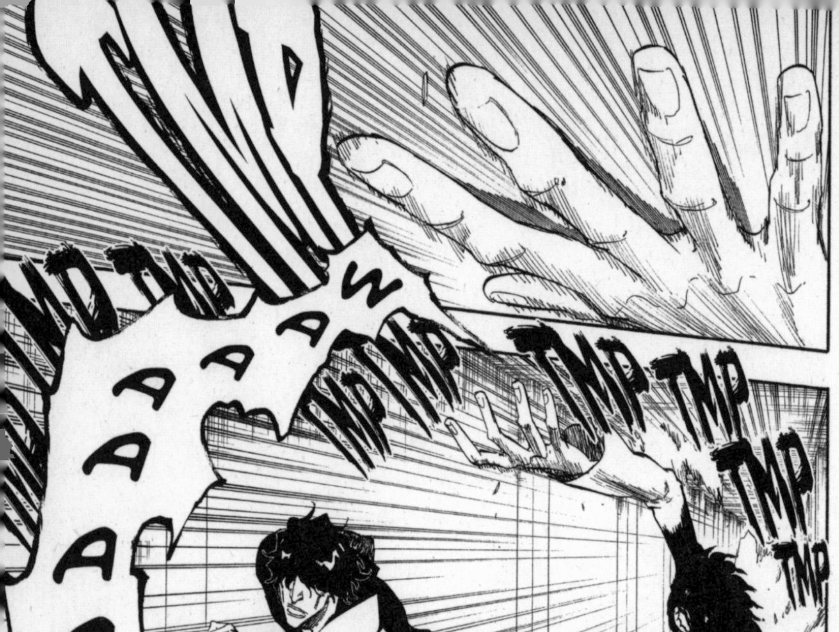
WAAAAAAAH!!
TMP TMP
TMP TMP
TMP TMP

242. TWO MEN ARE BURNING

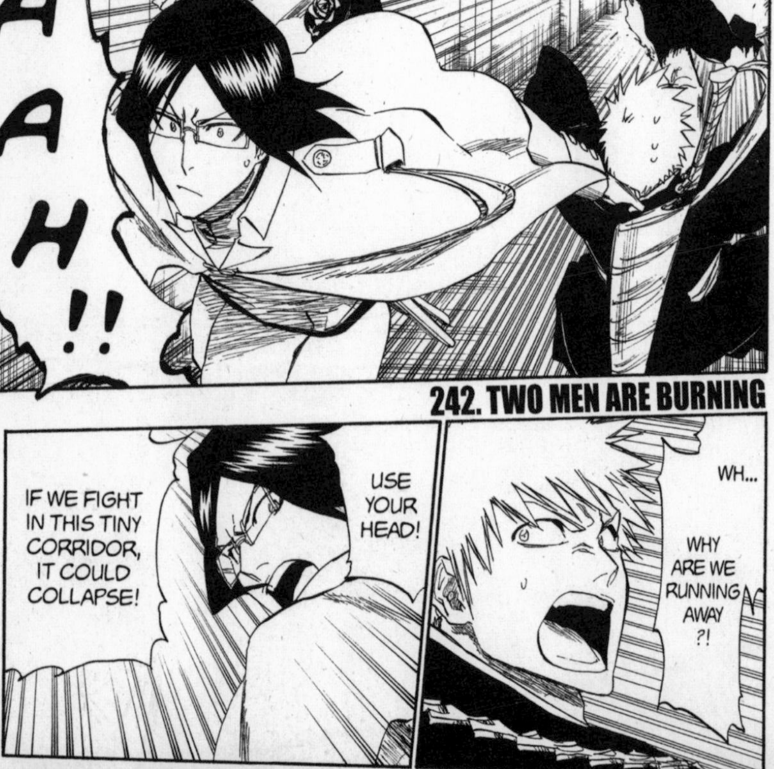
WH...
WHY ARE WE RUNNING AWAY?!
USE YOUR HEAD!
IF WE FIGHT IN THIS TINY CORRIDOR, IT COULD COLLAPSE!

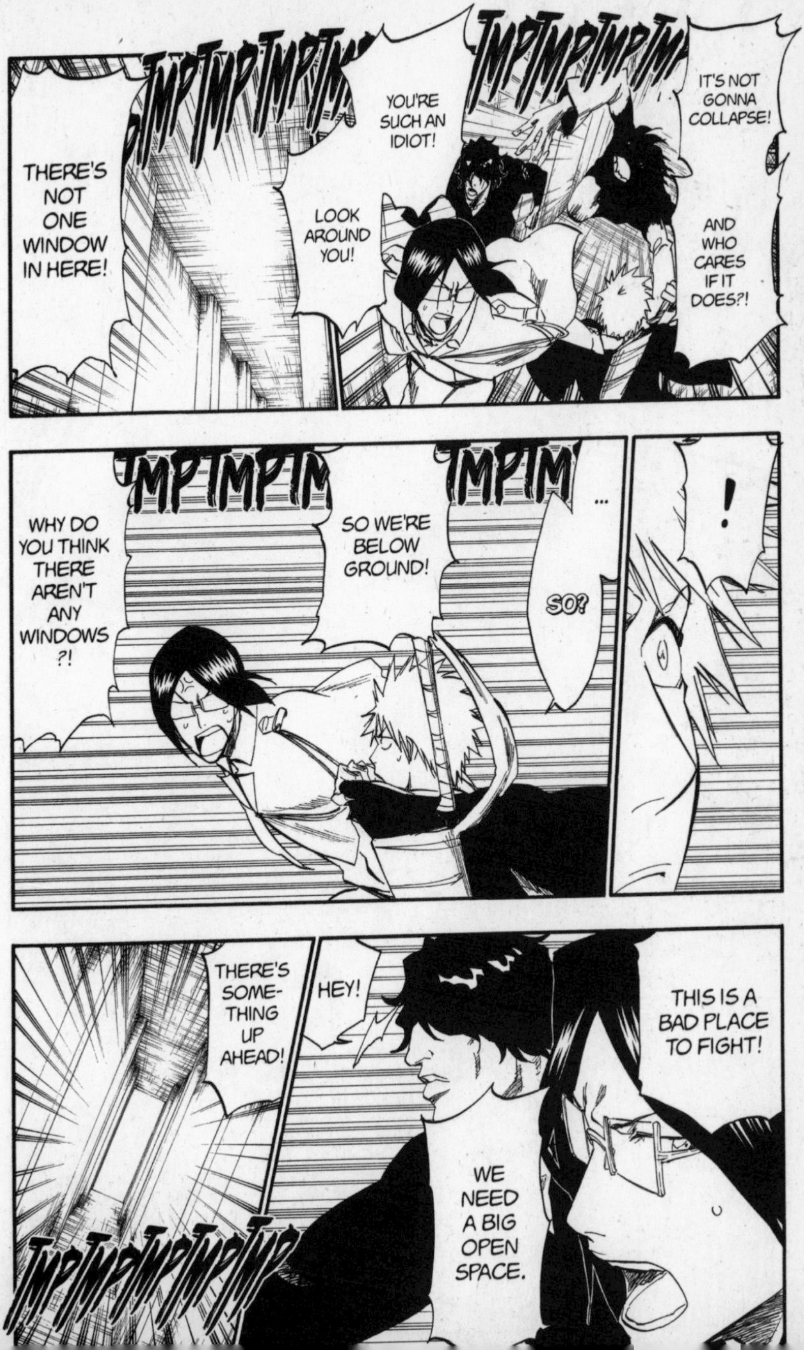
TMPTMPTMPTM
IT'S NOT GONNA COLLAPSE!
AND WHO CARES IF IT DOES?!
YOU'RE SUCH AN IDIOT!
LOOK AROUND YOU!
THERE'S NOT ONE WINDOW IN HERE!
TMPTMPTMPTM
!
TMPTM
...
SO?
SO WE'RE BELOW GROUND!
TMPTMPTM
WHY DO YOU THINK THERE AREN'T ANY WINDOWS?!
THIS IS A BAD PLACE TO FIGHT!
WE NEED A BIG OPEN SPACE.
HEY!
THERE'S SOME-THING UP AHEAD!
TMPTMPTMPTMPTMP

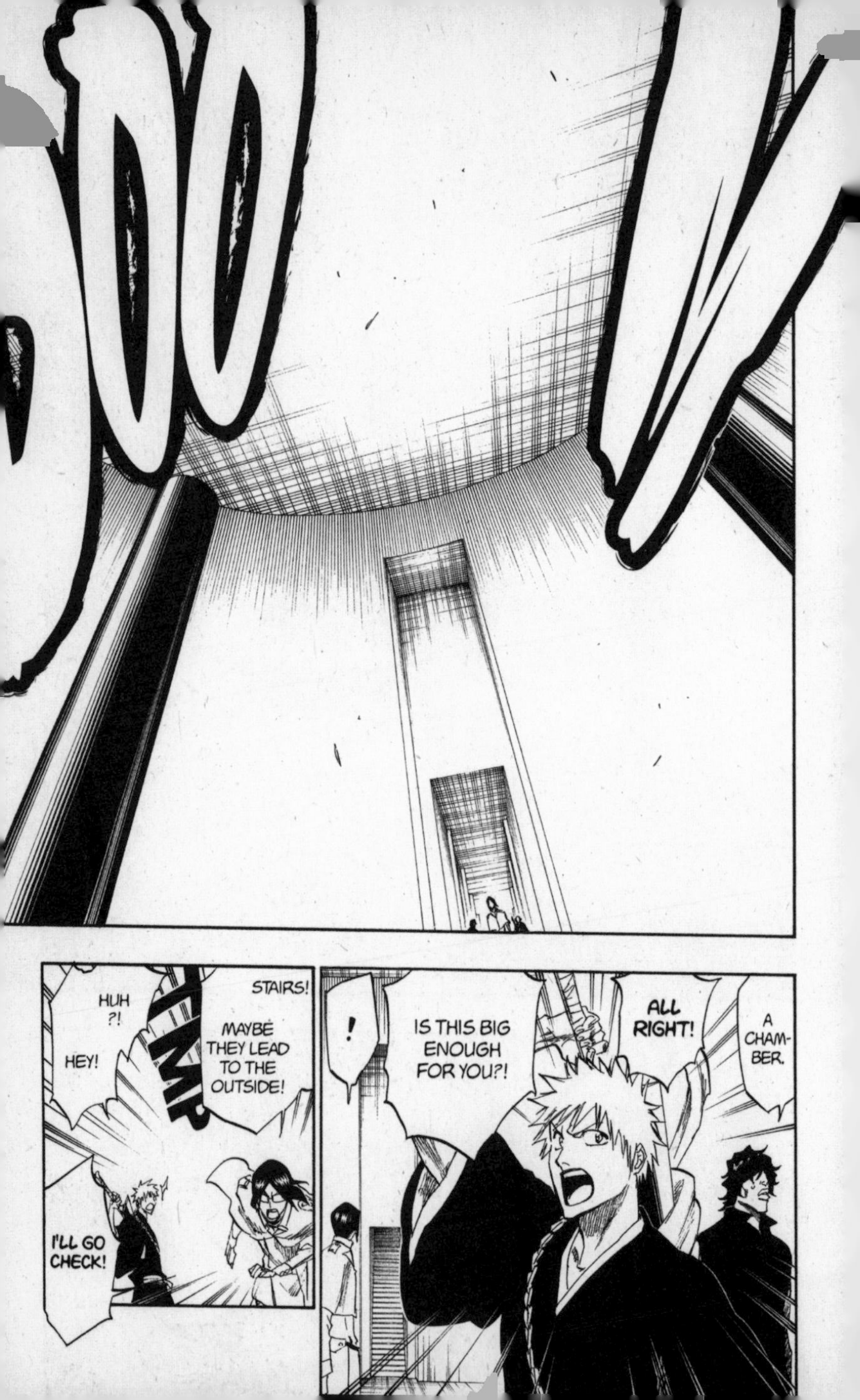
A CHAMBER.
ALL RIGHT!
IS THIS BIG ENOUGH FOR YOU?!
!
STAIRS!
MAYBE THEY LEAD TO THE OUTSIDE!
HUH ?!
HEY!
I'LL GO CHECK!

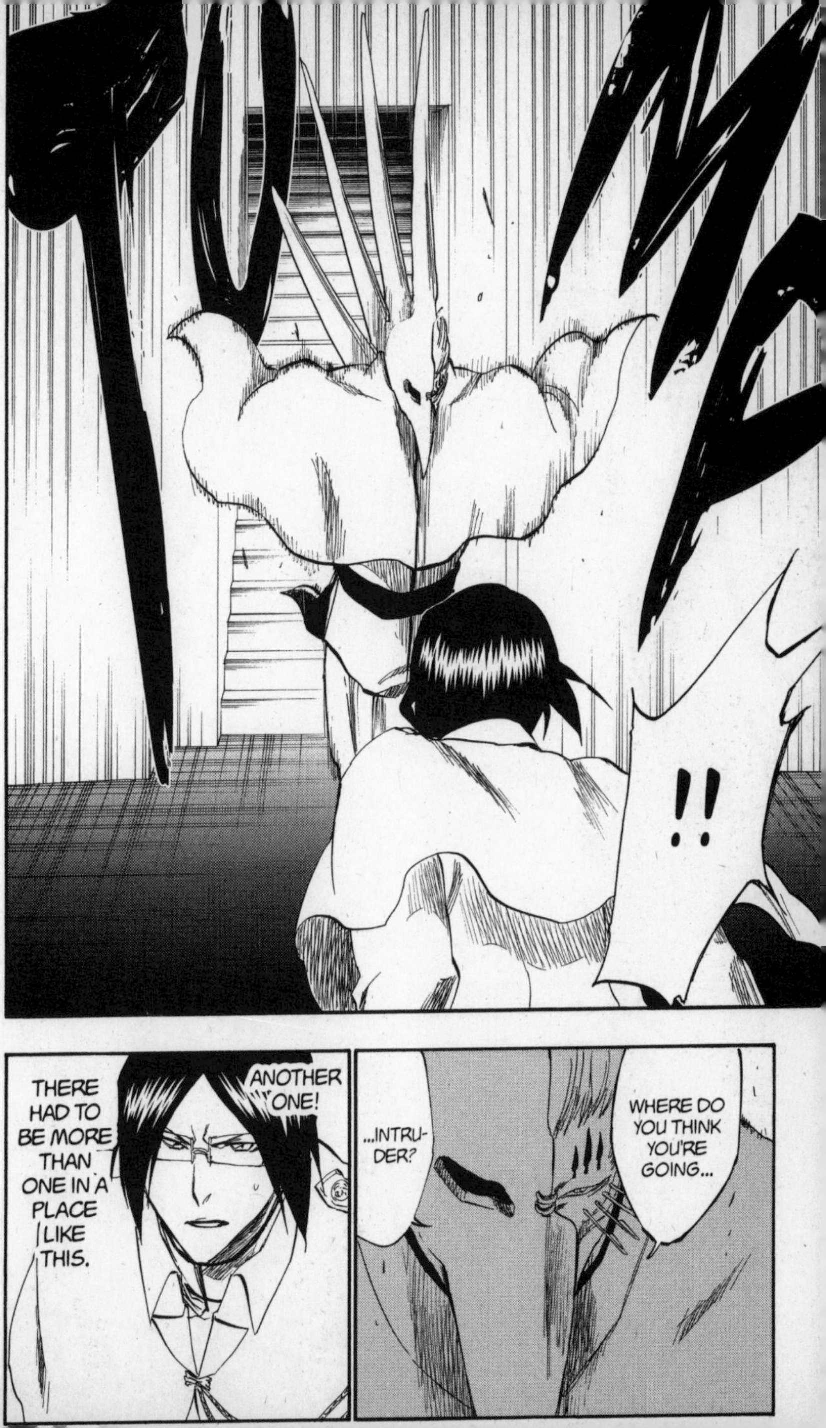
!!
WHERE DO YOU THINK YOU'RE GOING...
...INTRU-DER?
ANOTHER ONE!
THERE HAD TO BE MORE THAN ONE IN A PLACE LIKE THIS.

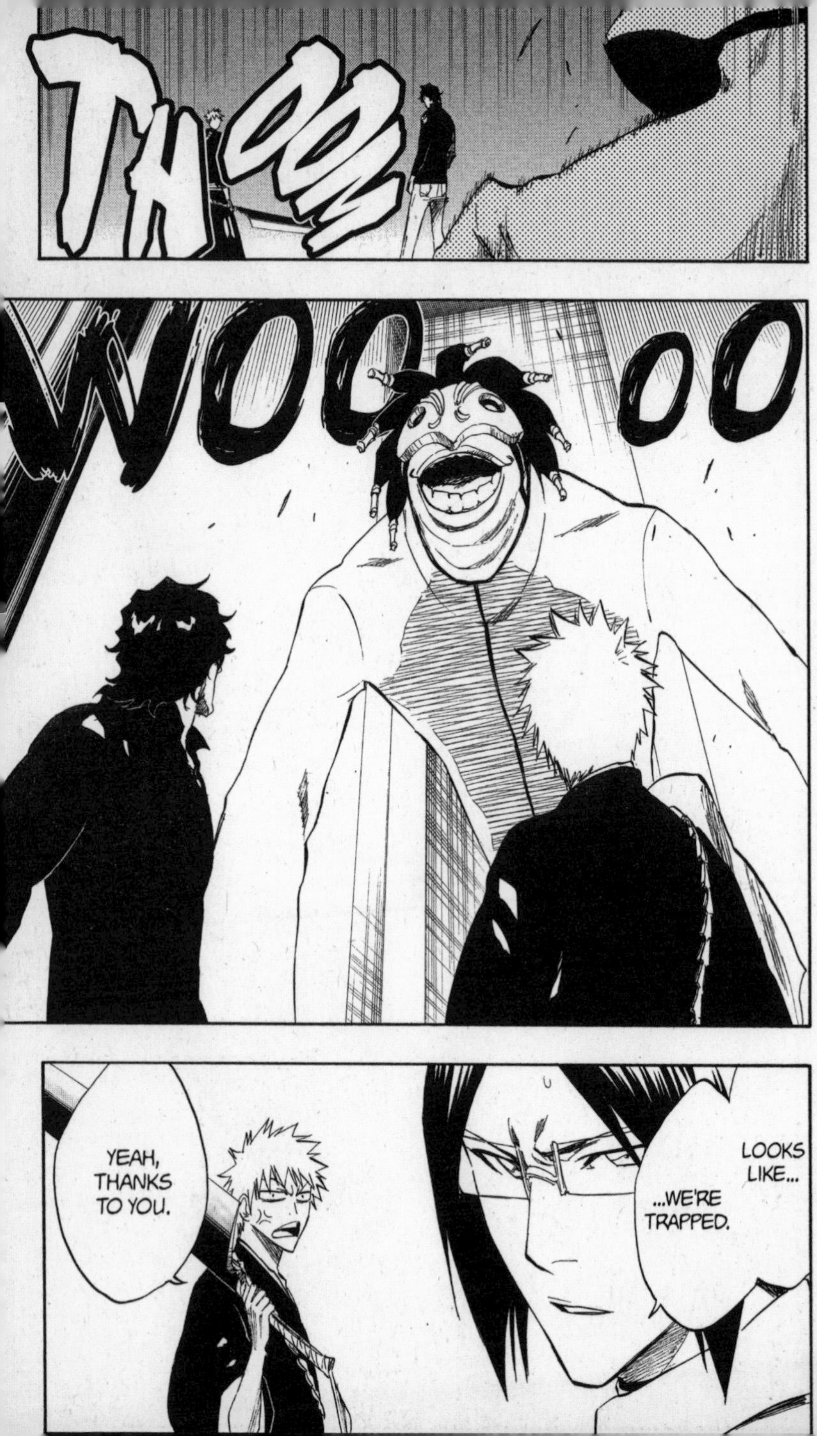
THOOM
WOOOOO
LOOKS LIKE...
...WE'RE TRAPPED.
YEAH, THANKS TO YOU.

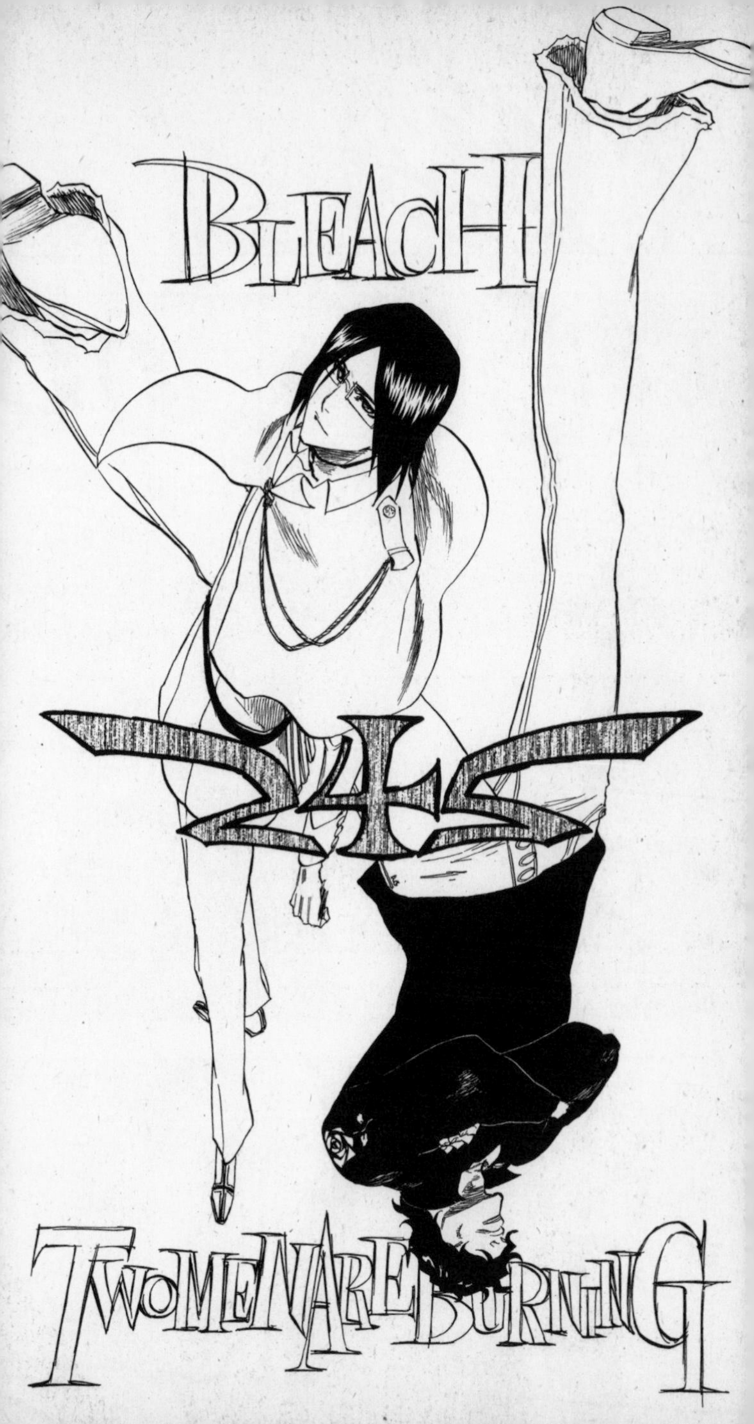
BLEACH
245
TWO MEN ARE BURNING

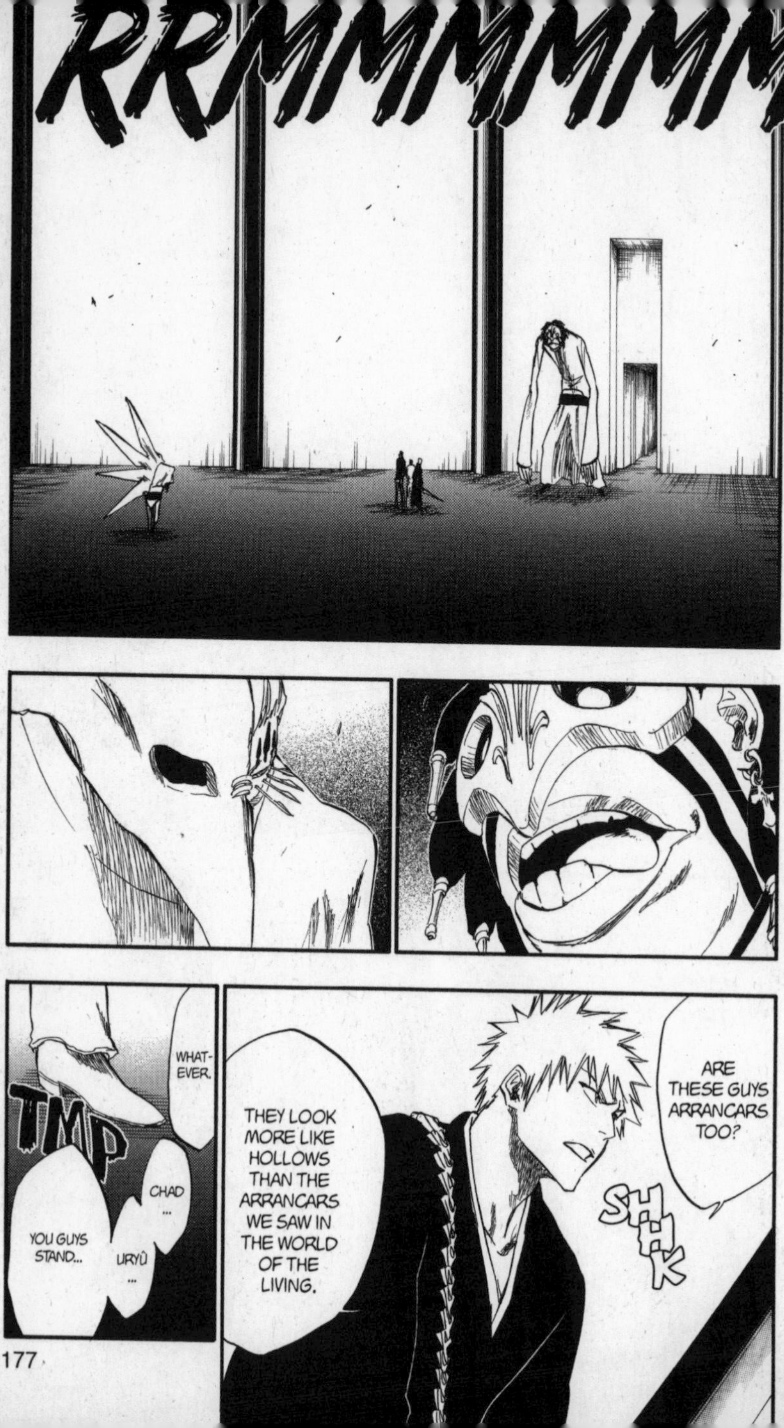
RRMMMMMM
ARE THESE GUYS ARRANCARS TOO?
SHHK
THEY LOOK MORE LIKE HOLLOWS THAN THE ARRANCARS WE SAW IN THE WORLD OF THE LIVING.
WHATEVER.
TMP
CHAD...
URYÛ...
YOU GUYS STAND...

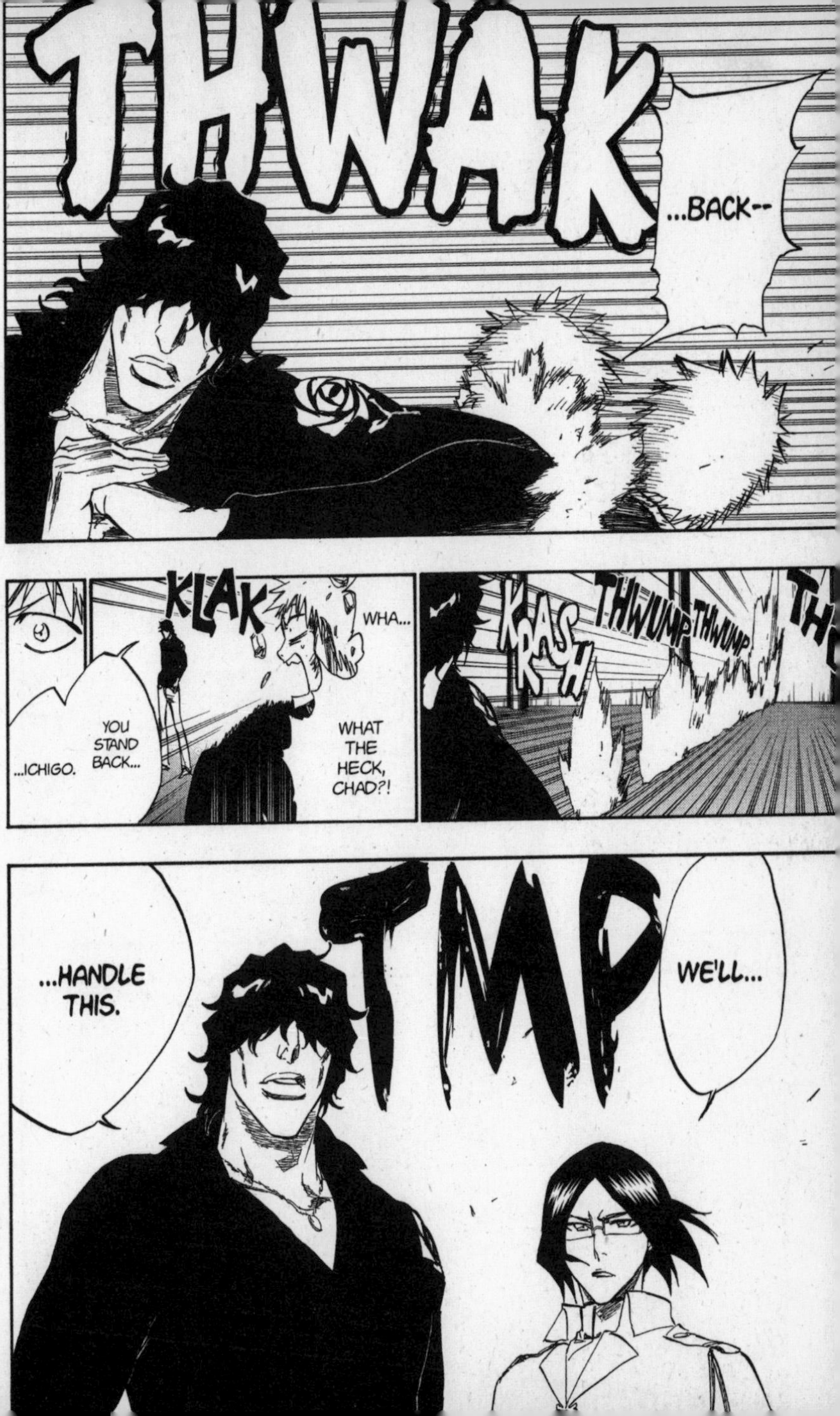
...BACK--
THWAK
KRASH
THWUMP
THWUMP
WHA...
WHAT THE HECK, CHAD?!
KLAK
YOU STAND BACK...
...ICHIGO.
WE'LL...
TMP
...HANDLE THIS.

READ THIS WAY

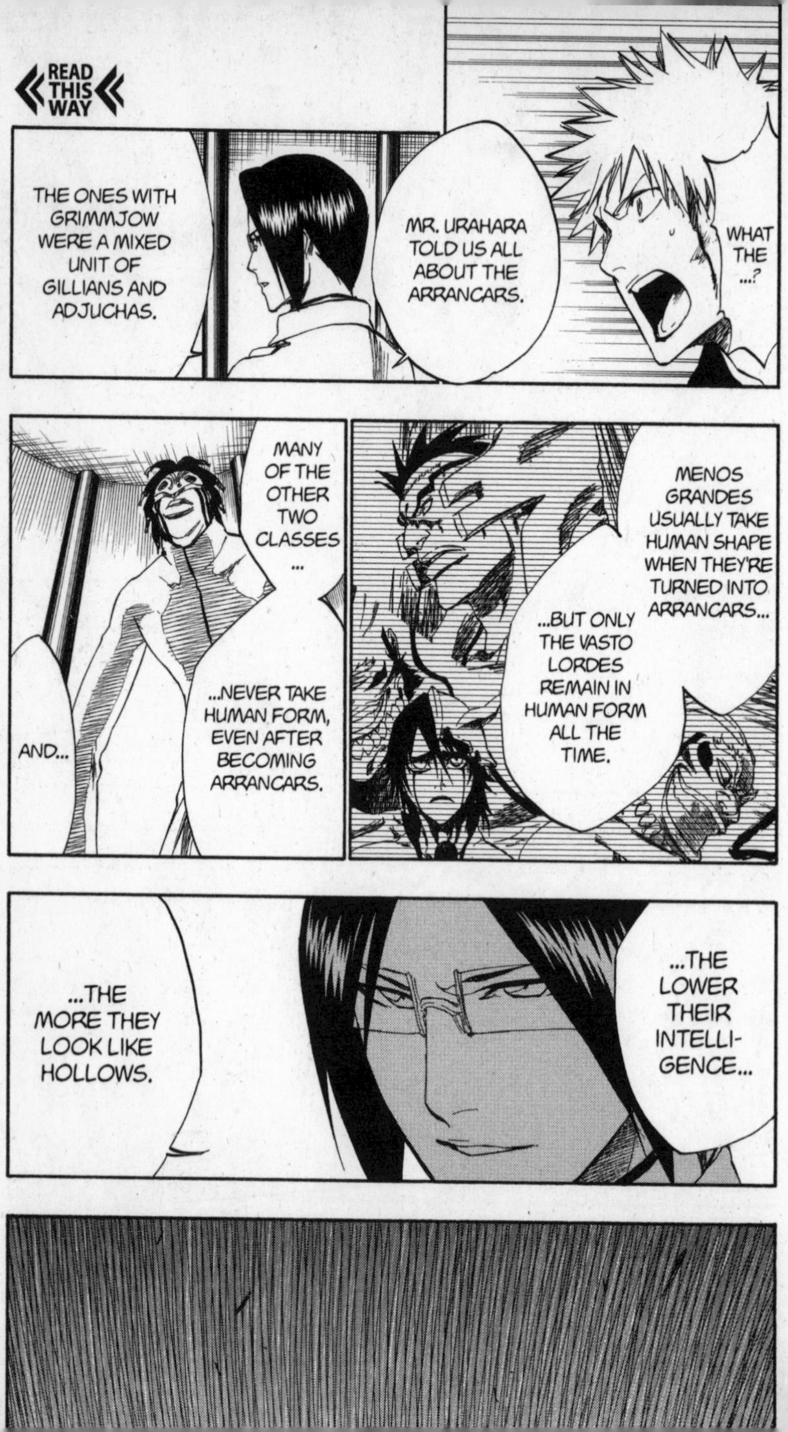
WHAT THE ...?
MR. URAHARA TOLD US ALL ABOUT THE ARRANCARS.
THE ONES WITH GRIMMJOW WERE A MIXED UNIT OF GILLIANS AND ADJUCHAS.
MENOS GRANDES USUALLY TAKE HUMAN SHAPE WHEN THEY'RE TURNED INTO ARRANCARS...
...BUT ONLY THE VASTO LORDES REMAIN IN HUMAN FORM ALL THE TIME.
MANY OF THE OTHER TWO CLASSES ...
...NEVER TAKE HUMAN FORM, EVEN AFTER BECOMING ARRANCARS.
AND...
...THE LOWER THEIR INTELLI-GENCE...
...THE MORE THEY LOOK LIKE HOLLOWS.

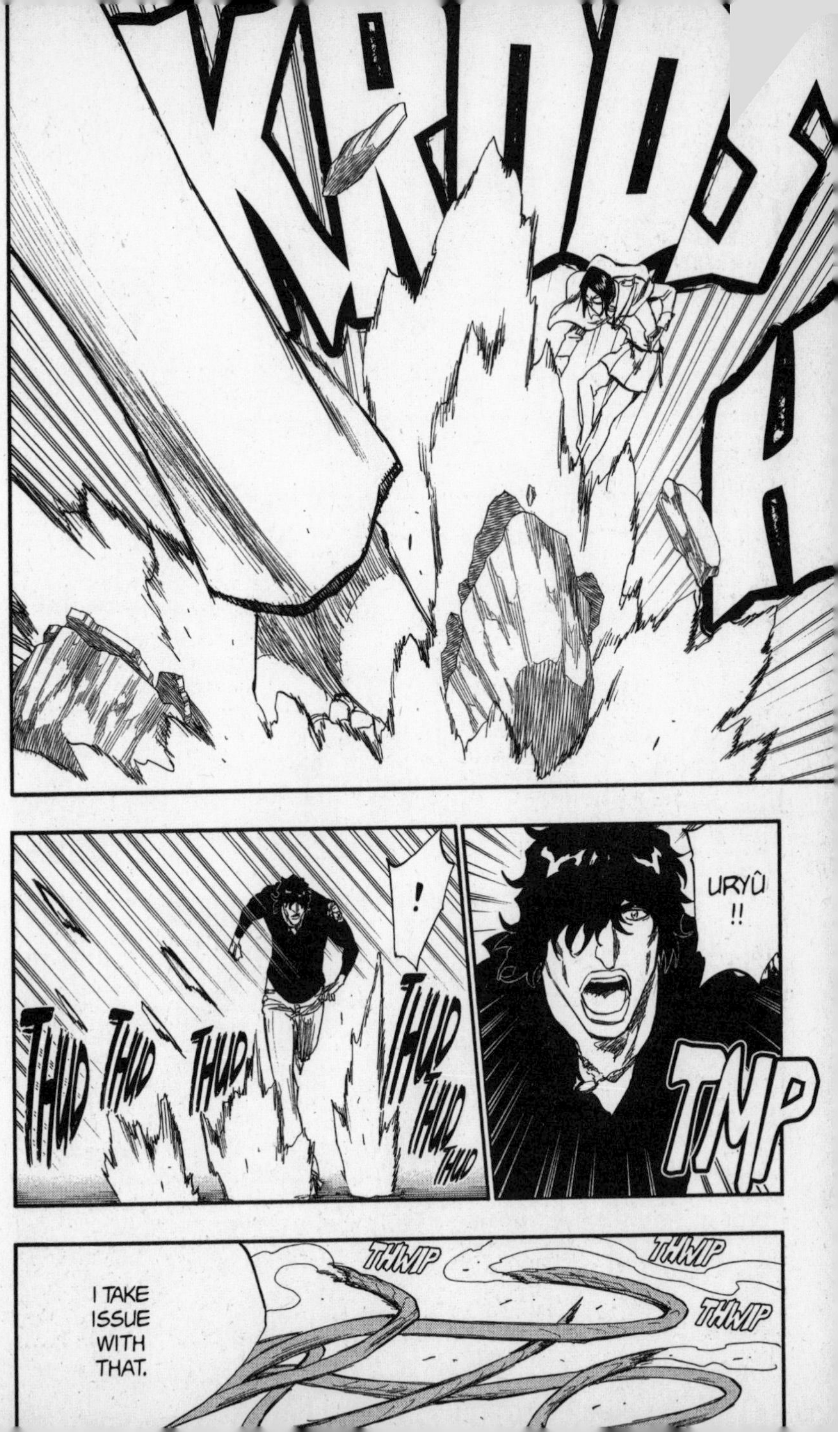
URYÛ !!
TMP
!
THUD THUD THUD THUD THUD THUD THUD
THWIP THWIP THWIP
I TAKE ISSUE WITH THAT.

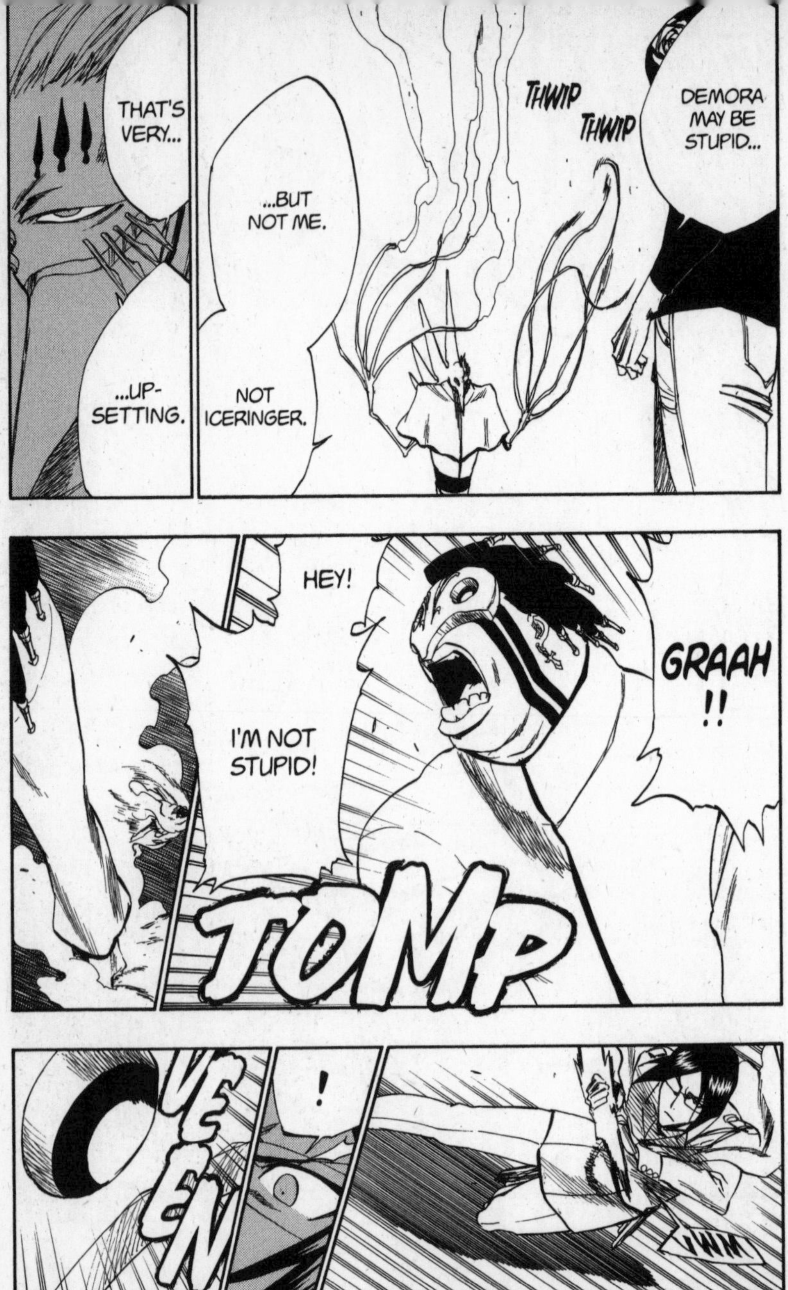

DEMORA MAY BE STUPID...
THWIP
THWIP
...BUT NOT ME.
NOT ICERINGER.
THAT'S VERY...
...UP-SETTING.
GRAAH!!
HEY!
I'M NOT STUPID!
TOMP
!
VEEN

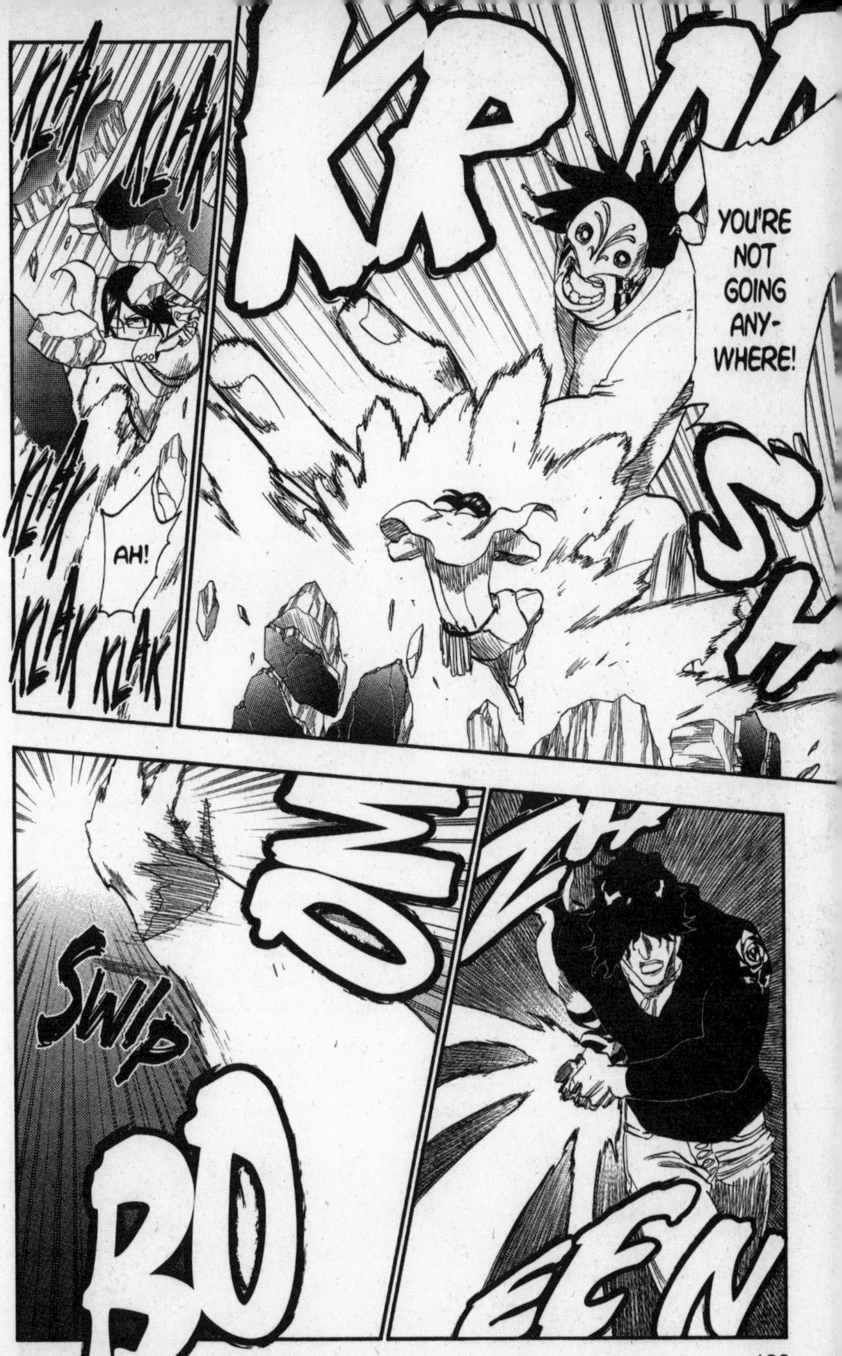
YOU'RE NOT GOING ANY-WHERE!
KLAK KLAK
KLAK KLAK
KLAK KLAK
AH!
SWIP

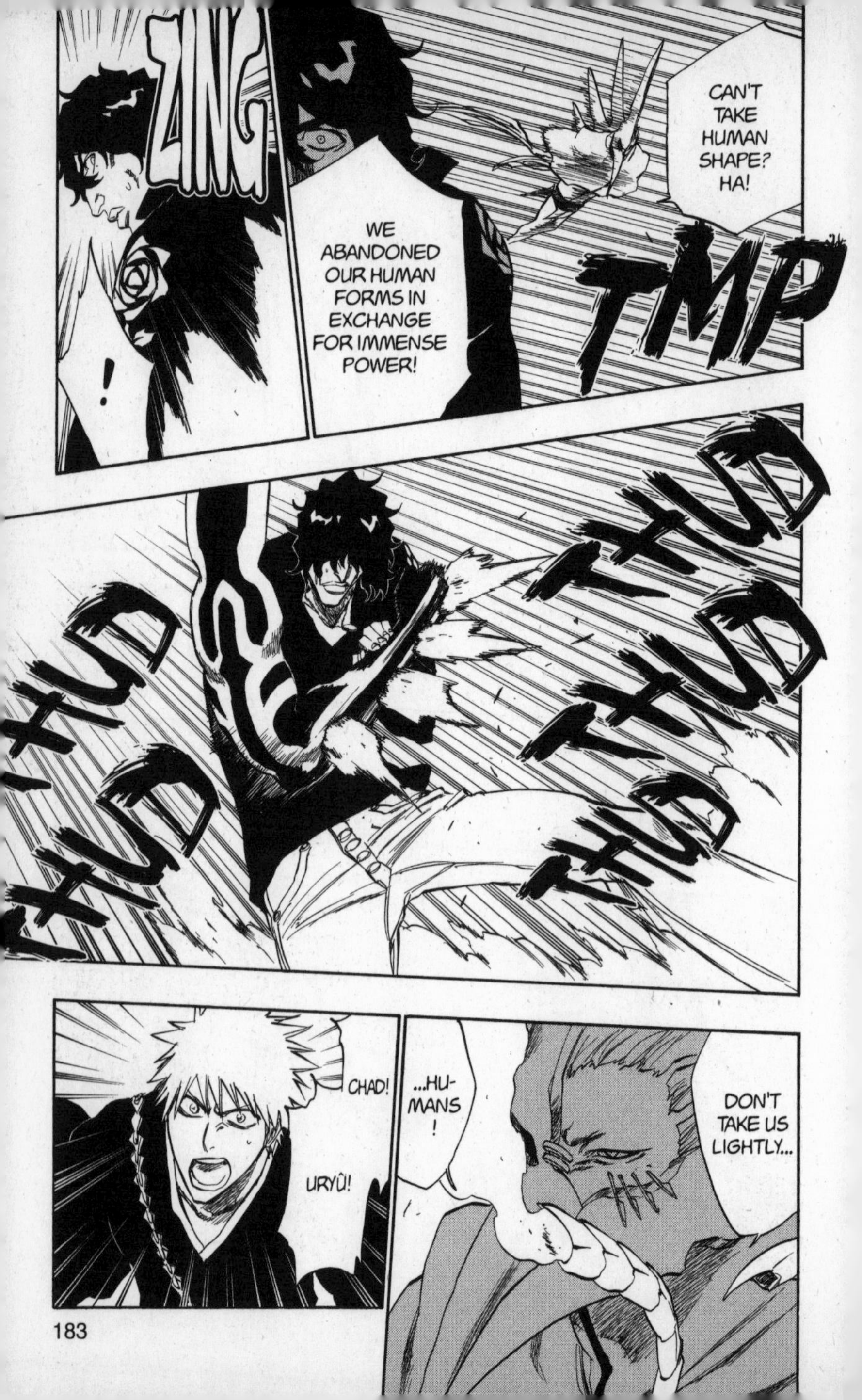
CAN'T TAKE HUMAN SHAPE? HA!
WE ABANDONED OUR HUMAN FORMS IN EXCHANGE FOR IMMENSE POWER!
TMP
ZING
!
THUD
THUD
THUD
DON'T TAKE US LIGHTLY...
...HU-MANS!
CHAD!
URYŪ!

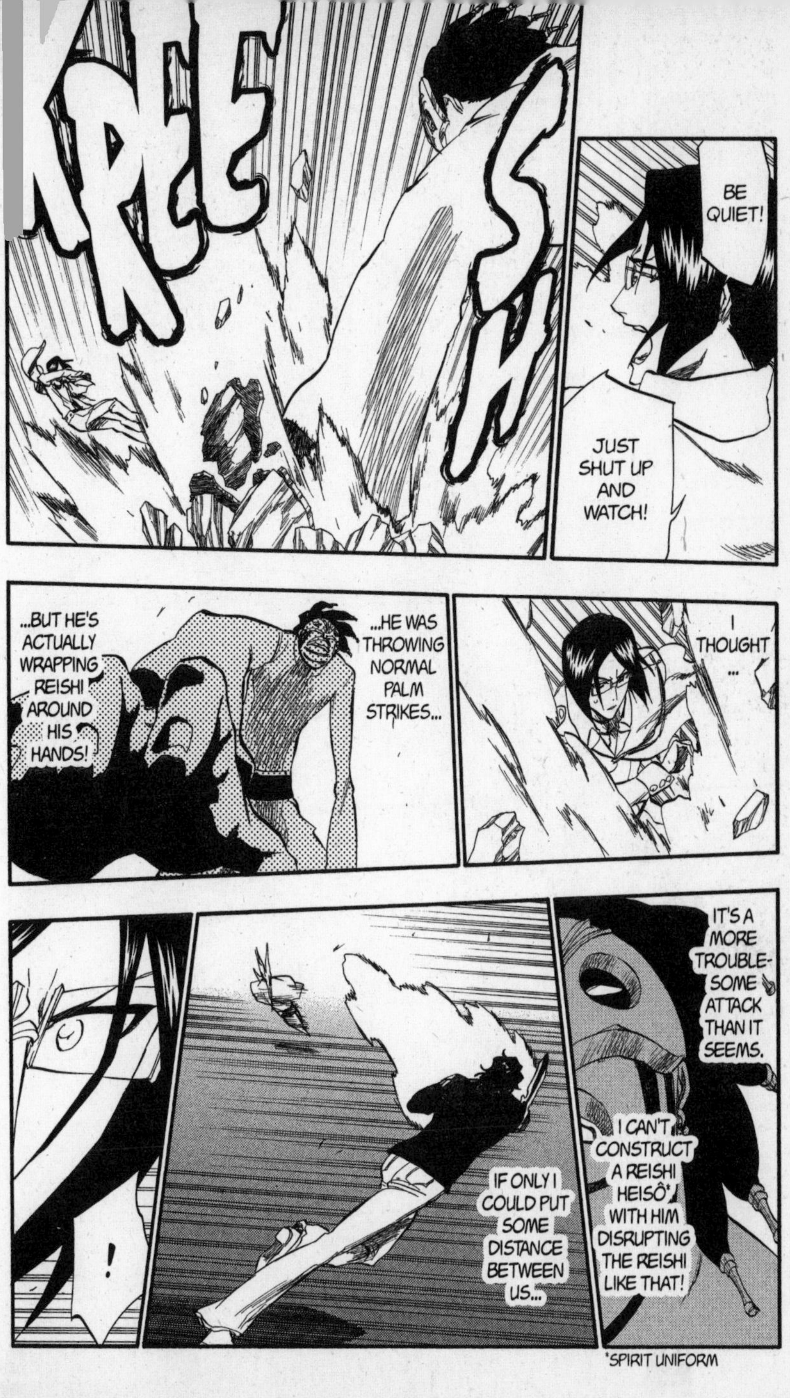
BE QUIET!
JUST SHUT UP AND WATCH!
I THOUGHT...
...HE WAS THROWING NORMAL PALM STRIKES...
...BUT HE'S ACTUALLY WRAPPING REISHI AROUND HIS HANDS!
IT'S A MORE TROUBLE-SOME ATTACK THAN IT SEEMS.
I CAN'T CONSTRUCT A REISHI HEISÔ* WITH HIM DISRUPTING THE REISHI LIKE THAT!
IF ONLY I COULD PUT SOME DISTANCE BETWEEN US...
!

*SPIRIT UNIFORM

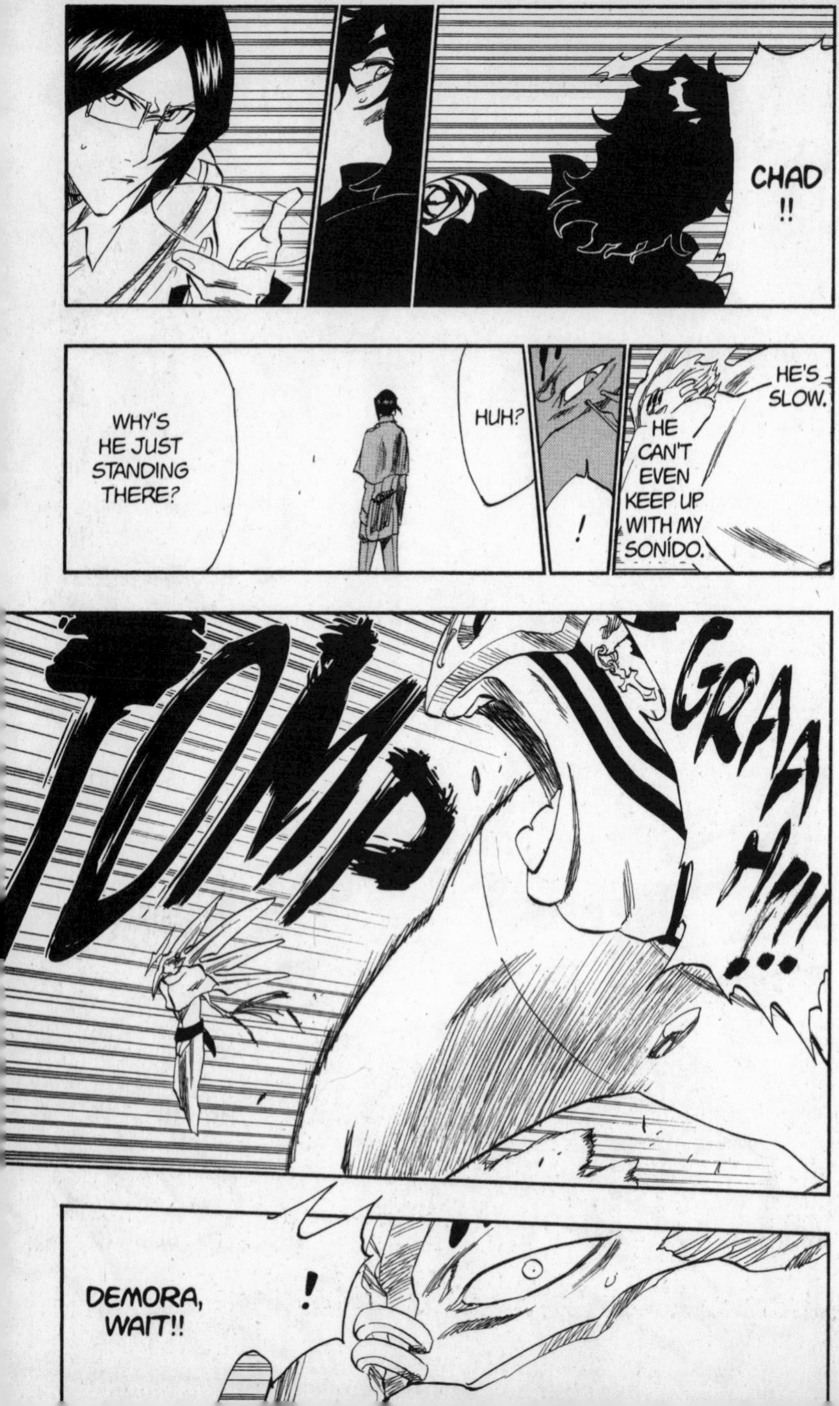
CHAD !!
HE'S SLOW.
HE CAN'T EVEN KEEP UP WITH MY SONÍDO.
!
HUH?
WHY'S HE JUST STANDING THERE?
GRAAH!!!!
DOMP
!
DEMORA, WAIT!!

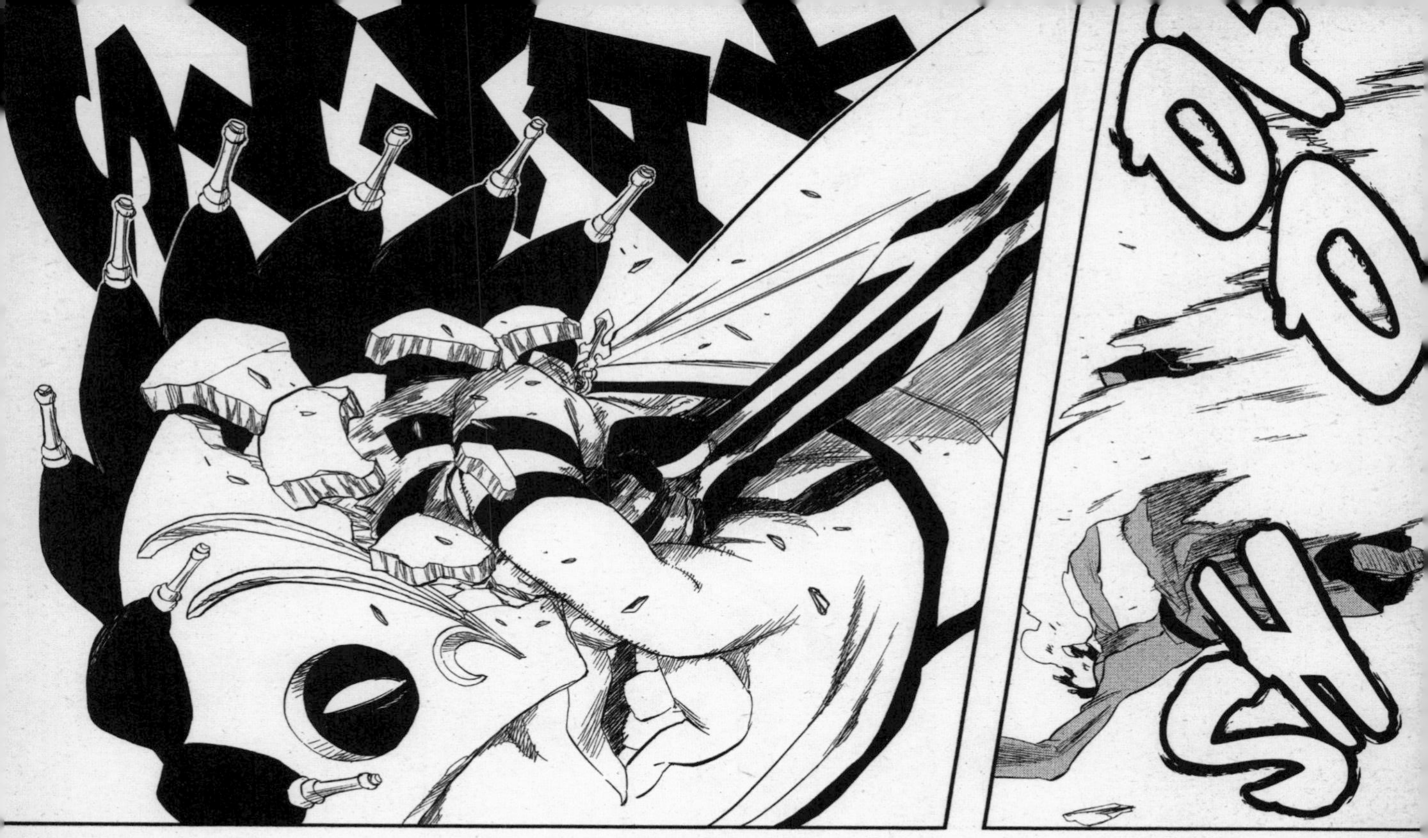

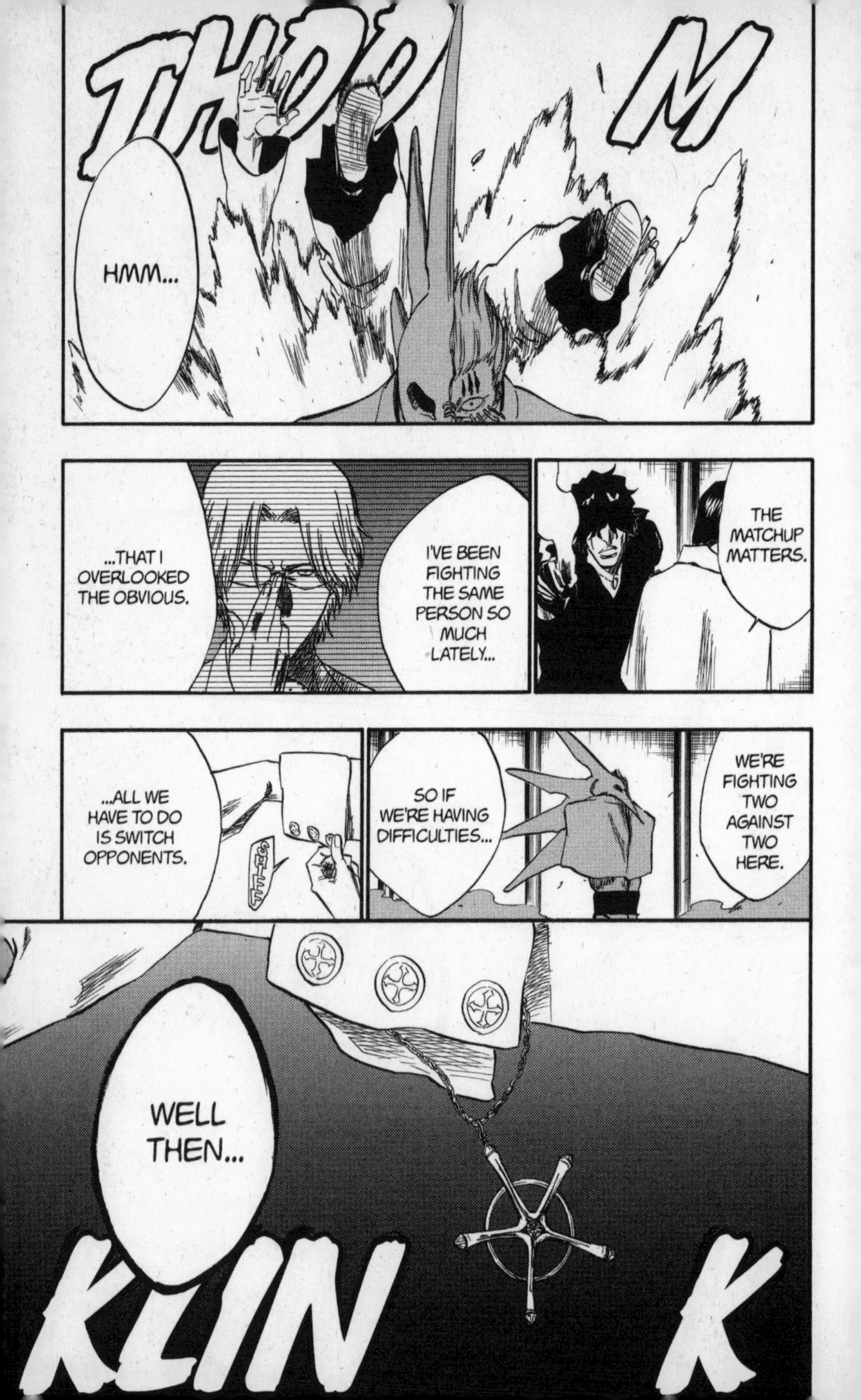
THOOM
HMM...
THE MATCHUP MATTERS.
I'VE BEEN FIGHTING THE SAME PERSON SO MUCH LATELY...
...THAT I OVERLOOKED THE OBVIOUS.
WE'RE FIGHTING TWO AGAINST TWO HERE.
SO IF WE'RE HAVING DIFFICULTIES...
...ALL WE HAVE TO DO IS SWITCH OPPONENTS.
WELL THEN...
KLINK

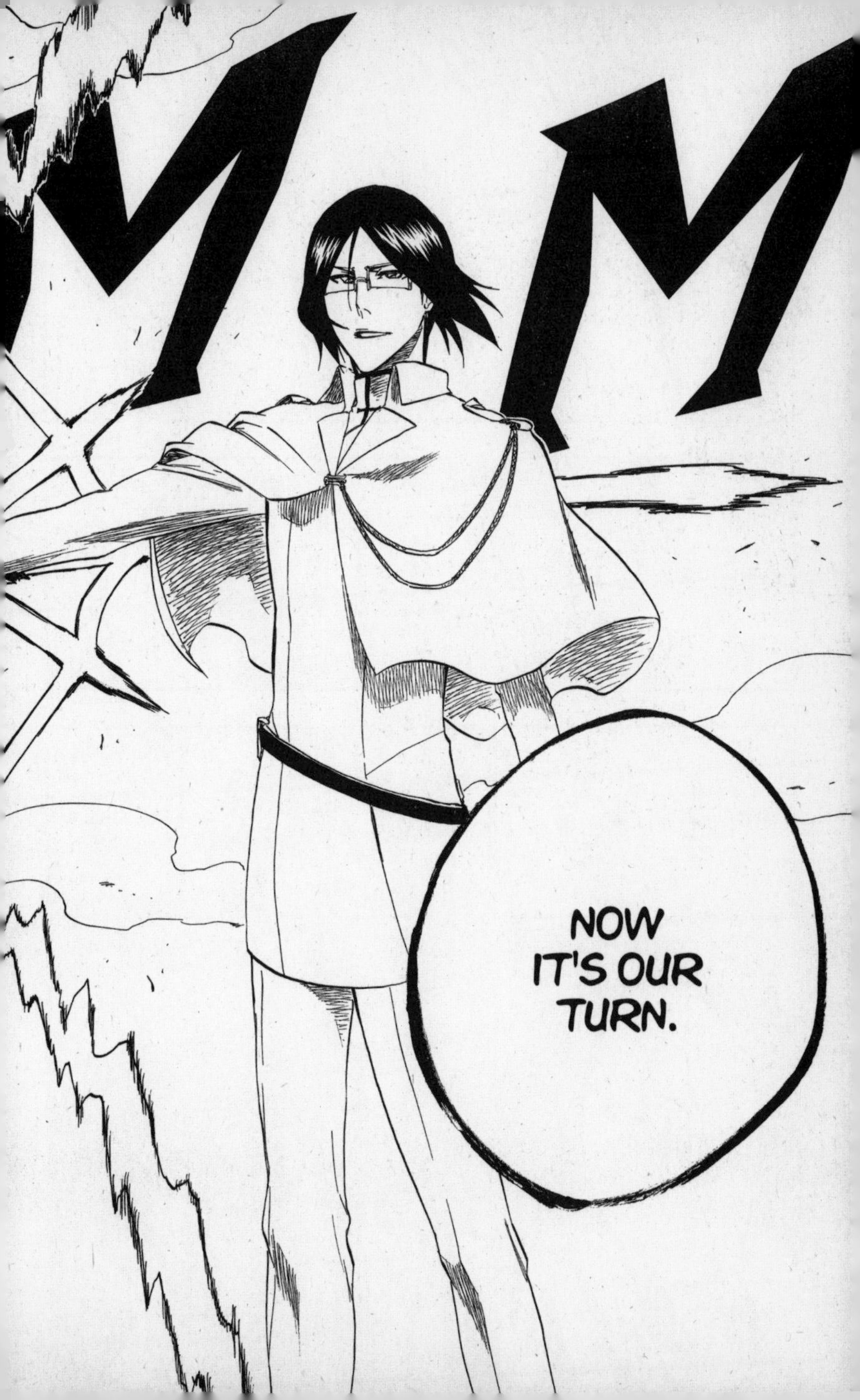
MM
NOW IT'S OUR TURN.

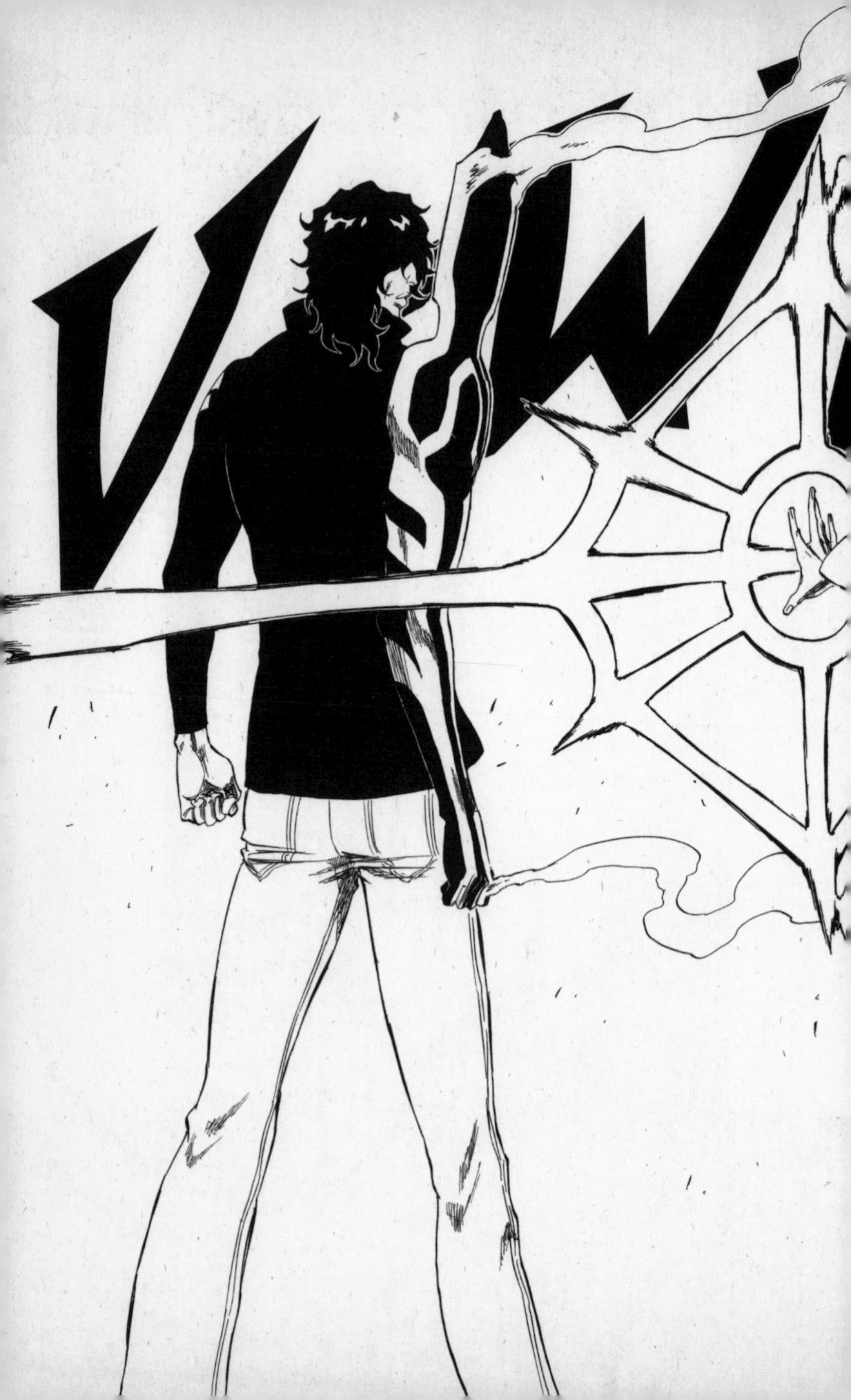

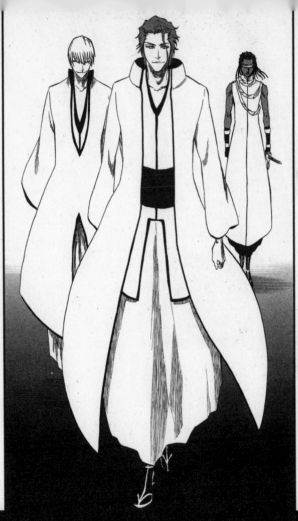

Ichigo, Chad and Uryû journey to Hueco Mundo to save the kidnapped Orihime. They may have made it past the gate, but now they're in Aizen's territory. What devious plans does the traitorous ex-Soul Reaper have up his sleeves?

Read it first in SHONEN JUMP magazine!

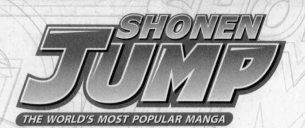
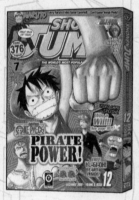
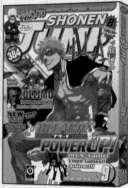
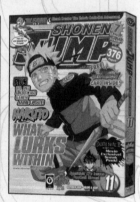